Your LSAT Journey Starts Here

Before you jump into the world check out our **FREE WEBINAR:**

5 Tips to ANNIHILATE the LSAT

Watch as Trent Teti, one of Blueprint's Founders, gives you the lowdown on the best way to approach the LSAT and shares some of our best practices. Don't miss this exclusive content!

Visit **blueprintlsat.com/free**

Should you have any questions as your work through the book, want more LSAT help or discounts on our courses, like our FB and follow us on Twitter!

f facebook.com/blueprintlsatprep   **🐦** @BlueprintLSAT

Don't forget your **FREE** online explanations!

This book contains 33 actual Reading Comprehension passages from recent tests that you'll work through according to the Blueprint method. Even better, you'll have access to detailed PDF explanations for every single one of the real Reading Comprehension passages, either in the book itself or in your MyBlueprint account. Yep. Every single one.

To access these explanations, visit:

blueprintlsat.com/login

On that page, you can create a MyBlueprint online account. Or, if you already have a MyBlueprint online account, you'll simply login to access this extra content.

More LSAT help from Blueprint

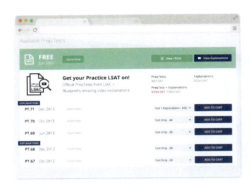

Free MyBlueprint Account

- **Free practice LSAT** (June 2007) to download, take, and see Blueprint's explanations for every question
- Score any LSAT and receive **detailed score reports**
- Articles on LSAT basics and advanced topics
- **Gauge your chances of admission** to any ABA-accredited law school in the nation with Blueprint's Law School Compass
- Try it out for free at **blueprintlsat.com/lsat/free-help/free-accounts**

The Blueprint for LSAT Logic Games

- **35 actual LSAT** Logic Games with video explanations
- The **Blueprint Building Blocks™** method for approaching Logic Games
- Written by Blueprint founder and Logic Games expert Matt Riley
- For more information, go to **blueprintlsat.com/lsat/books**

112-hour classroom course

- **76 hours** of live lectures, 6 proctored practice exam plus extra exams
- Access to the lessons from our online course, Blueprint: The Movie 2.0
- MyBlueprint iOS app study tool with comprehensive analytics
- **11-point average score increase** (measured first to best practice exam*)
- Instructors with an LSAT score of **170 or higher** on actual LSAT
- Online explanations for **every question in the homework**
- Course curriculum that utilizes a **full set of questions licensed from LSAC** (over 7,500)
- Learn more about our classroom course at **blueprintlsat.com/lsat/classroom/overview**

Blueprint: The Movie 2.0 (our online LSAT course)

- **Same curriculum** and format as Blueprint's classroom course
- 16 lessons, 3 workshops, 3 clinics, 6 practice exams plus extra exams
- **Fully animated**, HD, interactive lessons
- Taught by Blueprint founders Trent Teti and Matt Riley
- Access to the MyBlueprint iOS app with adaptive learning and interactive drills
- Online explanations for **every question in the homework**
- Curriculum that utilizes a **full set of licensed LSAC questions** (over 7,500)
- For more information, check out **blueprintlsat.com/lsat/online/overview**

the blueprint for
LSAT READING COMPREHENSION

blueprint
LSAT preparation

This book is printed on recycled paper.

Copyright © 2017 by Blueprint Test Preparation LLC. All rights reserved.

No part of this publication may be reproduced, stored in a retrieval system, or transmitted in any form or by any means, electronic, mechanical, photocopying, recording, scanning, or otherwise, without the prior written permission of Blueprint Test Preparation LLC.

All actual LSAT questions printed within this work are used with the permission of Law School Admission Council, Inc., Box 2000, Newtown, PA, 18940, the copyright owner. LSAC does not review or endorse specific test preparation materials or services, and inclusion of licensed LSAT questions within this work does not imply the review or endorsement of Law Services. LSAT is a registered trademark of Law Services.

For general information on our products and services or for technical support, please contact our customer service department at (888) 4-BP-PREP or (310) 477-8383.

Blueprint Test Preparation
110 S. Fairfax Blvd., Suite 250
Los Angeles, CA 90036

Email: info@blueprintlsat.com
Web: www.blueprintlsat.com

ISBN: 978-0-9842199-2-6

CONTENTS

1. Welcome 1
2. LSAT Basics 2
3. RC Time 13
4. Method 20
5. The Big Three 40
6. Comprehension While Reading 51
7. Main Point 61
8. Where's the Author 74
9. Primary Structure 84
10. Thesis Passages 88
11. Antithesis Passages 112
12. Synthesis Passages 133
13. Review Quiz 153
14. Tag and Mark 156
15. Secondary Structures 180
16. Cause and Effect 186
17. Example 204
18. Question and Answer 219
19. Classification 235
20. Review Quiz 252
21. Structure 255
22. Putting It All Together 282
23. Comparative Reading 312
24. Question Types 325
25. It's Go Time 341
26. More Practice 399
27. Keep Practicing 420
28. Timing 423
29. Tips for Saving Time 425
30. Appendix 435

1/WELCOME

THE BLUEPRINT

Welcome to *The Blueprint for LSAT Reading Comprehension*, the best guide to Reading Comprehension ever written, or at least we think it is. We are very pleased that you've chosen Blueprint and we're confident this book can help you improve your performance substantially on this challenging section of the LSAT.

A Word About Us

Blueprint was founded in 2005 by a group of people who believe that it's possible to learn difficult concepts and have fun at the same time. In general, LSAT prep materials are about as exciting as watching a late night skin care infomercial. At Blueprint, we believe students learn better when they're having fun. To that end, we've designed our live classes, online courses, and books to be entertaining as well as informative.

Now, don't get us wrong. Our first priority is the LSAT. And we definitely know the LSAT. We actually know far more than any group of people really should know about the LSAT (at least if they'd like to maintain healthy social lives and good hygiene). But this knowledge has enabled us to help thousands of students significantly improve their LSAT scores.

This book was written by Jodi Teti, author of the Reading Comprehension portion of the Blueprint curriculum and one of the Blueprint founders.* Jodi excels at three things in life: scrabble, lemon bars (use copious amounts of zest), and tackling Reading Comprehension passages. Jodi's reading acumen was sharpened while earning a BA in English Literature from Stanford University and an MA in 18th Century English Literature from the University of Virginia. Her academic experience also included teaching, which enables her not only to master this portion of the LSAT, but impart the ability to do so to others.

We're happy that you're here. Strap in, kick back, and grab a snack. It's going to be a fun and educational ride.

---

* Special thanks to Branden Frankel for helping with parts of the book and for reading more RC passages than someone really should in this life.

2/LSATbasics

LSAT OVERVIEW

The LSAT, for those of you who accidentally opened this book instead of *US Weekly*, is a standardized test that every student who wants to attend an ABA-approved law school[1] must take. It consists of **five timed sections of 35 minutes each** and a writing sample, which is also a 35-minute section. The test is scored on a scale of **120 (lowest) to 180 (highest)**.

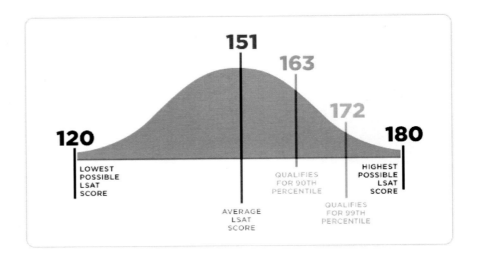

Sections of the LSAT

The scored sections of the LSAT include two sections of Logical Reasoning, one section of Reading Comprehension, and one section of Logic Games, not necessarily in that order. In addition to the four scored sections, there is an "experimental" section. If that sounds like a period of your youth that involved questionable decisions, not to worry: the experimental section is not scored. The section can vary between Logical Reasoning, Logic Games, and Reading Comprehension. The Law School Admission Council (LSAC), which administers the LSAT, uses this section to test future LSAT questions. In addition, the experimental section is not identified during the exam, so you will have the pleasure of expending energy on a portion of the test that in no way affects your score.

There is also a writing exercise at the end of the exam, which, as far as we can tell, tests your ability to write an essay long after your brain has died. Like the experimental section, the writing sample is not scored. However, it is sent to law schools along with your LSAT score. The writing sample challenges you to write with a pencil on paper for 35 minutes at the end of about three hours of testing, so your chances of suffering a major hand cramp are quite high.

---

[1] What is an ABA-approved law school, you ask? ABA stands for the American Bar Association, whose job it is (besides making your life relevant with a little thing called the Bar Exam) to make sure that law schools are reputable. If your law school is not ABA accredited, it means you may not be able to take the Bar Exam in any other state, thus potentially limiting your options for working as a lawyer in different states and purchasing very expensive automobiles.

Here's a table that illustrates the six different sections of the LSAT:

Section	Time	# of Questions
Logical Reasoning 1	35 Minutes	24 - 26
Logical Reasoning 2	35 Minutes	24 - 26
Logic Games	35 Minutes	22 - 24
Reading Comprehension	35 Minutes	26 - 28
Experimental (Not Scored)	35 Minutes	22 - 28
Writing Sample (Not Scored)	35 Minutes	N/A

READING COMPREHENSION

Reading Comprehension consists of three long passages and a Comparative Reading passage (itself made up of two, shorter passages). The subject matter is invariably riveting, encompassing everything from the oral traditions of Native American communities to various theories on the extinction of the dinosaurs. As a lawyer, you must wade through dense and sometimes poorly written judicial opinions and pick out the arguments of the plaintiff(s) and defendant(s), not to mention figure out the judge's position on a particular issue. The passages in Reading Comprehension test your ability to do all those things in a short amount of time.

Each passage is 50 to 65 lines long and is followed by five to eight questions. All told, Reading Comprehension is typically the longest section on the LSAT, totalling between 26 and 28 questions.

Reading Comprehension is an interesting beast because, of the three scored sections of the LSAT, it's the most familiar to most students. This, as with rings of power and immortality, can turn out to be a great boon or a great burden. More on this later.

LOGICAL REASONING

There are two scored sections of Logical Reasoning on the LSAT. Each one contains between 24 and 26 questions, so you'll answer approximately 50 Logical Reasoning questions, which means that **Logical Reasoning makes up approximately half of the test.**

In this section, you'll read a short passage followed by a question. On this page is a question about male sage grouse and their air sacs. Yep. It's an actual LSAT question. Because we here at Blueprint are perverse, we've also included a drawing of the male sage grouse with his air sacs inflated. No wonder sage grouse ladies can't resist.

Right now you're thinking, "What do sage grouse have to do with law school?" The answer is nothing. Absolutely nothing. However, Logical Reasoning tests your ability to make and understand arguments. What do you do all day in law school? Argue about things! If you can argue about the sage grouse, you can certainly argue about the First Amendment or contract language.

The male sage grouse has air sacs that, when not inflated, lie hidden beneath the grouse's neck feathers. During its spring courtship ritual, the male sage grouse inflates these air sacs and displays them to the female sage grouse. Some scientists hypothesize that this courtship ritual serves as a means for female sage grouse to select healthy mates.

Which one of the following, if true, most strongly supports the scientists' hypothesis?

(A) Some female sage grouse mate with unhealthy male sage grouse.
(B) When diseased male sage grouse were treated with antibiotics, they were not selected by female sage grouse during the courtship ritual.
(C) Some healthy male sage grouse do not inflate their air sacs as part of the courtship ritual.
(D) Male sage grouse are prone to parasitic infections that exhibit symptoms visible on the birds' air sacs.
(E) The sage grouse is commonly afflicted with a strain of malaria that tends to change as the organism that causes it undergoes mutation.

In Logical Reasoning, you'll experience the joy of questions like the sage grouse 24 to 26 times in the span of 35 minutes. The subject matter and the questions asked about it will vary. You might be asked what you can conclude from a series of propositions about Biba, a nice guy at the swimming pool. Or you might be asked how to strengthen an argument about diamond appraisal, or be required to find the main point of an argument about adjustable computer workstations.

An actual male sage grouse. Nice air sacs, no?

Whatever the topic or the question you're answering, the Logical Reasoning portion of the LSAT is testing your ability to assess information quickly. In this section, you'll be called upon to judge the validity of arguments without focusing on whether or not the statements they contain are true or false in the real world. In this way, Logical Reasoning prepares you quite well for being a lawyer.

LOGIC GAMES

Another scored section on the LSAT is known in fuddy-duddy parlance as Analytical Reasoning, but we, and most of the known world, affectionately refer to it as Logic Games. In this section, you will be presented with an introductory paragraph and rules, then asked questions about the way in which the variable sets can be organized. Logic Games might involve clowns getting out of cars, cereals displayed at grocery stores, or monkeys being placed in cages. Despite the wide-ranging and sometimes absurd nature of games, it turns out that the number of game types is actually quite small.

This section is often the most mystifying for future law students. LSAT takers rightfully wonder why they have to be able to figure out which clown gets out of the car seventh to go to law school. The key is in understanding that Logic Games are all about managing rules and information. How does this apply? Well, for instance, a statute (fancy word for a law) might be hundreds of pages long with interlocking parts that refer to or affect other parts of the statute or even other laws or regulations. Invoking one part of the law in your case could cause all sorts of other issues you never expected. (Still want to go to law school?) Your ability to understand how different rules interact with each other and with the given facts is crucial to navigating the pitfalls of law. This is what Logic Games are testing.

THE MOMENT OF TRUTH: SCORING

In order to understand scoring on the LSAT, we'll need to discuss the difference between a raw score and a scaled LSAT score. Your raw score refers to how many questions you answered correctly. Your scaled score refers to how this number compares against everyone else. The number relevant for law school admission is your scaled score.

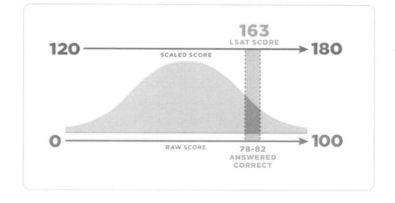

Let's use an example to show you how this works. **Meet Bob.** Bob quit his job parking cars at the local club to move into his parent's basement for three months to study for the LSAT. He was rewarded for his diligence on test day by answering 79 questions correctly out of a possible 101. After LSAT ran all of the tests through their fancy, 1970's-era Scantron machine, they determined that Bob and his 79 correct answers placed him in the 90th percentile. This means Bob beat out 90% of other test takers. LSAC then referenced his score against a percentile table and emailed Bob his final score: a 163. Go Bob!

By the way Bob, your mom told us to tell you: don't even think about moving back home into the basement.

---

* The LSAC scoring process is quite rigorous. For an incredibly dense article guaranteed to cure insomnia, you can learn more at blueprintlsat.com. Go to "Free Help," then "Advanced LSAT," and read the article "LSAT Scores and Curve Explained."

Raw Score	Scaled Score
99-101	180
*	175
89	170
82 - 83	165
74	160
65 - 66	155
56-57	150

Here is a truncated version of the score conversion chart from the **December 2014 LSAT**. The score conversion chart changes slightly for different LSATs depending on how the test-taking population performs, but it has stayed relatively consistent over the years.

Remember, your scaled score is determined by how you fare in comparison to thousands of other test takers. So you don't want an easy LSAT. Rather, you want to fare better than everyone else on the test you take.

What does the LSAT test?

Now that you have an understanding of how scoring on the LSAT works, it's quite natural to wonder what it tests. In a nutshell, the LSAT tests the skills you'll need as a law student and as a lawyer. This includes constructing and analyzing arguments (Logical Reasoning), understanding dense passages of material (Reading Comprehension), organizing information intelligibly (Logic Games), and how to bend a spoon with your mind.*

What the LSAT does not test, however, is rote memorization. Rather than asking you for the capital of North Dakota (Bismarck) or the German Chancellor during World War I (also Bismarck), the test challenges you to think in a certain way. This could involve weakening an argument about gem authenticity, identifying the main idea of a passage on Thurgood Marshall, or deciding whether or not the third mannequin wears a blue hat.

The downside of this method of testing is that you cannot "cram" for the LSAT; you must acquire the skills for it through diligence and repetition. While this is unfortunate news for those of you who scraped by in college writing your papers hours before they were due, it's good news for those of you who enjoy reading and thinking critically. Like all skills in life, some good practice can really enhance your abilities in these areas.

---

* This is not actually tested on the LSAT. But if you can do it, you should already be aware that none of this is real.

LSAT ADMINISTRATIONS

The LSAT is administered four times a year: February, June, September/October, and December.

As you can see, the Sept/Oct LSAT has historically been the most popular administration, followed by the December exam. The June and February LSATs have fewer test takers, but each still sees around 25,000 students.

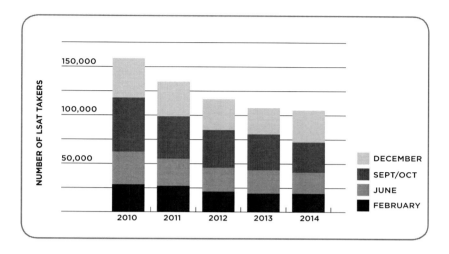

The LSAT is typically given early on a Saturday morning, due to LSAC's insidious plot to ruin your entire weekend. The June exam is the exception, as it is given on a Monday afternoon.* There are also Saturday Sabbath observers' tests that are administered on Mondays. These require a separate enrollment process through LSAC.

For exact LSAT dates and times, check the LSAC website at www.lsac.org.

Is there a "best" time to take the LSAT?

There is a "best" time to take the LSAT, but probably not in the way you're thinking. Unfortunately, it is not the case that one LSAT administration is easier than the others. If you ponder this for a second, you'll probably see why. If the February test, for example, were always easier than the December test, this would be spectacularly unfair for the December test takers. More to the point: no one would take the December test, and everyone would take the February exam. To guard against this, LSAC institutes elaborate procedures to ensure that all the exams are fairly equal.

However, the simple ease of the test isn't the only reason to take a particular administration. Most law schools work on a rolling admissions basis in which students are admitted as applications come in. It's generally better to apply earlier in the process because there are typically more seats available.

Law schools usually begin accepting applications in early fall, so taking the February, June, or Sept/Oct LSAT will ensure your score arrives early in the process. All law schools accept the December LSAT, but you'll want to be absolutely sure your applications are ready to go by the time you receive your LSAT score. Some schools will accept the February LSAT for the same

---

* If you need six cups of coffee and a defibrillator to wake up before 8 AM, the June exam might be for you.

LSATbasics / 7

year in which you're seeking to enroll, but many won't. Taking the February exam to matriculate the same year will generally ensure that you're at the bottom of a squirming, anxiety-ridden mass of applicants.

But whether you apply early or late, **the biggest component of your application is the LSAT score itself**. It is such an important piece, in fact, that applying later with a better LSAT score usually outweighs applying earlier with a lower score. To that end, the "best" time to take the LSAT is when you have the most time to prepare for it. That is why so many people take the Sept/Oct test, when the principal part of their study time falls during the summer months when school is out.

Everything else being equal, we here at Blueprint recommend taking the June test. This is because it's early enough in the process that you can take the test, see your score, determine to which schools you'll apply, and still have plenty of time to get your application together. In addition, if you cancel the test for any reason (off day, landslide blocking the road, unanticipated hangover, etc.) you can take the Sept/Oct test as a backup and still apply early in the admissions cycle. Plus, the June test is the only one given in the afternoon rather than in the morning. Since we Blueprinters haven't voluntarily seen 6 AM since standing in line for tickets to the last Jonas Brothers concert, we're fans of the midday starting time.

IS IT REALLY WORTH THE WORK?

The LSAT is the single most important piece of your law school application (apart from substantial donations to university library foundations from a wealthy family member). **Conventional wisdom holds that the LSAT carries the weight of about 60% of your application.** Because of its importance in the application process, the *better your LSAT score*, the better the law school you can typically attend. As law firms become increasingly selective in the hiring process, a *better law school* can mean a better job. A *better job* often equates to a *better-looking spouse*, which in turn can influence the attractiveness of your offspring.* In other words, a higher LSAT score can equate to an evolutionary advantage for passing on your genetic traits. That's just basic Darwinism.

Not only can a higher LSAT score get you into a better law school, it can also result in scholarship money once you're there. Why not save on tuition so you can use your money for better things, like purchasing a taco truck or an exotic pet farm?

Finally, more so than any other standardized test, better performance on the LSAT correlates to better performance in law school. So in studying for the LSAT, you have the satisfaction of knowing it can pay dividends in law school performance, as well.

---

* While we are very confident in our ability to improve your performance in Reading Comprehension, we cannot guarantee anything about the attractiveness of your significant other. You have to work a little bit, too.

Why devote a whole book to Reading Comprehension?

Of the different sections on the LSAT, we find that our students are typically least concerned about Reading Comprehension. This is precisely why this book is necessary.

Let's first take a look into why this phenomenon occurs. We find that, initially, our students tend to be the most scared of the Logic Games section of the LSAT. This is because the games are unlike anything students have seen before.

Here's a fairly standard Logic Game question: If the third dinosaur has a long neck and is mauve, then the first dinosaur must be what color? Typical newbie LSAT student answer: How can a dinosaur be mauve? Also, do you have any toilet paper? I think I just wet myself.

The horrified reaction engendered by the first encounter with Logic Games motivates students to study for it. The difficulty with Reading Comprehension, on the other hand, is that it consists of longer, academic passages of the kind with which most students are already familiar. There is typically no horrifying brush with confusion, no adult diaper moment, to prod students into studying.

To make matters worse, of all the sections on the LSAT, Reading Comprehension is the one that is becoming more difficult. In 2007, one of the four, longer passages was removed and replaced with two shorter "Comparative Reading" passages. The passages in general are also becoming increasingly dense with more difficult questions. Thus is the very section that is becoming more difficult the one that is often the most neglected. Yikes.

There is good news, however! Because other test-takers often don't put in the time to learn how to tackle Reading Comprehension correctly, you'll have a distinct advantage on the exam when you master this section. In addition, proficiency in Reading Comprehension will reward you on other sections of the LSAT. The ability to read critically will pay dividends in Logical Reasoning and Logic Games. For example, finding the main idea of a Reading Comprehension passage (which is a question that accompanies nearly every passage) correlates directly to Main Point questions in Logical Reasoning. That's a two-fer, people.

THE BLUEPRINT ADVANTAGE

Now that you're convinced you need to hone your Reading Comprehension skills, you might question why our Reading Comprehension method is better than other companies', or why you can't just tackle Reading Comprehension armed only with your common sense.

First, your common sense is crap. Remember your first trip to Vegas when you thought the dealer had to push at the blackjack table? That was where your common sense got you.

Second, Blueprint has devised the most effective approach to Reading Comprehension in existence. We break down all Reading Comprehension passages into just three categories, then provide you with the tools to:

> *1) recognize into which category the passage falls,*
> *2) mark it up to determine the important parts, and*
> *3) anticipate the questions likely to be asked, as well as their answers.*

As you will soon experience for yourself, our approach is simple, yet powerful. Rather than tossing random passages in your direction and explaining how to answer the questions after the fact (e.g. "this answer can be found in lines 4-5"), we've isolated the basic processes that motivate all Reading Comprehension passages. By helping you identify their salient features on your own, our methods will help you classify, then most efficiently assess, any Reading Comprehension passage thrown at you.

But there's something else that sets us apart. Other Reading Comprehension books will give you a passage, ask you to read it, then explain how to answer the questions. This means that readers have to reconstruct, as best they can, when they were supposed to know that a certain sentence constituted the main idea, or when it should have been evident that the author was providing an opinion. In *The Blueprint for LSAT Reading Comprehension*, however, we've broken down all the Reading Comprehension passages and their questions into their component parts. We teach you what to do the minute you receive new information. As soon as a sentence indicates something important in the passage, we walk you through the process of how to recognize it and what to do with it.

We call this step-by-step process **The Blueprint Reading Method™**. We've even trademarked it so that it sounds incredibly important and makes us look smart. What the method does is guide you through every moment of a Reading Comprehension passage. It's as close as you can get to having an instructor with you while you're reading. It also requires a lot of work on our end, which is our best guess as to why we haven't seen it anywhere else. Whereas other companies explain how to answer Reading Comprehension passage questions after the fact, we're able to work through Reading Comprehension passages with you, step by step, to show you the crucial maneuvers that occur at each stage.

After reading every single Reading Comprehension passage available to man, woman, or Komodo dragon (a gangster of a lizard), we've also figured out that there's a whole bunch of stuff the test makers ask about repeatedly. This means we'll also give you tips on how to look out for common patterns in Reading Comprehension passages and use them to your advantage. We've condensed all of this knowledge into this book so you'll completely kill Reading Comprehension on your own LSAT. And by "kill," we mean achieve a score that will get you a hot assistant and a vacation home in the Costa del Sol.

YOUR STUDY GROUP

Now that we've covered the basics of the LSAT and why your decision to study Reading Comprehension with Blueprint shows excellent judgment on your part, it's time to meet your study group. No one likes to study alone. You're probably reading this by yourself, possibly somewhere in the badlands of South Dakota. We all need friends, particularly for something as traumatic as LSAT study. Sit back and say hello to your new comrades.

The Ninja:

The Ninja is very powerful, as you can see by his extremely long sword. Your goal is to become the Ninja, for he knows Reading Comprehension like the back of his karate-chopping hand. At various points, he will contribute *Ninja Notes* to which you should pay close attention. These will be advanced comments about specific passages or techniques. Listen to the Ninja, and one day the Ninja you will become.

Cleetus:

Poor Cleetus. Unfortunately, not all of us can be born with the correct number of chromosomes. Or teeth. You see, Cleetus is not very skilled at Reading Comprehension, and thus you definitely do not want to be Cleetus. But Cleetus will commit some of the common mistakes that students make, and those are the same mistakes you need to learn to avoid.

Ditz McGee:

Say hello to Ditz. She doesn't really want to be here. Truth be told, Ditz wants to become a pop star, but the singing career has not quite taken off. So Ditz is thinking about law school as a backup plan. Since she is lazy and isn't committed to studying, Ditz will try to skate through and find ways around actually learning. Like Cleetus, Ms. McGee is the voice of mistakes you'll want to avoid. Remember, there is no quick fix for Reading Comprehension, just like there is no quick fix for poor career choices or tattoos of an ex-boyfriend's name.

BP Minotaur:

Finally, we come to the Minotaur. He's a master of erudition, and his study smells of rich mahogany. In case you were not aware, he's the figure from Greek mythology who dwelt in a maze and ate Athenian youths sent to Crete as tribute. Now, he's the perfect figure to lead you through the labyrinth of Reading Comprehension. The Minotaur will be the voice of Blueprint and lend helpful tactical hints along the way. Plus, he's got great horns and a stellar monocle.

So that's it for the introduction, people. As you know, the world of the LSAT and law school admissions is a competitive one. But there's a pot of gold at the end of the rainbow if you can beat out all the other pre-law leprechauns.

You've come to the right place to become an expert in Reading Comprehension. Someday, when you have grey hair and put your teeth in a glass at night, you'll look back on what you did here with this book and say: "Man, Blueprint %#*ing rocked."

3/RCtime

READING COMPREHENSION

In the Reading Comprehension section, there are always three long passages and one Comparative Reading passage (consisting of two shorter paired passages), for a total of four passages. **Each passage has two basic parts: the passage and the questions.**

Say hello to a Reading Comprehension passage.

In economics, the term "speculative bubble" refers to a large upward move in an asset's price driven not by the asset's fundamentals—that is, by the earnings derivable from the asset—but rather by
(5) mere speculation that someone else will be willing to pay a higher price for it. The price increase is then followed by a dramatic decline in price, due to a loss in confidence that the price will continue to rise, and the "bubble" is said to have burst. According to Charles
(10) Mackay's classic nineteenth-century account, the seventeenth-century Dutch tulip market provides an example of a speculative bubble. But the economist Peter Garber challenges Mackay's view, arguing that there is no evidence that the Dutch tulip market really
(15) involved a speculative bubble.

By the seventeenth century, the Netherlands had become a center of cultivation and development of new tulip varieties, and a market had developed in which rare varieties of bulbs sold at high prices. For example,
(20) a Semper Augustus bulb sold in 1625 for an amount of gold worth about U.S.$11,000 in 1999. Common bulb varieties, on the other hand, sold for very low prices. According to Mackay, by 1636 rapid price rises attracted speculators, and prices of many varieties
(25) surged upward from November 1636 through January 1637. Mackay further states that in February 1637 prices suddenly collapsed; bulbs could not be sold at 10 percent of their peak values. By 1739, the prices of all the most prized kinds of bulbs had fallen to no
(30) more than one two-hundredth of 1 percent of Semper Augustus's peak price.

Garber acknowledges that bulb prices increased dramatically from 1636 to 1637 and eventually reached very low levels. But he argues that this episode
(35) should not be described as a speculative bubble, for the increase and eventual decline in bulb prices can be explained in terms of the fundamentals. Garber argues that a standard pricing pattern occurs for new varieties of flowers. When a particularly prized variety
(40) is developed, its original bulb sells for a high price. Thus, the dramatic rise in the price of some original tulip bulbs could have resulted as tulips in general, and certain varieties in particular, became fashionable. However, as the prized bulbs become more readily
(45) available through reproduction from the original bulb, their price falls rapidly; after less than 30 years, bulbs sell at reproduction cost. But this does not mean that the high prices of original bulbs are irrational, for earnings derivable from the millions of bulbs
(50) descendent from the original bulbs can be very high, even if each individual descendent bulb commands a very low price. Given that an original bulb can generate a reasonable return on investment even if the price of descendent bulbs decreases dramatically, a
(55) rapid rise and eventual fall of tulip bulb prices need not indicate a speculative bubble.

---

22. Which one of the following most accurately expresses the main point of the passage?

    (A) The seventeenth-century Dutch tulip market is widely but mistakenly believed by economists to provide an example of a speculative bubble.
    (B) Mackay did not accurately assess the earnings that could be derived from rare and expensive seventeenth-century Dutch tulip bulbs.
    (C) A speculative bubble occurs whenever the price of an asset increases substantially followed by a rapid and dramatic decline.
    (D) Garber argues that Mackay's classic account of the seventeenth-century Dutch tulip market as a speculative bubble is not supported by the evidence.
    (E) A tulip bulb can generate a reasonable return on investment even if the price starts very high and decreases dramatically.

23. Given Garber's account of the seventeenth-century Dutch tulip market, which one of the following is most analogous to someone who bought a tulip bulb of a certain variety in that market at a very high price, only to sell a bulb of that variety at a much lower price?

    (A) someone who, after learning that many others had withdrawn their applications for a particular job, applied for the job in the belief that there would be less competition for it
    (B) an art dealer who, after paying a very high price for a new painting, sells it at a very low price because it is now considered to be an inferior work
    (C) someone who, after buying a box of rare motorcycle parts at a very high price, is forced to sell them at a much lower price because of the sudden availability of cheap substitute parts
    (D) a publisher who pays an extremely high price for a new novel only to sell copies at a price affordable to nearly everyone
    (E) an airline that, after selling most of the tickets for seats on a plane at a very high price, must sell the remaining tickets at a very low price

And when you are done, you get to do this three more times. All within 35 minutes. Sounds like fun, no?

The Passage

The passage consists of one or more paragraphs that present one or more points of view as well as evidence to support the view(s).

The Questions

Each passage has between five and eight questions. They are designed to test your knowledge of the passage, including viewpoints presented, how those viewpoints are supported, and particular details in the passage. If you've done what you're supposed to do in the passage, you should have anticipated a large number of the questions before you even reach them.

THIS LOOKS FAMILIAR

For most students, Reading Comprehension is not viewed as foreign territory. This is because you've probably taken at least one undergraduate class where you had to read an academic essay. (Please say you've taken at least one undergraduate class where you had to read an academic essay.) Since these types of academic essays are used to create Reading Comprehension passages, this section should feel familiar.

However, you're probably not used to reading those passages carefully and retaining information about them. How many times have you glanced at an assigned article for class and just skimmed it to get the gist? Or never read it all? This may work for you in History 101, but it will definitely fail you on the LSAT.

BP Minotaur: Reading comprehension is probably the most familiar section of the LSAT. This poses a problem, however, as you've developed reading habits that you're going to have to break in order to master the section.

THE MADNESS

In our experience, most people decide to learn how to tackle Reading Comprehension in the same way they learn how to play a game of poker. Namely, by pulling up a chair, dealing the cards, and just starting to play the game. While this might work for a trip to Vegas (we highly recommend Excalibur for its low ante blackjack tables and Tournament of Kings dinner), this tactic is highly unlikely to work on the LSAT.

This is because just reading passage after passage will only serve to reinforce the way you already approach this section of the test. Because your method isn't informed by a deeper understanding of the LSAT, it's unlikely to yield mastery on this section.

The seductive mistake is that tackling a series of Reading Comprehension passages without a method can give the illusion of learning. However, while familiarizing yourself with this section of the LSAT will undoubtedly yield a few points, continuing to attempt passage after passage without a method means you will plateau in this section relatively quickly. And not a plateau such as you might find high in the Himalayas, more like one in Holland.

The makers of the test count on this. Because most students don't take the time to understand the structures underlying Reading Comprehension passages, LSAC chooses a wide variety of subjects in Reading Comprehension, from Hopi personal names to steady-state economics, to make the section seem extremely varied and difficult.

BP Ninja: When you're done with this book, you'll find subject matter will fall away like cherry blossoms from a tree in spring. Only structure will matter.

At Blueprint, we have identified the general structures that underlie every Reading Comprehension passage in the history of the LSAT. As you'll soon see, there aren't very many. Fewer than there are fingers on your right hand. (Unless your right hand has three or fewer fingers, which would be unfortunate.) Once we walk you through these structures, you'll be able to understand Reading Comprehension passages on a theoretical level, and you won't be intimidated by its subject matter. However, it is our experience that we can talk about this until the cows come home and you still won't be convinced.

THE CHALLENGE

To that end, here is what's going to happen next: you're going to tackle a Reading Comprehension passage. Yep, you're going to attempt a passage with whatever unsystematic, cobbled-together, crap method you're currently using. (Don't be offended. You know it is.) If you ace the passage in five minutes, put down this book and start packing for Harvard Law School. But if you find the following passage painful, as nearly everyone in the world will, then when you're done we'll show you the correct way to approach this passage.

SEPTEMBER 2007 {PASSAGE 4}

This is the fourth passage from the September 2007 LSAT. On average, you'll have eight minutes and forty-five seconds to complete each Reading Comprehension passage on test day. So grab a watch, egg timer, or a sundial and set the clock. Your challenge is to complete this passage in the time allotted. Once you finish (or your time has expired), we'll discuss how Blueprint can help Reading Comprehension become a lot more efficient and, dare we say, even pleasant experience. *When you're ready, turn the page.*

16 / Chapter 3

*Take a deep breath.
It's about to get real.*

Most people acknowledge that not all governments have a moral right to govern and that there are sometimes morally legitimate reasons for disobeying the law, as when a particular law
(5) prescribes behavior that is clearly immoral. It is also commonly supposed that such cases are special exceptions and that, in general, the fact that something is against the law counts as a moral, as well as legal, ground for not doing it; i.e., we
(10) generally have a moral duty to obey a law simply because it is the law. But the theory known as philosophical anarchism denies this view, arguing instead that people who live under the jurisdiction of governments have no moral duty to those
(15) governments to obey their laws. Some commentators have rejected this position because of what they take to be its highly counterintuitive implications: (1) that no existing government is morally better than any other (since all are, in a sense, equally illegitimate),
(20) and (2) that, lacking any moral obligation to obey any laws, people may do as they please without scruple. In fact, however, philosophical anarchism does not entail these claims.

First, the conclusion that no government is
(25) morally better than any other does not follow from the claim that nobody owes moral obedience to any government. Even if one denies that there is a moral obligation to follow the laws of any government, one can still evaluate the morality of the policies and
(30) actions of various governments. Some governments do more good than harm, and others more harm than good, to their subjects. Some violate the moral rights of individuals more regularly, systematically, and seriously than others. In short, it is perfectly
(35) consistent with philosophical anarchism to hold that governments vary widely in their moral stature.

Second, philosophical anarchists maintain that all individuals have basic, nonlegal moral duties to one another—duties not to harm others in their lives,
(40) liberty, health, or goods. Even if governmental laws have no moral force, individuals still have duties to refrain from those actions that constitute crimes in the majority of legal systems (such as murder, assault, theft, and fraud). Moreover, philosophical
(45) anarchists hold that people have a positive moral obligation to care for one another, a moral obligation that they might even choose to discharge by supporting cooperative efforts by governments to help those in need. And where others are abiding by
(50) established laws, even those laws derived from mere conventions, individuals are morally bound not to violate those laws when doing so would endanger others. Thus, if others obey the law and drive their vehicles on the right, one must not endanger them by
(55) driving on the left, for, even though driving on the left is not inherently immoral, it is morally wrong to deliberately harm the innocent.

20. Which one of the following most accurately expresses the main point of the passage?

    (A) Some views that certain commentators consider to be implications of philosophical anarchism are highly counterintuitive.
    (B) Contrary to what philosophical anarchists claim, some governments are morally superior to others, and citizens under legitimate governments have moral obligations to one another.
    (C) It does not follow logically from philosophical anarchism that no government is morally better than any other or that people have no moral duties toward one another.
    (D) Even if, as certain philosophical anarchists claim, governmental laws lack moral force, people still have a moral obligation to refrain from harming one another.
    (E) Contrary to what some of its opponents have claimed, philosophical anarchism does not conflict with the ordinary view that one should obey the law because it is the law.

21. The author identifies which one of the following as a commonly held belief?

    (A) In most cases we are morally obligated to obey the law simply because it is the law.
    (B) All governments are in essence morally equal.
    (C) We are morally bound to obey only those laws we participate in establishing.
    (D) Most crimes are morally neutral, even though they are illegal.
    (E) The majority of existing laws are intended to protect others from harm.

22. The author's stance regarding the theory of philosophical anarchism can most accurately be described as one of

    (A) ardent approval of most aspects of the theory
    (B) apparent acceptance of some of the basic positions of the theory
    (C) concerned pessimism about the theory's ability to avoid certain extreme views
    (D) hesitant rejection of some of the central features of the theory
    (E) resolute antipathy toward both the theory and certain of its logical consequences

23. By attributing to commentators the view that philosophical anarchism has implications that are "counterintuitive" (line 17), the author most likely means that the commentators believe that

    (A) the implications conflict with some commonly held beliefs
    (B) there is little empirical evidence that the implications are actually true
    (C) common sense indicates that philosophical anarchism does not have such implications
    (D) the implications appear to be incompatible with each other
    (E) each of the implications contains an internal logical inconsistency

24. Which one of the following scenarios most completely conforms to the views attributed to philosophical anarchists in lines 37–44?

    (A) A member of a political party that is illegal in a particular country divulges the names of other members because he fears legal penalties.
    (B) A corporate executive chooses to discontinue her company's practice of dumping chemicals illegally when she learns that the chemicals are contaminating the water supply.
    (C) A person who knows that a coworker has stolen funds from their employer decides to do nothing because the coworker is widely admired.
    (D) A person neglects to pay her taxes, even though it is likely that she will suffer severe legal penalties as a consequence, because she wants to use the money to finance a new business.
    (E) A driver determines that it is safe to exceed the posted speed limit, in spite of poor visibility, because there are apparently no other vehicles on the road.

25. It can be inferred that the author would be most likely to agree that

    (A) people are subject to more moral obligations than is generally held to be the case
    (B) governments that are morally superior recognize that their citizens are not morally bound to obey their laws
    (C) one may have good reason to support the efforts of one's government even if one has no moral duty to obey its laws
    (D) there are some sound arguments for claiming that most governments have a moral right to require obedience to their laws
    (E) the theory of philosophical anarchism entails certain fundamental principles regarding how laws should be enacted and enforced

26. The author's discussion of people's positive moral duty to care for one another (lines 44–49) functions primarily to

    (A) demonstrate that governmental efforts to help those in need are superfluous
    (B) suggest that philosophical anarchists maintain that laws that foster the common good are extremely rare
    (C) imply that the theoretical underpinnings of philosophical anarchism are inconsistent with certain widely held moral truths
    (D) indicate that philosophical anarchists recognize that people are subject to substantial moral obligations
    (E) illustrate that people are morally obligated to refrain from those actions that are crimes in most legal systems

27. In the passage, the author seeks primarily to

    (A) describe the development and theoretical underpinnings of a particular theory
    (B) establish that a particular theory conforms to the dictates of common sense
    (C) argue that two necessary implications of a particular theory are morally acceptable
    (D) defend a particular theory against its critics by showing that their arguments are mistaken
    (E) demonstrate that proponents of a particular theory are aware of the theory's defects

4/METHOD

You may have experienced some difficulty with this passage. If you didn't, hurray for you and get a head start while those of us who found it difficult look for a blunt object with which to bludgeon you.

Most people who encounter this passage find it a painful task because the argument is laid out in an abstract and somewhat convoluted matter.

Ditz McGee: I stopped reading after the first paragraph.

That's a fairly typical reaction, Ditz. Most people find Reading Comprehension passages boring at best and intimidating at worst. As a consequence, they skim instead of read. We'll help you know what to read for so you no longer gloss over what you read without true comprehension. By applying the Blueprint method, which is all about unveiling structure, you'll find that the passage falls apart as easily as a Kardashian marriage.

We'll take you through the passage paragraph by paragraph to let you know what you should have gleaned from the passage, what marks to make in the passage itself (where to underline, etc.), what to tag in the space to the right of the passage, and how it all comes together to form what we call a Reading Comprehension markup.

You won't be called upon to make your own markups for quite some time, but we wanted to give you a sense of the entire Blueprint Reading Method™ before teaching you how to replicate the process yourself.

Note: If our assessment of the passage seems overwhelming and impossible right now, that's okay. The purpose of this exercise is to show you what you're aiming for, not what you should be able to do right now. To that end, you can skip to chapter 5 if you find you don't really understand what's happening in the explanation. However, if you can, it's a great exercise to read through to see what you'll be capable of doing by the end of the book.

How to Read This Passage

Paragraph 1

> Most people acknowledge that not all governments have a moral right to govern and that there are sometimes morally legitimate reasons for disobeying the law, as when a particular law
> (5) prescribes behavior that is clearly immoral. It is also commonly supposed that such cases are special exceptions and that, in general, the fact that something is against the law counts as a moral, as well as legal, ground for not doing it; i.e., we
> (10) generally have a moral duty to obey a law simply because it is the law. But the theory known as philosophical anarchism denies this view, [arguing instead that people who live under the jurisdiction of governments have no moral duty to those
> (15) governments to obey their laws.] Some commentators have rejected this position because of what they take to be its highly counterintuitive implications: (1) that no existing government is morally better than any other (since all are, in a sense, equally illegitimate),
> (20) and (2) that, lacking any moral obligation to obey any laws, people may do as they please without scruple. In fact, however, philosophical anarchism does not entail these claims.

Margin notes:
- MOST PEOPLE: LAWS AND MORALITY GENERALLY IN LINE
- DEF. OF PHILOSOPHICAL ANARCHISM
- COMMENTATORS' VIEWS
- AUTHOR'S CONCLUSION

The passage begins with a description of how "most people" (line 1) view government and its laws. Since in Reading Comprehension "views" equate to structure (we classify all of our Reading Comprehension passages by the number of views they have), it's important to keep track of every viewpoint you find. For this paragraph, the view should be noted by writing it down to the right of the passage.

It's very common for a Reading Comprehension passage to begin with a generally-held view as a point of departure for another, more interesting view that will ultimately be the one espoused by the author. Sure enough, we get a nice "but" in line 11 that lets us know that a different perception—that of philosophical anarchism—countermands the popular view held by "most people." A definition of philosophical anarchism is put forth, which lets us know that this view is going to be fairly important. We put [brackets] around the definition and tag this new view in the margin on the right.

Cleetus: Philosophical whatism?

METHOD / 21

Don't worry, Cleetus. It's common for LSAC writers to utilize elevated vocabulary and jargon to make passages more difficult. However, such vocabulary will always be defined for you, either explicitly, as it is here, or by context clues.

On line 15, yet another view is introduced, that of the "commentators." The commentators lay out two criticisms of philosophical anarchism, both stemming from the fact that philosophical anarchism is "counterintuitive" (line 17). As a high-level word, we circle "counterintuitive" and make a note of the third view—that of the commentators—in the margin.

We're not finished with the first paragraph and we already have three points of view regarding the government and laws. These include:

1. What "most people" believe (lines 1-11)
2. Philosophical anarchism (lines 11-15)
3. The commentators' views (lines 15-21)

But there's more! Because the first paragraph ends with ANOTHER view in lines 22 and 23: that philosophical anarchism "does not entail these claims."

Who is espousing this view and what does it mean?

The big question is who is putting forth the opinion that philosophical anarchism doesn't entail these claims. If you said it's the author, you would be correct. We know that it's the author because it's an opinion that isn't attributed to anyone else.

We also know that the author is rebutting the commentators' view that philosophical anarchism entails two very negative outcomes: that no government is better than any other and that people can do whatever they want.

Ditz: I agree that people should be able to do whatever they want.

Yes, Ditz. As evinced by your purple hair extensions and pink-sequined smartphone case.

At this point, we should assess all of the views in the paragraph. It's becoming clear that the first view held by "most people" (lines 1-11) is really just background for the passage. This is because the view is not developed further. Unless the view is revisited later, it's likely that it won't factor into the structure of the passage.

In contrast, philosophical anarchism is shaping up to be the main battleground for the passage. This is because it's defined (always a clue that something is important in a passage) and we have a view (the commentators') that argues against it. Moreover (and most importantly), the author weighs in on this view, defending it. Tracking the author's view always leads to the main idea since the author's main conclusion is ALWAYS the main point of a Reading Comprehension passage (unless there is no author present in the passage, which is a different story we'll discuss later).

BP Minotaur: Keep this important point in mind. In a passage with a present author, the author's primary conclusion is always the main point of a Reading Comprehension passage.

To that end, we can construct our primary structure diagram (you'll learn all about this later) in the lower, right-hand corner of the page. This structure may change, since we're only through the first paragraph of the passage, but at this point we can take an educated guess and change it later, if necessary.

Ninja: We use the lower, right-hand corner of the page to construct our primary structure diagram because it almost always has room on the test. Just as we store our katana in the southeast corner of the dojo. All items in their place.

Finally, whenever we see the author's opinion, we underline it. This is because it's extremely likely to be the main idea of the passage. Even if it's not, it still allows us to track the author's attitude, which is often asked about in the questions.

Now that we've dissected all of the information in the first paragraph, here is the mark-up for the first paragraph along with the primary structure diagram for the entire passage.

METHOD / 23

Most people acknowledge that not all governments have a moral right to govern and that there are sometimes morally legitimate reasons
(5) for disobeying the law, as when a particular law prescribes behavior that is clearly immoral. It is also commonly supposed that such cases are special exceptions and that, in general, the fact that something is against the law counts as a moral,
(10) as well as legal, ground for not doing it; i.e., we generally have a moral duty to obey a law simply because it is the law. But the theory known as philosophical anarchism denies this view, arguing instead that people who live under the jurisdiction of governments have no moral duty to those
(15) governments to obey their laws. Some commentators have rejected this position because of what they take to be its highly counterintuitive implications: (1) that no existing government is morally better than any other (since all are, in a sense, equally illegitimate),
(20) and (2) that, lacking any moral obligation to obey any laws, people may do as they please without scruple. In fact, however, philosophical anarchism does not entail these claims.

First, the conclusion that no government is
(25) morally better than any other does not follow from the claim that nobody has a moral duty to obey any government. Even if citizens do not have a moral obligation to follow the laws of their governments, one can still evaluate the morality of the
(30) actions of various governments; some governments do more good than harm, and others more harm than good, to their subjects; some respect the rights of individuals more regularly, systematically, and seriously than others. In short, it is perfectly
(35) consistent with philosophical anarchism to hold that governments vary widely in their moral stature.

Second, philosophical anarchists maintain that all individuals have basic, nonlegal moral duties to one another—duties not to harm others in their lives,
(40) liberty, health, or goods. Even if governmental laws have no moral force, individuals still have duties to refrain from those actions that constitute crimes in the majority of legal systems (such as murder, assault, theft, and fraud). Moreover, philosophical
(45) anarchists hold that people have a positive moral obligation to care for one another, a moral obligation that they might even choose to discharge by supporting cooperative efforts by governments to help those in need. And where others are abiding by
(50) established laws, even those laws derived from mere conventions, individuals are morally bound not to violate those laws when doing so would endanger others. Thus, if others obey the law and drive their vehicles on the right, one must not endanger them by
(55) driving on the left, for, even though driving on the left is not inherently immoral, it is morally wrong to deliberately harm the innocent.

Cleetus: There ain't no way I can do that.

Perhaps not right now, Cleetus. But fortified by squirrel gravy and this book, you should be able to in the near future. Now let's take a look at the next paragraph.

Paragraph 2

> (25) First, the conclusion that no government is morally better than any other does not follow from the claim that nobody owes moral obedience to any government. Even if one denies that there is a moral obligation to follow the laws of any government, one can still evaluate the morality of the policies and
> (30) actions of various governments. Some governments do more good than harm, and others more harm than good, to their subjects. Some violate the moral rights of individuals more regularly, systematically, and seriously than others. In short, it is perfectly
> (35) consistent with philosophical anarchism to hold that governments vary widely in their moral stature.

(1) IS INCORRECT

BECAUSE CAN JUDGE GOV'T

ATT.

Paragraph two begins by providing support for the author's view that philosophical anarchism does NOT entail the two claims that the "commentators" say it does. In fact, a quick glance at paragraph three, which begins with "Second," reveals the entire structure of the passage. The second paragraph is devoted to refuting the first of the commentators' two claims and the third paragraph is devoted to refuting the second of the commentators' two claims. This means we know all of our points of view, as well as what the author thinks.

Accordingly, we know that our primary structure is correct. We can now confidently identify that this is an Antithesis passage (one with two primary points of view) and that the author is firmly aligned with the second point of view: that the "counterintuitive" implications of philosophical anarchism put forth by the commentators are not, in fact, entailed by the view.

It's important to read paragraphs two and three thoroughly to glean specific information from them, but at this point you've cracked the passage code and should feel pretty darn good about your awesomeness.

To that end, paragraph two explains why the commentators' first criticism of philosophical anarchism (that no existing government is morally better than any other) is incorrect. The author explains that governments can be evaluated (one might think that Finland's government is a better one than say, Canada's) and that doing so is consistent with philosophical anarchism. This tag should be added to the right side of the passage.

We also see some author's attitude in the paragraph in lines 34-35 when she describes the ability to judge between governments as "perfectly consistent" with philosophical anarchism. It's the "perfectly" that lets us know our author's opinion on the matter: she's clearly espousing the view. We underline this phrase and tag it on the side of the passage because there are often questions about the author's attitude.

Compared to the first paragraph, paragraph two is mercifully short and relatively straightforward. Phew.

Most people acknowledge that not all governments have a moral right to govern and that there are sometimes morally legitimate reasons for disobeying the law, as when a particular law
(5) prescribes behavior that is clearly immoral. It is also commonly supposed that such cases are special exceptions and that, in general, the fact that something is against the law counts as a moral, as well as legal, ground for not doing it; i.e., we
(10) generally have a moral duty to obey a law simply because it is the law. But the theory known as philosophical anarchism denies this view, arguing instead that people who live under the jurisdiction of governments have no moral duty to those
(15) governments to obey their laws. Some commentators have rejected this position because of what they take to be its highly counterintuitive implications: (1) that no existing government is morally better than any other (since all are, in a sense, equally illegitimate),
(20) and (2) that, lacking any moral obligation to obey any laws, people may do as they please without scruple. In fact, however, philosophical anarchism does not entail these claims.

First, the conclusion that no government is
(25) morally better than any other does not follow from the claim that nobody owes moral obedience to any government. Even if one denies that there is a moral obligation to follow the laws of any government, one can still evaluate the morality of the policies and
(30) actions of various governments. Some governments do more good than harm, and others more harm than good, to their subjects. Some violate the moral rights of individuals more regularly, systematically, and seriously than others. In short, it is perfectly
(35) consistent with philosophical anarchism to hold that governments vary widely in their moral stature.

Second, philosophical anarchists maintain that all individuals have basic moral duties toward one another—duties not to harm others in their
(40) liberty, health, or goods are paramount among these. Governments have no moral force behind them, but people are bound to refrain from those actions that violate such duties, and in the majority of legal systems, things like murder,
(45) assault, theft, and fraud are illegal. Further, anarchists hold that individuals have some moral obligation to care for one another, which means that they might even have moral reasons for supporting cooperative arrangements to
(50) help those in need. And where others are abiding by established laws, even those laws derived from mere conventions, individuals are morally bound not to violate those laws when doing so would endanger others. Thus, if others obey the law and drive their
(55) vehicles on the right, one must not endanger them by driving on the left, for, even though driving on the left is not inherently immoral, it is morally wrong to deliberately harm the innocent.

Paragraph 3

> (40) Second, philosophical anarchists maintain that all individuals have basic, nonlegal moral duties to one another—duties not to harm others in their lives, liberty, health, or goods. Even if governmental laws have no moral force, individuals still have duties to refrain from those actions that constitute crimes in the majority of legal systems (such as murder, assault, theft, and fraud). Moreover, philosophical
> (45) anarchists hold that people have a positive moral obligation to care for one another, a moral obligation that they might even choose to discharge by supporting cooperative efforts by governments to help those in need. And where others are abiding by
> (50) established laws, even those laws derived from mere conventions, individuals are morally bound not to violate those laws when doing so would endanger others. Thus, if others obey the law and drive their vehicles on the right, one must not endanger them by
> (55) driving on the left, for, even though driving on the left is not inherently immoral, it is morally wrong to deliberately harm the innocent.

Margin notes:
(2) IS INCORRECT BECAUSE:
1. MORAL DUTIES
2. MUST CARE FOR OTHERS
3. CAN'T ENDANGER OTHERS
 EX.

As we've already noted, paragraph three begins by addressing the commentators' second criticism of philosophical anarchism (that without moral obligation to obey laws, people will do whatever they please). The author explains that even without laws, philosophical anarchists have moral duties not to harm each other, positive obligations to care for each other, and moral obligations to uphold laws when violating these laws would endanger others. This final point is illustrated with an example involving driving.

We'll learn in later chapters that the support for the author's view lists several items and so is a Classification structure, which we number and tag in the margin. We also note the example since examples are often asked about in the questions.

 **BP Minotaur:** Both Classification and Example structures provide support for conclusions. By noting them, you're learning to read for structure. Here, you've found premises that support the conclusion of an argument.

The markup for the entire passage thus looks like...

Most people acknowledge that not all governments have a moral right to govern and that there are sometimes morally legitimate reasons for disobeying the law, as when a particular law
(5) prescribes behavior that is clearly immoral. It is also commonly supposed that such cases are special exceptions and that, in general, the fact that something is against the law counts as a moral, as well as legal, ground for not doing it; i.e., we
(10) generally have a moral duty to obey a law simply because it is the law. But the theory known as philosophical anarchism denies this view, arguing instead that people who live under the jurisdiction of governments have no moral duty to those
(15) governments to obey their laws. Some commentators have rejected this position because of what they take to be its highly counterintuitive implications: (1) that no existing government is morally better than any other (since all are, in a sense, equally illegitimate),
(20) and (2) that, lacking any moral obligation to obey any laws, people may do as they please without scruple. In fact, however, philosophical anarchism does not entail these claims.

First, the conclusion that no government is
(25) morally better than any other does not follow from the claim that nobody owes moral obedience to any government. Even if one denies that there is a moral obligation to follow the laws of any government, one can still evaluate the morality of the policies and
(30) actions of various governments. Some governments do more good than harm, and others more harm than good, to their subjects. Some violate the moral rights of individuals more regularly, systematically, and seriously than others. In short, it is perfectly
(35) consistent with philosophical anarchism to hold that governments vary widely in their moral stature.

Second, philosophical anarchists maintain that all individuals have basic, nonlegal moral duties to one another—duties not to harm others in their lives,
(40) liberty, health, or goods. Even if governmental laws have no moral force, individuals still have duties to refrain from those actions that constitute crimes in the majority of legal systems (such as murder, assault, theft, and fraud). Moreover, philosophical
(45) anarchists hold that people have a positive moral obligation to care for one another, a moral obligation that they might even choose to discharge by supporting cooperative efforts by governments to help those in need. And where others are abiding by
(50) established laws, even those laws derived from mere conventions, individuals are morally bound not to violate those laws when doing so would endanger others. Thus, if others obey the law and drive their vehicles on the right, one must not endanger them by
(55) driving on the left, for, even though driving on the left is not inherently immoral, it is morally wrong to deliberately harm the innocent.

September 2007 Passage 4

MOST PEOPLE: GENERALLY LAWS AND MORALITY IN LINE

DEF. OF PHILOSOPHICAL ANARCHISM

COMMENTATORS' VIEWS

AUTHOR'S CONCLUSION

(1) IS INCORRECT

BECAUSE CAN JUDGE GOV'T

ATT.

(2) IS INCORRECT BECAUSE:

1. MORAL DUTIES

2. MUST CARE FOR OTHERS

3. CAN'T ENDANGER OTHERS

EX.

PHILOSOPHICAL ANARCHISM

COUNTERINTUITIVE IMPLICATIONS (COMMENTATORS) → CLAIMS DON'T FOLLOW

Cleetus: That was more painful than the rash Auntie Brody gave me.

Well, Cleetus, it certainly was a difficult passage in the first paragraph. But once we untangled the structure, paragraphs two and three were a breeze. Think how many students gave up because the first paragraph was difficult and just began skimming. Those students essentially threw away eight points on the LSAT.

We've finished our Reading Comprehension markup, but we're not quite done. To wrap up our Reading Comprehension passage analysis, we need to perform the following tasks before moving to the questions. We do this because these are common themes across all Reading Comprehension passages that are frequently asked about.

> 1. Anticipate the main idea
> 2. Anticipate the primary purpose
> 3. Anticipate the author's attitude
> 4. Anticipate anything to which the passage lends itself
> 5. Summarize the entire passage in a sentence

Ninja: Shinobi alway know what their enemies will do before they act. You anticipate so you know the answers before you read the questions.

Many of the above should be answered by the markup we've made for the passage. However, this checklist will allow you to evaluate how well you understand the passage and how good your markup is. If you're not sure what the main idea of the passage is by the end of the passage, for instance, then you know your head is up your hiney and you're staring at your lower intestine and you need to go back and figure out what the main point is.

30 / Chapter 4

For our passage, the five steps look like this:

1. Anticipate the main idea

The main idea is in our primary structure diagram, which is that for philosophical anarchism, the implications put forth by the commentators are not warranted.

2. Anticipate the primary purpose

The primary purpose answers the question of why the passage was written. It is intimately tied to the main idea and so can usually be found in the primary structure diagram. Here, the author wrote the passage to refute the position of the commentators.

3. Anticipate the author's attitude

For the author's attitude we track two things: with which view the author is aligned and any other instances of her opinion in the passage. The former is tracked in the primary structure diagram and the latter is tracked when we underline moments of attitude, as in lines 34-35 when the author uses the term "perfectly consistent." For this passage, the author clearly supports philosophical anarchism and her tone is scholarly. We describe it as scholarly because she's never excessively positive or negative in her views but rather measured, which is the hallmark of an academic tone.

4. Anticipate anything to which the passage lends itself

This moment allows you to note anything unusual in the passage (excessively emotional attitude or an unusually large number of examples, for instance). This passage has a definition, a Classification structure that explains how the second of the commentators' views is incorrect, and an example that further supports this.

5. Summarize the entire passage in a sentence

This is an important thing to do before moving to the answer choices because it lets you know whether or not you really understand the structure of the passage. It can also help you nail Organization questions (more on this in a later chapter) that come up from time to time. For this passage, the summary would be something like: commentators levy two criticisms against philosophical anarchism, and the author defends against these criticisms.

Now that we've analyzed the passage, marked it up according to the Blueprint Reading Method™, and anticipated our important points, we're finally ready to move on to the questions!

Ditz: That was, like, a totally huge amount of, like, work.

Yes it was, Ditz. But remember, this is the first time you've done it so it's going to take more time. With practice, this will become an automatic process that you'll perform much more quickly. Also, when you're really good at it, you won't have to write everything down.

20. Which one of the following most accurately expresses the main point of the passage?

(A) Some views that certain commentators consider to be implications of philosophical anarchism are highly counterintuitive.
(B) Contrary to what philosophical anarchists claim, some governments are morally superior to others, and citizens under legitimate governments have moral obligations to one another.
(C) It does not follow logically from philosophical anarchism that no government is morally better than any other or that people have no moral duties toward one another.
(D) Even if, as certain philosophical anarchists claim, governmental laws lack moral force, people still have a moral obligation to refrain from harming one another.
(E) Contrary to what some of its opponents have claimed, philosophical anarchism does not conflict with the ordinary view that one should obey the law because it is the law.

Question #20

The main point question! Accompanying almost every Reading Comprehension passage in existence, the main point question is as ubiquitous as it is tasty. This is because, when you've done the Blueprint method correctly, the correct answer should leap at you like a lemur on a juicy tamarind. Since we have an author in the passage, her conclusion is that philosophical anarchism does *not* entail that 1) no government is morally better than another and 2) people may do as they please. That's (C).

Answer choice (A) incorrectly uses the commentators' point of view as the main idea. We can throw out answer choice (B) immediately because the first six words "contrary to what philosophical anarchists claim" let us know it's wrong. We know the author is aligned with philosophical anarchism since she defends it against the commentators, so this is an easy exclusion. Answer choice (D) focuses far too narrowly on a detail of the passage to be the main idea. Finally, answer choice (E) gives us a payoff for tracking all of the views. We know that the original view held by "most people" isn't significant because it was immediately dropped. We know it can't be the main idea and so can exclude (E) handily.

Please note that question 20 was easily answered from the primary structure diagram we constructed in the lower, right-hand side of the passage.

Cleetus: I guess I kinda see where you're going with this whole markup thing.

Why thank you, Cleetus.

Question #21

21. The author identifies which one of the following as a commonly held belief?

    (A) In most cases we are morally obligated to obey the law simply because it is the law.
    (B) All governments are in essence morally equal.
    (C) We are morally bound to obey only those laws we participate in establishing.
    (D) Most crimes are morally neutral, even though they are illegal.
    (E) The majority of existing laws are intended to protect others from harm.

This question can be easily answered from our tagging to the right of the passage. The phrase "commonly held belief" lets us know we're in the first paragraph, which is tagged with "laws and morality generally in line." Once there, lines 9-11 contain the sentence "It is also commonly supposed that...we generally have a moral duty to obey a law simply because it is the law." This leads us to answer choice (A) like a bloodhound on the trail of a pungent raccoon.

Answer choice (B) describes the criticism the commentators have of philosophical anarchism, rather than the generally held view for which we're looking, so it's not the correct answer choice. Answer choices (C), (D), and (E) aren't mentioned in the passage, so they can't be something the author identified as a belief.

BP Minotaur: This is a common theme in Reading Comprehension answers. If the question asks us to identify something from the passage, the correct answer has to be in the passage. If you find yourself making an assumption for an answer choice to be correct, you are committing an error more grave than thinking Umberto from your summer abroad program wants to be in a committed relationship.

Question #22

22. The author's stance regarding the theory of philosophical anarchism can most accurately be described as one of

   (A) ardent approval of most aspects of the theory
   (B) apparent acceptance of some of the basic positions of the theory
   (C) concerned pessimism about the theory's ability to avoid certain extreme views
   (D) hesitant rejection of some of the central features of the theory
   (E) resolute antipathy toward both the theory and certain of its logical consequences

Here we have an attitude question, which is a very common question to see in Reading Comprehension passages. We know from the primary structure that the author agrees with philosophical anarchism and, from lines 34-35 where we underlined the author's attitude, that our author's approval is clear but measured. Accordingly, we can scan the answer choices for something that fits with this. Sure enough, answer choice (B) with its "apparent acceptance" is correct.

Answer choice (A) is a bit too ebullient with its "ardent approval" and answer choices (C), (D), and (E) can easily be ruled out because they're all negative toward philosophical anarchism in some way, which is clearly at odds with what our author thinks. Pro tip: if you're short on time, tackling the attitude questions first can often yield easy points.

Question #23

Question 23 draws on the high-level word we circled, "counterintuitive." If you didn't know that counterintuitive meant "contrary to common sense," you could divine from the passage that the implications of philosophical anarchism are counterintuitive to what "most people" from the first view believe (i.e. that because something is against the law, we shouldn't do it on moral grounds, as well). This leads us to answer choice (A) because the implications of philosophical anarchism run counter to what "most people" believe of laws.

23. By attributing to commentators the view that philosophical anarchism has implications that are "counterintuitive" (line 17), the author most likely means that the commentators believe that

   (A) the implications conflict with some commonly held beliefs
   (B) there is little empirical evidence that the implications are actually true
   (C) common sense indicates that philosophical anarchism does not have such implications
   (D) the implications appear to be incompatible with each other
   (E) each of the implications contains an internal logical inconsistency

Don't let answer choice (C), with its discussion of common sense, pull you in.
The latter part of the answer choice states: "...philosophical anarchism does not have such implications." The NOT ruins this answer choice as, according to the commentators, common

sense dictates that philosophical anarchism *does* have such implications. Oh the difference a single word makes. Just think if Nike changed "it" to "me." Talk about questionable slogans.

> 24. Which one of the following scenarios most completely conforms to the views attributed to philosophical anarchists in lines 37–44?
>
> (A) A member of a political party that is illegal in a particular country divulges the names of other members because he fears legal penalties.
> (B) A corporate executive chooses to discontinue her company's practice of dumping chemicals illegally when she learns that the chemicals are contaminating the water supply.
> (C) A person who knows that a coworker has stolen funds from their employer decides to do nothing because the coworker is widely admired.
> (D) A person neglects to pay her taxes, even though it is likely that she will suffer severe legal penalties as a consequence, because she wants to use the money to finance a new business.
> (E) A driver determines that it is safe to exceed the posted speed limit, in spite of poor visibility, because there are apparently no other vehicles on the road.

Answer choices (B), (D), and (E) each miss the mark because they all stray widely from the topic of what people commonly believe, or what common sense tells us.

Question #24

Question 24 nicely gives us the line numbers regarding where we should look for the answer. Since that directs us to the third paragraph, which is tagged with the idea that the commentators' second criticism is wrong because people have a duty not to harm others, we shouldn't lose time by re-reading the paragraph. Instead, we should look through the answer choices to see if one of them personifies the idea of not harming others.

Answer choice (B) is the correct answer because it fulfills the philosophical anarchist's criteria of not harming others. The executive stops dumping chemicals that are contaminating the water supply and thus causing harm to others. Don't let the "illegal" fool you—whether it's being dumped legally or illegally, the chemicals are harming others and stopping that is clearly in line with philosophical anarchism.

Answer choices (A) and (D) can quickly be eliminated because they involve cases where an individual fails to act for selfish reasons, rather than to refrain from harming others. Answer choice (C) can be eliminated because the person fails to stop a harm, which is against the dictates of philosophical anarchism. Answer choice (E) can be eliminated because the driver's actions may cause harm to others.

> **Ninja:** Here again, tagging the passage, like sharpening your throwing stars before a fight, pays off. Rather than wasting time locating the line numbers and re-reading that part of the paragraph, you can proceed immediately to the answer choices and answer the question just based on your tags.

Question #25

Question 25 asks us with what the author would agree. Hurray! We know from our primary structure diagram that our author agrees with philosophical anarchism, so we're searching for an answer choice that promotes its tenets. Remember, these tenets are that 1) governments can be evaluated and 2) people have a duty not to harm others.

> 25. It can be inferred that the author would be most likely to agree that
>
> (A) people are subject to more moral obligations than is generally held to be the case
> (B) governments that are morally superior recognize that their citizens are not morally bound to obey their laws
> (C) one may have good reason to support the efforts of one's government even if one has no moral duty to obey its laws
> (D) there are some sound arguments for claiming that most governments have a moral right to require obedience to their laws
> (E) the theory of philosophical anarchism entails certain fundamental principles regarding how laws should be enacted and enforced

Sure enough, answer choice (C) gives us the second. Philosophical anarchists don't care whether you follow the government's laws or not, just as long as you don't harm others. In fact, the example we tagged really helps us here: people should follow laws in order not to harm others.

We don't know whether (A) is correct since the passage doesn't discuss how people generally feel about moral obligations—we only know how they feel about following the law. Answer choice (B) is similar in that we don't know anything about it from the passage. The passage doesn't mention anything about "morally superior" governments. Answer choice (D) can be eliminated for the same reason: there are no arguments either way discussing whether or not governments have a moral right to require obedience to their laws. Answer choice (E) commits the same error by discussing how laws should be enacted and enforced according to philosophical anarchism, something about which the passage is silent.

Please note that ALL of the incorrect answer choices contained information about which we could know nothing from the passage. In Reading Comprehension, it's just as important to know what you *don't* as what you *do*.

Question #26

As with question 24, we're nicely directed to the part of the passage where we should look. That's the third paragraph, which is tagged with the moral obligations philosophical anarchists claim we have, including caring for others and not harming others. We outlined all of these in the margin with our numbered Classification structure. Armed with this information, the first thing to do is scan the answer choices to see if anything corresponds to this idea. Sure enough, answer choice (D) fits the bill. "Substantial moral obligations" encompasses both of these.

Only answer choice (E) comes close with its discussion of harms, but it describes the moral

26. The author's discussion of people's positive moral duty to care for one another (lines 44-49) functions primarily to

   (A) demonstrate that governmental efforts to help those in need are superfluous
   (B) suggest that philosophical anarchists maintain that laws that foster the common good are extremely rare
   (C) imply that the theoretical underpinnings of philosophical anarchism are inconsistent with certain widely held moral truths
   (D) indicate that philosophical anarchists recognize that people are subject to substantial moral obligations
   (E) illustrate that people are morally obligated to refrain from those actions that are crimes in most legal systems

27. In the passage, the author seeks primarily to

   (A) describe the development and theoretical underpinnings of a particular theory
   (B) establish that a particular theory conforms to the dictates of common sense
   (C) argue that two necessary implications of a particular theory are morally acceptable
   (D) defend a particular theory against its critics by showing that their arguments are mistaken
   (E) demonstrate that proponents of a particular theory are aware of the theory's defects

obligation as refraining from crimes, which is not what philosophical anarchism espouses. Answer choices (A), (B), and (C) all miss the mark because they don't discuss a duty not to harm others. Please note that, just like question 24, we answered that question without looking back at the passage at all. This tactic will save you valuable time on test day.

Question #27

This question is a Purpose question, which, if you remember, we anticipated before tackling the questions. We know that the author wrote the passage in order to refute the commentators' criticisms of philosophical anarchism. This leads us to (D) as handily as Hansel and Gretel following breadcrumbs in the forest. Only without a witch, or the threat of eating children.

Answer choice (A) can be eliminated because the passage fails to "describe the development" of any theory. Answer choice (B) can be eliminated because philosophical anarchism specifically fails to conform to common sense (remember that word "counterintuitive")? Answer choice (C) is close because it discusses two implications, which our passage does as well. However, our author objects to the fact that the implications outlined by the commentators are warranted, so this is the opposite of our author's purpose. Answer choice (E) is wrong because the only proponent of our theory of philosophical anarchism is the author and she argues that the defects the commentators put forth aren't present at all.

METHOD / 37

Ditz McGee: Okay, okay. We get it. We take time up front to mark up the passage to save time in the questions.

Very good, Ditz. Now you're getting it.

And that, kids, is how you tackle a Reading Comprehension passage according to the Blueprint method. Dissecting the passage in the Blueprint way enables you to analyze the passage as you read it as well as anticipate the answers to many questions before they're even asked. Much better than just skimming a bunch of information without really understanding it, no?

You should also have noticed that by using the Blueprint method, our markup led us to the correct answers to *ALL EIGHT QUESTIONS*. This means that, rather than running back to the passage to re-read lines or paragraphs and trying find the answer, you can quickly reference your markup, then answer the question.

BP Minotaur: You might be beginning to see that the extra time you spend marking up the passage will be more than compensated for by the time you save in the questions.

To be fair, this is a Reading Comprehension passage that has two great qualities: (1) It's fairly difficult for students the first time around, and (2) it breaks down quite nicely using the Blueprint method. However, we think you'll find that ALL of the passages on the test will become much easier by using our method. This exercise is designed to contrast your current, haphazard approach with the most effective way to tackle this passage so you'll understand that there is light at the end of the Reading Comprehension tunnel. Dim and seemingly very far away right now, but light nonetheless.

Can I get better?

That's a fair question. A lot of students think that, even though our method helped with *this particular* passage, it won't help with others. Because one passage discusses the homing mechanism of pigeons and another parses Thurgood Marshall's skills as a litigator, it can be difficult to recognize any similarities between passages. In fact, you might be tempted to think each passage is very different and what worked for one won't work for others. Thankfully, the writers of the LSAT appear to be stuck in a rut. Like your grandfather who eats the same early bird special for dinner every night, watches re-runs of *Seinfeld*, and won't be seen without his grey fedora, the Reading Comprehension section has a limited number of tricks up its sleeve. However, this book will give you the tools to recognize the repetitive features in the passages you encounter. **Once you realize that you are seeing the same structures over and over again, your performance will improve dramatically.**

So how do I get there?

As we stated earlier, the difficult part for students is usually that they feel they already know how to read so they resist applying the Blueprint methods. However, if the way you read was sufficient to get you a great score on the Reading Comprehension section of the LSAT, then you wouldn't be here, now would you?

On the previous pages, you saw the proper way to tackle a Reading Comprehension passage. But there is no quick and easy guide for mastering this strategy (as evinced by the size of this book). For instance, it's highly unlikely that you'll see another passage about philosophical anarchism again, and your work for this particular passage is done.

However, you will see a passage with two points of view along with an author aligning herself with one particular side. The purpose of this book is to train you to look past the subject matter of the passages to see the structure underneath. This is an abstract way of thinking that is incredibly powerful, but can also be difficult to learn. We will teach you how to read this way, but you have to be patient. In addition, you have to give up your old way of reading and trust that our method will work, even if it feels like it's taking longer and is less efficient in the beginning.

We will do plenty of passages throughout this book, but not right up front. There will be a number of chapters that discuss general strategy and focused drills before we set you free to battle passages about a platypus's hunting abilities and Korean labor force movements.

So let's start at the beginning...

5/theBIGthree

CAN IT REALLY BE THAT SIMPLE?

It's time to talk strategy. When you're first confronted with Reading Comprehension passages, they might seem overwhelming. This is largely because there appears to be hundreds of different types of passages. One minute, you're reading about whether or not Byron is a great poet. (Hint: he's not). The next, you're finding out about fractals. Then, you find yourself delving into the dearth of writing about women in medieval English law.

Cleetus: I ain't got no shot at learnin' all them things.

Cleetus, you might be right. However, here's the great news: you don't have to! It turns out that, in Reading Comprehension, you don't have to figure out hundreds of different topics. The masterminds who make this test just want you to think you do. While the subject matter may vary widely from passage to passage, this is completely irrelevant to the task at hand. The subject matter of a passage may be interesting as the love hexagon on last season's *Ice Road Bachelorette Truckers* or as dry as the Gobi desert, but the topic never determines how you approach a Reading Comprehension passage. Rather, the number of views in the passage is what actually defines a passage.

BP Minotaur: Most excellent news. After intensive analysis, Blueprint has discovered there are only a small number of Reading Comprehension passage types on the LSAT.

You might find this difficult to believe, but there aren't hundreds of types of Reading Comprehension passages. There aren't even twenty, or ten, or even five. Hold on to your seat...

At Blueprint, our revolutionary approach classifies every single passage in the history of the LSAT according to how many viewpoints it contains: one, two, or three.

Yes, just three. All of the hundreds of passages in the history of the LSAT can be organized into three different structures. Put simply, you are looking for one point of view, two points of view, or three points of view. Once you recognize this fact, Reading Comprehension becomes much more manageable. Perhaps (dare we say it?) even pleasurable.

① Thesis (1)
② anti-thesis (2)
③ synthesis (3)

THREE PRIMARY STRUCTURES

As we mentioned, all Reading Comprehension passages can be broken down into three categories according to the number of their points of view. At Blueprint, we call these categories *PRIMARY STRUCTURES*. Here's how they break down:

THESIS — one point of view

We begin with the Thesis passage, the most basic category in Reading Comprehension. Thesis passages contain one point of view. The following are samples of the main idea from real Thesis passages.

"The Pico workers' campaign thus offers an important lesson…"

"Recent studies have confirmed the ability of leading questions to alter the details of our memories…"

"Only recently, however, have biologists concluded on the basis of new evidence that the animal uses its bill to locate its prey while underwater…"

Ninja: There has been at least one Thesis passage on 86% of LSATs since the June 1991 exam. This means you're very likely to get a Thesis passage on your own LSAT.

The following are some examples of Thesis passages:

The paintings of Romare Bearden (1914-1988) represent a double triumph. At the same time that Bearden's work reflects a lifelong commitment to perfecting the innovative painting techniques he pioneered, it also reveals an artist engaged in a search
(5) for ways to explore the varieties of African-American experience.

By presenting scene, character, and mood using a unique layered and fragmented style that
(10) combines elements of painting with elements of collage, Bearden suggested some of the ways in which commonplace subjects could be forced to undergo a metamorphosis when filtered through the techniques available to the resourceful artist. Bearden knew that
(15) regardless of individual painters' personal histories, tastes, or points of view, they must pay their craft the respect of approaching it through an acute awareness of the resources and limitations of the form to which they have dedicated their creative energies.

(20) But how did Bearden, so passionately dedicated to solving the more advanced problems of his painting technique, also succeed so well at portraying the realities of African-American life? During the Great Depression of the 1930's, Bearden painted scenes of
(25) the hardships of the period; the work was powerful, the scenes grim and brooding. Through his depiction of the unemployed in New York's Harlem he was able to move beyond the usual "protest painting" of the period to reveal instances of individual human suffering. His
(30) human figures, placed in abstract yet mysteriously familiar urban settings, managed to express the complex social reality lying beyond the borders of the canvas without compromising their integrity as elements in an artistic composition. Another important element of
(35) Bearden's compositions was his use of muted colors, such as dark blues and purples, to suggest moods of melancholy or despair. While functioning as part of the overall design, these colors also served as symbols of the psychological effects of debilitating social processes.

(40) During the same period, he also painted happier scenes—depictions of religious ceremony, musical performance, and family life—and instilled them with the same vividness that he applied to his scenes of suffering. Bearden sought in his work to reveal in all its
(45) fullness a world long hidden by the clichés of sociology and rendered cloudy by the simplifications of journalism and documentary photography. Where any number of painters have tried to project the "prose" of Harlem, Bearden concentrated on releasing its poetry—its family
(50) rituals and its ceremonies of affirmation and celebration. His work insists that we truly see the African-American experience in depth, using the fresh light of his creative vision. Through an act of artistic will, he created strange visual harmonies out of the mosaic of the African-
(55) American experience, and in doing so reflected the multiple rhythms, textures, and mysteries of life.

Viewpoint (Thesis)

The okapi, a forest mammal of central Africa, has presented zoologists with a number of difficult questions since they first learned of its existence in 1900. The first was how to classify it. Because it is horselike in dimension, and because it sports a hide similar to a zebra's (a relative of the horse), zoologists first classified it as a member of the horse (5) family. But further studies showed that, despite its coloration and short necks, their closest relatives were (10) giraffes. The okapi's rightful place within the giraffe family is confirmed by its skin-covered horns (in males), two-lobed canine teeth, and long prehensile tongue.

The next question was the size of the okapi (15) population. Because okapis were infrequently captured by hunters, some zoologists believed that they were rare; however, others theorized that their habits simply kept them out of sight. It was not until 1985, when zoologists started tracking okapis by affixing collars (20) equipped with radio transmitters to briefly captured specimens, that reliable information about okapi numbers and habits began to be collected. It turns out that while okapis are not as rare as some zoologists suspected, their population is concentrated in an (25) extremely limited chain of forestland in northeastern central Africa, surrounded by savanna.

One reason for their seeming scarcity is that their coloration allows okapis to camouflage themselves even at close range. Another is that okapis do not (30) travel in groups or with other large forest mammals, and neither frequent open riverbanks nor forage at the borders of clearings, choosing instead to keep to the forest interior. This is because okapis, unlike any other animal in the central African forest, subsist entirely (35) on leaves: more than one hundred species of plants have been identified as part of their diet, and about twenty of these are preferred. Okapis never eat one plant to the exclusion of others; even where preferred foliage is abundant, okapis will leave much of it (40) uneaten, choosing to move on and sample other leaves. Because of this, and because of the distribution of their food, okapis engage in individual rather than congregated foraging.

But other questions about okapi behavior arise. (45) Why for example, do they prefer to remain within forested areas when many of their favorite plants are found in the open border between forest and savanna? One possibility is that this is a defense against predators; another is that the okapi was pushed into the (50) forest by competition with other large, hoofed animals, such as the bushbuck and bongo, that specialize on the forest edges and graze them more efficiently. Another question is why okapis are absent from other nearby forest regions that would seem hospitable to them. (55) Zoologists theorize that okapis are relicts of an era when forestland was scarce and that they continue to respect those borders even though available forestland has long since expanded.

December 1999 Passage 1

The okapi, a forest mammal of central Africa, has presented zoologists with a number of difficult questions since they first learned of its existence in 1900.

Viewpoint (Thesis)

At first glance, these passages might seem to be quite distinct from each other. However, the basic process in each passage is the same: there is only one point of view being espoused.

Thesis passages will be the first challenge we tackle in this book. They come in many shapes and sizes, but the underlying structure is always the same.

ANTITHESIS

(handwritten annotations: "usually about conflict"; "two points of view - one viewpoint espoused and another typically conflicts with it - the author sides with one")

The second type of passage for you to conquer has two points of view. These are Antithesis passages. These are the most common type of Reading Comprehension passage and you are nearly guaranteed to see one and likely more on test day. In an Antithesis passage, one point of view is espoused and a second point of view conflicts with it. Antithesis passages are thus two arguments, with the author typically siding with one side or the other.

> "Most of what has been written about Thurgood Marshall... has just focused on his judicial record...But when Marshall's career is viewed from a technical perspective, his work with the NAACP reveals a strategic and methodological legacy to the field of public interest law."

> Andres Duany, Elizabeth Plater-Zyberk, and Jeff Speck, a group of prominent town planners belonging to a movement called New Urbanism, contend that suburban sprawl contributes to the decline of civic life and civility...Opponents of New Urbanism claim that migration to sprawling suburbs is an expression of people's legitimate desire to secure the enjoyment and personal mobility provided by the automobile and the lifestyle that it makes possible.

> "Recently, a new school of economics called steady-state economics has seriously challenged neoclassical economics, the reigning school in Western economic decision making."

Ninja: There has been at least one Antithesis passage on 97% of the LSATs since June 1991 and at least two 71% of the time. You're almost guaranteed to get an Antithesis passage on your LSAT, and quite likely to get two.

Antithesis passages differ from Thesis passages in that they include an opposing point of view. The following are samples of the two points of view expressed in real Antithesis passages:

Traditionally, members of a community such as a town or neighborhood share a common location and a sense of necessary interdependence that includes, for example, mutual respect and emotional support. (5) But as modern societies grow more technological and sometimes more alienating, people tend to spend less time in the kinds of interactions that their communities require in order to thrive. Meanwhile, technology has made it possible for individuals to interact via personal (10) computer with others who are geographically distant. Advocates claim that these computer conferences, in which large numbers of participants communicate by typing comments that are immediately read by other participants and responding immediately to those (15) comments they read, function as communities that can substitute for traditional interactions with neighbors.

What are the characteristics that advocates claim allow computer conferences to function as communities? For one, participants often share (20) common interests or concerns; conferences are frequently organized around specific topics such as music or parenting. Second, because conferences are conversations, participants have adopted conventions in recognition of the importance of (25) respecting each others' sensibilities. Abbreviations are used to convey commonly expressed sentiments of courtesy such as "pardon me for cutting in" ("pmfci") or "in my humble opinion" ("imho"). Because a humorous tone can be difficult to communicate in (30) writing, participants will often end an intentionally humorous comment with a set of characters that, when looked at sideways, resembles a smiling or winking face. Typing messages entirely in capital letters is avoided, because its tendency to demand the attention (35) of a reader's eye is considered the computer equivalent of shouting. These conventions, advocates claim, constitute a form of etiquette, and with this etiquette as a foundation, people often form genuine, trusting relationships, even offering advice and support during (40) personal crises such as illness or the loss of a loved one.

But while it is true that conferences can be both respectful and supportive, they nonetheless fall short of communities. For example, computer conferences (45) discriminate along educational and economic lines because participation requires a basic knowledge of computers and the ability to afford access to conferences. Further, while advocates claim that a shared interest makes computer conferences similar (50) to traditional communities—insofar as the shared interest is analogous to a traditional community's shared location—this analogy simply does not work. Conference participants are a self-selecting group; they are drawn together by their shared interest in (55) the topic of the conference. Actual communities, on the other hand, are "nonintentional": the people who inhabit towns or neighborhoods are thus more likely to exhibit genuine diversity—of age, career, or personal interests—than are conference participants. It (60) might be easier to find common ground in a computer conference than in today's communities, but in so doing it would be unfortunate if conference participants cut themselves off further from valuable interactions in their own towns or neighborhoods.

Many people complain about corporations, but there are also those whose criticism goes further and who hold corporations morally to blame for many of the problems in Western society. Their criticism is
(5) not reserved solely for fraudulent or illegal business activities, but extends to the basic corporate practice of making decisions based on what will maximize profits without regard to whether such decisions will contribute to the public good. Others, mainly
(10) economists, have responded that this criticism is flawed because it inappropriately applies ethical principles to economic relationships.

It is only by extension that we attribute the quality of morality to corporations, for corporations are not
(15) persons. Corporate responsibility is an aggregation of the responsibilities of those persons employed by the corporation when they act in and on behalf of the corporation. Some corporations are owner-operated, but in many corporations and in most larger ones there
(20) is a syndicate of owners to whom the chief executive officer, or CEO, who runs the corporation is said to have a fiduciary obligation.

The economists argue that a CEO's sole responsibility is to the owners, whose primary interest,
(25) except in charitable institutions, is the protection of their profits. CEOs are bound, as a condition of their employment, to seek a profit for the owners. But suppose a noncharitable organization is owner-operated, or, for some other reason, its CEO is not
(30) obligated to maximize profits. The economists' view is that even if such a CEO's purpose is to look to the public good and nothing else, the CEO should still work to maximize profits, because that will turn out best for the public anyway.

(35) But the economists' position does not hold up under careful scrutiny. For one thing, although there are, no doubt, strong underlying dynamics in national and international economies that tend to make the pursuit of corporate interest contribute to the public
(40) good, there is no guarantee—either theoretically or in practice—that a given CEO will benefit the public by maximizing corporate profit. It is absurd to deny the possibility, say, of a paper mill legally maximizing its profits over a five year period by decimating a forest
(45) for its wood or polluting a lake with its industrial waste. Furthermore, while obligations such as those of corporate CEOs to corporate owners are binding in a business or legal sense, they are not morally paramount. The CEO could make a case to the owners
(50) that certain profitable courses of action should not be taken because they are likely to detract from the public good. The economic consequences that may befall the CEO for doing so, such as penalty or dismissal, ultimately do not excuse the individual from the
(55) responsibility for acting morally.

Synthesis passages are all about HARMONY
- *two conflicting views are brought into harmony or reconciled by a third viewpoint - usually the author's*

SYNTHESIS — three points of view

While Antithesis passages are all about conflict, Synthesis passages, which contain three points of view, are all about harmony. In Synthesis passages, two views are espoused and a third view—typically that of the author—reconciles those views. Synthesis passages are the least common type of Reading Comprehension structure but they're fun when you get them since they're typically quite easy to spot.*

The following are samples of Synthesis conclusions as expressed in real Synthesis passages.

> "Most interesting and controversial cases will occur in the penumbra of both rules and principles."

> "His persistent use of comic-art conventions demonstrates a faith in reconciliation, not only between cartoons and fine art, but between parody and true feeling."

> "An effort should be made to dispel the misunderstandings that still prevent the much-needed synthesis and mutual supplementation of science and the humanities."

Cleetus: Is a penumbra one of them umbrellas for pens?

No, Cleetus. A penumbra is a shadowy or indefinite area. Remember, kids, look up words you don't understand now so you don't get caught by them on test day. That would be unpropitious indeed.

Ninja: 32% of LSATs since June of 1991 have at least one Synthesis passage. You're likely to get one or none of these passage types on your LSAT.

Next are some examples of synthesis passages.

---

* And by fun we mean "tending to yield easy points."

Countee Cullen (Countee Leroy Porter, 1903–1946) was one of the foremost poets of the Harlem Renaissance, the movement of African American writers, musicians, and artists centered in the Harlem section of New York City during the 1920s. Beginning with his university years, Cullen strove to establish himself as an author of romantic poetry on abstract, universal topics such as love and death. Believing poetry should consist of "lofty thoughts beautifully expressed," Cullen preferred controlled poetic forms. He used European forms such as sonnets and designs such as quatrains, couplets, and conv[...] and he frequently employed classical [...] Christian religious imagery, which we[...] the product both of his university edu[...] his upbringing as the adopted son of [...] Episcopal reverend.

Some literary critics have praised [...] at writing European-style verse, findi[...] in "The Ballad of the Brown Girl" an artful use of diction and a rhythm and sonority that allow him [...] capture the atmosphere typical of the English ba[...] form of past centuries. Others have found Culle[...] use of European verse forms and techniques un[...] to treating political or racial themes, such as the themes in "Uncle Jim," in which a young man is [...] by his uncle of the different experiences of Afri[...] Americans and whites in United States society, [...] "Incident," which relates the experience of an e[...] year-old child who hears a racial slur. One such [...] has complained that Cullen's persona as express[...] in his work sometimes seems to vacillate between aesthete and spokesperson for racial issues. But Cullen himself rejected this dichotomy, m[...] interest in romantic poetry was qu[...] his concern over racial issues. He [...] between poetry of solely political [...] work, which he believed reflected [...] African American. As the heartfelt [...] his personality accomplished by means of careful attention to his chosen craft, his work could not help but do so.

Explicit references to racial matters do in fact decline in Cullen's later work, but not because he felt any less passionately about these matters. Rather, Cullen increasingly focused on the religious dimension of his poetry. In "The Black Christ," in which the poet imagines the death and resurrection of a rural African American, and "Heritage," which expresses the tension between the poet's identification with Christian traditions and his desire to stay close to his African heritage, Cullen's thoughts on race were subsumed within what he conceived of as broader and more urgent questions about the suffering and redemption of the soul. Nonetheless, Cullen never abandoned his commitment to the importance of racial issues, reflecting on one occasion that he felt "actuated by a strong sense of race consciousness" that "grows upon me, I find, as I grow older."

Wherever the crime novels of P. D. James are
discussed by critics, there is a tendency on the one
hand to exaggerate her merits and on the other to
castigate her as a genre writer who is getting above
(5) herself. Perhaps underlying the debate is the
false opposition set up between different kinds of
fiction, according to which enjoyable novels are
to be somehow slightly lowbrow, and a novel is not
considered true literature unless it is a tiresome chore.
(10) Those commentators who would elevate P. D.
James's books to the status of high literature point
to her painstakingly constructed characters, her
elaborate settings, her sense of place, and her love
of abstractions: notions about morality, duty, pain,
(15) and pleasure are never far from the lips of her police
officers and murderers. Others find her pretentious
and tiresome; an inverted snobbery accuses her of
abandoning the time honored conventions of the
detective genre in favor of a highbrow literary style.
(20) The critic Harriet Waugh wants P. D. James to get
on with "the more taxing business of laying a tricky
trail and then fooling the reader"; Philip Oakes in *The
Literary Review* groans, "Could we please proceed
with the business of clapping the handcuffs on the
(25) killer?"
James is certainly capable of strikingly good
writing. She takes immense trouble to provide her
characters with convincing histories and passions.
Her descriptive digressions are part of the pleasure
(30) of her books and give them dignity and weight. But
it is equally true that they frequently interfere with
the story; the patinas and aromas of a country kitchen
receive more loving attention than does the plot itself.
Her devices to advance the story can be shameless and
(35) thin, and it is often impossible to see how her detective
arrives at the truth; one is left to conclude that the
detective solves crimes through intuition. At this stage
in her career P. D. James seems to be less interested
in the specifics of detection than in her characters'
(40) vulnerabilities and perplexities.
However, once the rules of a chosen genre
cramp creative thought, there is no reason why an
able and interesting writer should accept them. In her
latest book, there are signs that P. D. James is starting
(45) to feel constrained by the crime-novel genre, as
her determination to leave areas of ambiguity in the
solution of the crime and to distribute guilt among
murderer, victim, and bystander amounts to a kind of
rebellion against the traditional neatness of detective
(50) fiction. It is fashionable, though reprehensible, for one
writer to prescribe to another. But perhaps the time has
come for P. D. James to slide out of her handcuffs and
stride into the territory of the mainstream novel.

June 1996 Passage 1

The makers of the test go to great lengths to make the passages seem difficult. However, when you clear away the detritus and obfuscation, there are only three things happening on the most basic level in Reading Comprehension. By focusing on structure, rather than subject, you'll have a huge advantage over other test takers.

Up next, we are going to delve into important basic skills for any passage. First up: comprehending what you read. Let's go.

6/COMPREHENSIONwhile READING

LET'S START AT THE VERY BEGINNING...

You might think that the next step, after learning about the three types of Reading Comprehension passages, will be to begin practice categorizing passages into types. You would be wrong. Before we teach you more of the Blueprint method, it's important to have some basic skills you'll need on this section of the test. We begin with the most basic of these: understanding what it is you're reading. This seems totally reasonable in the abstract, but we've found that many test takers blow through passages without understanding the text in its entirety, either from reading too quickly and skipping information, or from not taking the time to understand recondite terminology from context clues.

BP Minotaur: Stop reading immediately if you don't comprehend something in the passage. Otherwise, you're just wasting your time.

Ninja: Grasshoppers who failed to look up the word "recondite" shall be beaten with nunchaku until further notice.

But I need to read quickly, don't I?

Eventually, yes. But not yet. For now, and up until a few weeks before the actual LSAT, you should practice reading slowly and thoroughly. Even if it takes you forty-five minutes or more to read and understand one passage, that's perfectly fine. In fact, that's great, because it means you're taking the time to understand what you read, look up any unfamiliar vocabulary, and anticipate the questions likely to be asked about the passage.

After you've learned how to read a passage thoroughly and effectively, then it's time to work on your speed. Practice Reading Comprehension as though you were learning to operate a buzz saw: eventually, you'll be a master, but, if you go too fast too soon, you'll have fewer fingers, and, if things go really badly, you could bleed out.

PRACTICE, PRACTICE, PRACTICE

The following exercises are designed to test your ability to comprehend what you are reading. You should understand each sentence before proceeding to the next, and, if you don't understand any portion of the sentence, read it again. This may seem laborious and painstaking, but practice it now so that you form the habit of understanding what you're reading early in the process.

These passages are intentionally dense and wordy and difficult because the passages on the LSAT are dense and wordy and difficult. If you don't know a word, look it up. Not only is it always a good idea to expand your vocabulary, the word might just show up on test day.

To be perfectly clear, you should either understand each sentence of each passage before finishing the exercise, or someone should find your dusty skeleton years from now, with this book open to this page.

For passages 1-5, read the passage and select the answer that best summarizes it. Passages 6-10 increase the challenge by giving you a space to summarize the passage in your own words.

Question #1

The Lascaux Cave, set in the hilly Montignac region of Southern France, is one of the oldest art installations in the world. Current estimates date its creation to around 15,000 B.C. The cave, which is decorated with over 2,000 images of animals, humans, and abstract symbols, was discovered in late summer of 1940 by Marcel Ravidat, a local teenager. It was briefly opened to the public in 1948, but carbon dioxide from human respiration caused damage to the paintings, and the cave was closed to the public thereafter. A destructive black fungus has overrun the cave since 1998, and that state of affairs has been attributed to a new air conditioning system installed in the cave around that time. This has sparked discussion among paleo-anthropologists over the question, "Why the hell do you need A/C in a cave nobody visits?" The best answer so far has been supplied by an anonymous stoner in Portland, Oregon who responded, "Because, then you could, like, get really high and not get hot, and those paintings are soooooo old, dude, and you could just sit there and trip out, and be like, 'Dude, cavemen lived here!'"

(A) A stoner from Portland, Oregon is believed to be the guerilla artist behind an art installation in southwestern France.
(B) In 1940, a teenager in southwestern France was busy installing air conditioning in his house when he fell through the floor and found a cave full of old paintings.
(C) In 1940, a cave was discovered in southwestern France, and it contained paintings from 15,000 B.C. Fungus attributed to human respiration covered the walls shortly after it was opened in 1948, and it was closed. Carbon dioxide later caused further damage.
(D) That guy is totally right. Cavemen did live there. That is awesome. Know what else is awesome? Chips and guacamole.
(E) In 1940, a cave was discovered in southwestern France that contained paintings from 15,000 B.C. It was briefly opened to the public in 1948, but carbon dioxide attributed to human respiration caused damage. It was closed thereafter. More recently, fungus has sprouted on the cave walls, probably as a result of a new air conditioning system.

Question #2

> Scholars of the Law and Economics school of thought believe, in essence, that the legal system's primary purpose is to produce outcomes that maximize economic efficiency. The ideal rule of law, according to these scholars, is one that achieves Pareto efficiency, named after Italian economist Vilfredo Pareto. In sum, Pareto efficiency applied to legal rules identifies a situation in which the rule could not be changed to make one person better off economically without making another person worse off economically. The implications of applying this idea to legal rules are counterintuitive to some. For example, it has been argued that there should be no penalty for breach of contract where both parties will be better off economically for the breach, even if the other party opposes the breach. To illustrate this concept, under Pareto efficiency, a contractor could agree to build a house for a certain sum and then walk away, with some money in his pocket after having done no work, if there were a cheaper alternative for the homeowner for getting the work done. To scholars outside the Law and Economics school, this notion has been described as "theft" and "total bull$#!@."

(A) Scholars of the Law and Economics school believe that legal rules should work to make both sides of a dispute as economically well off as possible, even if that state of affairs seems unfair to some.

(B) Scholars of the Law and Economics school believe that many, if not most, students go to law school for economic reasons, i.e. to make serious money.

(C) Scholars of the Law and Economics school believe in the Pareto efficiency concept, which holds that laws should be as efficient as possible.

(D) Pareto efficiency is ridiculous because it was thought up by an Italian, and Italy is inherently inefficient. If Italy was efficient, then Rome would've been built in a day, which it wasn't.

(E) Scholars of the Law and Economics movement are primarily concerned with letting contractors take advantage of homeowners.

Question #3

In 1905, the United States Supreme Court handed down its decision in the case United States v. Winans, which interpreted the application of the Treaty Clause of the U.S. Constitution to a treaty entered into in 1855 between the United States government and the Yakima Indians of what is now the state of Washington. The tribe sued the Winans brothers, accusing them of violating the provision of the treaty providing the tribe with "the right of taking fish at all usual and accustomed places in common with the citizens of the territory." The brothers operated a fish wheel, which allowed them to catch several tons of fish at a time, decimating the population of fish upon which the Yakima survived. The Winans brothers also prevented the Yakima from crossing their property to access certain traditional fishing grounds. The Court held that the Winans brothers could continue to operate the fish wheel, but could not prevent the Yakima from accessing traditional fishing grounds.

(A) In U.S. v. Winans, the Supreme Court decided that the Yakima treaty prevented the Winans brothers from operating a fish wheel, but that they could continue to block access to their property.
(B) In U.S. v. Winans, the Supreme Court decided that the Yakima treaty prevented the Winans brothers from operating a fish wheel and from blocking access to their property.
(C) In U.S. v. Winans, the Supreme Court decided that the Yakima treaty allowed the Winans brothers to operate a fish wheel, but that they could not continue to block access to their property.
(D) In U.S. v. Winans, the Supreme Court decided that the Yakima treaty allowed the Winans brothers to operate a fish wheel, and that they could continue to block access to their property.
(E) In U.S. v. Winans, the Supreme Court decided that the Yakima Treaty violated the Treaty Clause of the U.S. Constitution.

Question #4

> Scholars of the Revanchist School argue that the Symbolist Movement developed in response to the Realist Movement, which predominated French poetry in the first half of the Nineteenth Century. Scholars of the Complementalist School take the opposite position, i.e. that the Symbolist Movement dovetails with the Realist Movement in a way that is complementary rather than antagonistic. Critics from both schools cite Les Fleurs du mal (The Flowers of Evil), a volume of poetry by the Frenchman Charles Baudelaire, to support their positions. Fleurs presents a dream-like depiction of a rapidly modernizing Paris in the mid-Nineteenth Century. That dream-like quality, Revanchists argue, is evidence that Symbolists like Baudelaire were in open rebellion against Realists. Complementalists, however, claim that the somber tone of the work and its exposition of the inner states of its characters intentionally incorporate the Realist movement's literalism to great effect.

(A) Revanchists and Complementalists agree that Les Fleur du mal was the first and most important example of French Symbolism.
(B) Realist and Symbolist scholars are at odds over whether Complementalism emerged as a response to Revanchism or as the inevitable next step in Revanchism.
(C) Les Fleur du mal was widely regarded as the first Symbolist work at the time of its publishing.
(D) Charles Baudelaire wrote Les Fleur du mal both as an extension of Realism and a challenge to it.
(E) Revanchists and Complementalists both cite Les Fleur du mal as supporting their own interpretations of the relationship between Symbolism and Realism, even though those interpretations are opposed.

Question #5

> Until recently, the early hominid Homo neanderthalensis, commonly referred to as the "Neanderthal," was classified by paleontologists as a separate species from Homo sapiens, i.e. modern day humans. Other paleontologists have challenged this notion in recent years, arguing that the Neanderthal is a human subspecies. They point to the recent discovery that DNA believed to be unique to Neanderthals resides in the genetic code of all modern humans, ranging anywhere from 0.5% of a strand of DNA to as much as 3% in some humans. This evidence, they argue quite convincingly, shows extensive interbreeding among humans and Neanderthals. I submit, however, that both of these theories are wrong. Humans are, in fact, a devolved subspecies of Neanderthal—an evolutionary step backward. I need only note the popularity of Justin Bieber or the practice, popular in Europe, of eating French fries with mayonnaise, to conclude definitively that humans are nothing more than hairless apes.

(A) I don't know. I stopped reading at Homo neanderthalensis.
(B) Certain paleontologists believe that humans and Neanderthals are related, but they are actually different species.
(C) Eating French fries with mayonnaise is an abomination, and anyone caught in the act of consuming it should be summarily executed for the good of humanity.
(D) Scientists have disagreed over whether Neanderthals are a subspecies of human, or a separate species. However, the truth is that humans are actually a subspecies of Neanderthal.
(E) Seriously. French fries with mayonnaise?

Question #6

In his 1936 treatise, The General Theory of Employment, Interest and Money, economist John Maynard Keynes disputed pre-Depression Era economic orthodoxy, which held that a drop in consumption due to savings, like the stock market selloff that ensued after the 1929 Black Tuesday crash of the U.S. stock market, would cause interest rates to fall. Falling interest rates, those economists believed would, in turn, lead businesses to borrow money, and increase investment spending and demand for products and services. The market would, in other words, correct itself in times of crisis. Keynes disagreed, arguing instead that lower interest rates by themselves do not increase spending by firms, but, rather, firms invest only when they expect demand for their products in the future. Pessimism about future demand, according to Keynes, causes a retrenchment in spending, independent of interest rates, which in turn lowers overall demand in the economy. The result is a vicious cycle, like the Great Depression, that can only be addressed by increased expenditures, which, in such a situation, can only be expected from the government.

SUMMARIZE THE PASSAGE: _____
_____
_____
_____
_____
_____

Question #7

The narwhal, an Arctic-dwelling whale whose closest relative is the beluga whale, has been hunted to near extinction. Although some Inuit peoples hunt the narwhal for subsistence, its status as an endangered species is primarily a function of the market value of its tusk. Male narwhals grow spiraled tusks that can be up to ten feet in length, and those tusks have long been prized curiosities. In the 16th century, Queen Elizabeth I was presented with a bejeweled narwhal tusk by an admirer who paid some £10,000, or approximately $4 million in today's dollars. Another reason for the narwhal's status as an endangered species is that it is a highly specialized species. They live only in the Arctic Circle, making them particularly susceptible to the effects of climate change. More importantly, the narwhal has reduced dentition and cannot chew its food. Instead, it sucks up its prey, and suitable prey is also highly susceptible to the effects of climate change.

SUMMARIZE THE PASSAGE: _____
_____
_____
_____
_____
_____

Question #8

When Igor Stravinsky's ballet, Rite of Spring, debuted in Paris in 1913, the audience booed and hissed, and eventually the scene devolved into something like a riot, with spectators fighting one another and threatening the orchestra. The piece's chaotic dissonance and confounding rhythms assaulted the listeners in a way for which they were not prepared. Ironically, when Rite subsequently became a fixture of the musical canon, it lost its ability to shock and to move, its primary contribution to the orchestral landscape of the early Twentieth Century. Half a century later, the great composer and conductor Leonard Bernstein reimagined Rite in a way that would make it relevant in perpetuity, a way that took into account more than its propensity to disorient the listener. Bernstein brought to the fore the lyrical quality of the music and its previously underemphasized tonality, summoning beauty out of chaos, in a way that evoked deeper emotion in the listener than mere shock.

SUMMARIZE THE PASSAGE: _____

Question #9

On June 30, 1908, at 7:14 a.m. local time, a deafening explosion occurred in the skies over the Podkamennaya Tunguska River in Siberia, flattening 770 square miles of forest, and knocking over some 80 million trees. The Tunguska Event, as it is now known, was caused by a meteor measuring somewhere between 200 and 800 feet in length. The explosion contained destructive power more than a thousand times greater than the nuclear bomb dropped on Hiroshima in 1945. It is interesting to note that, strictly speaking, the comet did not impact the earth, instead breaking up into millions of smaller chunks that rained down on a wide swath of the Siberian wilderness. Giuseppe Longo, an Italian scientist, hypothesized that a previously undiscovered, bowl-shaped lake a few miles north of the epicenter, Lake Cheko, was created by a fragment of the meteor, about three feet square, that survived the explosion and impacted the ground. Dating of the sediment found at the bottom of the lake, as well as sonic readings determining the shape of the lakebed, provide support for Longo's hypothesis.

SUMMARIZE THE PASSAGE: _____

Question #10

Although much is now known about their genesis, the mo'ai—giant carved statues that dot the landscape of far-flung Easter Island—remain mysterious in certain respects, as does the Rapa Nui civilization, which created the statues. It is now known that the mo'ai were carved in place at a quarry on a different island and transported on vessels to their final location. It is, however, still unknown exactly how they were transported to and from the vessels. Easter Island has been completely deforested, which has engendered speculation that the statues were rolled over land on felled trees. When Jacob Roggeveen, a Dutch explorer, became the first westerner to find Easter Island in 1722, there was a thriving population on the island. However, in the greatest of mysteries relating to the mo'ai, by 1868, the island was abandoned and the statues had all been knocked down. The quarry where the statues were carved appeared to have been abandoned in haste, with statues in varying states of completion and tools strewn about. Various theories have been put forward to explain this abandonment, including that the population starved, having used the trees that they needed to make vessels for rolling the statues. This theory, however, can't account for the rapidity of the departure of the Rapa Nui from the island or the fact that the statues were knocked over.

SUMMARIZE THE PASSAGE: _____

ANSWER KEY

1. e, 2. a, 3. c, 4. e, 5. d.

6. Pre-Depression economists believed that lower spending by consumers would lead to lower interest rates, and, because of that, businesses would borrow money to spend, thereby boosting the economy. Keynes, however, believed that businesses only spend in response to demand, which, in a recession or depression, can only be created by government spending.

7. The narwhal is a whale with a tusk. It is an endangered species because it has been hunted for its tusk and because it and the prey it consumes are susceptible to the effects of climate change.

8. Rite of Spring was controversial when it premiered because it shocked listeners, but it lost its relevance until Leonard Bernstein was able to find the beauty in it.

9. A large meteor exploded in the skies of Siberia, destroying a wide swath of the countryside as well as millions of trees. An Italian scientist believes that a fragment that survived the explosion created a lake nearby, a theory supported by various pieces of evidence.

10. The *mo'ai* are giant statues on an abandoned island. Much about them is a mystery, including how they were moved and what happened to the people who created them.

7/mainPOINT

WHATCHA TRYIN' TO SAY?

In Chapter 5 we discussed the three primary structures. Remember that? Golly, that was fun! (Don't argue.) The primary structure of a passage, you'll remember, is the number of **points of view** in the passage. Well, let's get down to brass tacks. Just what is a point of view?

> **BP Minotaur:** A point of view is a conclusion, and the conclusion is the most important part of an argument. As a lawyer, you will make your own arguments and rebut your opponent's arguments. RC passages test your ability to identify and understand arguments.

Let's take a lawyerly example. You are the prosecutor in a murder trial. You are making an argument to the jury. Your conclusion—your point of view—is that the defendant is guilty of murder. Everything else you tell the jury—his DNA was found at the crime scene, he confessed to the crime, his alibi didn't check out—is support for that point of view. And that's all an argument is: a conclusion, and some stuff that provides support for it.

Before we continue, a note on the terminology used in this book. We use the following terms to identify conclusions: **point of view, viewpoint, main idea, claim, and main point**. While these terms are more or less interchangeable in real life, there are subtle differences for Reading Comprehension.

- *Claim, point of view, and viewpoint refer to the conclusions of the parties in the passage.* So, for example, in a Synthesis passage, there are three viewpoints/points of view.
- *Main idea and main point refer to the overall conclusion of the passage as a whole.* When the author expresses a point of view (a concept we will discuss in depth in the next chapter) the author's point of view is the main point of the passage. So, even though there are three viewpoints in a Synthesis passage, there is only one main point when the author expresses a point of view. When the author does not express a point of view, the main point is a summary of all the points of view in a passage.

If this isn't totally clear right now, that's okay. The differences in terminology will be reinforced throughout the book.

So, now that you know what a conclusion is, you must learn to identify one. The good news is that we can help you develop this skill. The even better news is that learning how to locate conclusions will have a huge payoff on the Logical Reasoning section of the test, as well.

Cleetus: It's like when you buy a grape slushy at the Gas n' Gulp and they throw in a Slim Jim for free.

Precisely, Cleetus.

Two Parts of An Argument

Arguments come with just two primary parts:

- *Premise(s)*
- *Conclusion*

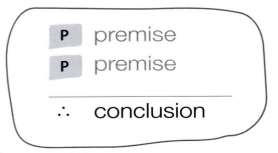

Logical Reasoning questions usually have a complete argument in the stimulus: premise(s) and conclusion. Take a look at the following problem, give 'er a try, and then we'll talk about it just a bit.

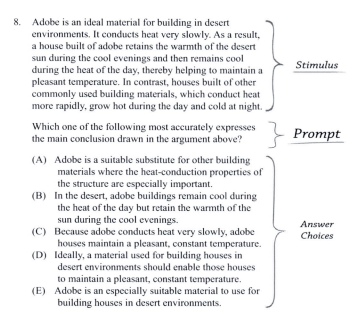

If someone were to walk up to you on the street and say to you what is said in the stimulus of this question you'd think, "This guy must sell adobe or something." Well, even in this question, the author is more or less trying to sell you adobe. His conclusion is that adobe is a great material to use for buildings in the desert. The rest of the stimulus gives support for that idea: cool during the day, warm at night, and all that good stuff. Those are premises. That's why (E) is the right answer.

It's the same thing with finding the conclusion of an RC passage. Look for the statement that is supported by other statements.

Premises provide support for conclusions. The main conclusion of an argument—also known as the main point—does not support anything else in the argument. Think of a house on a foundation. The house (conclusion) is supported by the foundation (premise), but the house supports nothing else. (Subsidiary conclusions, discussed later, are both supported and provide support, a sort of first story in a two-story house, if you will.)

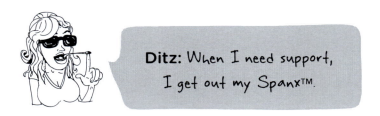

Ditz: When I need support, I get out my Spanx™.

First, let's all agree that Spanx™ is the best invention for women since the push-up bra and Ryan Gosling. Second, let's focus, Ditz.

INDICATOR WORDS

In order to truly master Reading Comprehension, you'll need to be able to understand the difference between premises (that which supports) and conclusions (that which is supported). On the way to mastery, however, indicator words can offer a helpful hint.

Premises		Conclusions	
Since	After all	Therefore	As a result
Because	Moreover	Thus	Consequently
For	In addition	Hence	It follows that
As	Given that	So	It is clear that

Though indicator words can help you track conclusions and premises, they, like politicians and professional athletes with smartphones, can have their shortcomings. Many Reading Comprehension passages don't use indicator words to indicate a conclusion. Or, even more nefariously, there are passages that use indicator words like "hence" or "therefore" to indicate a subsidiary conclusion while the main conclusion isn't introduced with any indicator word at all.

Nevertheless, it is important to learn these words' meanings and be on the lookout for them as they can be supremely helpful in locating conclusions.

> **Ninja:** The words "because" and "since" always introduce a premise, and the other half of the sentence—right or left—is a conclusion. For example: "(Since) he's afraid of the dark, he cannot train to be a ninja," or "It's time to clean the dojo (because) it smells like feet."

THE USUAL SUSPECTS

Looking for supported statements and finding key words are not the only ways of finding conclusions. The makers of the LSAT fear change, and they come back to the same well again and again for conclusions. The following items are the LSAT's "greatest hits" of ways it likes to introduce conclusions, so be on the lookout for them.

Value judgments/Opinions — *introduce conclusion(s)*

If a passage says that something is "unfair" or "morally wrong" or expresses an opinion, that's a value judgment. Look for something that supports the opinion to determine whether or not you have a conclusion.

> The court's decision to deny the plaintiff's motion was unfair because the judge flipped a coin to make his decision.

The conclusion here is that the decision was not fair. There's a very good reason, i.e. a premise, supporting that conclusion: the judge flipped a coin. Bad judge.

Predictions — *introduce conclusion(s)*

Whether they're spot on or way off base, predictions are conclusions.

> Chuck told me that the world was about to end. When I asked him where he got this information, he pointed to the sky and screamed, "Asteroid!"

Here, Chuck is concluding that the world will end at a particular time. The premise supporting that prediction is the information that an asteroid is headed toward earth.

Causal statements — *introduce conclusion(s)*

The statement that X causes Y is often a conclusion.

> The incidence of brain cancer is ten times greater in cities near toxic waste dumps than it is in cities that are not located near such dumps. Therefore, toxic waste causes brain cancer.

The author concludes that toxic waste causes brain cancer and supports that notion by presenting evidence that cancer rates are higher near toxic waste dumps.

Conclusions can be (& often) introduced through...
1. value judgements/opinions
2. predictions
3. Causal statements (X causes Y)
4. hypothese/theories
5. comparisions
6. perscriptive statements
   — a conclusion recommending some action be taken
7. indirect conclusions (not explicitly stated, but signal a shift in attitude, signaled by words such as however or but)

mainPOINT / 65

Hypotheses/Theories

Both hypotheses and theories are explanations of a phenomenon that require support if people are to believe them.

> Scientists hypothesize that the universe was created in a gigantic explosion - the Big Bang. As evidence, they point to the fact that all objects in the universe are continuously moving away from one another as though they all started from the same point.

Scientists conclude that a giant explosion created the universe. The premise supporting this conclusion is the fact that all the objects in the universe are moving away from one another.

Comparisons

While comparisons are often conclusions, they are sometimes premises. In fact, comparison conclusions are often supported by comparison premises. For this category, be sure to be precise when considering what supports what.

> Bill is taller than Phil. Therefore, Bill is a better basketball player than Phil.

Both of these statements contain comparisons. In order to determine which is the conclusion and which is the premise, ask yourself which statements supports the other. The fact that Bill is taller than Phil provides support for the conclusion that Bill is the better basketball player. However, the fact that Bill is a better basketball player does not support the fact that he is taller than Phil. Note that the indicator word "Therefore" helped us to hone in on the conclusion as well.

Prescriptive statements

The makers of the LSAT looooove to tell you what to do. "This nation must continue to fund space-based research." "The court should rule in favor of the defendants." "You ought to lower your cholesterol intake." "Don't pose naked on a wrecking ball if you want to appear demure." A prescriptive statement is a conclusion that recommends some action be taken.

> You look horrible, Stanley. You should get lipo and a facelift.

The extremely rude conclusion here is that Stanley should get some work done. The premise supporting that idea is that he looks horrible.

Indirect conclusions

marked by a shift in attitude signaled by words such as "however" and "but"

Finally, there is the "indirect conclusion," which occurs when the conclusion is a refutation of another assertion.

> Some people believe that all trees have leaves, but this is not the case with *Pinus aphremphous* or the common pine tree.

Note that the conclusion, that pine trees don't have leaves, is never explicitly stated. Indirect conclusions tend to be more difficult to spot, which is almost certainly why LSAC uses them. These are often marked by a shift in attitude signaled by words such as "but" and "however" and are extremely common on the LSAT in general and in Reading Comprehension in particular.

Cleetus: Hooooeey doggy! I really gotta learn all them ways of spotting conclusions? That's more work than greasing a hog.

It is, Cleetus. But spotting conclusions is the number one skill tested on the LSAT as a whole. Not only is it crucial in Reading Comprehension, it's an important skill for virtually every Logical Reasoning question type.

SUBSIDIARY CONCLUSIONS

Ever wonder what happens when something is supported by something, and also supports something else in turn? Enter the subsidiary conclusion. These happen a lot on the LSAT and you'll need to be able to spot them. Here's an example of a subsidiary conclusion:

> Wilma picked up soap at the store, so she must be washing her hair today. Whenever Wilma washes her hair, she has a date with Fred. Therefore, Wilma has a date with Fred tonight.

There are two conclusions in this paragraph. The first is that Wilma must be washing her hair today. Not only does the indicator word "so" help us locate the conclusion, it's also supported by the premise that "Wilma picked up soap at the store." However, the argument doesn't end there. We also have the conclusion (nicely tagged with a "therefore"), that Wilma has a date with Fred.

BP Minotaur: A subsidiary conclusion is a conclusion that is supported by premises, but that itself supports another conclusion.

The question is: how can we tell which conclusion is the main conclusion and which conclusion is the subsidiary conclusion? Ask yourself which conclusion supports which. Does the fact that Wilma has a date with Fred support the fact that Wilma is washing her hair today? Or does the fact that Wilma is washing her hair today support the fact that she has a date with Fred tonight? You don't have to live in Bedrock to know it's the latter.

CONCLUSION DRILL

The following drill will test your ability to understand the difference between main or primary conclusions, premises, subsidiary conclusions, and indirect conclusions. If the conclusion is expressly stated in the paragraph, simply underline it. If it is an indirect conclusion, write out the conclusion in your own words in the space provided. If there is no conclusion, write "no conclusion" in the space provided.

1. Seven-time Tour de France winner Lance Armstrong was stripped of his titles after it was found that he had used performance-enhancing drugs during the races. When asked whether or not he thought the decision was fair, Armstrong replied, "I have one testicle, people, cut me some slack."

Indirect, value judgement. Lance doesn't think the decision was fair.

2. Thomas Ravenswing wears a linen shirt and short pants to Renaissance Fairs, enjoys LARPING, and is currently the mediator of an online "Avatar" chat forum.

no conclusion

3. You can't get a seat in this damn coffee shop because there's a thousand-and-one losers writing screenplays! Not one of these bozos is ever going to get a bite from a producer. No, instead, they'll slink back to Wichita Falls or Enid or whatever hole they come from, or they'll end up breaking their mothers' hearts making dirty movies to pay the rent. Since they're all just wasting perfectly good table space, the management ought to board up the outlets so they'll buzz off.

Perscriptive statement - management ought to board up the outlets - you can't get a seat... subsidiary conclusion supporting main conclusion that people are wasting space?

4. The anglerfish has an unusual way of ensuring procreation. After locating a female anglerfish, the male anglerfish burrows into the female and emits an enzyme that digests the skin of his mouth and the skin of her body, fusing the pair together. The male then receives food and oxygen via the shared circulatory system. In return for sustaining the male, the female has access to sperm to fertilize her eggs whenever she needs it.

no conclusion

mainPOINT / 69

5. Showering is for suckers. I just squirt a little window cleaner under my pits—and a shot down my trousers for good measure—and I'm good for a week! The money I save on water and soap and dates goes right into the ol' piggy bank. I'm saving up for one of them beer helmets!

showering is for suckers

6. While many consider zombies to be the stuff of horror fiction and nothing else, this is not the case in Haiti. In *The Serpent and the Rainbow*, Harvard ethnobotanist Wade Davis explains how, in Haiti, the use of a certain drug can create the realistic illusion of death. A second drug then makes the person dazed and highly susceptible to suggestion. The result has all the hallmarks of zombitude.

indirect conclusion - people in Haiti think zombies are real

7. A recent study by prison researchers showed that those inmates who had frequent visits from friends and/or family—defined as at least one visit per month incarcerated—were only half as likely to reoffend upon release as those who were visited less frequently. While it might seem that the emotional support received in prison is what makes the difference, psychological studies showed no relevant difference in the psychological states of the two groups after release. The better explanation is that offenders with an existing social network are better able to find jobs and housing than those without such a network.

hypothesis/theory conclusion

8. Hundreds of thousands of tourists visit Yellowstone National Park each year, and the hot springs and geysers that dot the landscape here and there are major draws. Few people know, however, that these hot springs and geysers are merely the visible indicators of a supervolcano—a caldera, in scientific terms—that covers nearly 1,600 square miles, most of it underneath the park. The caldera erupts, on average, once every 600,000 years. Since it has been 640,000 years since its last eruption, it's bound to go off any day now, and we'll all be goners.

we'll all be goners - prediction hypothesis - conclusion

9. Phobos and Deimos—named after the Greek gods of Fear and Panic, respectively—are Mars' only moons. They are, in comparison with Earth's moon, extraordinarily tiny. While our moon is well over 2,000 miles in diameter, Phobos is less than fourteen miles in diameter, and miniscule Deimos is less than eight miles in diameter. They are so small, in fact, that neither had sufficient gravity to collapse into a sphere, and both are oblong.

no conclusion

10. When asked if he thought Justin Bieber was a musical genius, world-renowned cellist Yo-Yo Ma screamed incoherently and then passed out.

Justin Bieber is not a musical genius. - indirect/value judgement conclusion. Yo-Yo-ma was asked what he thought about Justin and responded negatively

ANSWER KEY

1) INDIRECT CONCLUSION: The decision was unfair.

Lance responded negatively to a question about whether the decision was fair. That means he believes it was unfair. Note that this is a value judgment.

2) NO CONCLUSION.

As much as we might want to conclude that Monsieur Ravenswing will never, ever get a date, the paragraph merely lists a number of facts about him. However, none of these facts provides support for anything else.

3) The management ought to board up the outlets.

This is a prescriptive statement. The sentence begins with the word "since," meaning that what comes directly after is a premise. The idea that these people are wasting space provides support for the idea that the outlets should be boarded up.

4) NO CONCLUSION.

The paragraph lists a number of facts about the anglerfish, but nothing provides support for anything else.

5) Showering is for suckers.

All other statements in this paragraph give reasons for believing that showering is unnecessary.

6) INDIRECT CONCLUSION: People in Haiti believe that zombies are real.

A point of view held by people outside of Haiti is offered, and reasons are given supporting the idea that such a point of view is not shared by Haitians.

7) The better explanation is that offenders with an existing social network are better able to find jobs and housing than those without such a network.

The conclusion is a hypothesis. Note that there is an indirect conclusion - that emotional support is not the correct explanation - that functions as a subsidiary conclusion. After dispensing with the emotional support idea, the argument gives reason to believe that something else is the cause of the difference between the two groups, i.e. the social network.

8) We'll all be goners.

This is a prediction. As with question three, the conclusion sentence contains the word "since." The first half of the sentence -that it's been an unusually long time since the last eruption- provides support for the idea that we'll all be goners.

9) NO CONCLUSION.

The paragraph lists a number of facts about the moons of Mars, but nothing provides support for anything else.

10) INDIRECT CONCLUSION: Justin Bieber is not a musical genius.

Yo-Yo Ma was asked a question about the Biebs, and he responded negatively to that question.

8/WHERE'S the AUTHOR

HIDE AND SEEK

Now that we've learned to find the conclusion of an argument, we will spend the next several chapters learning to identify precisely who is making the argument. You might ask to whom* we are referring? Why the author, of course.

While there may be more than one argument in a passage, and, therefore, more than one conclusion, it is the author's conclusion—the author's opinion, to put it another way—that is the main point of the passage as a whole. (As long as the author is present. There are passages without present authors and we'll discuss those in a bit.)

The first question of any passage usually asks for the main point of the passage, and other questions will require you to know the main point of the passage to answer them correctly. While we'll talk specifically about addressing particular question types later in the book, it's important to get into the habit of identifying the author's opinion early on as it will have a huge payoff on test day.

When the author comes out and says something like, "I believe..." or, "In my humble opinion...," finding the author's opinion is a snap. However, it's not always so easy.

BP Minotaur: In fact, there are very few instances of the use of the word "I" or "me" in Reading Comprehension passages. It is extremely uncommon for the author to signal his or her point of view so obviously.

- Whenever we can find the authors conclusion (or the authors opinion) that is the main point of the whole passage.
  - If an opinion in a passage is not attributed to anyone else it must be the authors opinion.

---

* In order to distinguish "who" from "whom," just ask yourself if the answer would be "she" or "her." She is who and her is whom. Who's taking the LSAT? She is. From whom are you learning the LSAT? From her. This isn't important on the test but it will probably come in handy in law school and as a lawyer.

If you see an opinion in the passage, and it is not assigned to anyone else, that is the author's opinion. Here's an example:

> A group of paleontologists has recently concluded that dinosaurs became extinct as a result of a giant asteroid impact at the end of the Cretaceous period. But this cannot be right, because the evidence indicates that the asteroid they point to impacted Earth nearly one million years after the dinosaurs died out. Instead, it is more likely that the dinosaurs went extinct as the result of a new viral strain to which their immune systems were unable to adapt.

Because the opinion about the paleontologists ("But this cannot be right") is not attributed to anyone, we can conclude that it's the opinion of the person writing the paragraph: the author.

It might seem strange that an opinion that isn't assigned to anyone must be the author's, but think of it this way: do you always identify yourself before you venture an opinion on something? No. Say you think that kale chips are slightly less appetizing than bunion shavings. You might say, "Kale chips should be outlawed." In doing so, you'd be expressing your own opinion, and nobody would spend precious moments wondering if that opinion was yours or someone else's.

BUT I LOOKED EVERYWHERE!

Sometimes the author does not actually have an opinion. If the only conclusion(s) is/are assigned to another party or parties, the author is absent. You must determine whether a passage has a present author (the author has an opinion) or an absent author (the author has no opinion) before heading into the questions. Every time.

When the author is absent, the correct answer to the main point question will summarize the point(s) of view expressed in the passage. If there is more than one point of view, it will summarize both without choosing between them.

BP Minotaur: Sometimes a question will mention an author, even though the author is absent. Don't let this throw you. Someone wrote the passage, even though that person did not express his or her own opinion in the passage.

A NOTE ON ATTITUDE

Some questions ask about the author's attitude. Author's attitude is not the same as the author's opinion. When the author believes something, that's the author's opinion. When the author likes or dislikes something, that's the author's attitude.

Suppose the author of the passage says, "The Earth is round." The author has an opinion on the shape of the Earth, but it's hard to say that she feels any particular way about it.

Suppose the author says, "The discovery that the Earth is round was a profound leap forward in science." Here, the topic is the same, but the author approves of the discovery. In this case, the author has a positive attitude about this discovery.

An author may have a negative attitude about something as well. Suppose the author says, "Those who continue to believe that the Earth is flat are ignorant." Again, we have the same topic, but here the author dislikes something.

Ninja: When the author's attitude shows up in a passage, you are very likely to see a question about it.

PRACTICE, PRACTICE, PRACTICE

In the following drills, determine whether the author is present or absent, and circle the word "PRESENT" or "ABSENT" accordingly. If the author is present, underline the author's opinion. Circle any words indicating the author's attitude.

1. The aye-aye (Daubentonia madagascariensis) is a lemur found only in Madagascar. There is debate as to how the aye-aye got its odd name. According to some scholars, the name is an approximation of the aye-aye's vocalization. Another set of scholars believes that aye-aye is derived from Malagasy, the language of the native population. "Heh-heh" is Malagasy for "I don't know." The scholars advancing this hypothesis believe that the Malagasy people regarded the aye-aye as a fearful, magical animal, and as a result refused to tell European explorers the actual name, instead saying that they didn't know.

PRESENT / **ABSENT**

2. Historiography is the study of the methodology and development of history. It can be summarized generally as the history of history. Historians agree that no particular account of history is entirely objective. The more interesting question is whether or not there is an objective history independent of humanity's attempts to record it. Some historiographers believe that history, and indeed time itself, are human constructs, and, without beings to comprehend it, there can be no such thing as history. But this argument assigns an importance to humanity that is not warranted. There is exactly one way events in the past have played out, and there is therefore such a thing as objective history.

PRESENT / ABSENT

3. So, Pauly calls me up and says to me, "Hey! Vinny! Did you take care of that thing?" And I says, "Yeah! Of course. What am I, some kinda mook? Of course I took care of that thing!" I see him a week or two later, and he says to me, "Vincenzo, you broke my heart. You did not take care of that thing. We agreed that the D.A. had to go." But Pauly's got it all wrong. We referred to the hit on the D.A. as "that *situation*." "That thing" was burning down the Cuban restaurant for the insurance money. And I did take care of that thing. It was Jimmy Two-Fingers' job to take care of that situation, and that dingus is at the bottom of the East River now because he f*@!ed it up.

PRESENT / ABSENT

WHERE'StheAUTHOR / 77

4. Who is the best superhero? Plenty of people love Superman, but let's dispense with him right off the bat. First of all, the guy is basically invincible, except he falls apart when you flash a green rock at him. A superhero isn't interesting unless he's vulnerable, and a green rock doesn't cut it. This very complaint about Superman forms the basis for fans' love of Batman. He doesn't have super powers. He's a regular guy—except for the whole billionaire thing—and he still kicks ass. That's all fine and well; we can all agree that Batman is awesome. But really, at the end of the day, the best superhero is clearly The Thing. First off, he's a boulder in a speedo. Second, his battle cry is "It's clobberin' time!" Case closed.

PRESENT / ABSENT

5. Theseus, the mythical founder of Athens and slayer of the Minotaur, had one mother, Aethra, and two fathers, Aegeus and Poseidon. Although this seems to be the stuff of fantasy, biologists have argued that this situation, however unlikely, is actually possible. Many instances of heteropaternal superfecundation (HS) have been documented: usually, fraternal twins have the same father; however, two ova can be fertilized in separate acts of intercourse, and so fraternal twins may have different fathers. But how can one person have two fathers? The other half of the equation is tetragametic chimerism (TG), wherein two separately fertilized zygotes fuse into one organism. Biologists have concluded that the combination of these two processes could, in theory, produce one person with two fathers.

PRESENT / ABSENT

BP Minotaur: "Slayer of the Minotaur?" Not cool, people.

6. How old is the Grand Canyon? The debate has raged unchecked since geologists sank the first pickax into the canyon wall. One set of scientists believes the Grand Canyon formed recently, at least by geological standards, around six million years ago. Sediment found at the bottom of the canyon dates to around that time. However, a more recent theory is that the Colorado River, which formed the canyon, took advantage of existent low-lying areas, some of which were 70 million years old, and those scientists use that as the measure of the canyon's age. However, both of these theories are wrong, Paul Bunyan dug the canyon with his ax a mere 150 years ago. How do we know this? Someone "axed" him. Get it?

PRESENT / ABSENT

7. Those who eat a diet heavy in saturated fats are more likely to suffer from diabetes, high blood pressure, lethargy, and even live shorter lives. But who wants to give up fatty, greasy foods? Anyone who wants to live a long and healthy life without the hassle of making responsible lifestyle choices should try the brand new weight loss miracle, The Digestive Tracuum! Using a patented process that is too disgusting to describe in polite company, the Tracuum sucks the fat, as well as some of the lining, from your whole digestive tract. Eat as much as you want! The Digestive Tracuum has your backside!

PRESENT / ABSENT

8. The mayor has spent much of his tenure arguing for expanded access to public records at City Hall. That is all well and good, but it is not enough. The records of public officials—the Mayor, City Councilmen, and the Chief of Police among them—as well as those of high-level administrative officials such as the Controller and the Custodian of Records, must be disclosed to the public. Only then can the corruption that plagues this city be dislodged, root and branch.

PRESENT / ABSENT

9. Which president had the worst facial hair? Some experts on presidential aesthetics believe that title should go to Martin Van Buren. His wispy, white sideburns were combed outward as were the remains of his hair, achieving a kind of white rectangle flanking each side of his face. This ridiculousness was exaggerated by the fact that he was only 5'6, leaving the impression that he was a child in a Halloween costume, rather than the Commander in Chief. Others cite Chester Arthur for his embarrassingly thin and curly sideburn-mustache combo. A third set of experts thinks that the real issue is which president has the stupidest face, regardless of facial hair.

PRESENT / ABSENT

Van Buren *Arthur*

BP Minotaur: Because of course, you need to see the pictures. If you think you have even more ridiculous facial hair or hairstyle (ladies), upload a pic to our Facebook page, facebook.com/blueprintlsatprep. If we agree, we'll send you a Starbucks giftcard.

10. Clemente Perez, the plaintiff in *Perez v. Brownell*, was born in the United States but lived and voted in Mexico. The government revoked his citizenship, and the Supreme Court ruled that the action was constitutional. ~~The Court corrected this grievous mistake in a subsequent case~~ with nearly identical facts, *Afroyim v. Rusk*, paving the way for greater acceptance of dual citizenship.

PRESENT/ABSENT

The earliest surviving cookbook dates from 1390 and includes dishes made from swan and peacock.

ANSWER KEY

1) ABSENT.

The two points of view about how the aye-aye got its names are assigned to two different sets of scholars.

2) PRESENT.

> 2. Historiography is the study of the methodology and development of history. It can be summarized generally as the history of history. Historians agree that no particular account of history is entirely objective. The more interesting question is whether or not there is an objective history independent of humanity's attempts to record it. Some historiographers believe that history, and indeed time itself, are human constructs, and, without beings to comprehend it, there can be no such thing as history. <u>But this argument assigns an importance to humanity that is not warranted</u>. There is exactly one way events in the past have played out, and <u>there is therefore such a thing as objective history.</u>

3) PRESENT.

> 3. So, Pauly calls me up and says to me, "Hey! Vinny! Did you take care of that thing?" And I says, "Yeah! Of course. What am I, some kinda mook? Of course I took care of that thing!" I see him a week or two later, and he says to me, "Vincenzo, you broke my heart. You did not take care of that thing. We agreed that the D.A. had to go." <u>But Pauly's got it all wrong.</u> We referred to the hit on the D.A. as "that *situation*." "That thing" was burning down the Cuban restaurant for the insurance money. And I did take care of that thing. It was Jimmy Two-Fingers' job to take care of that situation, and (that dingus) is at the bottom of the East River now because he f*@!ed it up.

4) PRESENT.

> 4. Who is the best superhero? Plenty of people love Superman, but let's dispense with him right off the bat. First of all, the guy is basically invincible, except he falls apart when you flash a green rock at him. A superhero isn't interesting unless he's vulnerable, and (a green rock doesn't cut it.) This very complaint about Superman forms the basis for fans' love of Batman. He doesn't have super powers. He's a regular guy—except for the whole billionaire thing—and he still kicks ass. That's all fine and well; we can all agree that (Batman is awesome.) But really, at the end of the day, <u>the best superhero is clearly The Thing.</u> First off, he's a boulder in a speedo. Second, his battle cry is "It's clobberin' time!" Case closed.

5) ABSENT.

The only point of view in the passage is assigned to biologists, and their conclusion is that it is possible that Theseus had two fathers.

6) PRESENT.

> 6. How old is the Grand Canyon? The debate has raged unchecked since geologists sank the first pickax into the canyon wall. One set of scientists believes the Grand Canyon formed recently, at least by geological standards, around six million years ago. Sediment found at the bottom of the canyon dates to around that time. However, a more recent theory is that the Colorado River, which formed the canyon, took advantage of existent low-lying areas, some of which were 70 million years old, and those scientists use that as the measure of the canyon's age. However, <u>both of these theories are wrong. Paul Bunyan dug the canyon with his ax a mere 150 years ago.</u> How do we know this? Someone "axed" him. Get it?

7) PRESENT.

> 7. Those who eat a diet heavy in saturated fats are more likely to suffer from diabetes, high blood pressure, lethargy, and even live shorter lives. But who wants to give up fatty, greasy foods? <u>Anyone who wants to live a long and healthy life without the hassle of making responsible lifestyle choices should try the brand new weight loss miracle, The Digestive Tracuum!</u> Using a patented process that is too disgusting to describe in polite company, the Tracuum sucks the fat, as well as some of the lining, from your whole digestive tract. Eat as much as you want! The Digestive Tracuum has your backside!

8) PRESENT.

> 8. The mayor has spent much of his tenure arguing for expanded access to public records at City Hall. That is all well and good, <u>but it is not enough. The records of public officials—the Mayor, City Councilmen, and the Chief of Police among them—as well as those of high-level administrative officials such as the Controller and the Custodian of Records, must be disclosed to the public.</u> Only then can the corruption that plagues this city be dislodged, root and branch.

9) ABSENT.

There are three different opinions about presidential mustaches, and all of them are assigned to various experts.

10) PRESENT.

> 10. Clemente Perez, the plaintiff in *Perez v. Brownell*, was born in the United States but lived and voted in Mexico. The government revoked his citizenship, and the Supreme Court ruled that the action was constitutional. <u>The Court corrected this (grievous mistake) in a subsequent case with nearly identical facts, *Afroyim v. Rusk*,</u> paving the way for greater acceptance of dual citizenship.

9/PRIMARYstructure

A PRIMER ON PRIMARY STRUCTURE

Now that you've learned how to read for comprehension (no skimming!), how to spot conclusions and their support, and how to track the author, it's time to return to the Blueprint method for Reading Comprehension. Hurray!

We're going to begin with what we here at Blueprint call primary structure, which is what we use to categorize Reading Comprehension passages.

Let's be very clear about what exactly constitutes the primary structure of a passage: it's the number of developed views present. (More on the "developed" part in a bit.)

To find the primary structure of a passage, you must answer the following two questions:

> 1) How many viewpoints are there?
> 2) Who is arguing for each particular viewpoint?

If you can't remember how to go about finding viewpoints, go back and review Chapter 7. We'll wait. *Checks watch; rolls eyes.* When you have answered (1) and (2), you've identified the conclusions to the different arguments that are being made in the passage, and understanding argumentation is the key to the LSAT door.

Record the view(s) in the passage, the topic of the passage, and with which view the author agrees (if the author is present) in what we call the primary structure diagram. The primary structure diagram consists of the topic of the passage, any views in the passage along with their advocates, and the presence of the author. We use an arrow to show which view the author espouses. The point of writing all of this information down is so you'll have it for easy reference when you tackle the questions.

> **Cleetus:** I'm guessin' here's where you say all that work pays off later, kinda like slow cookin' gator meat.

That's right, Cleetus. It may take more time up front, but when you get proficient at making primary structure diagrams, recording that information will save you a ton of time in the questions.

Here's an example of a Reading Comprehension passage with an Antithesis primary structure, along with its primary structure diagram.

With their recognition of Maxine Hong Kingston as a major literary figure, some critics have suggested that her works have been produced almost *ex nihilo*, saying that they lack a large traceable body of direct
(5) literary antecedents especially within the Chinese American heritage in which her work is embedded. But these critics, who have examined only the development of written texts, the most visible signs of a culture's narrative production, have overlooked Kingston's
(10) connection to the long Chinese tradition of a highly developed genre of song and spoken narrative known as "talk-story" (*gong gu tsai*).

Traditionally performed in the dialects of various ethnic enclaves, talk-story has been maintained within
(15) the confines of the family and has rarely surfaced into print. The tradition dates back to Sung dynasty (A.D. 970–1279) storytellers in China, and in the United States it is continually revitalized by an overlapping sequence of immigration from China.
(20) Thus, Chinese immigrants to the U.S. had a fully established, sophisticated oral culture, already ancient and capable of producing masterpieces, by the time they began arriving in the early nineteenth century. This transplanted oral heritage simply embraced new
(25) subject matter or new forms of Western discourse, as in the case of Kingston's adaptations written in English.

Kingston herself believes that as a literary artist she is one in a long line of performers shaping a recalcitrant history into talk-story form. She
(30) distinguishes her "thematic" storytelling memory processes, which sift and reconstruct the essential elements of personally remembered stories, from the memory processes of a print-oriented culture that emphasizes the retention of precise sequences of
(35) words. Nor does the entry of print into the storytelling process substantially change her notion of the character of oral tradition. For Kingston, "writer" is synonymous with "singer" or "performer" in the ancient sense of privileged keeper, transmitter, and creator of stories
(40) whose current stage of development can be frozen in print, but which continue to grow both around and from that frozen text.

Kingston's participation in the tradition of talk-story is evidenced in her book *China Men*, which
(45) utilizes forms typical of that genre and common to most oral cultures including: a fixed "grammar" of repetitive themes; a spectrum of stock characters; symmetrical structures, including balanced oppositions (verbal or physical contests, antithetical characters,
(50) dialectical discourse such as question-answer forms and riddles); and repetition. In *China Men*, Kingston also succeeds in investing idiomatic English with the allusive texture and oral-aural qualities of the Chinese language, a language rich in aural and visual puns,
(55) making her work a written form of talk-story.

As discussed in Chapter 5, there are three different primary structures. Thesis Passages have one developed point of view, Antithesis passages have two, and Synthesis passages have three.

If the author is absent, the main point of the passage is a summary of the point(s) of view expressed in the passage. If the author is present, the author's point of view is the main point.

The makers of the LSAT are keen to test you in a number of ways on the points of view and who holds them. They will often ask you what the main point of the passage is and what other views are present in the passage. Additionally, questions related to viewpoints are often posed. These include asking for the primary purpose of the passage, as well as the author's opinion on various facets of the passage.

Tracking the primary structure allows you to answer these questions readily. It also allows you to do a whole lot more. For instance, knowing the primary structure additionally allows you to eliminate answer choices in other questions. If a question asks what can be inferred from the passage (a Reading Comprehension question as maddeningly vague as it is ubiquitous), you can eliminate any answer choices that don't reflect the point of view you know is being espoused in the passage.

Handwritten notes:

① Thesis
② antithesis
③ synthesis

- If author present their viewpoint/opinion is the main point, if author not present the main point is the summary of different viewpoints

Rank the order of places you'd post a dating profile:

_____ **DEAD-MEET.COM**
A dating and networking site for death industry professionals.

_____ **STACHEPASSIONS.COM**
A 100% free social networking and online dating site specifically for singles with a passion for the Stache.

_____ **SINGLESWITHFOODALLERGIES.COM**
Singles with Food Allergies allows people from across the country to date, communicate, and develop lasting relationships based around the food allergy lifestyle our members share.

_____ **EQUESTRIANCUPID.COM**
The best, largest, and most effective dating site for single horse lovers and friends in the world!

_____ **BIKERKISS.COM**
Two wheels, two hearts, one road.

10/THESISpassages

Thesis passages are those with just one point of view. They're not the most common type of passage in Reading Comprehension (they constitute approximately 33% of passages) but we start with them because they're typically very straightforward (only having one point of view and all). In fact, Thesis passages have an average difficulty rating of 2.9*, which means they're historically among the easiest type of passage. (Only Synthesis passages, with a difficulty rating of 2.56, have a lower average rating.)

In a moment, you will be turned loose on a few Thesis passages to test your burgeoning Reading Comprehension superpowers, but first, let's discuss exactly what a Thesis passage looks like and why it's important to be able to identify a Thesis passage. Also, see how many times you can say "Thesis passage" in a row without it turning into "this is pasta."

Take the following example:

> Mr. James Boddy was found dead in the kitchen of his mansion last night. Solving such a mystery usually takes time, but Detective Frank Gumshoe announced today at an early morning news conference on the steps of City Hall that the mystery had been solved. Although Boddy was found in the kitchen, Gumshoe firmly believes that Professor Peter Plum killed Boddy in the drawing room with a knife.
>
> Gumshoe reasoned that the puncture wounds indicated a knife attack—as did the 13" kitchen knife protruding from Boddy's chest. He further reasoned that the bloodstains leading from the drawing room to the kitchen indicated that the murder had taken place in the drawing room. Finally, he reasoned that Plum was the culprit because Plum was covered in blood, sitting next to the victim, shouting, "I did it!" over and over again.
>
> Given the strength of the evidence and Gumshoe's impressive track record, it is clear that Plum killed Boddy in the location and manner Gumshoe alleged.

In the passage above, there is one point of view: Plum killed Boddy with a knife in the drawing room. Gumshoe holds this point of view, and the author endorses it in the last paragraph. That point of view is, of course, supported by the evidence offered in the second paragraph.

---

*What's this? To calculate the average difficulty of Thesis passages, a team of experts (read the BP founders and an instructor they inveigled into the job with the promise of free booze) assigned a rating of 1-5 for each Reading Comprehension passage *in the history of the test*. Yep; it was as much fun as it sounds like. A rating of one was assigned to the easiest passages (your dog has a fair shot at it) and five was assigned to the most difficult (Einstein would struggle). We then added up the values assigned to all Thesis passages and divided by the number of passages to arrive at the average difficulty rating. Voila.

For this passage, the primary structure diagram would look like the following:

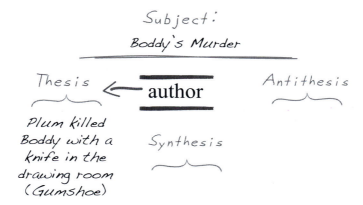

ATTITUDE

It is also important to keep track of the attitude of the various parties present in the passage. In this case, if you were asked about the author's attitude toward Gumshoe, the answer would look something like "confident of his abilities." This is evident from the fact that the author calls Gumshoe's track record "impressive."

BP Minotaur: If you are keeping track of the view(s) and attitude of the parties in a passage as well as the author's, you will be performing the most important bit of analysis the LSAT tests in Reading Comprehension.

A NOTE ON DEVELOPMENT

Remember earlier when we said that the primary structure could be determined by the number of developed views present? Well, the reason we say "developed" is that occasionally a passage will contain a viewpoint that serves only to introduce the topic at hand, or that functions as a simple summary of a position against which the rest of the passage argues.

In either case, we don't count the undeveloped view as part of the structure, since it is just used as a setup to introduce the real view.

The following passage from December 2003 is an example of such an instance.

THESISpassages / 89

Because the market system enables entrepreneurs and investors who develop new technology to reap financial rewards from their risk of capital, it may seem that the primary result of this activity is that
(5) some people who have spare capital accumulate more. But in spite of the fact that the profits derived from various technological developments have accrued to relatively few people, the developments themselves have served overall as a remarkable democratizing
(10) force. In fact, under the regime of the market, the gap in benefits accruing to different groups of people has been narrowed in the long term.

    This tendency can be seen in various well-known technological developments. For example, before
(15) the printing press was introduced centuries ago, few people had access to written materials, much less to scribes and private secretaries to produce and transcribe documents. Since printed materials have become widely available, however, people without
(20) special position or resources—and in numbers once thought impossible—can take literacy and the use of printed texts for granted. With the distribution of books and periodicals in public libraries, this process has been extended to the point where people in general
(25) can have essentially equal access to a vast range of texts that would once have been available only to a very few. A more recent technological development extends this process beyond printed documents. A child in school with access to a personal computer
(30) and modem—which is becoming fairly common in technologically advanced societies—has computing power and database access equal to that of the best-connected scientists and engineers at top-level labs of just fifteen years ago, a time when relatively few
(35) people had personal access to any computing power. Or consider the uses of technology for leisure. In previous centuries only a few people with abundant resources had the ability and time to hire professional entertainment, and to have contact through travel
(40) and written communication—both of which were prohibitively expensive—with distant people. But now broadcast technology is widely available, and so almost anyone can have an entertainment cornucopia unimagined in earlier times. Similarly,
(45) the development of inexpensive mail distribution and telephone connections and, more recently, the establishment of the even more efficient medium of electronic mail have greatly extended the power of distant communication.

(50)   This kind of gradual diffusion of benefits across society is not an accident of these particular technological developments, but rather the result of a general tendency of the market system. Entrepreneurs and investors often are unable to maximize financial
(55) success without expanding their market, and this involves structuring their prices to the consumers so as to make their technologies genuinely accessible to an ever-larger share of the population. In other words, because market competition drives prices down, it
(60) tends to diffuse access to new technology across society as a result.

December 2003 Passage 3

Ninja: It's perfectly acceptable to include an undeveloped point of view in your initial primary structure diagram and then erase it later. In fact, it's a sign that you're reading closely and tracking the passage, much like a jaguar on the trail of a capybara.

YOUR TURN

Attack!

Now it's your turn. The following passages are Thesis passages. We have supplied you with a blank primary structure diagram. Read the passage and identify the argument(s), filling in the diagram as you go. When you see a point of view, underline it and identify in the margin exactly who is espousing that particular point of view. If you see an indication that the author or another party has a positive or negative attitude toward something, underline the word or words that indicate the attitude and tag the side of the passage with "Att."

So far we have learned to identify the main point/conclusion of an argument, and we have learned to identify author's attitude. Answer the questions in black at the end of the passages, for they test those concepts. The other questions have been greyed out. You may attempt them if you wish but we have not included explanations for them here because you don't yet know the Blueprint methodology for addressing them.

After each passage we've included a paragraph-by-paragraph explanation so you can review what you should have gleaned from each paragraph. Study it carefully when you are done reading and answering the questions to make sure you correctly identified all the relevant points of view and instances of attitude. Good luck!

EXERCISE 1: OCT. 2013 PASSAGE 2

One of the more striking developments in modern North American dance was African American choreographer Katherine Dunham's introduction of a technique known as dance-isolation, in which one
(5) part of the body moves in one rhythm while other parts are kept stationary or are moved in different rhythms. The incorporation of this technique into North American and European choreography is relatively recent, although various forms of the technique have
(10) long been essential to traditional dances of certain African, Caribbean, and Pacific-island cultures. Dunham's success in bringing dance-isolation and other traditional techniques from those cultures into the mainstream of modern North American dance is due
(15) in no small part to her training in both anthropological research and choreography.

As an anthropologist in the 1930s, Dunham was one of the pioneers in the field of dance ethnology. Previously, dance had been neglected as an area of
(20) social research, primarily because most social scientists gravitated toward areas likely to be recognized by their peers as befitting scientifically rigorous, and therefore legitimate, modes of inquiry. Moreover, no other social scientist at that time was sufficiently trained in dance to
(25) be able to understand dance techniques, while experts in dance were not trained in the methods of social research.

Starting in 1935, Dunham conducted a series of research projects into traditional Caribbean dance
(30) forms, with special interest in their origins in African culture. Especially critical to her success was her approach to research, which diverged radically from the methodology that prevailed at the time. Colleagues in anthropology advised her not to become too closely
(35) involved in the dances she was observing, both because of the extreme physical demands of the dances, and because they subscribed to the long-standing view, now fortunately recognized as unrealistic, that effective data gathering can and must be conducted from a position of
(40) complete detachment. But because of her interest and her skill as a performer, she generally eschewed such caution and participated in the dances herself. Through prolonged immersion of this kind, Dunham was able not only to comprehend various dances as complex
(45) cultural practices, but also to learn the techniques well enough to teach them to others and incorporate them into new forms of ballet.

Between 1937 and 1945, Dunham developed a research-to-performance method that she used to
(50) adapt Caribbean dance forms for use in theatrical performance, combining them with modern dance styles she learned in Chicago. The ballets she created in this fashion were among the first North American dances to rectify the exclusion of African American
(55) themes from the medium of modern dance. Her work was thus crucial in establishing African American dance as an art form in its own right, making possible future companies such as Arthur Mitchell's Dance Theater of Harlem.

8. Which one of the following most accurately expresses the main point of the passage?

(A) Katherine Dunham transformed the field of anthropology by developing innovative research methodologies for studying Caribbean and other traditional dance styles and connecting them with African American dance.
(B) Katherine Dunham's ballets were distinct from others produced in North America in that they incorporated authentic dance techniques from traditional cultures.
(C) Katherine Dunham's expertise as an anthropologist allowed her to use Caribbean and African dance traditions to express the aesthetic and political concerns of African American dancers and choreographers.
(D) The innovative research methods of Katherine Dunham made possible her discovery that the dance traditions of the Caribbean were derived from earlier African dance traditions.
(E) Katherine Dunham's anthropological and choreographic expertise enabled her to make contributions that altered the landscape of modern dance in North America.

9. According to the passage, Dunham's work in anthropology differed from that of most other anthropologists in the 1930s in that Dunham

(A) performed fieldwork for a very extended time period
(B) related the traditions she studied to those of her own culture
(C) employed a participative approach in performing research
(D) attached a high degree of political significance to her research
(E) had prior familiarity with the cultural practices of the peoples she set out to study

14. The passage suggests that the author would be most likely to agree with which one of the following statements about the colleagues mentioned in line 33?

    (A) They were partly correct in recommending that Dunham change her methods of data collection, since injury sustained during fieldwork might have compromised her research.
    (B) They were partly correct in advising Dunham to exercise initial caution in participating in the Caribbean dances, since her skill in performing them improved with experience.
    (C) They were incorrect in advising Dunham to increase the degree of her detachment, since extensive personal investment in fieldwork generally enhances scientific rigor.
    (D) They were incorrect in assuming that researchers in the social sciences are able to gather data in an entirely objective manner.
    (E) They were incorrect in assuming that dance could be studied with the same degree of scientific rigor possible in other areas of ethnology.

EXPLANATION {BROKEN DOWN BY PARAGRAPH}

Paragraph 1

> One of the more <u>striking</u> developments in modern North <u>American dance was</u> African American choreographer [Katherine Dunham's] introduction of a technique known as dance-isolation, in which one
> (5) part of the body moves in one rhythm while other parts are kept stationary or are moved in different rhythms. The incorporation of this technique into North American and European choreography is relatively recent, although various forms of the technique have
> (10) long been essential to traditional dances of certain African, Caribbean, and Pacific-island cultures. <u>Dunham's success in bringing dance-isolation and other traditional techniques from those cultures into the mainstream of modern North American dance is due
> (15) in no small part to her training in both anthropological research and choreography.</u>

ATT.

AUTHOR'S CONCLUSION: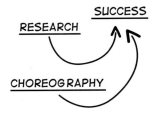

We've got a great indicator of author's attitude right at the top. Dunham's work is a "striking development." This is strongly positive language, showing us that the author is interested and excited about Dunham. We therefore underline and mark it with "Att."

The last sentence is a causal statement, and a causal statement is very often a conclusion to an argument. Let's be very clear about what the causal statement is. The effect is "success in bringing...traditional techniques into the mainstream...." The cause? There are two: Dunham's "training in both anthropological research and choreography."

> **BP Ninja:** Keeping track of cause and effect is as important as keeping your throwing stars sharp. It's so important that, in a later chapter, we discuss how to diagram it in detail.

This cause and effect statement is a good candidate for the Thesis point of view. If we find support for it in subsequent paragraphs, we can fill in our primary structure diagram.

Paragraph 2

>   As an anthropologist in the 1930s, Dunham was
> one of the pioneers in the field of dance ethnology.
> Previously, dance had been neglected as an area of
> (20) social research, primarily because most social scientists
> gravitated toward areas likely to be recognized by their
> peers as befitting scientifically rigorous, and therefore
> legitimate, modes of inquiry. Moreover, no other social
> scientist at that time was sufficiently trained in dance to
> (25) be able to understand dance techniques, while experts
> in dance were not trained in the methods of social
> research.

BACKGROUND

WHY DANCE HAD BEEN NEGLECTED

This paragraph is heavy on facts, and its primary function in the passage is to provide background information. Here, we are talking about the state of affairs *before* Dunham came on the scene. While it is important to understand the situation in which the arguments occur, it is the arguments that are of primary importance. Accordingly, let's tag the paragraph with a description of what it's doing and move on.

Paragraph 3

>   Starting in 1935, Dunham conducted a series
> of research projects into traditional Caribbean dance
> (30) forms, with special interest in their origins in African
> culture. Especially critical to her success was her
> approach to research, which diverged radically from
> the methodology that prevailed at the time. Colleagues
> in anthropology advised her not to become too closely
> (35) involved in the dances she was observing, both because
> of the extreme physical demands of the dances, and
> because they subscribed to the long-standing view, now
> <u>fortunately recognized as unrealistic,</u> that effective data
> gathering can and must be conducted from a position of
> (40) complete detachment. But because of her interest and
> her skill as a performer, she generally eschewed such
> caution and participated in the dances herself. <u>Through
> prolonged immersion of this kind, Dunham was able
> not only to comprehend various dances as complex
> (45) cultural practices, but also to learn the techniques well
> enough to teach them to others and incorporate them
> into new forms of ballet.</u>

COLLEAGUES: JOINING IN IS DANGEROUS AND WRECKS OBJECTIVITY

ATT.

RESEARCH → SUCCESS

In the first two sentences of this paragraph, we have two—count them, two!—words that play pivotal roles in the cause and effect statement in paragraph one. Specifically, the author asserts

Dunham's training in "research" was one of the two causes of her "success." It's a good bet that we will find some facts (premises) supporting that idea later in this paragraph. Let's read on.

The portion of the paragraph starting at line 33 functions a lot like the second paragraph, i.e. background. It's telling us what people *other than* Dunham were thinking. We have other anthropologists' opinion, but nothing supporting that opinion, so it's not an argument. There is more author's attitude here as well. The word "fortunately" shows that the author thinks that their opinion was not a good one.

> **BP Minotaur:** This is an undeveloped view, as discussed earlier in this chapter. It is, therefore, not part of the primary structure of the passage.

Reading on, the author tells us that "prolonged immersion of this kind"—her method of research—allowed Dunham to comprehend the cultural importance and teach the dances to others. In layman's terms, her method of research caused her success. This provides support for the causal statement—one half of it, at least. This means we can now place it into our primary structure diagram.

That's one half of the causal statement. The other half was that Dunham's training in choreography caused her success. There's one paragraph left, and it's near certain that it will address the other half. Aren't you excited? Let's read on!

Paragraph 4

>   Between 1937 and 1945, Dunham developed
> a research-to-performance method that she used to
> (50) adapt Caribbean dance forms for use in theatrical
> performance, combining them with modern dance
> styles she learned in Chicago. <u>The ballets she created
> in this fashion were among the first North American
> dances to rectify the exclusion of African American
> (55) themes from the medium of modern dance.</u> Her work
> was thus crucial in establishing African American
> dance as an art form in its own right, making possible
> future companies such as Arthur Mitchell's Dance
> Theater of Harlem.

EX. OF SUCCESS

It would be nice if the paragraph used the word "choreography" to tie this puppy up in a neat package, but it doesn't. Instead, the passage lets us know that Dunham created ballets. That, kiddos, is choreography. And when she used that training in choreography to create ballets, those ballets helped address the fact that African American themes were absent from modern dance.

That's success, any way you slice it. We now know that the cause and effect statement in the first paragraph is definitely our conclusion. It has tons of support.

So, let's recap. In the first paragraph, we found a cause and effect statement, and it looked like a good candidate for a conclusion. Specifically, we found a statement that said that there were two causes—research and choreography—responsible for Dunham's success. After one background paragraph, we went on to find a paragraph providing support for the first cause and a final paragraph providing support for the second cause.

When there is a conclusion and support for that conclusion, you have a point of view that should show up in your primary structure diagram. Since we only found one supported conclusion, this is a Thesis passage. Hooray!

The completed markup looks like this:

One of the more striking developments in modern North American dance was African American choreographer Katherine Dunham's introduction of a technique known as dance-isolation, in which one
(5) part of the body moves in one rhythm while other parts are kept stationary or are moved in different rhythms. The incorporation of this technique into North American and European choreography is relatively recent, although various forms of the technique have
(10) long been essential to traditional dances of certain African, Caribbean, and Pacific-island cultures. Dunham's success in bringing dance-isolation and other traditional techniques from those cultures into the mainstream of modern North American dance is due
(15) in no small part to her training in both anthropological research and choreography.
As an anthropologist in the 1930s, Dunham was one of the pioneers in the field of dance ethnology. Previously, dance had been neglected as an area of
(20) social research, primarily because most social scientists gravitated toward areas likely to be recognized by their peers as befitting scientifically rigorous, and therefore legitimate, modes of inquiry. Moreover, no other social scientist at that time was sufficiently trained in dance to
(25) be able to understand dance techniques, while experts in dance were not trained in the methods of social research.
Starting in 1935, Dunham conducted a series of research projects into traditional Caribbean dance
(30) forms, with special interest in their origins in African culture. Especially critical to her success was her approach to research, which diverged radically from the methodology that prevailed at the time. Colleagues in anthropology advised her not to become too closely
(35) involved in the dances she was observing, both because of the extreme physical demands of the dances, and because they subscribed to the long-standing view, now fortunately recognized as unrealistic, that effective data gathering can and must be conducted from a position of
(40) complete detachment. But because of her interest and her skill as a performer, she generally eschewed such caution and participated in the dances herself. Through prolonged immersion of this kind, Dunham was able not only to comprehend various dances as complex
(45) cultural practices, but also to learn the techniques well enough to teach them to others and incorporate them into new forms of ballet.
Between 1937 and 1945, Dunham developed a research-to-performance method that she used to
(50) adapt Caribbean dance forms for use in theatrical performance, combining them with modern dance styles she learned in Chicago. The ballets she created in this fashion were among the first North American dances to rectify the exclusion of African American
(55) themes from the medium of modern dance. Her work was thus crucial in establishing African American dance as an art form in its own right, making possible future companies such as Arthur Mitchell's Dance Theater of Harlem.

ATT.

AUTHOR'S CONCLUSION:

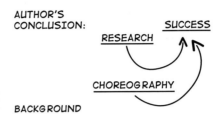

BACKGROUND

WHY DANCE HAD BEEN NEGLECTED

COLLEAGUES: JOINING IN IS DANGEROUS AND WRECKS OBJECTIVITY

This is the way we diagram causal statements. This is shorthand for "Training in anthropological research and choreography were the causes for Dunham's success."

ATT.

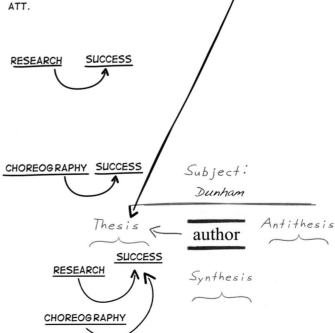

98 / Chapter 10

Don't worry if you found some of the tagging difficult or confusing. At this point we just want you to be able to fill in the primary structure diagram and locate instances of attitude in the passage. Everything else you'll learn later. Now, to the questions:

Question #8

We got this one. We filled in our diagram, noting exactly one point of view—that Dunham's training in research and choreography caused her success. That is the author's point of view, which means it's the main point. Answer choice (E) says exactly that, albeit in different (and wordier!) language.

We can generally get rid of answers to Main Point questions on two different grounds: the answer is too narrow, or it misrepresents the contents of the passage.

8. Which one of the following most accurately expresses the main point of the passage?

(A) Katherine Dunham transformed the field of anthropology by developing innovative research methodologies for studying Caribbean and other traditional dance styles and connecting them with African American dance.

(B) Katherine Dunham's ballets were distinct from others produced in North America in that they incorporated authentic dance techniques from traditional cultures.

(C) Katherine Dunham's expertise as an anthropologist allowed her to use Caribbean and African dance traditions to express the aesthetic and political concerns of African American dancers and choreographers.

(D) The innovative research methods of Katherine Dunham made possible her discovery that the dance traditions of the Caribbean were derived from earlier African dance traditions.

(E) Katherine Dunham's anthropological and choreographic expertise enabled her to make contributions that altered the landscape of modern dance in North America.

Dunham brought African American dance into modern dance where it did not before exist. Answer choice (A) is saying she brought Caribbean dance into African American dance, so it misrepresents the passage. Answer choice (B) also misrepresents the passage. While traditional African American dance might not have been incorporated, it's not clear that no traditional cultures were represented. Answer choice (C) talks about political concerns, which are not addressed in the passage. If it's not in the passage, it certainly can't be the main point. Answer choice (D) says that Dunham herself discovered the link between Caribbean and African dances. As with (C), there's no indication of that in the passage.

Question #9

Here, we are being asked about the other anthropologists, which the author discusses in paragraphs two and three. By glancing at our tagged paragraphs, we see the most notable characteristic of the other anthropologists is that our author doesn't agree with their view. We marked this with an "Att." at line 38, which is where the correct answer lies. The author doesn't like the view of the other anthropologists because they didn't participate in the cultures they studied. The fact that Dunham did participate is exactly what the author likes about Dunham. Answer choice (C) draws on our knowledge of the author's attitude to yield the correct answer.

Question #14

This question once again addresses the author's attitude toward other researchers. Let's get rid of (A) and (B) right off the bat because the author never agrees with anything these other researchers do, even partly.

Answer choice (C) is tempting, because the author does indeed think the colleagues' advice was bad. But we don't necessarily know, as the answer choice asserts, that extensive personal investment in fieldwork *generally* enhances scientific rigor. It might have in this particular case, even though it would do the opposite 99% of the time. Answer choice (E) is wrong because it misrepresents the colleagues' point of view. They thought the opposite.

(D) is the right answer. The passage says that the idea that "effective data gathering can...be conducted from a position of complete detachment" (lines 37-40), is not true. Answer choice (D) says that exactly.

9. According to the passage, Dunham's work in anthropology differed from that of most other anthropologists in the 1930s in that Dunham

   (A) performed fieldwork for a very extended time period
   (B) related the traditions she studied to those of her own culture
   (C) employed a participative approach in performing research
   (D) attached a high degree of political significance to her research
   (E) had prior familiarity with the cultural practices of the peoples she set out to study

14. The passage suggests that the author would be most likely to agree with which one of the following statements about the colleagues mentioned in line 33?

   (A) They were partly correct in recommending that Dunham change her methods of data collection, since injury sustained during fieldwork might have compromised her research.
   (B) They were partly correct in advising Dunham to exercise initial caution in participating in the Caribbean dances, since her skill in performing them improved with experience.
   (C) They were incorrect in advising Dunham to increase the degree of her detachment, since extensive personal investment in fieldwork generally enhances scientific rigor.
   (D) They were incorrect in assuming that researchers in the social sciences are able to gather data in an entirely objective manner.
   (E) They were incorrect in assuming that dance could be studied with the same degree of scientific rigor possible in other areas of ethnology.

Looking for the explanations for questions 10 through 13? Since you haven't learned the methods to attack those questions yet, we have not included them here. You can find them on your online *MyBlueprint* account.

ANSWER KEY

8. e, 9. c, 10. c, 11. d, 12. e, 13. d, 14. d

EXERCISE 2: JUNE 2012 PASSAGE 3

Music and literature, rivals among the arts, have not coexisted without intruding on each other's terrain. Ever since what we think of as "literature" developed out of the sounds of spoken, sung, and chanted art,
(5) writing has aspired to the condition of music, in which form contributes significantly to content. Nowhere is this truer than in the African American tradition, whose music is often considered its greatest artistic achievement and one of the greatest contributions to
(10) North American art. But while many African American writers have used musicians and music as theme and metaphor in their writing, none had attempted to draw upon a musical genre as the structuring principle for an entire novel until Toni Morrison did so in her 1992
(15) novel *Jazz*, a novel set in the Harlem section of New York City in 1926.

In *Jazz*, the connection to music is found not only in the novel's plot but, more strikingly, in the way in which the story is told. The narration slips easily
(20) from the third-person omniscience of the narrator's disembodied voice—which, though sensitive and sympathetic, claims no particular identity, gender, or immersion in specific social circumstances—to the first-person lyricism of key characters. But throughout
(25) these shifts, the narrator is both generous with the characters' voices and protective of his or her mastery over the narrative as a whole. On the one hand, the central characters are given the responsibility of relating their parts of the overarching story, but on
(30) the other hand, their sections are set off by quotation marks, reminders that the narrator is allowing them to speak. In this way, the narrative is analogous in structure to the playing of a jazz band which intertwines its ensemble sound with the individuality
(35) of embedded solo performances.

In jazz, composer and conductor Duke Ellington was the first to construct his compositions with his individual musicians and their unique "voices" in mind. Yet no matter how lengthy his musicians'
(40) improvisations, no matter how bold or inventive their solos might be, they always performed within the undeniable logic of the composer's frame—they always, in other words, performed as if with quotation marks around their improvisations and solos. It is this
(45) same effect that Toni Morrison has achieved in *Jazz*, a literary rendering of an art of composition that Duke Ellington perfected around the time in which *Jazz* is set.

In this novel, Morrison has found a way,
(50) paradoxically, to create the sense of an ensemble of characters improvising within the fixed scope of a carefully constructed collective narration. By simulating the style of a genius of music while exhibiting Morrison's own linguistic virtuosity,
(55) *Jazz* serves to redefine the very possibilities of narrative point of view.

15. Which one of the following most accurately states the main point of the passage?

(A) In *Jazz*, Morrison has realized a significant artistic achievement in creating the first African American work of fiction whose plot, themes, and setting are all drawn from the world of jazz.

(B) Morrison's striking description of a musical ensemble performance containing solo improvisations constitutes an important artistic innovation and makes *Jazz* an important model for other writers.

(C) Although many African American writers have used music as a central metaphor in their works, Morrison's 1992 novel is unique and innovative for using jazz as its central metaphor.

(D) Building on the works of many African American writers and musical composers, Morrison has over the years developed an innovative jazzlike style of narration, which she used especially effectively in the novel *Jazz*.

(E) In *Jazz*, Morrison has succeeded in creating an original and effective narrative strategy that is a literary analogue of Duke Ellington's style of musical composition.

16. The author's discussion in the first paragraph proceeds in which one of the following ways?

(A) from a common claim about the arts, to a denial of this claim as applied to a particular artistic tradition, to a hypothesis about a particular individual

(B) from a general remark about two art forms, to a similar observation about a particular artistic tradition, to a specific comment about a particular work that exemplifies the prior remarks

(C) from a description of a common claim about two art forms, to some specific evidence that supports that claim, to an inference regarding a particular individual to whom that claim applies

(D) from an observation about a specific art form, to a more general claim about the applicability of that observation to other art forms, to a particular counterexample to the first observation

(E) from general comments about the arts, to a purported counterexample to the general comments as applied to a particular artistic tradition, to a description of a particular work that bears out the original comments

17. The author's assertion in lines 10–16 would be most called into question if which one of the following were true?

    (A) Every casual reading of *Jazz* makes it evident that the author has intentionally tried to simulate a style of jazz performance in the narration of the story.
    (B) A small number of African American novelists writing earlier in the twentieth century sought to base the form of their work on the typical structure of blues music.
    (C) All novels about nonliterary arts and artists appear as if their authors have tried to make their narrative styles reminiscent of the arts in question.
    (D) Depending partly on whether or not it is read aloud, any novel can be found to be somewhat musical in nature.
    (E) A smaller number of African American writers than of non-African American writers in North America have written novels whose plots and characters have to do with music.

18. The information in the passage most supports which one of the following statements regarding Ellington?

    (A) Morrison has explicitly credited him with inspiring the style of narration that she developed in *Jazz*.
    (B) He prevented his musicians from performing lengthy solos in order to preserve the unity of his compositions.
    (C) He is a minor character in Morrison's *Jazz*.
    (D) He composed music that was originally intended to be performed by the specific musicians he conducted.
    (E) Though he composed and conducted primarily jazz, he also composed some music of other genres.

19. The author's primary purpose in the passage is to

    (A) analyze and commend the variety of contributions to the art of the novel made by a particular writer
    (B) contrast a particular African American writer's work with the work of African American practitioners of another art
    (C) describe a particular aspect of one work by a particular writer
    (D) demonstrate the ways in which two apparently dissimilar arts are, on a deeper analysis, actually quite similar
    (E) detail the thematic concerns in the work of a particular writer and identify the sources of those concerns

20. Each of the following excerpts from the passage exhibits the author's attitude toward the novel *Jazz* EXCEPT:

    (A) "...whose music is often considered its greatest artistic achievement and one of the greatest contributions to North American art" (lines 8–10)
    (B) "In *Jazz*, the connection to music is found not only in the novel's plot but, more strikingly, in the way in which the story is told" (lines 17–19)
    (C) "The narration slips easily from the third-person omniscience of the narrator's disembodied voice..." (lines 19–21)
    (D) "...Morrison has found a way, paradoxically, to create the sense of an ensemble of characters improvising within the fixed scope..." (lines 49–51)
    (E) "By simulating the style of a genius of music while exhibiting Morrison's own linguistic virtuosity..." (lines 52–54)

21. It can be inferred from the passage that the author would be most likely to believe which one of the following?

    (A) In *Jazz*, Morrison has perfected a style of narration that had been attempted with little success by other North American writers in the twentieth century.
    (B) Because of its use of narrative techniques inspired by jazz, Morrison's novel represents the most successful representation to date of the milieu in which jazz musicians live and work.
    (C) In *Jazz*, Morrison develops her narrative in such a way that the voices of individual characters are sometimes difficult to distinguish, in much the same way that individual musicians' voices merge in ensemble jazz playing.
    (D) The structural analogy between *Jazz* and Duke Ellington's compositional style involves more than simply the technique of shifting between first-person and third-person narrators.
    (E) Morrison disguises the important structural connections between her narrative and Duke Ellington's jazz compositions by making the transitions between first- and third-person narrators appear easy.

22. The passage contains information that most helps to answer which one of the following questions?

    (A) Do any African American visual artists also attempt to emulate African American music in their work?
    (B) In what way is *Jazz* stylistically similar to other literary works by Morrison?
    (C) After the publication of *Jazz*, did critics quickly acknowledge the innovative nature of the narrative style that Morrison uses in that novel?
    (D) How many works by African American writers have been inspired by the music of Duke Ellington?
    (E) What characteristic of *Jazz* is also present in the work of some other African American writers?

EXPLANATION

Paragraph 1

> Music and literature, rivals among the arts, have not coexisted without intruding on each other's terrain. Ever since what we think of as "literature" developed out of the sounds of spoken, sung, and chanted art,
> (5) writing has aspired to the condition of music, in which form contributes significantly to content. Nowhere is this truer than in the African American tradition, whose music is often considered its greatest artistic achievement and one of the greatest contributions to
> (10) North American art. But while many African American writers have used musicians and music as theme and metaphor in their writing, none had attempted to draw upon a musical genre as the structuring principle for an entire novel until Toni Morrison did so in her 1992
> (15) novel *Jazz*, a novel set in the Harlem section of New York City in 1926.

CHARACTERISTIC OF MUSIC (lines 5-6)

AUTHOR'S CONCLUSION

As is often the case, the passage begins with some background, which helps us to fill in the subject of our primary structure diagram. Here, we have a comparison between music and literature. In music, form contributes to content (lines 5-6) and literature is trying to do the same.

A few lines later, we get what looks like a conclusion. Toni Morrison's *Jazz* seems to fit the form-contributing-to-content principle of music we got earlier in the paragraph. This is because a musical genre provides the structuring principle for the novel. This is an example where form (the musical genre jazz) contributes to content (a fictional narrative).

Cleetus: I'm still having trouble with this conclusion bidness. How do you know it's a conclusion?

Good question, Cleetus. The author is expressing the *opinion* that this particular novel fits the definition of music. As you'll remember from Chapter 7, opinions are very often conclusions. Another indicator is the word "but," which starts off this sentence. A change in attitude ("but," "however," "nonetheless," etc.) is often a good conclusion indicator. We've identified a conclusion, and, if we find support for it elsewhere in the passage, it should be the Thesis position in our primary structure diagram.

Paragraph 2

> In *Jazz*, the connection to music is found not only in the novel's plot but, more strikingly, in the way in which the story is told. The narration slips easily
> (20) from the third-person omniscience of the narrator's disembodied voice—which, though sensitive and sympathetic, claims no particular identity, gender, or immersion in specific social circumstances—to the first-person lyricism of key characters. But throughout
> (25) these shifts, the narrator is both generous with the characters' voices and protective of his or her mastery over the narrative as a whole. On the one hand, the central characters are given the responsibility of relating their parts of the overarching story, but on
> (30) the other hand, their sections are set off by quotation marks, reminders that the narrator is allowing them to speak. In this way, the narrative is analogous in structure to the playing of a jazz band which intertwines its ensemble sound with the individuality
> (35) of embedded solo performances.

ATT.

LIKE MUSIC, THE BOOK HAS ENSEMBLE AND SOLO PERFORMANCES

The second paragraph is entirely devoted to providing support for the conclusion in the first paragraph that, in the novel *Jazz*, form contributes to content. How does it do that? The author asserts that the narration in *Jazz* is sometimes omniscient, third person narrative—analogous to the harmonious sound of a jazz ensemble—and at other times the characters are allowed to narrate tracts of the novel—analogous to solo performances in the context of the jazz ensemble. This gives us very good reason to believe that, in *Jazz* as in music, form contributes to content.

Since we have found substantial support for the conclusion in paragraph one, we can be sure that the conclusion is a viewpoint that ought to be represented in our primary structure diagram. This is the Thesis point of view.

Paragraph 3

> In jazz, composer and conductor Duke Ellington was the first to construct his compositions with his individual musicians and their unique "voices" in mind. Yet no matter how lengthy his musicians'
> (40) improvisations, no matter how bold or inventive their solos might be, they always performed within the undeniable logic of the composer's frame—they always, in other words, performed as if with quotation marks around their improvisations and solos. It is this
> (45) same effect that Toni Morrison has achieved in *Jazz*, a literary rendering of an art of composition that Duke Ellington perfected around the time in which *Jazz* is set.

DUKE ELLINGTON'S ACHIEVEMENTS

AUTHOR'S CONCLUSION

In this paragraph, the author continues to provide support for the idea that *Jazz* fits the definition of music, using the music of Duke Ellington as an example with which to compare *Jazz*. Ellington composed songs with the performers of his band in mind. The solos of those performers always fit into the overall song structure that Ellington envisioned. *Jazz*, the author explains, is set up the same way. The characters of the novel engage in extended narration solos, as described in the previous paragraph, but those solos fit into the overall structure that Morrison has designed. The paragraph concludes with a reiteration of our Thesis: Morrison's book is the literary equivalent of a composition. It's rare for a conclusion to be stated twice but very nice when it happens as it gives you a second chance to spot the author's conclusion.

Paragraph 4

> In this novel, Morrison has found a way,
> (50) paradoxically, to create the sense of an ensemble of characters improvising within the fixed scope of a carefully constructed collective narration. By simulating the style of a genius of music while exhibiting Morrison's own linguistic virtuosity,
> (55) *Jazz* serves to redefine the very possibilities of narrative point of view.

ATT.

ATT.

The final paragraph continues to support the conclusion in the first paragraph, but it is mostly devoted to emphasizing the author's attitude toward *Jazz*. That attitude is very, very positive. Morrison was able to recreate "the style of a genius of music," she displays "linguistic virtuosity," and she has "redefine[d] the very possibilities of the narrative point of view." In other words, the author luuuuvs Ms. Morrison.

So, let's summarize what happens in this passage. We have a conclusion expressed by the author (it is not assigned to anybody else) in the first paragraph. The next two paragraphs provide support for that conclusion. Finally, the last paragraph gives us strong, positive author's attitude regarding the subject of the passage.

When the author is present—when the author expresses an opinion—the author's opinion is the main point of the passage. In this case, the main point of the passage is that, in *Jazz* as in music in general, form contributes to content. Since it's the only point of view, this is a Thesis passage.

The completed markup looks like this:

> Music and literature, rivals among the arts, have not coexisted without intruding on each other's terrain. Ever since what we think of as "literature" developed out of the sounds of spoken, sung, and chanted art,
> (5) writing has aspired to the condition of music, in which form contributes significantly to content. Nowhere is this truer than in the African American tradition, whose music is often considered its greatest artistic achievement and one of the greatest contributions to
> (10) North American art. But while many African American writers have used musicians and music as theme and metaphor in their writing, none had attempted to draw upon a musical genre as the structuring principle for an entire novel until Toni Morrison did so in her 1992
> (15) novel *Jazz*, a novel set in the Harlem section of New York City in 1926.
>   In *Jazz*, the connection to music is found not only in the novel's plot but, more strikingly, in the way in which the story is told. The narration slips easily
> (20) from the third-person omniscience of the narrator's disembodied voice—which, though sensitive and sympathetic, claims no particular identity, gender, or immersion in specific social circumstances—to the first-person lyricism of key characters. But throughout
> (25) these shifts, the narrator is both generous with the characters' voices and protective of his or her mastery over the narrative as a whole. On the one hand, the central characters are given the responsibility of relating their parts of the overarching story, but on
> (30) the other hand, their sections are set off by quotation marks, reminders that the narrator is allowing them to speak. In this way, the narrative is analogous in structure to the playing of a jazz band which intertwines its ensemble sound with the individuality
> (35) of embedded solo performances.
>   In jazz, composer and conductor Duke Ellington was the first to construct his compositions with his individual musicians and their unique "voices" in mind. Yet no matter how lengthy his musicians'
> (40) improvisations, no matter how bold or inventive their solos might be, they always performed within the undeniable logic of the composer's frame—they always, in other words, performed as if with quotation marks around their improvisations and solos. It is this
> (45) same effect that Toni Morrison has achieved in *Jazz*, a literary rendering of an art of composition that Duke Ellington perfected around the time in which *Jazz* is set.
>   In this novel, Morrison has found a way,
> (50) paradoxically, to create the sense of an ensemble of characters improvising within the fixed scope of a carefully constructed collective narration. By simulating the style of a genius of music while exhibiting Morrison's own linguistic virtuosity,
> (55) *Jazz* serves to redefine the very possibilities of narrative point of view.

Margin annotations:
- CHARACTERISTIC OF MUSIC
- AUTHOR'S CONCLUSION
- ATT.
- LIKE MUSIC, THE BOOK HAS ENSEMBLE AND SOLO PERFORMANCES
- DUKE ELLINGTON'S ACHIEVEMENTS
- AUTHOR'S CONCLUSION
- ATT.
- ATT.

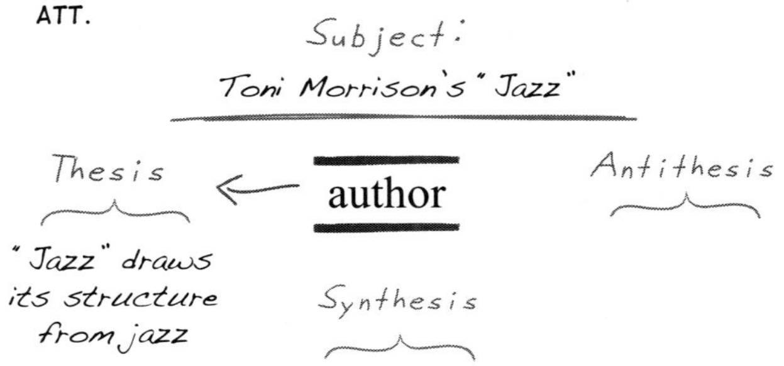

Subject: Toni Morrison's "Jazz"

Thesis ← author → Antithesis

"Jazz" draws its structure from jazz

Synthesis

And now, on to the questions.

Question #15

We already have anticipated the correct answer to the Main Point question by filling in our primary structure diagram. Answer choice (E) is the correct answer because it says, in so many words, that *Jazz* fits the definition of music. It does so by calling it the "literary analogue" of Duke Ellington's compositions. Not sure what an "analogue" is? Remember to always look up unfamiliar words! An analogue is "something similar to something else." As in "dragons are Comic Con's *analogue* of a mascot."

Answer choice (A) is wrong because it mischaracterizes the passage. There's no indication in the passage that Morrison was the first to write about jazz. It's that she writes *in the style of jazz*. Answer choice (B) also mischaracterizes the passage. There's no indication in the passage that Morrison ever actually describes musical ensemble performances in the novel. Instead, her characters fit into the novel in a way that is analogous (there's that word again!) to jazz. Answer choice (C) similarly mischaracterizes the passage. There's no indication that Morrison was the first to use jazz as a central metaphor. Answer choice (D) is tempting because it asserts that the narration is like jazz, but there's no indication in the passage that this narration style is used in any of her other books.

15. Which one of the following most accurately states the main point of the passage?

(A) In *Jazz*, Morrison has realized a significant artistic achievement in creating the first African American work of fiction whose plot, themes, and setting are all drawn from the world of jazz.

(B) Morrison's striking description of a musical ensemble performance containing solo improvisations constitutes an important artistic innovation and makes *Jazz* an important model for other writers.

(C) Although many African American writers have used music as a central metaphor in their works, Morrison's 1992 novel is unique and innovative for using jazz as its central metaphor.

(D) Building on the works of many African American writers and musical composers, Morrison has over the years developed an innovative jazzlike style of narration, which she used especially effectively in the novel *Jazz*.

(E) In *Jazz*, Morrison has succeeded in creating an original and effective narrative strategy that is a literary analogue of Duke Ellington's style of musical composition.

Question #20

It need not be said that the author thinks *Jazz* is a pretty darn good book. Since this is an EXCEPT question, we are looking for the answer that does *not* express that attitude. Answer choice (A) is the right answer simply because that part of the passage is discussing the African American tradition rather than *Jazz*. You just can't express your opinion on one thing by talking about a whole other thing.

20. Each of the following excerpts from the passage exhibits the author's attitude toward the novel *Jazz* EXCEPT:

    (A) "...whose music is often considered its greatest artistic achievement and one of the greatest contributions to North American art" (lines 8–10)
    (B) "In *Jazz*, the connection to music is found not only in the novel's plot but, more strikingly, in the way in which the story is told" (lines 17–19)
    (C) "The narration slips easily from the third-person omniscience of the narrator's disembodied voice..." (lines 19–21)
    (D) "...Morrison has found a way, paradoxically, to create the sense of an ensemble of characters improvising within the fixed scope..." (lines 49–51)
    (E) "By simulating the style of a genius of music while exhibiting Morrison's own linguistic virtuosity..." (lines 52–54)

Ninja: You would be surprised at how many grasshoppers skip over the EXCEPT in the question prompt and choose (B) as the correct answer. This is why it's important to read every answer choice. If you read to (C), you would see that it, too, would be correct, prompting you to re-read the question and see the EXCEPT. Like a sharp blade in a lychee-cutting contest, thoroughness pays off, young grasshopper.

Answer choice (B) reveals the authors attitude with the word "strikingly." Answer choice (C) reveals the attitude with the assertion that the novel "slips easily" from one voice to another. Answer choice (D) is praising Morrison's ability to put together things that it seems impossible to put together. Answer choice (E) says she is "simulating the style of a genius." Folks, it doesn't get much more boot-lickingly positive than that.

Question #21

This question is fairly wide open, because the author is present throughout the entire passage. Answer choice (D) is the right answer, and tracking the author's attitude in paragraph three helped us get here. The author asserts that Morrison, like Ellington, crafted a structure within which the characters could improvise (lines 39-48). That's more than just shifting between the first- and third-person narrators.

Answer choice (A) is wrong because it goes directly against the author's assertion that Morrison was the first to attempt this style of narration (lines 10-16). Look at answer choice (B). The test writers love to do this to you. The author says that *Jazz* is good, and they want you to conclude that it is the absolute best there ever was. This is a comparison for which there is no support. Answer choice (C) is wrong because it mischaracterizes the analogy between jazz and *Jazz*. The ensemble part of the book is where Morrison narrates in the third-person. And, with answer choice (E), there is no indication in the passage that Morrison was trying to hide what she was doing.

21. It can be inferred from the passage that the author would be most likely to believe which one of the following?

(A) In *Jazz*, Morrison has perfected a style of narration that had been attempted with little success by other North American writers in the twentieth century.
(B) Because of its use of narrative techniques inspired by jazz, Morrison's novel represents the most successful representation to date of the milieu in which jazz musicians live and work.
(C) In *Jazz*, Morrison develops her narrative in such a way that the voices of individual characters are sometimes difficult to distinguish, in much the same way that individual musicians' voices merge in ensemble jazz playing.
(D) The structural analogy between *Jazz* and Duke Ellington's compositional style involves more than simply the technique of shifting between first-person and third-person narrators.
(E) Morrison disguises the important structural connections between her narrative and Duke Ellington's jazz compositions by making the transitions between first- and third-person narrators appear easy.

The explanations for questions 16-18 and 22 are in your online *MyBlueprint* account. Since you have not learned the methods needed to answer those questions yet, we didn't include them, but there are some little rascals who just can't help themselves.

ANSWER KEY

15. e, 16. b, 17. b, 18., d, 19. c, 20. a, 21. d, 22. e

11/ANTITHESISpassages

Wanna fight?

You're going to law school because you like to argue. Well, Antithesis passages should be right up your alley.

Cleetus: Hold up jest a sec'! I gotta get my tire iron and my beer helmet if we gonna go at it.

Take it easy there, Cleetus. We're not talking about real live fisticuffs here. We're talking scholarly debate.

When you tackle Reading Comprehension passages, you get to read about scholars arguing about super important things like whether the extinction of the dodo bird led to a near extinction of a particular tree found only on the island of Mauritius or whether a forgery can be classified as art. We here at Blueprint call them Antithesis passages because it's not just that there are two points of view; those points of view are usually in opposition to each other, just like a plaintiff and a defendant. One view is the antithesis of the other.

Antithesis passages are by far the most common passage type on the LSAT, comprising just over 50% (50.34% to be exact) of all of Reading Comprehension. This makes sense because, for the most part, your compulsory reading material in law school will be judicial opinions, and those almost always include two points of view: plaintiff and defendant.

Antithesis passages have an average difficulty rating of 2.93, the highest of the three primary structures. This, too, makes sense as it's typically more difficult to keep track of multiple views.

Most Antithesis passages have a present author, meaning that the author either introduces or adopts one of the points of view. This also makes sense because, in a judicial opinion, the judge ends up ruling that one party is right and the other one is wrong. In an Antithesis passage, it is your job to identify both arguments, as well as identify with which point of view the author is aligned.

BP Minotaur: Sometimes a passage will identify a particular point of view that the author says is wrong. If there is no support for that point of view, the author is probably just using it as a background to introduce her conclusion. In such a case, you don't have two full arguments and the passage is a Thesis passage, rather than an Antithesis passage.

Like the previous chapter on Thesis passages, the important thing to take from this chapter is that you must track points of view as well as the author's attitude (where applicable). Let's take an example.

> Carol and I are trying to figure out the best way to explain the birds and the bees to little Johnny, but, so far, we're stumped. When we talked about it a few days back, she said we should tell him—get this!—it's like jumping on a trampoline, and then there's a baby in mommy's tummy.
>
> When I heard that, I couldn't help myself. I told her it was the dumbest idea I'd ever heard! I mean, c'mon! If he doesn't understand now, that's only going to make it worse. Trampoline! What does that even mean?! And the next time he jumps on the trampoline with his little friend Sally, he's going to be running around telling everyone they're making babies together.
>
> Then I looked up the subject on Yahoo!™ Answers. I've never face-palmed so hard in my life. I think I broke my nose. What a wasteland of insanity and misinformation.
>
> My mechanic Chuck agreed that Carol's idea was a total loser. He told me the best way to go is just explain it all and let the kid process the trauma. He says it'll make a man out of him. I'm inclined to agree. Better than letting Johnny be the idiot who walks around telling people that babies come from trampolines.

Cleetus: You mean they don't come from a trampoline?

There are two points of view here about the best way to explain the birds and the bees. The first is Carol's trampoline idea, and the other is Chuck's idea to just be straightforward. These are, respectively, the Thesis and Antithesis positions. Carol espouses Thesis, and Chuck espouses Antithesis. Importantly, the author adopts Chuck's position ("I'm inclined to agree."). Take a look at the primary structure diagram for this incredibly scholarly passage.

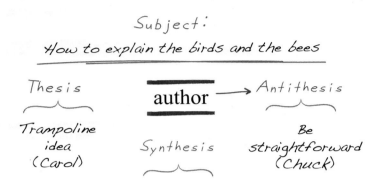

Now, let's talk about attitude. The author strongly disapproves of Carol's point of view ("dumbest idea I've ever heard"). So does Chuck ("a total loser").

Finally, it's important to note that, while the author consulted Yahoo!™ Answers, no point of view on how to talk to Johnny comes from it. The author does, however, express strong negative attitude toward it ("...wasteland of insanity and misinformation").

YOUR TURN

Attack!

The following passages are Antithesis Passages, and we have supplied you with a blank primary structure diagram. Read each passage and identify the arguments, filling in the diagram as you go. When you see a point of view, underline it and identify in the margins exactly who holds what particular point of view. If you see an indication that the author or a party has a positive or negative attitude toward something, underline the word or words that indicate the attitude and tag it in the margins with an "Att."

Answer the questions in black—Main Point, Primary Purpose, Author's Attitude, and Viewpoint—at the end of the passages. The other questions have been greyed out. You may attempt them if you wish, but we will learn to address them in later chapters so we have not included explanations for them here. A paragraph-by-paragraph explanation follows. Study it carefully when you are done reading and answering the questions to make sure you correctly identified all the relevant points of view. Good luck!

Did you know your brain is the fattest organ in your body? It's approximately 60% fat. So don't diet before the LSAT!

EXERCISE 1: JUNE 1999 PASSAGE 3

Recently, a new school of economics called steady-state economics has seriously challenged neoclassical economics, the reigning school in Western economic decision making. According to the
(5) neoclassical model, an economy is a closed system involving only the circular flow of exchange value between producers and consumers. Therefore, no noneconomic constraints impinge upon the economy and growth has no limits. Indeed, some neoclassical
(10) economists argue that growth itself is crucial, because, they claim, the solutions to problems often associated with growth (income inequities, for example) can be found only in the capital that further growth creates.
Steady-state economists believe the neoclassical
(15) model to be unrealistic and hold that the economy is dependent on nature. Resources, they argue, enter the economy as raw material and exit as consumed products or waste; the greater the resources, the greater the size of the economy. According to these
(20) economists, nature's limited capacity to regenerate raw material and absorb waste suggests that there is an optimal size for the economy, and that growth beyond this ideal point would increase the cost to the environment at a faster rate than the benefit to
(25) producers and consumers, generating cycles that impoverish rather than enrich. Steady-state economists thus believe that the concept of an ever growing economy is dangerous, and that the only alternative is to maintain a state in which the economy remains in
(30) equilibrium with nature. Neoclassical economists, on the other hand, consider nature to be just one element of the economy rather than an outside constraint, believing that natural resources, if depleted, can be replaced with other elements—i.e., human-made
(35) resources-that will allow the economy to continue with its process of unlimited growth.
Some steady-state economists, pointing to the widening disparity between indices of actual growth (which simply count the total monetary value of
(40) goods and services) and the index of environmentally sustainable growth (which is based on personal consumption, factoring in depletion of raw materials and production costs), believe that Western economies have already exceeded their optimal size. In response
(45) to the warnings from neoclassical economists that checking economic growth only leads to economic stagnation, they argue that there are alternatives to growth that still accomplish what is required of any economy: the satisfaction of human wants. One of
(50) the alternatives is conservation. Conservation—for example, increasing the efficiency of resource use through means such as recycling–differs from growth in that it is qualitative, not quantitative, requiring improvement in resource management rather than an
(55) increase in the amount of resources. One measure of the success of a steady-state economy would be the degree to which it could implement alternatives to growth, such as conservation, without sacrificing the ability to satisfy the wants of producers and consumers.

14. Which one of the following most completely and accurately expresses the main point of the passage?

(A) Neoclassical economists, who, unlike steady-state economists, hold that economic growth is not subject to outside constraints, believe that nature is just one element of the economy and that if natural resources in Western economies are depleted they can be replaced with human-made resources.

(B) Some neoclassical economists, who, unlike steady-state economists, hold that growth is crucial to the health of economies, believe that the solutions to certain problems in Western economies can thus be found in the additional capital generated by unlimited growth.

(C) Some steady-state economists, who, unlike neoclassical economists, hold that unlimited growth is neither possible nor desirable, believe that Western economies should limit economic growth by adopting conservation strategies, even if such strategies lead temporarily to economic stagnation.

(D) Some steady-state economists, who, unlike neoclassical economists, hold that the optimal sizes of economies are limited by the availability of natural resources, believe that Western economies should limit economic growth and that, with alternatives like conservation, satisfaction of human wants need not be sacrificed.

(E) Steady-state and neoclassical economists, who both hold that economies involve the circular flow of exchange value between producers and consumers, nevertheless differ over the most effective way of guaranteeing that a steady increase in this exchange value continues unimpeded in Western economies.

15. Based on the passage, neoclassical economists would likely hold that steady-state economists are wrong to believe each of the following EXCEPT:

(A) The environment's ability to yield raw material is limited.
(B) Natural resources are an external constraint on economies.
(C) The concept of unlimited economic growth is dangerous.
(D) Western economies have exceeded their optimal size.
(E) Economies have certain optimal sizes.

16. According to the passage, steady-state economists believe that unlimited economic growth is dangerous because it

    (A) may deplete natural resources faster than other natural resources are discovered to replace them
    (B) may convert natural resources into products faster than more efficient resource use can compensate for
    (C) may proliferate goods and services faster than it generates new markets for them
    (D) may create income inequities faster than it creates the capital needed to redress them
    (E) may increase the cost to the environment faster than it increases benefits to producers and consumers

17. A steady-state economist would be LEAST likely to endorse which one of the following as a means of helping a steady-state economy reduce growth without compromising its ability to satisfy human wants?

    (A) a manufacturer's commitment to recycle its product packaging
    (B) a manufacturer's decision to use a less expensive fuel in its production process
    (C) a manufacturer's implementation of a quality-control process to reduce the output of defective products
    (D) a manufacturer's conversion from one type of production process to another with greater fuel efficiency
    (E) a manufacturer's reduction of output in order to eliminate an overproduction problem

18. Based on the passage, a steady-state economist is most likely to claim that a successful economy is one that satisfies which one of the following principles?

    (A) A successful economy uses human-made resources in addition to natural resources.
    (B) A successful economy satisfies human wants faster than it creates new ones.
    (C) A successful economy maintains an equilibrium with nature while still satisfying human wants.
    (D) A successful economy implements every possible means to prevent growth.
    (E) A successful economy satisfies the wants of producers and consumers by using resources to spur growth.

19. In the view of steady-state economists, which one of the following is a noneconomic constraint as referred to in line 7?

    (A) the total amount of human wants
    (B) the index of environmentally sustainable growth
    (C) the capacity of nature to absorb waste
    (D) the problems associated with economic growth
    (E) the possibility of economic stagnation

20. Which one of the following most accurately describes what the last paragraph does in the passage?

    (A) It contradicts the ways in which the two economic schools interpret certain data and gives a criterion for judging between them based on the basic goals of an economy.
    (B) It gives an example that illustrates the weakness of the new economic school and recommends an economic policy based on the basic goals of the prevailing economic school.
    (C) It introduces an objection to the new economic school and argues that the policies of the new economic school would be less successful than growth-oriented economic policies at achieving the basic goal an economy must meet.
    (D) It notes an objection to implementing the policies of the new economic school and identifies an additional policy that can help avoid that objection and still meet the goal an economy must meet.
    (E) It contrasts the policy of the prevailing economic school with the recommendation mentioned earlier of the new economic school and shows that they are based on differing views on the basic goal an economy must meet.

21. The passage suggests which one of the following about neoclassical economists?

    (A) They assume that natural resources are infinitely available.
    (B) They assume that human-made resources are infinitely available.
    (C) They assume that availability of resources places an upper limit on growth.
    (D) They assume that efficient management of resources is necessary to growth.
    (E) They assume that human-made resources are preferable to natural resources.

EXPLANATION

Paragraph 1

> Recently, a new school of economics called steady-state economics has seriously challenged neoclassical economics, the reigning school in Western economic decision making. According to the
> (5) neoclassical model, an economy is a closed system involving only the circular flow of exchange value between producers and consumers. <u>Therefore, no noneconomic constraints impinge upon the economy and growth has no limits.</u> Indeed, some neoclassical
> (10) economists argue that growth itself is crucial, because, they claim, the solutions to problems often associated with growth (income inequities, for example) can be found only in the capital that further growth creates.

NEOCLASSICAL ECONOMISTS' CONCLUSION

Let the battle of the econ nerds begin! In this corner, the upstart challenger, steady-state economics! And in this corner, the reigning champion of kickin' it solo in the library on Friday night, neoclassical economics! Okay, okay. Enough of that. Let's get down to business. The first sentence screams out Antithesis because there are two points of view, and one is challenging the other. However, we should wait and see if there is support for these points of view before we place them into our primary structure diagram.

The rest of this paragraph is devoted to explaining neoclassical economics. Neoclassical economists believe that nothing other than the transactions between buyers and sellers matters to an economy. Some of these economists believe that, as a result, an economy can and often should grow infinitely. There's nothing that constrains growth, in other words. Since the neoclassical point of view is fleshed out in detail, let's put it into our primary structure diagram as the Thesis point of view.

Paragraph 2

> Steady-state economists believe the neoclassical (15) model to be <u>unrealistic</u> and hold that the economy is dependent on nature. Resources, they argue, enter the economy as raw material and exit as consumed products or waste; the greater the resources, the greater the size of the economy. According to these (20) economists, nature's limited capacity to regenerate raw material and absorb waste suggests that there is an optimal size for the economy, and that growth beyond this ideal point would increase the cost to the environment at a faster rate than the benefit to (25) producers and consumers, generating cycles that impoverish rather than enrich. <u>Steady-state economists thus believe that the concept of an ever growing economy is dangerous, and that the only alternative is to maintain a state in which the economy remains in (30) equilibrium with nature.</u> Neoclassical economists, on the other hand, consider nature to be just one element of the economy rather than an outside constraint, believing that natural resources, if depleted, can be replaced with other elements—i.e., human-made (35) resources-that will allow the economy to continue with its process of unlimited growth.

ATT.

STEADY-STATE ECONOMISTS' CONCLUSION

The steady-state economists disagree with the point of view espoused by the neoclassical economists. Note that, not only do steady-state economists disagree, they think that the neoclassicists are "unrealistic." This is a pretty harsh criticism, and it's always important to note when a party in a passage has a strong attitude.

The steady-state economists believe that something other than transactions has an effect on an economy, namely nature. There's only so much good stuff we can take from, and bad stuff we can put back in to, nature. Instead of growth always being good, like the neoclassicists believe, growth can be, not just bad, but downright dangerous (more strong attitude). Thus, the steady-staters believe that there is an optimal size for an economy. Because there's support for it, let's put this point of view into our diagram as the Antithesis.

At the very end of the second paragraph, the neoclassical economists counter, saying that nature is really just part of the economy. If we destroy nature, hey, no big deal. We'll just make something better.

Paragraph 3

> (40) Some steady-state economists, pointing to the widening disparity between indices of actual growth (which simply count the total monetary value of goods and services) and the index of environmentally sustainable growth (which is based on personal consumption, factoring in depletion of raw materials and production costs), believe that Western economies have already exceeded their optimal size. In response
> (45) to the warnings from neoclassical economists that checking economic growth only leads to economic stagnation, they argue that there are alternatives to growth that still accomplish what is required of any economy: the satisfaction of human wants. One of
> (50) the alternatives is conservation. Conservation—for example, increasing the efficiency of resource use through means such as recycling–differs from growth in that it is qualitative, not quantitative, requiring improvement in resource management rather than an
> (55) increase in the amount of resources. One measure of the success of a steady-state economy would be the degree to which it could implement alternatives to growth, such as conservation, without sacrificing the ability to satisfy the wants of producers and consumers.

Annotations: STEADY-STATE CONCERN / CRITICISM OF STEADY-STATE / EX. / RESPONSE TO CRITICISM

At the beginning of the third paragraph, steady-state economists provide support for their view: actual growth is outstripping environmentally sustainable growth at an ever-increasing rate, and some economies are already too big. Uh-oh! So what do we do? The neoclassical economists warn that, if we stop growing, we will stagnate.

The steady-state economists believe there are alternatives to growth that will prevent stagnation without destroying the environment. Conservation, they say, is like growth in that we get more stuff (hooray for more stuff!), and we don't even need to destroy forests or mow down furry, adorable, woodland critters to do it. Win-win!

Before moving on to the questions, let's just be sure to summarize the passage. Paragraph one introduces two points of view, and fleshes out the first. Paragraph two elaborates on the second point of view and, at the end, describes the response of the proponents of the first point of view. Finally, paragraph three shows how the second point of view can address a concern expressed by those holding the first point of view. Nowhere in the passage do we ever see the author, so we know he or she isn't present.

The completed markup looks like this:

Recently, a new school of economics called steady-state economics has seriously challenged neoclassical economics, the reigning school in Western economic decision making. According to the
(5) neoclassical model, an economy is a closed system involving only the circular flow of exchange value between producers and consumers. Therefore, <u>no noneconomic constraints impinge upon the economy and growth has no limits</u>. Indeed, some neoclassical
(10) economists argue that growth itself is crucial, because, they claim, the solutions to problems often associated with growth (income inequities, for example) can be found only in the capital that further growth creates.

Steady-state economists believe the neoclassical
(15) model to be <u>unrealistic</u> and hold that the economy is dependent on nature. Resources, they argue, enter the economy as raw material and exit as consumed products or waste; the greater the resources, the greater the size of the economy. According to these
(20) economists, nature's limited capacity to regenerate raw material and absorb waste suggests that there is an optimal size for the economy, and that growth beyond this ideal point would increase the cost to the environment at a faster rate than the benefit to
(25) producers and consumers, generating cycles that impoverish rather than enrich. Steady-state economists thus believe that <u>the concept of an ever growing economy is dangerous, and that the only alternative is to maintain a state in which the economy remains in
(30) equilibrium with nature</u>. Neoclassical economists, on the other hand, consider nature to be just one element of the economy rather than an outside constraint, believing that natural resources, if depleted, can be replaced with other elements—i.e., human-made
(35) resources-that will allow the economy to continue with its process of unlimited growth.

Some steady-state economists, pointing to the widening disparity between indices of actual growth (which simply count the total monetary value of
(40) goods and services) and the index of environmentally sustainable growth (which is based on personal consumption, factoring in depletion of raw materials and production costs), believe that Western economies have already exceeded their optimal size. In response
(45) to the warnings from neoclassical economists that checking economic growth only leads to economic stagnation, they argue that there are alternatives to growth that still accomplish what is required of any economy: the satisfaction of human wants. One of
(50) the alternatives is conservation. Conservation—for example, increasing the efficiency of resource use through means such as recycling–differs from growth in that it is qualitative, not quantitative, requiring improvement in resource management rather than an
(55) increase in the amount of resources. One measure of the success of a steady-state economy would be the degree to which it could implement alternatives to growth, such as conservation, without sacrificing the ability to satisfy the wants of producers and consumers.

NEOCLASSICAL ECONOMISTS' CONCLUSION

ATT.

STEADY-STATE ECONOMISTS' CONCLUSION

STEADY-STATE CONCERN

CRITICISM OF STEADY-STATE

EX.

RESPONSE TO CRITICISM

Subject: Economic Growth

Thesis — author — Antithesis

Growth is unlimited (Neoclassical economists)

Synthesis

Growth is limited (Steady-state economists)

ANTITHESISpassages / 121

Question #14

14. Which one of the following most completely and accurately expresses the main point of the passage?

    (A) Neoclassical economists, who, unlike steady-state economists, hold that economic growth is not subject to outside constraints, believe that nature is just one element of the economy and that if natural resources in Western economies are depleted they can be replaced with human-made resources.
    (B) Some neoclassical economists, who, unlike steady-state economists, hold that growth is crucial to the health of economies, believe that the solutions to certain problems in Western economies can thus be found in the additional capital generated by unlimited growth.
    (C) Some steady-state economists, who, unlike neoclassical economists, hold that unlimited growth is neither possible nor desirable, believe that Western economies should limit economic growth by adopting conservation strategies, even if such strategies lead temporarily to economic stagnation.
    (D) Some steady-state economists, who, unlike neoclassical economists, hold that the optimal sizes of economies are limited by the availability of natural resources, believe that Western economies should limit economic growth and that, with alternatives like conservation, satisfaction of human wants need not be sacrificed.
    (E) Steady-state and neoclassical economists, who both hold that economies involve the circular flow of exchange value between producers and consumers, nevertheless differ over the most effective way of guaranteeing that a steady increase in this exchange value continues unimpeded in Western economies.

This is a Main Point question. This passage has an absent author, and so neither point of view is endorsed. In such a case, the main point of the passage is a summary of the points of view. The passage spends much more time on the views of the steady-state economists than those of the neoclassical economists, and the answer choice reflects that. (D) is the right answer because it describes steady-state economists' view in detail. It also encompasses the Antithesis point of view by saying they are "unlike neoclassical economists."

Both (A) and (B) are wrong because they miss important parts of the steady-state view, including everything in the third paragraph. There's no indication in the passage that steady-state economists think that conservation entails the possibility of temporary economic stagnation, so (C) mischaracterizes the passage. Steady-state economists do not believe that economies are circular flow models. That's the view of neoclassical economists (lines 4-7), so (E) cannot be correct.

17. A steady-state economist would be LEAST likely to endorse which one of the following as a means of helping a steady-state economy reduce growth without compromising its ability to satisfy human wants?

(A) a manufacturer's commitment to recycle its product packaging
(B) a manufacturer's decision to use a less expensive fuel in its production process
(C) a manufacturer's implementation of a quality-control process to reduce the output of defective products
(D) a manufacturer's conversion from one type of production process to another with greater fuel efficiency
(E) a manufacturer's reduction of output in order to eliminate an overproduction problem

Question #17

This question is going to throw four things at us that a steady-state economist would love—those are the wrong answers—and one with which a steady-state economist would either disagree or have no opinion. That leads to answer choice (B) because it's talking about saving money rather than conserving resources. We are never told whether the steady-state economists have any particular opinion on whether it's important for manufacturers to save money.

All the other answers address the conservation of resources, which the steady-state economists love. Recycling shows up in answer choice (A). Love it! Answer choice (C) talks about reducing the wastefulness associated with producing defective (i.e. unusable) products. Love it! In (D) we've got greater fuel efficiency. Doubly love it! And answer choice (E) talks about eliminating overproduction. Oh jeez, love it so so so much!

BP Minotaur: If you missed the word LEAST in the prompt you might be tempted to choose (A), as it aligns with the steady-state economists' view. This is why you should read every answer choice as you would see (C), (D), and (E) all align with that view as well, prompting you to re-read the question and arrive at correct answer choice (B).

Once again, you'll find the answers to the greyed-out questions on your online *MyBlueprint* account.

ANSWER KEY

14. d, 15. a, 16. e, 17. b, 18. c, 19. c, 20. d, 21. b

EXERCISE 2: OCT. 2004 PASSAGE 4

The proponents of the Modern Movement in architecture considered that, compared with the historical styles that it replaced, Modernist architecture more accurately reflected the functional
(5) spirit of twentieth-century technology and was better suited to the newest building methods. It is ironic, then, that the Movement fostered an ideology of design that proved to be at odds with the way buildings were really built.
(10) The tenacious adherence of Modernist architects and critics to this ideology was in part responsible for the Movement's decline. Originating in the 1920s as a marginal, almost bohemian art movement, the Modern Movement was never very popular with
(15) the public, but this very lack of popular support produced in Modernist architects a high-minded sense of mission—not content merely to interpret the needs of the client, these architects now sought to persuade, to educate, and, if necessary, to dictate.
(20) By 1945 the tenets of the Movement had come to dominate mainstream architecture, and by the early 1950s, to dominate architectural criticism—architects whose work seemed not to advance the evolution of the Modern Movement tended to be dismissed by
(25) proponents of Modernism. On the other hand, when architects were identified as innovators—as was the case with Otto Wagner, or the young Frank Lloyd Wright—attention was drawn to only those features of their work that were "Modern"; other aspects were
(30) conveniently ignored.
The decline of the Modern Movement later in the twentieth century occurred partly as a result of Modernist architects' ignorance of building methods, and partly because Modernist architects
(35) were reluctant to admit that their concerns were chiefly aesthetic. Moreover, the building industry was evolving in a direction Modernists had not anticipated: it was more specialized and the process of construction was much more fragmented
(40) than in the past. Up until the twentieth century, construction had been carried out by a relatively small number of tradespeople, but as the building industry evolved, buildings came to be built by many specialized subcontractors working independently.
(45) The architect's design not only had to accommodate a sequence of independent operations, but now had to reflect the allowable degree of inaccuracy of the different trades. However, one of the chief construction ideals of the Modern Movement was to
(50) "honestly" expose structural materials such as steel and concrete. To do this and still produce a visually acceptable interior called for an unrealistically high level of craftmanship. Exposure of a building's internal structural elements, if it could be achieved
(55) at all, could only be accomplished at considerable cost—hence the well-founded reputation of Modern architecture as prohibitively expensive.
As Postmodern architects recognized, the need to expose structural elements imposed unnecessary
(60) limitations on building design. The unwillingness of architects of the Modern Movement to abandon their ideals contributed to the decline of interest in the Modern Movement.

21. Which one of the following most accurately summarizes the main idea of the passage?

(A) The Modern Movement declined because its proponents were overly ideological and did not take into account the facts of building construction.
(B) Rationality was the theoretical basis for the development of the Modern Movement in architecture.
(C) Changes in architectural design introduced by the Modern Movement inspired the development of modern construction methods.
(D) The theoretical bases of the Modern Movement in architecture originated in changes in building construction methods.
(E) Proponents of the Modern Movement in architecture rejected earlier architectural styles because such styles were not functional.

22. Which one of the following is most similar to the relationship described in the passage between the new methods of the building industry and pre-twentieth century construction?

(A) Clothing produced on an assembly line is less precisely tailored than clothing produced by a single garment maker.
(B) Handwoven fabric is more beautiful than fabric produced by machine.
(C) Lenses ground on a machine are less useful than lenses ground by hand.
(D) Form letters produced by a word processor elicit fewer responses than letters typed individually on a typewriter.
(E) Furniture produced in a factory is less fashionable than handcrafted furniture.

23. With respect to the proponents of the Modern Movement, the author of the passage can best be described as

    (A) forbearing
    (B) defensive
    (C) unimpressed
    (D) exasperated
    (E) indifferent

24. It can be inferred that the author of the passage believes which one of the following about Modern Movement architects' ideal of exposing structural materials?

    (A) The repudiation of the ideal by some of these architects undermined its validity.
    (B) The ideal was rarely achieved because of its lack of popular appeal.
    (C) The ideal was unrealistic because most builders were unwilling to attempt it.
    (D) The ideal originated in the work of Otto Wagner and Frank Lloyd Wright.
    (E) The ideal arose from aesthetic rather than practical concerns.

25. Which one of the following, in its context in the passage, most clearly reveals the attitude of the author toward the proponents of the Modern Movement?

    (A) "functional spirit" (lines 4–5)
    (B) "tended" (line 24)
    (C) "innovators" (line 26)
    (D) "conveniently" (line 30)
    (E) "degree of inaccuracy" (line 47)

26. The author of the passage mentions Otto Wagner and the young Frank Lloyd Wright (lines 27–28) primarily as examples of

    (A) innovative architects whose work was not immediately appreciated by the public
    (B) architects whom proponents of the Modern Movement claimed represented the movement
    (C) architects whose work helped to popularize the Modern Movement
    (D) architects who generally attempted to interpret the needs of their clients, rather than dictating to them
    (E) architects whose early work seemed to architects of the Modern Movement to be at odds with the principles of Modernism

27. The author of the passage is primarily concerned with

    (A) analyzing the failure of a movement
    (B) predicting the future course of a movement
    (C) correcting a misunderstanding about a movement
    (D) anticipating possible criticism of a movement
    (E) contrasting incompatible viewpoints about a movement

EXPLANATION

Paragraph 1

> The proponents of the Modern Movement in architecture considered that, compared with the historical styles that it replaced, <u>Modernist architecture more accurately reflected the functional
> (5) spirit of twentieth-century technology and was better suited to the newest building methods.</u> It is <u>ironic, then, that the Movement fostered an ideology of design that proved to be at odds with the way buildings were really built.</u>

MODERNISTS' CONCLUSION

AUTHOR'S CONCLUSION
ATT.

Didn't think you'd need to hear about Modernist architecture to get into law school, did you? Ha! Well, let's get to it then.

By now you should know that the passage begins with a point of view. Proponents of Modernist architecture had the opinion that Modernism was a better representation of the time and better suited to the newest building methods than what came before. And then, in the next sentence, the author smacks the Modernists right in the face, saying that they were wrong. So very wrong. Note the author's attitude that it was "ironic" because Modernist architecture was actually at odds with the new building methods. Our author is clearly not impressed with the Modernists.

As we've seen before, there are opinions at the beginning of a passage. Here, they are opposed to one another. That makes it a good possibility that we have the Thesis position followed right on its heels by the Antithesis position. Let's read on to make sure we're right.

Paragraph 2

(10) The tenacious adherence of Modernist architects and critics to this ideology was in part responsible for the Movement's decline. Originating in the 1920s as a marginal, almost bohemian art movement, the Modern Movement was never very popular with
(15) the public, but this very lack of popular support produced in Modernist architects a high-minded sense of mission—not content merely to interpret the needs of the client, these architects now sought to persuade, to educate, and, if necessary, to dictate.
(20) By 1945 the tenets of the Movement had come to dominate mainstream architecture, and by the early 1950s, to dominate architectural criticism—architects whose work seemed not to advance the evolution of the Modern Movement tended to be dismissed by
(25) proponents of Modernism. On the other hand, when architects were identified as innovators—as was the case with Otto Wagner, or the young Frank Lloyd Wright—attention was drawn to only those features of their work that were "Modern"; other aspects were
(30) conveniently ignored.

SUPPORT FOR MODERNISTS' CONCLUSION

ATT.

This paragraph explains the ideology and actions of the Modernists. The public didn't like Modernist architecture. But did the architects cry about it like babies? Heck, no! They pushed for Modernist architecture, and boy did they push hard, dictating (line 19) if necessary. Modernism eventually came to dominate both architecture and architectural criticism. Since it expands on the view introduced in the first paragraph, we know this is the Thesis position. Let's put it into our primary structure diagram: Modernism is better for the times and methods.

We also get the author's attitude toward the Modernist movement. The movement dismissed architecture that didn't advance Modernism, and it "conveniently" overlooked the non-Modernist impulses of architects it wanted to claim as its own. In other words, the author thinks they are hypocrites.

> **Ditz:** I looked up "tenacious adherence" and it means "a firm hold." Like the grip I keep on my Louis Vuitton on the subway.

Kudos to you, Ditz! You looked up the high-level words and you practice subway safety. Nice work.

Paragraph 3

> The decline of the Modern Movement later in the twentieth century occurred partly as a result of Modernist architects' <u>ignorance</u> of building methods, and partly because Modernist architects
> (35) were reluctant to admit that their concerns were chiefly aesthetic. Moreover, the building industry was evolving in a direction Modernists had not anticipated: it was more specialized and the process of construction was much more fragmented
> (40) than in the past. Up until the twentieth century, construction had been carried out by a relatively small number of tradespeople, but as the building industry evolved, buildings came to be built by many specialized subcontractors working independently.
> (45) The architect's design not only had to accommodate a sequence of independent operations, but now had to reflect the allowable degree of inaccuracy of the different trades. However, one of the chief construction ideals of the Modern Movement was to
> (50) "honestly" expose structural materials such as steel and concrete. To do this and still produce a visually acceptable interior called for an <u>unrealistically</u> high level of craftsmanship. Exposure of a building's internal structural elements, if it could be achieved
> (55) at all, could only be accomplished at considerable cost—hence the <u>well-founded reputation</u> of Modern architecture as prohibitively expensive.

Annotations: ATT. (line 33); SUPPORT FOR AUTHOR'S CONCLUSION; ATT. (line 52); ATT. (line 56)

If this is going to be an Antithesis passage, we'd expect support for the second point of view right about now. Sure enough, the third paragraph is devoted to explaining why Modernists were wrong that Modernism was better suited to newer building methods. To sum it up, newer building methods entailed utilizing subcontractors who specialized in different areas of building. Because of that, there was a degree of inaccuracy in the use of newer building methods. Unlike a craftsman who builds the entire thing to exacting specifications, you have to fit together pieces made by different people.

The Modernists thought that building materials should be exposed, but that butted up against the level of inaccuracy that modern building methods had to incorporate. Therefore, according to the author, Modernism was actually not at all well suited to newer building methods. Let's get that into our primary structure diagram as the Antithesis position.

Take note of all the instances of the author's attitude toward the Modernists: "ignorance of building methods" (lines 33-34), "unrealistically high level of craftsmanship" (lines 52-53), and "the well-founded reputation of Modern architecture as prohibitively expensive" (lines 56-57). Our author really, REALLY doesn't like Modernist architecture.

Cleetus: Yeah, whoa. Like, chill out author guy. It's just a building. It's not like a gator's nippin' at your toes.

We're glad you noticed how opinionated the author is, Cleetus. Count yourself lucky when you find examples of strong author's attitude. When the author feels strongly about something, there is almost always at least one question about it. By taking note of it, you'll be ready when the question comes.

Paragraph 4

> As Postmodern architects recognized, the need to expose structural elements imposed unnecessary
> (60) limitations on building design. The unwillingness of architects of the Modern Movement to abandon their ideals contributed to the decline of interest in the Modern Movement.

Not much to see here. The guys who came after the Modernists recognized what the Modernists refused to recognize, and that's why Modernism was consigned to the dust bin of history.

Let's summarize the passage before moving to the questions, paying particular attention to the points of view. Two opposing views are introduced in paragraph one, the latter of which is strongly endorsed by the author. In paragraph two, the first view is put forward and a criticism mentioned. In paragraphs three and four, the second view is strongly endorsed.

The completed markup looks like this:

>   The proponents of the Modern Movement
> in architecture considered that, compared with
> the historical styles that it replaced, <u>Modernist
> architecture more accurately reflected the functional
> (5) spirit of twentieth-century technology and was
> better suited to the newest building methods.</u> It is
> ironic, then, that the <u>Movement fostered an ideology
> of design that proved to be at odds with the way
> buildings were really built.</u>
> (10)   The tenacious adherence of Modernist architects
> and critics to this ideology was in part responsible
> for the Movement's decline. Originating in the 1920s
> as a marginal, almost bohemian art movement, the
> Modern Movement was never very popular with
> (15) the public, but this very lack of popular support
> produced in Modernist architects a high-minded
> sense of mission—not content merely to interpret
> the needs of the client, these architects now sought
> to persuade, to educate, and, if necessary, to dictate.
> (20) By 1945 the tenets of the Movement had come to
> dominate mainstream architecture, and by the early
> 1950s, to dominate architectural criticism—architects
> whose work seemed not to advance the evolution of
> the Modern Movement tended to be dismissed by
> (25) proponents of Modernism. On the other hand, when
> architects were identified as innovators—as was the
> case with Otto Wagner, or the young Frank Lloyd
> Wright—attention was drawn to only those features
> of their work that were "Modern"; other aspects were
> (30) <u>conveniently ignored.</u>
>   The decline of the Modern Movement later
> in the twentieth century occurred partly as a result
> of Modernist architects' <u>ignorance</u> of building
> methods, and partly because Modernist architects
> (35) were reluctant to admit that their concerns were
> chiefly aesthetic. Moreover, the building industry
> was evolving in a direction Modernists had not
> anticipated: it was more specialized and the
> process of construction was much more fragmented
> (40) than in the past. Up until the twentieth century,
> construction had been carried out by a relatively
> small number of tradespeople, but as the building
> industry evolved, buildings came to be built by many
> specialized subcontractors working independently.
> (45) The architect's design not only had to accommodate
> a sequence of independent operations, but now
> had to reflect the allowable degree of inaccuracy
> of the different trades. However, one of the chief
> construction ideals of the Modern Movement was to
> (50) "honestly" expose structural materials such as steel
> and concrete. To do this and still produce a visually
> acceptable interior called for an <u>unrealistically</u> high
> level of craftmanship. Exposure of a building's
> internal structural elements, if it could be achieved
> (55) at all, could only be accomplished at considerable
> cost—hence the <u>well-founded reputation</u> of Modern
> architecture as prohibitively expensive.
>   As Postmodern architects recognized, the need
> to expose structural elements imposed unnecessary
> (60) limitations on building design. The unwillingness of
> architects of the Modern Movement to abandon their
> ideals contributed to the decline of interest in the
> Modern Movement.

Annotations:
- MODERNISTS' CONCLUSION
- AUTHOR'S CONCLUSION
- ATT.
- SUPPORT FOR MODERNISTS' CONCLUSION
- ATT.
- ATT.
- SUPPORT FOR AUTHOR'S CONCLUSION
- ATT.
- ATT.

Subject: Modernist Architecture

Thesis: Construction better suited to methods

author → Antithesis: Construction ill suited to methods

Synthesis

130 / Chapter 11

Question #21

When the author is present, as is the case here, the author's point of view is the main point of the passage. We know from our diagram that's answer choice (A).

We are never told anywhere in the passage that rationality was the basis of this movement, and in fact, the author calls modernism "an ideology of design...at odds with the way buildings were really built" (lines 7-9), so (B) is going pretty strongly against the passage and is certainly not the main point. There's no information in the passage on what inspired modern construction methods; there's only the Modernists' claim that their designs were suited to those methods. This knocks out (C). Conversely, there's no indication that changes in building methods actually brought about Modernism, and so (D) is out. Finally, (E) assumes that we know why the earlier styles were rejected, which could've been any number of things. All we know is that Modernists thought their designs were more in line with the "functional spirit" (lines 4-5) of the time.

21. Which one of the following most accurately summarizes the main idea of the passage?

    (A) The Modern Movement declined because its proponents were overly ideological and did not take into account the facts of building construction.
    (B) Rationality was the theoretical basis for the development of the Modern Movement in architecture.
    (C) Changes in architectural design introduced by the Modern Movement inspired the development of modern construction methods.
    (D) The theoretical bases of the Modern Movement in architecture originated in changes in building construction methods.
    (E) Proponents of the Modern Movement in architecture rejected earlier architectural styles because such styles were not functional.

Question #23

Ohhhhh... we've so got this. The author thinks that Modernism is as lame as lame can be. The author is, in a word, unimpressed. We tracked a number of examples of author's attitude, and are rewarded here with the easy point. Answer choice (C) is correct.

23. With respect to the proponents of the Modern Movement, the author of the passage can best be described as

    (A) forbearing
    (B) defensive
    (C) unimpressed
    (D) exasperated
    (E) indifferent

"Forbearing" means patient and restrained, and the author is neither patient nor restrained. The author is critical, and so (A) is wrong. The author is not happy with Modernism, but "defensive" does not describe his attitude, seeing as he more or less spends the whole passage on the offensive against Modernists. So chuck (B). You might be tempted by (D) because the author is really not pleased with Modernism. But this answer implies that the author is just irritated rather than having a rational basis for his opinion. Pro tip: such an answer won't ever be right because the author of any passage always has reasons for his or her point of view. Finally, the author is anything but indifferent (he HATES the Modern Movement), so (E) is wrong.

Question #25

More author's attitude! Hooray! The right answer points at the criticism in paragraph two—that Modernists were hypocrites who "conveniently" ignored the parts of Wagner's and Wright's work that didn't fit their theory. That's answer choice (D).

> 25. Which one of the following, in its context in the passage, most clearly reveals the attitude of the author toward the proponents of the Modern Movement?
>
> (A) "functional spirit" (lines 4–5)
> (B) "tended" (line 24)
> (C) "innovators" (line 26)
> (D) "conveniently" (line 30)
> (E) "degree of inaccuracy" (line 47)

"Functional spirit" is something the Modernists' think they have a lock on, but the author disagrees. So answer choice (A) is not identifying the author's attitude. Answer choice (B) refers back to a portion of the passage explaining the Modernists' opinion, not the author's. Answer choice (C) is wrong for the same reason as (B), which is that it's describing the Modernists' position rather than the author's. Answer choice (E) is tempting because it's negative language, just like the author's attitude toward Modernism. But that part of the passage is talking factually about how building methods had changed, and not how Modernists operated. So (E) is wrong.

BP Minotaur: Things that are emphasized in the passage often equate to questions. This passage is unusual in that it has so much strong author's attitude. Consequently, the fact that there are two questions about it comes as no surprise.

Looking for the remaining answer explanations? You'll find them on your online *MyBlueprint* account.

ANSWER KEY

21. a, 22. a, 23. c, 24. e, 25. d, 26. b, 27. a

12/SYNTHESISpassages

Now, kiss and make up

Antithesis passages were all about the thrill of the fight. Synthesis passages, on the other hand, are all about the make up. No, it won't feel quite as good as when you and your significant other make up, and you, well, y'know... AWOOOGAH!

Anyway, Synthesis passages are so called because they take two points of view that are at odds with one another, like those in Antithesis passages, and synthesize those points of view into a third point of view that reconciles the two.

We discussed in the previous chapter that Antithesis passages are structured much like judicial opinions. Well, in a good number of judicial opinions, the judge does his or her best to craft a solution that satisfies both parties, i.e. a synthesis of their two views. Also, there's a whole area of law—mediation and arbitration—that is geared toward finding a middle ground between parties that are in disagreement with one another.

Just so you know, what you are learning here and now will be quite useful in law school and beyond. You're welcome!

Synthesis passages are, on average, the easiest of the three passage types. Their average difficulty rating is a 2.56. This might seem at odds with the fact that these passages have the most points of view (so you'd think they'd be difficult). But it turns out they're typically easy to spot and decipher. Unfortunately, they're also the least common of all the primary structures, only showing up 8.45% of the time.

By now you should know how important it is to track points of view and attitude, and with three points of view in a Synthesis passage, you'll have your work cut out for you. Let's take a look at the following example.

> It's Saturday night, and Frank and Bill are bored out of their minds. They've done just about all there is to do in the sleepy town of Waukesha, WI. "Hey," says Bill, endlessly walking a quarter back and forth over his knuckles, "there's a new petting zoo in town! That sounds like a laugh. We should go!"
>
> Frank raises an eyebrow, peering at Bill from behind the latest issue of Cat Fancy™ magazine. "That's really weird. You're weird." A few moments pass, and then Frank says, "Hey, wanna wrestle?"
>
> "No," says Bill. "You think I'm weird? That's weird. Hey, let's call Dale. He always knows of fun stuff to do."
>
> Ten minutes later, Dale sits before them, absorbed in thought. He has heard their ideas: petting zoo vs. wrestling. "There is a third way," he says. "We should all go cow tipping. Bill, you get to touch farm animals much like you would at a petting zoo, and Frank, you get to burn off some energy like you would wrestling."
>
> "Sweet!" shout Frank and Bill in unison. High fives are traded, and a night of cow tipping has begun.

In this passage, there are two points of view that are at odds with one another. Frank proposes going to a petting zoo, and Bill proposes wrestling. Each of them has a negative attitude toward the other's idea, calling it "weird." Dale comes along with a third point of view that synthesizes the first two. Cow tipping is an activity that combines (synthesizes) the best elements of petting zoos and wrestling. Frank and Bill both have a positive attitude toward this proposal, as indicated by the shouting and high-fives. The diagram, tracking the points of view, would look like this.

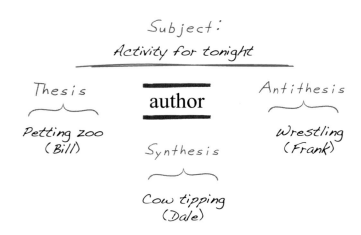

Since the author is absent, there's no arrow pointing to any view. If you were keeping track of points of view and attitude, you would be ready for the questions that test you on them.

YOUR TURN

Attack!

You know the drill by now. The following passages are Synthesis passages, and we have supplied you with a blank primary structure diagram. Read the passage and identify the arguments, filling in the diagram as you go. When you see a point of view, underline it and identify in the margins exactly who believes that particular point of view. If you see an indication that the author or a party has a positive or negative attitude toward something, note that as well with "Att."

Answer the questions in black at the end of the passages, for they test your ability to track point of view and attitude. The other questions have been greyed out. You may attempt them if you wish, but we will learn to address them in later chapters. If you're burning up with curiosity, explanations of these questions may be found on your *MyBlueprint* account. A paragraph-by-paragraph explanation follows. Study it carefully when you are done reading and answering the questions to make sure you correctly identified all the relevant information. Good luck!

EXERCISE 1: DEC. 1999 PASSAGE 2

Tragic dramas written in Greece during the fifth century B.C. engender considerable scholarly debate over the relative influence of individual autonomy and the power of the gods on the drama's action. One early
(5) scholar, B. Snell, argues that Aeschylus, for example, develops in his tragedies a concept of the autonomy of the individual. In these dramas, the protagonists invariably confront a situation that paralyzes them, so that their prior notions about how to behave or think
(10) are dissolved. Faced with a decision on which their fate depends, they must reexamine their deepest motives, and then act with determination. They are given only two alternatives, each with grave consequences, and they make their decision only after a tortured internal
(15) debate. According to Snell, this decision is "free" and "personal" and such personal autonomy constitutes the central theme in Aeschylean drama, as if the plays were devised to isolate an abstract model of human action. Drawing psychological conclusions from this
(20) interpretation, another scholar, Z. Barbu, suggests that "[Aeschylean] drama is proof of the emergence within ancient Greek civilization of the individual as a free agent."

To A. Rivier, Snell's emphasis on the decision
(25) made by the protagonist, with its implicit notions of autonomy and responsibility, misrepresents the role of the superhuman forces at work, forces that give the dramas their truly tragic dimension. These forces are not only external to the protagonist; they
(30) are also experienced by the protagonist as an internal compulsion, subjecting him or her to constraint even in what are claimed to be his or her "choices." Hence all that the deliberation does is to make the protagonist aware of the impasse, rather than motivating one
(35) choice over another. It is finally a necessity imposed by the deities that generates the decision, so that at a particular moment in the drama necessity dictates a path. Thus, the protagonist does not so much "choose" between two possibilities as "recognize" that there is
(40) only one real option.

A. Lesky, in his discussion of Aeschylus' play *Agamemnon*, disputes both views. Agamemnon, ruler of Argos, must decide whether to brutally sacrifice his own daughter. A message from the deity Artemis has
(45) told him that only the sacrifice will bring a wind to blow his ships to an important battle. Agamemnon is indeed constrained by a divine necessity. But he also deeply desires a victorious battle: "If this sacrifice will loose the winds, it is permitted to desire it fervently,"
(50) he says. The violence of his passion suggests that Agamemnon chooses a path—chosen by the gods for their own reasons—on the basis of desires that must be condemned by us, because they are his own. In Lesky's view, tragic action is bound by the constant tension
(55) between a self and superhuman forces.

7. Based on the information presented in the passage, which one of the following statements best represents Lesky's view of Agamemnon?

    (A) Agamemnon's motivations are identical to those of the gods.
    (B) The nature of Agamemnon's character solely determines the course of the tragedy.
    (C) Agamemnon's decision-making is influenced by his military ambitions.
    (D) Agamemnon is concerned only with pleasing the deity Artemis.
    (E) Agamemnon is especially tragic because of his political position.

8. Which one of the following paraphrases most accurately restates the quotation from Agamemnon found in lines 48-49 of the passage?

    (A) If the goddess has ordained that the only way I can evade battle is by performing this sacrifice, then it is perfectly appropriate for me to deeply desire this sacrifice.
    (B) If the goddess has ordained that the only way I can get a wind to move my ships to battle is by performing this sacrifice, then it is perfectly appropriate for me to deeply desire victory in battle.
    (C) If the goddess has ordained that the only way I can get a wind to move my ships to battle is by performing this sacrifice, then it is perfectly appropriate for me to deeply desire this sacrifice.
    (D) As I alone have determined that only this sacrifice will give me victory in battle, I will perform it, without reservations.
    (E) As I have determined that only deeply desiring victory in battle will guarantee the success of the sacrifice, I will perform it as ordained by the goddess.

9. Which one of the following statements best expresses Rivier's view, as presented in the passage, of what makes a drama tragic?

    (A) The tragic protagonist is deluded by the gods into thinking he or she is free.
    (B) The tragic protagonist struggles for a heroism that belongs to the gods.
    (C) The tragic protagonist wrongly seeks to take responsibility for his or her actions.
    (D) The tragic protagonist cannot make a decision that is free of divine compulsion.
    (E) The tragic protagonist is punished for evading his or her responsibilities.

11. Which one of the following summaries of the plot of a Greek tragedy best illustrates the view attributed to Rivier in the passage?

(A) Although she knows that she will be punished for violating the law of her city, a tragic figure bravely decides to bury her dead brother over the objections of local authorities.
(B) Because of her love for her dead brother, a tragic figure, although aware that she will be punished for violating the law of her city, accedes to the gods' request that she bury his body.
(C) After much careful thought, a tragic figure decides to disobey the dictates of the gods and murder her unfaithful husband.
(D) A tragic figure, defying a curse placed on his family by the gods, leads his city into a battle that he realizes will prove futile.
(E) After much careful thought, a tragic figure realizes that he has no alternative but to follow the course chosen by the gods and murder his father.

EXPLANATION

Paragraph 1

> Tragic dramas written in Greece during the fifth century B.C. engender considerable scholarly debate over the relative influence of individual autonomy and the power of the gods on the drama's action. One early scholar, B. Snell, argues that Aeschylus, for example, <u>develops in his tragedies a concept of the autonomy of the individual.</u> In these dramas, the protagonists invariably confront a situation that paralyzes them, so that their prior notions about how to behave or think are dissolved. Faced with a decision on which their fate depends, they must reexamine their deepest motives, and then act with determination. They are given only two alternatives, each with grave consequences, and they make their decision only after a tortured internal debate. According to Snell, this decision is "free" and "personal" and such personal autonomy constitutes the central theme in Aeschylean drama, as if the plays were devised to isolate an abstract model of human action. Drawing psychological conclusions from this interpretation, another scholar, <u>Z. Barbu, suggests that "[Aeschylean] drama is proof of the emergence within ancient Greek civilization of the individual as a free agent."</u>

(Annotations: "SNELL'S CONCLUSION" and "BARBU'S OPINION")

So, apparently scholars of Greek tragedy don't have first names. Just letters. Who knew? The gods, that's who! This paragraph tees up the debate quite nicely: who runs the show in Greek tragedy, the protagonist or the gods? Well, meet B. Snell (terrible name). Snell, using Aeschylus as an example, argues that the protagonist makes his decision freely. After having his world torn asunder, the protagonist agonizes over a dilemma, ultimately choosing a course of action. This, Snell says, is the central theme in Aeschylean drama. Z. Barbu (an even more terrible name) agrees with Snell, arguing that this interpretation accurately reflects Greek society of the time. Because his position is substantiated in the passage, let's get Snell's point of view into our diagram as the Thesis position.

Paragraph 2

> (25) To A. Rivier, Snell's emphasis on the decision made by the protagonist, with its implicit notions of autonomy and responsibility, misrepresents the role of the superhuman forces at work, forces that give the dramas their truly tragic dimension. These
> (30) forces are not only external to the protagonist; they are also experienced by the protagonist as an internal compulsion, subjecting him or her to constraint even in what are claimed to be his or her "choices." Hence all that the deliberation does is to make the protagonist
> (35) aware of the impasse, rather than motivating one choice over another. It is finally a necessity imposed by the deities that generates the decision, so that at a particular moment in the drama necessity dictates a path. Thus, the protagonist does not so much "choose" between two possibilities as "recognize" that there is
> (40) only one real option.

RIVIER'S CONCLUSION

Hold your horses, says A. Rivier (terrible French name). Not only do the gods set up the dilemma, they also manipulate the protagonist as he considers the dilemma. The gods eventually force the protagonist's hand, and, instead of choosing, the protagonist goes forward with what was really the only option available to him. It would seem we have a developed opinion diametrically opposed to that in paragraph one. So let's put it in our diagram as the Antithesis position.

Paragraph 3

> A. Lesky, in his discussion of Aeschylus' play *Agamemnon*, disputes both views. Agamemnon, ruler of Argos, must decide whether to brutally sacrifice his own daughter. A message from the deity Artemis has
> (45) told him that only the sacrifice will bring a wind to blow his ships to an important battle. Agamemnon is indeed constrained by a divine necessity. But he also deeply desires a victorious battle: "If this sacrifice will loose the winds, it is permitted to desire it fervently,"
> (50) he says. The violence of his passion suggests that Agamemnon chooses a path—chosen by the gods for their own reasons—on the basis of desires that must be condemned by us, because they are his own. In Lesky's view, tragic action is bound by the constant tension
> (55) between a self and superhuman forces.

LESKY'S CONCLUSION

Just when we reach an impasse between Snell and Rivier, here comes A. Lesky (not *the* Lesky, mind you, just *a* Lesky). Lesky argues that these positions are reconcilable. He synthesizes them, if you will. We get an example, the play *Agamemnon*. There is a necessity imposed by Artemis: to get to battle, Agamemnon must sacrifice his daughter. Ultimately, Agamemnon takes the course settled on by the gods, but, because he's so amped up about getting to the battle, he actually *wants* to sacrifice his daughter. Ouch. According to Lesky, we can condemn Agamemnon, even if his choice wasn't entirely free. Let's get this into our diagram as the Synthesis position.

Let's sum up, keeping track of the points of view. The first paragraph identifies two sides of a debate, then fleshes out the first side. The second paragraph fleshes out the other side. The third paragraph offers an argument that the two sides can be reconciled. The author doesn't poke her head into the passage at any point, so we're dealing with an absent author.

The completed markup looks like this:

Tragic dramas written in Greece during the fifth century B.C. engender considerable scholarly debate over the relative influence of individual autonomy and the power of the gods on the drama's action. One early (5) scholar, <u>B. Snell, argues that Aeschylus, for example, develops in his tragedies a concept of the autonomy of the individual.</u> In these dramas, the protagonists invariably confront a situation that paralyzes them, so that their prior notions about how to behave or think (10) are dissolved. Faced with a decision on which their fate depends, they must reexamine their deepest motives, and then act with determination. They are given only two alternatives, each with grave consequences, and they make their decision only after a tortured internal (15) debate. According to Snell, this decision is "free" and "personal" and such personal autonomy constitutes the central theme in Aeschylean drama, as if the plays were devised to isolate an abstract model of human action. Drawing psychological conclusions from this (20) interpretation, another scholar, <u>Z. Barbu, suggests that "[Aeschylean] drama is proof of the emergence within ancient Greek civilization of the individual as a free agent."</u>

To A. Rivier, Snell's emphasis on the decision (25) made by the protagonist, with its implicit notions of autonomy and responsibility, misrepresents the role of the superhuman forces at work, forces that give the dramas their truly tragic dimension. These forces are not only external to the protagonist; they (30) are also experienced by the protagonist as an internal compulsion, subjecting him or her to constraint even in what are claimed to be his or her "choices." Hence all that the deliberation does is to make the protagonist aware of the impasse, rather than motivating one (35) choice over another. It is finally a necessity imposed by the deities that generates the decision, so that at a particular moment in the drama necessity dictates a path. <u>Thus, the protagonist does not so much "choose" between two possibilities as "recognize" that there is (40) only one real option.</u>

A. Lesky, in his discussion of Aeschylus' play *Agamemnon*, disputes both views. Agamemnon, ruler of Argos, must decide whether to brutally sacrifice his own daughter. A message from the deity Artemis has (45) told him that only the sacrifice will bring a wind to blow his ships to an important battle. Agamemnon is indeed constrained by a divine necessity. But he also deeply desires a victorious battle: "If this sacrifice will loose the winds, it is permitted to desire it fervently," (50) he says. The violence of his passion suggests that Agamemnon chooses a path—chosen by the gods for their own reasons—on the basis of desires that must be condemned by us, because they are his own. In Lesky's view, <u>tragic action is bound by the constant tension (55) between a self and superhuman forces.</u>

SNELL'S CONCLUSION

BARBU'S OPINION

RIVIER'S CONCLUSION

LESKY'S CONCLUSION

Subject: Greek Tragedy

Thesis — author — Antithesis

Protagonist chooses (Snell and Barbu)

Synthesis

Gods choose (Rivier)

Both choose (Lesky)

Question #7

Lesky is the Synthesis position in the passage, and he characterizes Agamemnon as not merely choosing the path the gods desire, but fervently desiring it himself. Answer choice (C) is correct because it identifies the underlying reason that Agamemnon fervently desires to sacrifice his daughter: he wants to get to the battle.

7. Based on the information presented in the passage, which one of the following statements best represents Lesky's view of Agamemnon?

    (A) Agamemnon's motivations are identical to those of the gods.
    (B) The nature of Agamemnon's character solely determines the course of the tragedy.
    (C) Agamemnon's decision-making is influenced by his military ambitions.
    (D) Agamemnon is concerned only with pleasing the deity Artemis.
    (E) Agamemnon is especially tragic because of his political position.

We can sometimes eliminate incorrect answer choices simply by noting that they identify a different point of view. In answer choice (A), Agamemnon's motivations are his own, even though he chooses the path the gods desire, so (A) is wrong. Answer choice (B) lines up with Snell's view, i.e. Thesis, which is a different point of view than that we are being asked about. Answer choice (D) is wrong for the same reason that (A) is wrong. Agamemnon has his own reasons for what he chooses. Finally, Lesky thinks that the "tension between a self and superhuman forces" is what makes for true tragedy (lines 54-55). Political position is a different matter, so (E) is wrong.

Question #9

Rivier is the Antithesis in the passage, and he argues that the protagonist doesn't really have a choice. Answer choice (D) says just that.

Answer choice (A) runs counter to Rivier's assertion that the protagonist recognizes that he has only one option. So that's out. There's no indication in the passage that heroism belongs to the gods, so (B) is just not supported anywhere. There's no mention in the passage of the protagonist actually taking personal responsibility for his actions, and answer choice (C) equivocates between being responsible for something and taking responsibility. Rivier believes that the protagonist is not capable of evading the choice that has been made for him, so he cannot evade his responsibilities as mentioned in (E).

9. Which one of the following statements best expresses Rivier's view, as presented in the passage, of what makes a drama tragic?

    (A) The tragic protagonist is deluded by the gods into thinking he or she is free.
    (B) The tragic protagonist struggles for a heroism that belongs to the gods.
    (C) The tragic protagonist wrongly seeks to take responsibility for his or her actions.
    (D) The tragic protagonist cannot make a decision that is free of divine compulsion.
    (E) The tragic protagonist is punished for evading his or her responsibilities.

Cleetus: I looked up "evade" and it means "to avoid." Kinda like the time I evaded the skunk spray by climbing up a tree.

Exactly like that, Cleetus.

Question #11

This is a Parallel question (which will be addressed in a later chapter), and we are looking for something that resembles the Antithesis view. That view, remember, is that the protagonist ultimately realizes what must be done rather than choosing a course of action. Answer choice (E) looks just like that.

Answer choice (A) is wrong because it identifies the protagonist as making a choice, and because the choice is in defiance of the government, not the gods. Answer choices (B), (C), and (D) identify the protagonist as making a free choice. That's not Rivier's view.

11. Which one of the following summaries of the plot of a Greek tragedy best illustrates the view attributed to Rivier in the passage?

   (A) Although she knows that she will be punished for violating the law of her city, a tragic figure bravely decides to bury her dead brother over the objections of local authorities.
   (B) Because of her love for her dead brother, a tragic figure, although aware that she will be punished for violating the law of her city, accedes to the gods' request that she bury his body.
   (C) After much careful thought, a tragic figure decides to disobey the dictates of the gods and murder her unfaithful husband.
   (D) A tragic figure, defying a curse placed on his family by the gods, leads his city into a battle that he realizes will prove futile.
   (E) After much careful thought, a tragic figure realizes that he has no alternative but to follow the course chosen by the gods and murder his father.

Looking for the explanations to the remaining questions? You'll find them online in your *MyBlueprint* account.

ANSWER KEY
7. c, 8. c, 9. d, 10. c, 11. e, 12. d, 13. b, 14. c

EXERCISE 2: DEC. 2006 PASSAGE 1

The work of South African writer Ezekiel Mphahlele has confounded literary critics, especially those who feel compelled to draw a sharp distinction between autobiography and fiction. These critics
(5) point to Mphahlele's best-known works—his 1959 autobiography *Down Second Avenue* and his 1971 novel *The Wanderers*—to illustrate the problem of categorizing his work. While his autobiography traces his life from age five until the beginning of his
(10) self-imposed 20-year exile at age thirty-eight, *The Wanderers* appears to pick up at the beginning of his exile and go on from there. Critics have variously decried the former as too fictionalized and the latter as too autobiographical, but those who focus
(15) on traditional labels inevitably miss the fact that Mphahlele manipulates different prose forms purely in the service of the social message he advances.

Even where critics give him a favorable reading, all too often their reviews carry a negative subtext.
(20) For example, one critic said of *The Wanderers* that if anger, firsthand experiences, compassion, and topicality were the sole requirements for great literature, the novel might well be one of the masterpieces of this declining part of the twentieth
(25) century. And although this critic may not have meant to question the literary contribution of the novel, there are those who are outright dismissive of *The Wanderers* because it contains an autobiographical framework and is populated with real-world
(30) characters. Mphahlele briefly defends against such charges by pointing out the importance of the fictional father-son relationship that opens and closes the novel. But his greater concern is the social vision that pervades his work, though it too is prone to
(35) misunderstandings and underappreciation. Mphahlele is a humanist and an integrationist, and his writings wonderfully articulate his vision of the future; but critics often balk at this vision because Mphahlele provides no road maps for bringing such a future
(40) about.

Mphahlele himself shows little interest in establishing guidelines to distinguish autobiography from fiction. Though he does refer to *Down Second Avenue* as an autobiography and *The Wanderers* as a
(45) novel, he asserts that no novelist can write complete fiction or absolute fact. It is the nature of writing, at least the writing he cares about, that the details must be drawn from the writer's experiences, and thus are in some sense fact, but conveyed in such a way as
(50) to maximize the effectiveness of the social message contained in the work, and thus inevitably fiction. As he claims, the whole point of the exercise of writing has nothing to do with classification; in all forms writing is the transmission of ideas, and important
(55) ideas at that: "Whenever you write prose or poetry or drama you are writing a social criticism of one kind or another. If you don't, you are completely irrelevant—you don't count."

1. Based on the passage, with which one of the following statements would Mphahlele be most likely to agree?

    (A) All works of literature should articulate a vision of the future.
    (B) It is not necessary for a writer to write works to fit predetermined categories.
    (C) Literary categories are worth addressing only when literary works are being unjustifiably dismissed.
    (D) Most works of literature that resemble novels could accurately be classified as autobiographies.
    (E) The most useful categories in literature are those that distinguish prose from poetry and poetry from drama.

2. The passage states that Mphahlele believes which one of the following?

    (A) Writing should provide a guide for achieving social change.
    (B) Writing should have as its goal the transmission of ideas.
    (C) Writing is most effective when it minimizes the use of real people and events to embellish a story.
    (D) Good writing is generally more autobiographical than fictional.
    (E) Fiction and autobiography are clearly identifiable literary forms if the work is composed properly.

3. In lines 18–25, the author uses the phrase "negative subtext" in reference to the critic's comment to claim that

   (A) the critic believes that Mphahlele himself shows little interest in establishing guidelines that distinguish fact from fiction in literature
   (B) the comment is unfairly one-sided and gives no voice to perspectives that Mphahlele might embrace
   (C) the requirement of firsthand experiences mentioned in the comment is in direct contradiction to the requirements of fiction
   (D) the requirements for great literature mentioned in the comment are ill conceived, thus the requirements have little bearing on what great literature really is
   (E) the requirements for great literature mentioned in the comment are not the sole requirements, thus Mphahlele's work is implied by the critic not to be great literature

6. Which one of the following aspects of Mphahlele's work does the author of the passage appear to value most highly?

   (A) his commitment to communicating social messages
   (B) his blending of the categories of fiction and autobiography
   (C) his ability to redefine established literary categories
   (D) his emphasis on the importance of details
   (E) his plan for bringing about the future he envisions

EXPLANATION

Paragraph 1

> The work of South African writer Ezekiel Mphahlele has confounded literary critics, especially those who feel compelled to draw a sharp distinction between autobiography and fiction. These critics
> (5) point to Mphahlele's best-known works—his 1959 autobiography *Down Second Avenue* and his 1971 novel *The Wanderers*—to illustrate the problem of categorizing his work. While his autobiography traces his life from age five until the beginning of his
> (10) self-imposed 20-year exile at age thirty-eight, *The Wanderers* appears to pick up at the beginning of his exile and go on from there. <u>Critics have variously decried the former as too fictionalized and the latter as too autobiographical,</u> but those who focus
> (15) on traditional labels inevitably miss the fact that <u>Mphahlele manipulates different prose forms purely in the service of the social message he advances.</u>

CRITICS' TWO CONCLUSIONS

AUTHOR'S CONCLUSION

Can fiction be autobiography? Or autobiography fiction? The head swims...unless, of course, you are the unparalleled wit, Ezekiel Mphahlele! But you're not, so pay attention.

In this paragraph, we are introduced to the critics and their understandable confusion. They don't like the alleged autobiography *Down Second Avenue* because it is "too fictionalized," and they don't like the novel *The Wanderers* because, even though it's nominally fiction, it picks up from the autobiography. The author comes in at the end of the paragraph (we know it's the author since it's an opinion without a named proponent) and says that both of these complaints are wrong. The point is not to fit into a particular genre, but rather to use whatever means serves Mphahlele's social message.

This already looks like a Synthesis passage. Two points of view—his autobiography is too fictional, and his fiction is too autobiographical—are put forth, and the author gives us a good reason to believe that they can be reconciled. However, let's make sure these points of view are fleshed out before we throw them into our primary structure diagram.

Paragraph 2

> Even where critics give him a favorable reading, all too often their reviews carry a negative subtext. (20) For example, one critic said of *The Wanderers* that if anger, firsthand experiences, compassion, and topicality were the sole requirements for great literature, the novel might well be one of the masterpieces of this declining part of the twentieth (25) century. And although this critic may not have meant to question the literary contribution of the novel, there are those who are <u>outright dismissive</u> of *The Wanderers* because it contains an autobiographical framework and is populated with real-world (30) characters. Mphahlele briefly defends against such charges by pointing out the importance of the fictional father-son relationship that opens and closes the novel. But his greater concern is the social vision that pervades his work, though it too is prone to (35) misunderstandings and underappreciation. Mphahlele is a humanist and an integrationist, and his writings <u>wonderfully articulate</u> his vision of the future; but critics often balk at this vision because Mphahlele provides no road maps for bringing such a future (40) about.

Margin notes:
- SUPPORT FOR CRITICS' CONCLUSIONS
- ATT.
- MPHAHLELE'S OPINION
- ATT.

This paragraph deals primarily with the second point of view, that the novel *The Wanderers* is too autobiographical. The author identifies the point of view of a particular critic, who gives a backhanded compliment: this book does some things well, but it's missing basic requirements to be great literature. Other critics are even more negative in their views of *The Wanderers*, for no other reason than there are real world elements.

> **Ninja:** A ninja must be a master of tracking: enemy footprints, the spoor of prey animals, and points of view. Just as it is important to track author's attitude, it is important to track the attitude of third parties. Strongly positive or negative opinions often form the basis for Viewpoint questions.

Mphahlele (can someone please tell us how to pronounce that?) pops up here to defend himself, lining up perfectly with the author's opinion we identified at the end of paragraph one (lines 14-17). Mphahlele provides a vision of the future in his books, regardless of how they are classified. The author is really excited about how awesome Mphahlele is, calling his writing "wonderfully articulate." That's strong author's attitude, and we should make a note of it. By this point, it is clear that we have a Synthesis passage. There are two points of view that can be reconciled into a third and all have support. Let's get it all into the diagram.

At the very end of this paragraph, we get one more criticism from the critics. Mphahlele may paint a nice picture of the future, but he doesn't tell us how to get there. Some guys are never satisfied.

Ditz: Tell me about it.

Moving on, Ditz. Moving on.

Paragraph 3

> Mphahlele himself shows little interest in establishing guidelines to distinguish autobiography from fiction. Though he does refer to *Down Second Avenue* as an autobiography and *The Wanderers* as a
> (45) novel, he asserts that no novelist can write complete fiction or absolute fact. It is the nature of writing, at least the writing he cares about, that the details must be drawn from the writer's experiences, and thus are in some sense fact, but conveyed in such a way as
> (50) to maximize the effectiveness of the social message contained in the work, and thus inevitably fiction. As he claims, the whole point of the exercise of writing has nothing to do with classification; in all forms writing is the transmission of ideas, and important
> (55) ideas at that: "Whenever you write prose or poetry or drama you are writing a social criticism of one kind or another. If you don't, you are completely irrelevant— you don't count."

MPHAHLELE'S OPINION

This paragraph explains Mphahlele's views in detail. It's not just that his writing is both fact and fiction—*any good writing incorporates both.* Mind. Completely. Blown. This is because, as the author asserts in the first paragraph, the most important thing to Mphahlele is advancing his social message, not fitting neatly into any particular category. It's important to take notice of the fact that Mphahlele agrees that his books can be classified as autobiography or novel, so he isn't just saying that there's no difference whatsoever.

As we always do, let's sum up, focusing on the points of view. Paragraph one sets up two points of view advanced by critics, both of which claim that two things are in conflict with one another, and the author gives a reason at the end of the paragraph to believe that these things can indeed be reconciled. Paragraph two focuses on the opinion of the critics, and paragraph three gives a further reason to believe that the points of view may be reconciled.

The completed markup looks like this:

The work of South African writer Ezekiel Mphahlele has confounded literary critics, especially those who feel compelled to draw a sharp distinction between autobiography and fiction. These critics
(5) point to Mphahlele's best-known works—his 1959 autobiography *Down Second Avenue* and his 1971 novel *The Wanderers*—to illustrate the problem of categorizing his work. While his autobiography traces his life from age five until the beginning of his
(10) self-imposed 20-year exile at age thirty-eight, *The Wanderers* appears to pick up at the beginning of his exile and go on from there. <u>Critics have variously decried the former as too fictionalized and the latter as too autobiographical,</u> but those who focus
(15) on traditional labels inevitably miss the fact that <u>Mphahlele manipulates different prose forms purely in the service of the social message he advances.</u>
  Even where critics give him a favorable reading, all too often their reviews carry a negative subtext.
(20) For example, one critic said of *The Wanderers* that if anger, firsthand experiences, compassion, and topicality were the sole requirements for great literature, the novel might well be one of the masterpieces of this declining part of the twentieth
(25) century. And although this critic may not have meant to question the literary contribution of the novel, there are those who are <u>outright dismissive</u> of *The Wanderers* because it contains an autobiographical framework and is populated with real-world
(30) characters. Mphahlele briefly defends against such charges by pointing out the importance of the fictional father-son relationship that opens and closes the novel. But his greater concern is the social vision that pervades his work, though it too is prone to
(35) misunderstandings and underappreciation. Mphahlele is a humanist and an integrationist, and his writings <u>wonderfully articulate</u> his vision of the future; but critics often balk at this vision because Mphahlele provides no road maps for bringing such a future
(40) about.
  Mphahlele himself shows little interest in establishing guidelines to distinguish autobiography from fiction. Though he does refer to *Down Second Avenue* as an autobiography and *The Wanderers* as a
(45) novel, he asserts that no novelist can write complete fiction or absolute fact. It is the nature of writing, at least the writing he cares about, that the details must be drawn from the writer's experiences, and thus are in some sense fact, but conveyed in such a way as
(50) to maximize the effectiveness of the social message contained in the work, and thus inevitably fiction. As he claims, the whole point of the exercise of writing has nothing to do with classification; in all forms writing is the transmission of ideas, and important
(55) ideas at that: "Whenever you write prose or poetry or drama you are writing a social criticism of one kind or another. If you don't, you are completely irrelevant—you don't count."

CRITICS' TWO CONCLUSIONS

AUTHOR'S CONCLUSION

SUPPORT FOR CRITICS' CONCLUSIONS

ATT.

MPHAHLELE'S OPINION

ATT.

MPHAHLELE'S OPINION

Note the arrow that shows us the author is present and aligned with the Synthesis position.

Subject: Ezekiel Mphahlele

Thesis — author — Antithesis

Autobiography shouldn't be fictional (Critics)

Synthesis — Blending is okay

Fiction shouldn't be autobiographical (Critics)

Question #1

You prepared yourself for the main point question, but it's nowhere to be found. Not to worry. You tracked the viewpoints and attitudes in the passage, which will get you the right answers. Mphahlele's point of view shows up at the end of paragraph two, starting at line 30, and continues until the end of the passage. Answer choice (B) is the correct answer, and it is just another way of expressing Mphahlele's view that "the whole point of the exercise of writing has nothing to do with classification."

1. Based on the passage, with which one of the following statements would Mphahlele be most likely to agree?

    (A) All works of literature should articulate a vision of the future.
    (B) It is not necessary for a writer to write works to fit predetermined categories.
    (C) Literary categories are worth addressing only when literary works are being unjustifiably dismissed.
    (D) Most works of literature that resemble novels could accurately be classified as autobiographies.
    (E) The most useful categories in literature are those that distinguish prose from poetry and poetry from drama.

While Mphahlele believes that all important writing is an exercise in social criticism (lines 55-57), it is not the case that it must take the form of a vision of the future, as (A) says. Mphahlele never says when, if ever, literary categories are worth addressing, and he certainly never pins down a certain context in which it should happen, so (C) is wrong. Answer choice (D) is way too broad because, while Mphahlele believes good writing includes both fact and fiction, there's no way to know what he thinks about works other than his. It's the "most" that kills this answer choice. Mphahlele does not really think categories are too useful (lines 41-43), so answer choice (E) is wrong.

Question #2

Another Viewpoint question asking about Mphahlele. Because we were meticulous about noting his views, the right answer ought to pop out at us, and indeed it does in answer choice (B) which states Mphahlele's view from the passage almost verbatim (lines 51-54).

2. The passage states that Mphahlele believes which one of the following?

    (A) Writing should provide a guide for achieving social change.
    (B) Writing should have as its goal the transmission of ideas.
    (C) Writing is most effective when it minimizes the use of real people and events to embellish a story.
    (D) Good writing is generally more autobiographical than fictional.
    (E) Fiction and autobiography are clearly identifiable literary forms if the work is composed properly.

Mphahlele declines to provide a guide to social change; that is the complaint of the critics (lines 37-40), and one that Mphahlele never disputes. So clearly (A) does not reflect his views. Mphahlele uses real people in both his autobiography (duh) and his fiction (lines 29-30), so he does not minimize the use of real people as (C) says. Good writing, according to Mphahlele, is about conveying social criticism, and the categories are irrelevant, so (D) is at odds with his views. Answer choice (E) again makes it seem like Mphahlele is concerned with categories, which is a misreading of his views.

Question #3

This question is asking us about the backhanded compliment supplied by the critic. Remember, the critic implies that Mphahlele is missing basic requirements of great literature, even though the critic acknowledges that the things Mphahlele actually does he does well. Answer choice (E) says this exactly.

3. In lines 18–25, the author uses the phrase "negative subtext" in reference to the critic's comment to claim that

   (A) the critic believes that Mphahlele himself shows little interest in establishing guidelines that distinguish fact from fiction in literature
   (B) the comment is unfairly one-sided and gives no voice to perspectives that Mphahlele might embrace
   (C) the requirement of firsthand experiences mentioned in the comment is in direct contradiction to the requirements of fiction
   (D) the requirements for great literature mentioned in the comment are ill conceived, thus the requirements have little bearing on what great literature really is
   (E) the requirements for great literature mentioned in the comment are not the sole requirements, thus Mphahlele's work is implied by the critic not to be great literature

The critic never comments on Mphahlele's motivations, only his execution, so (A) is wrong. The critic, unlike the other critics mentioned later in the paragraph, is not one-sided. The author accepts that the critic praises some aspects of Mphahlele's work, making (B) the wrong answer. The author never expresses disapproval of the requirements that Mphahlele does fulfill. The author never expresses disapproval of the requirements that Mphahlele does fulfill. Answer choice (C) is out because the author never indicates that there are contradictions in the requirements of fiction. Instead, the author expresses disapproval of the idea that Mphahlele fails to fulfill other requirements. So (C) and (D) are both wrong.

BP Minotaur: With so many points of view in a Synthesis passage, it's not surprising we got three questions about them. When there's lots of something in a passage, it's likely to be asked about!

6. Which one of the following aspects of Mphahlele's work does the author of the passage appear to value most highly?

   (A) his commitment to communicating social messages
   (B) his blending of the categories of fiction and autobiography
   (C) his ability to redefine established literary categories
   (D) his emphasis on the importance of details
   (E) his plan for bringing about the future he envisions

Question #6

The author's main point in the passage is that Mphahlele's writing works across genres because it is aimed at conveying a social message. That's answer choice (A).

Answer choice (B) is tempting because the author does suggest that Mphahlele blends fiction and autobiography within his work. However, the author seems to agree with Mphahlele that categorizing works of literature is pretty irrelevant to the overall effectiveness of the work. So anything involving genres (even one that talks about blending genres together) is unlikely to be the author's favorite part of Mphahlele's writing. Answer choice (C) assumes that Mphahlele redefined literary categories, which is too strong. He just used elements of one in the other. Details are discussed in the last paragraph (lines 46-51). Specifically, Mphahlele believes that they must come from the writer's experience, but there's no indication that they must be emphasized. So (D) is out. Mphahlele has no plan to bring about the future he envisions, something Mphahlele admits (lines 41-43), so (E) is just factually wrong.

Interested in the explanations for the other questions? You know where to go. blueprintlsat.com/login, my precious.

ANSWER KEY

1. b, 2. b, 3. e, 4. a, 5. c, 6. a, 7. d

13/REVIEW QUIZ

Congratulations! You've learned enough about Reading Comprehension and the Blueprint method to be tested on it. Keep in mind that some questions may have more than one correct answer. So without further ado:

1. What determines a passage's primary structure?
    (A) Whether or not the author is present
    (B) Its exoskeleton
    (C) The number of developed views
    (D) The number of conclusions

2. What is a subsidiary conclusion?
    (A) A conclusion that is both a premise and a conclusion.
    (B) A conclusion that's not very important.
    (C) The author's second conclusion.
    (D) The main point of the passage.

3. Which of the following are good candidates for the main idea of a passage?
    (A) A cause and effect statement
    (B) An opinion
    (C) Something supported by examples
    (D) A prediction

4. How many points of view are in an Antithesis passage?
    (A) One
    (B) Two
    (C) Three
    (D) None

5. Why do we track the author's opinion?
    (A) Because there will likely be a question about it
    (B) Because the author wrote the passage
    (C) Because authors don't get enough respect
    (D) Because the author's opinion is the main idea of the passage

6. When studying for Reading Comprehension, what do you do when you come across a word you don't know?
    (A) Keep reading
    (B) Look it up online
    (C) Ask your mom what it means
    (D) Curse the RC gods for their cruelty

ANSWER KEY

1. c, 2. a, 3. [a, b, c, d], 4. b, 5. [a, d], 6. [b, c (but only if your mom is smart)]

Hopefully, you answered all of these correctly. If not, well, there's always truck driving school. Kidding! Go back and review the relevant chapters since this is important stuff.

OFF WITH YOUR TRAINING WHEELS!

Up until now, the Primary Structure diagram we've provided has been large and fully labeled. Because the features of these diagrams should become second nature to you, from here on out, you'll see stripped down versions of the primary structure diagram that consist of only text and an arrow. Things still line up the same — Subject up top; Thesis to the left; Antithesis to the right; Synthesis below; and an arrow indicating the Author's position — but the labels are gone. Below you'll see how a passage discussing the tastiest beverage would be diagrammed using the full diagram and the streamlined diagram.

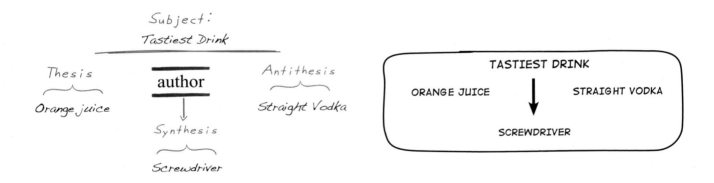

If you have questions going forward, come back to this page for clarification. Now get a move on!

Did you know: William H. Taft was the only president to also serve as a Supreme Court Justice?

14/tagANDmark

You now have a good overview of how to identify the underlying primary structure of a passage and how that translates to answering questions correctly. While that's a good start, there's still a lot more to understand about Reading Comprehension.

You must also be able to identify and mark relevant portions of the passage. In many cases, these marks will enable you to answer a question just by quickly referring to them. In others, they'll let you know where to read so that you don't have to search through the entire passage, thus saving you valuable time.

In this chapter, we'll teach you how to both tag the passage and mark it up. Tagging refers to writing short notes to the right of the passage in the margin while marking up refers to any type of writing you do on the actual passage itself, such as underlining or circling.

Here's a passage that's been tagged, marked up, and has a completed primary structure diagram. Hopefully, this should look familiar at this point. If it doesn't, you've skipped chapters and deserve to have taffy stuck to your hair. Like, deep in the back, not just on the ends.

The paintings of Romare Bearden (1914-1988) represent a double triumph. At the same time that Bearden's work reflects a lifelong commitment to perfecting the innovative painting techniques he
(5) pioneered, it also reveals an artist engaged in a search for ways to explore the varieties of African-American experience.

By presenting scene, character, and atmosphere using a unique layered and fragmented style that
(10) combines elements of painting with elements of collage, Bearden suggested some of the ways in which commonplace subjects could be forced to undergo a metamorphosis when filtered through the techniques available to the resourceful artist. Bearden knew that
(15) regardless of individual painters' personal histories, tastes, or points of view, they must pay their craft the respect of approaching it through an acute awareness of the resources and limitations of the form to which they have dedicated their creative energies.

(20) But how did Bearden, so passionately dedicated to solving the more advanced problems of his painting technique, also succeed so well at portraying the realities of African-American life? During the Great Depression of the 1930's, Bearden painted scenes of
(25) the hardships of the period; the work was powerful, the scenes grim and brooding. Through his depiction of the unemployed in New York's Harlem he was able to move beyond the usual "protest painting" of the period to reveal instances of individual human suffering. His
(30) human figures, placed in abstract yet mysteriously familiar urban settings, managed to express the complex social reality lying beyond the borders of the canvas without compromising their integrity as elements in an artistic composition. Another important element of
(35) Bearden's compositions was his use of muted colors, such as dark blues and purples, to suggest moods of melancholy or despair. While functioning as part of the overall design, these colors also served as symbols of the psychological effects of debilitating social processes.

(40) During the same period, he also painted happier scenes—depictions of religious ceremony, musical performance, and family life—and instilled them with the same vividness that he applied to his scenes of suffering. Bearden sought in his work to reveal in all its
(45) fullness a world long hidden by the clichés of sociology and rendered cloudy by the simplifications of journalism and documentary photography. Where any number of painters have tried to project the "prose" of Harlem, Bearden concentrated on releasing its poetry—its family
(50) rituals and its ceremonies of affirmation and celebration. His work insists that we truly see the African-American experience in depth, using the fresh light of his creative vision. Through an act of artistic will, he created strange visual harmonies out of the mosaic of the African-
(55) American experience, and in doing so reflected the multiple rhythms, textures, and mysteries of life.

October 2001 Passage 2

TAGGING

Remember when your probation officer told you that, if he found you tagging again, you'd be back in jail before you could say YOLO? Good news! You're about to learn to tag in a constructive and completely lawful manner!

Tagging consists of short notes written in the margin to the right of the passage. We tag in order to:

> 1) answer questions without having to re-read anything in the passage
> 2) know where to go to answer a question without re-reading the entire passage

There's a third reason that you should learn how to tag. Tagging the passage forces you to understand what you've read before moving on. As we discussed in previous chapters, reading without true understanding (skimming or not bothering to look up difficult words) is a big reason that students perform poorly on this section of the LSAT.

Tagging ensures that you've understood what you've read (otherwise, you wouldn't know what to tag) and that you can quickly refer back to important ideas in the passage. If you learn to tag the passage correctly, the questions will fall quivering before you like so many hapless rodents at the mercy of a honey badger.

Ditz: But won't it take forever to do all those things to the passage? I need to go faster, not take longer.

It's true that tagging takes time, Ditz. But it more than pays off in time saved. Also, the more you practice tagging, the quicker you'll be.

ROLE TAGGING AND SUBJECT TAGGING

The purpose of tagging is to make sure you've captured the structure and general topic of a paragraph. The former allows you to understand its overall purpose (e.g. providing support for the main idea) while the latter allows you to know what it's discussing (e.g. macropterous insects). Thus, you should be tagging in two different ways: by role and by subject.

Role Tagging

To the extent possible, you want to engage in role tagging.

Cleetus: I like it when my date tells me to dress up like a nurse.

Role tagging, Cleetus, not role playing. Role tagging is a logical extension of what you've learned in the past few chapters. In a Synthesis passage, for example, there are three points of view. Part of your role tagging would include noting each point of view and its proponent. If one of the points of view is the author's, you should underline it, as well (since, you know, it's the main idea of the passage and all). You should also fill in your primary structure diagram as you identify these points of view.

Here's an example of a role tag:

> The delegates to the convention from Candyland were unhappy with the resolution, noting that it did not mention the fact that certain nations—including the Republic of Molasses Swamp—had placed tariffs on the importation of gingerbread houses.

DELEGATES' VIEW

There are also role tags that are not points of view but nonetheless identify important structural components of the passage:

> The resolution also failed to take into account the strategic significance of lollipop woods or the peppermint stick forest. The delegates' argument is that, because both are key areas for entry to the crooked old peanut brittle house, this oversight is unacceptable.

SUPPORT FOR DELEGATES' VIEW

Subject Tagging

You should also tag for subject matter. While not structural in the way role tags are, subject tags can help you locate information quickly.

Here's an example of a subject tag:

> The eastern snake-neck turtle (Chelodina longicollis) has a neck that takes up approximately half its body length. It also ejects a foul-smelling liquid from its glands when is threatened.

EASTERN SNAKE-NECK TURTLE

Cleetus: How do I know what's important enough to tag? Also, them long necks make good eatin'.

First, it's good to know you've got dinner covered, Cleetus. Second, tagging the passage properly is a skill that takes time to develop. We'll tell you what to look for and give you plenty of examples to practice. We will see a little later in the chapter how both role and subject tags can help us anticipate and answer questions.

MARKING UP THE PASSAGE

In addition to making notes to the right of the passage, you'll also want to make certain marks on the passage itself. It is absolutely necessary to have a standardized method of marking up the passage. Otherwise, you run the risk of having a randomly underlined, highlighted, and generally unhelpful mess of a passage when you're done reading.

You can spend time inventing your own method, or you can use this one. You choose. (Just kidding, use this one.) As with all things in life including sexy time and LSAT prep, more time up front might appear burdensome at first, but, once you practice it enough, it will save time overall and make the process much more pleasurable.

The following list is very specific about what you want to mark up in the passage, as well as the tags that can accompany certain marks, and how to do it. *Memorize this method and use it religiously.*

- *Place a box around proper names such as* Scooby Doo *or* Kim Jong Un
- *Underline words or phrases that indicate the author's attitude such as regrettable or laudable. Tag these places with "Att."*
- *Circle high level words such as* indefatigable *or* hagiography *(except scientific terminology).*
- *Note weaknesses in arguments, including assumptions and criticisms. Tag assumptions and criticisms with "Ass." and "Crit.".**
- *Underline conclusions and note who advocates that particular conclusion.*
- *Tag research and studies (they support conclusions).*
- *Tag hypotheses with Hyp. (they can turn out to be conclusions)*
- *Bracket definitions such as [a crapella: singing out loud while listening to music with your headphones on].*
- *Note examples (they also support conclusions) with an "Ex."*

---

* Yes, we just used the word ass. If you come up with a better tag for assumption, let us know.

Ditz: Can't I just use my own method, like highlighting the author's attitude instead of underlining it?

That's a good question, Ditz, and the answer is yes, you can modify these rules as long as you consistently note these elements in the same manner. So if you want to circle proper names instead of boxing them, that's fine. Just make sure you're consistently marking it the same way. However, we recommend sticking with our method since all of our explanations use this symbology.

NOW IT'S YOUR TURN

Tag the following passages using the method above. This includes tagging, marking up the passage, and filling in the primary structure diagram. When you're finished, check your markups against ours, which have been provided, along with a brief explanation, at the end of the chapter.

1. Pluto, discovered in 1930, had a brief turn as a for-real planet before it was rudely kicked out of the planet club in 2006. So how did this happen? Pluto was always something of a mystery: a tiny, rocky object on the edge of the solar system, whereas all the other rocky planets are all close to the sun. Nevertheless, it was round and orbited the sun, and so scientists agreed that it was a planet.
    Then, in 2005, a similar but larger object, Eris, was discovered further out. More such discoveries followed in rapid succession. Some scientists believed that all such objects should be classified as planets. But the majority of scientists objected that inclusion of these objects would dilute the meaning of the word "planet."
    There had never been a clear definition of planet, and so, in 2006, the International Astronomical Union (IAU) developed the following formulation: A "planet" is a celestial body that: (a) is in orbit around the Sun, (b) has sufficient mass for its self-gravity to overcome rigid body forces so that it assumes a hydrostatic equilibrium (nearly round) shape, and (c) has cleared the neighborhood around its orbit. Pluto satisfies conditions (a) and (b), but, because it has not cleared its neighborhood, Pluto is not a planet.

Annotations:

- Att
- scientists view Pluto planet
- Debate
- Def
- author's conclusion

Subject: PLUTO

Thesis — planet (scientists)

author → Synthesis

Antithesis — not a planet (majority)

2. One of the main tactics people employ to lose weight is switching from sugary soda to diet soda. A single, 20-oz. bottle of sugary soda contains the equivalent of seventeen teaspoons of sugar. As such, one would assume that cutting such a significant source of calories out of one's diet would result in weight loss. However, in a recently completed, ten year study, the National Institute of Health determined that those who drank diet soda rather than regular soda actually lost less weight than their counterparts who continued to drink sugary soda. (To control for differences in body type, weight loss was defined in terms of percentage of body mass lost/gained, rather than a straight comparison between relative amounts of weight lost/gained.)

So why is there this discrepancy? A colleague of mine, Dr. Fielgud, hypothesized that the sugar substitute in diet soda triggers a slowdown in the metabolism just like real sugar. Look, I love to party with Dr. Fielgud, but he's missing the point. Even if the effect on the metabolism is the same, there should still be greater weight loss due to the elimination of the calories in the soda. Instead, it is more likely that those who switch to diet soda feel liberated to eat less healthy food, and so they more than make up the calories they avoid by forgoing sugary soda.

3. The literature of the Harlem Renaissance is unique in the history of African American literature, spanning, as it does, the gap between the Reconstruction Era and the Civil Rights Movement. Much of it retains the stylistic reservation of Reconstruction Era literature, and yet it explores, albeit obliquely, the attitude of resistance that would define the Civil Rights Era.

   Historian Franklin Brandon, an expert on African American history and literature at the University of Virginia and a fellow at the Alliance Foundation, asserts that this duality in Harlem Renaissance literature is primarily a function of the Great Migration, which reached its peak during the Harlem Renaissance.

   The Great Migration refers to the diaspora of African Americans, moving from the South to other places in the United States, primarily urban centers, in search of work and to leave behind the injustices of Jim Crow. Between 1910 and 1930, more than 1.3 million African Americans made their way out of the South.

   Brandon believes that the attitude held by by these "migrants" is reflected in the seemingly contradictory nature of Harlem Renaissance literature. In short, those participating in the Great Migration were both moving hopefully toward places less affected by the legacy of slavery to start a new life, but, at the same time, they were fleeing entrenched racism; their journey was therefore influenced both positively and negatively by their perception of the world around them.

   In a recent lecture, Brandon offered an example of this dichotomy captured in Countee Cullen's 1925 poem, "Yet I do marvel," in which the narrator acknowledges his powerlessness before some circumstances and yet expresses gratitude for the opportunities he does have.

4. So, "selfie" is now an entrenched part of the English language; the Oxford English Dictionary—the OED, to those in the know—made it an official entry in 2013. But the button down etymologists at the OED didn't stop there. "Selfie" was the winner of the Word of the Year Award for 2013.

    For those who have been living under a rock, a selfie is…well, let's just let the OED explain. The OED definition of selfie is, "a photograph that one has taken of oneself, typically one taken with a smartphone or webcam and uploaded to a social media website."

    Some are quick to blame the OED for legitimizing the narcissism pervasive among today's youth. But the OED is a repository of language, not an arbiter of culture, and so it records trends without necessarily affirming them. As evidence, one need only look at the OED's example for using the word in a sentence: "Occasional selfies are acceptable, but posting a new picture of yourself everyday isn't necessary."

    Right you are, OED. Right you are.

5. On April 26, 1937, German warplanes carpet-bombed the Basque city of Guernica, which was a safe haven for Republican forces, who battled the Nationalists during the Spanish Civil War. Guernica was annihilated, and there were heavy civilian casualties. Unfortunately, this tactic was to be used on a wide scale in World War II.

   Less than a week after the bombing, Pablo Picasso, the famous artist, read a firsthand account of the attack by George Steer published in the New York Times. The very same day, Picasso created preliminary sketches of a mural that would become one of the great anti-war works of art.

   "Guernica," a gigantic oil-on-canvas some eleven feet high and twenty-five feet wide, is an abstract rendering of the gruesome firebombing of the city of Guernica. Beyond these basic facts, art experts have been in sharp disagreement over its content and meaning, a disagreement that Picasso reluctantly weighed in on during his lifetime.

   The painting is rife with representations that have been potent symbols in art for eons: a bull, a horse, an eye, a broken sword. The contorted stance of the bull, often a symbol of aggression, was interpreted by art historian Janet Horowitz to indicate that Picasso believed the bombing would ultimately prove self-defeating for the Germans. This particularity presumes too much, however, as Picasso himself attested. When asked about this interpretation, Picasso did not dismiss it, but claimed that he "paints the objects for what they are" and asserted that any interpretations emerged later, after the image was created.

   P. Johnson asserts it's never a good idea to ask artists their intent. His conclusion is that Picasso left the moral open to interpretation so that an interpretation of either ultimate German defeat or not could be plausible.

ANSWER KEY

1. [Pluto,] discovered in 1930, had a brief turn as a for-real planet before it was <u>rudely</u> kicked out of the planet club in 2006. So how did this happen? Pluto was always something of a mystery: a tiny, rocky object on the edge of the solar system, whereas all the other rocky planets are all close to the sun. Nevertheless, it was round and orbited the sun, and <u>so scientists agreed that it was a planet.</u>

   Then, in 2005, a similar but larger object, [Eris,] was discovered further out. More such discoveries followed in rapid succession. <u>Some scientists believed that all such objects should be classified as planets. But the majority of scientists objected that inclusion of these objects would dilute the meaning of the word "planet."</u>

   There had never been a clear definition of planet, and so, in 2006, the International Astronomical Union (IAU) developed the following formulation: [A "planet" is a celestial body that: (a) is in orbit around the Sun, (b) has sufficient mass for its self-gravity to overcome rigid body forces so that it assumes a hydrostatic equilibrium (nearly round) shape, and (c) has cleared the neighborhood around its orbit.] <u>Pluto satisfies conditions (a) and (b), but, because it has not cleared its neighborhood, Pluto is not a planet.</u>

ATT.

SCIENTISTS' VIEW:
PLUTO IS A PLANET

DEBATE AMONG
SCIENTISTS

DEF.

AUTHOR'S CONCLUSION:
PLUTO IS NOT A PLANET

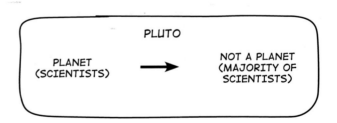

1) There are two points of view here—Pluto is a planet, espoused by some scientists, and that Pluto isn't a planet, championed by a majority of scientists. With two points of view, we know we have an Antithesis passage. Like many passages, it starts off with some background about the issue. There is a definition, and the author applies that definition to come to a conclusion, i.e. Pluto is not a planet, hence the author is aligned with the majority of scientists. Poor Pluto. Once so vaunted, now so low.

2. One of the main tactics people employ to lose weight is switching from sugary soda to diet soda. A single, 20-oz. bottle of sugary soda contains the equivalent of seventeen teaspoons of sugar. As such, one would assume that cutting such a significant source of calories out of one's diet would result in weight loss.

    However, in a recently completed, ten year study, the National Institute of Health determined that those who drank diet soda rather than regular soda actually lost less weight than their counterparts who continued to drink sugary soda. (To control for differences in body type, weight loss was defined in terms of percentage of body mass lost/gained, rather than a straight comparison between relative amounts of weight lost/gained.)

    So why is there this discrepancy? A colleague of mine, Dr. Fielgud, hypothesized that the sugar substitute in diet soda triggers a slowdown in the metabolism just like real sugar. Look, I love to party with Dr. Fielgud, but he's missing the point. Even if the effect on the metabolism is the same, there should still be greater weight loss due to the elimination of the calories in the soda. Instead, it is more likely that those who switch to diet soda feel liberated to eat less healthy food, and so they more than make up the calories they avoid by forgoing sugary soda.

ASS.

CUT SODA TO LOSE WEIGHT

STUDY

DIET SODA DRINKERS LOST **LESS** WEIGHT

DR. FIELGUD'S CONCLUSION

CRIT.

AUTHOR'S CONCLUSION: PEOPLE WHO QUIT SODA EAT MORE

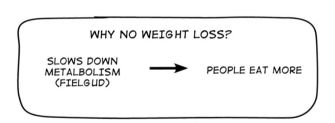

2) The passage begins with some background information on diet soda. The paragraph ends with an assumption: switching to diet soda will result in weight loss. This is followed by a study, which is always important to identify. The study casts doubt on the assumption and introduces a strange phenomenon that must be explained: why do people who quit soda lose less weight? Dr. Fielgud proposes an answer to that question, and that answer is his conclusion. The author criticizes Fielgud's conclusion, and then offers his own.

3. The literature of the Harlem Renaissance is unique in the history of African American literature, spanning, as it does, the gap between the Reconstruction Era and the Civil Rights Movement. Much of it retains the stylistic reservation of Reconstruction Era literature, and yet it explores, albeit obliquely, the attitude of resistance that would define the Civil Rights Era.

    Historian Franklin Brandon, an expert on African American history and literature at the University of Virginia and a fellow at the Alliance Foundation, asserts that this duality in Harlem Renaissance literature is primarily a function of the Great Migration, which reached its peak during the Harlem Renaissance.

    The Great Migration refers to the diaspora of African Americans, moving from the South to other places in the United States, primarily urban centers, in search of work and to leave behind the injustices of Jim Crow. Between 1910 and 1930, more than 1.3 million African Americans made their way out of the South.

    Brandon believes that the attitude held by by these "migrants" is reflected in the seemingly contradictory nature of Harlem Renaissance literature. In short, those participating in the Great Migration were both moving hopefully toward places less affected by the legacy of slavery to start a new life, but, at the same time, they were fleeing entrenched racism; their journey was therefore influenced both positively and negatively by their perception of the world around them.

    In a recent lecture, Brandon offered an example of this dichotomy captured in Countee Cullen's 1925 poem, "Yet I do marvel," in which the narrator acknowledges his powerlessness before some circumstances and yet expresses gratitude for the opportunities he does have.

HARLEM RENAISSANCE LITERATURE

BRANDON'S CONCLUSION: H.R. LITERATURE INFLUENCED BY GREAT MIGRATION

DEF.

GREAT MIGRATION BACKGROUND

SUPPORT FOR BRANDON'S CONCLUSION

EX.

POEM SUPPORTS BRANDON'S CONCLUSION

HARLEM RENAISSANCE LITERATURE

INFLUENCED BY
GREAT MIGRATION
(BRANDON)

---

3) The first paragraph identifies a feature of Harlem Renaissance literature which is that is combines both attitudes of reservation and resistance. The rest of the passage is devoted to explaining the reason that feature exists, which is that it was influenced by the Great Migration. We get Brandon's conclusion at the end of paragraph two, and paragraphs three through five support his conclusion. It's important to note that we are discussing Brandon's opinion, and the author does not express any. For this reason, there is no arrow in our primary structure diagram.

4. So, "selfie" is now an entrenched part of the English language; the Oxford English Dictionary—the OED, to those in the know—made it an official entry in 2013. But the button down (etymologists) at the OED didn't stop there. "Selfie" was the winner of the Word of the Year Award for 2013.   OED RECOGNIZES "SELFIE"

For those who have been living under a rock, a selfie is…well, let's just let the OED explain. The OED definition of [selfie is, "a photograph that one has taken of oneself, typically one taken with a smartphone or webcam and uploaded to a social media website."]   DEF.

DEFINITION OF "SELFIE"

Some are quick to blame the OED for legitimizing the narcissism pervasive among today's youth. But the OED is a repository of language, not an arbiter of culture, and so it records trends without necessarily affirming them. As evidence, one need only look at the OED's example for using the word in a sentence: "Occasional selfies are acceptable, but posting a new picture of yourself everyday isn't necessary."   CRIT.

AUTHOR'S CONCLUSION

EX.

Right you are, OED. Right you are.

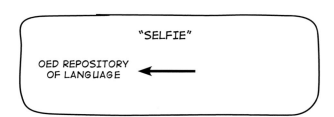

4) Like so many passages, we begin paragraph one with some background of the issue. The next paragraph identifies a definition. Paragraph three introduces a criticism of the OED including "selfie." However, the author quickly responds that it's perfectly proper given the dictionary's mandate. This response is a conclusion, supported in paragraph four with an example. The criticism is not recorded as a view since there is no support for it. It's not until paragraph three that we get the author's conclusion. That conclusion is a response to criticism. The support for the conclusion is that it's not the OED's job to influence culture. There is an example that supports this idea.

5. On April 26, 1937, German warplanes carpet-bombed the Basque city of Guernica, which was a safe haven for Republican forces, who battled the Nationalists during the Spanish Civil War. Guernica was annihilated, and there were heavy civilian casualties. Unfortunately, this tactic was to be used on a wide scale in World War II.

   Less than a week after the bombing, Pablo Picasso, the famous artist, read a firsthand account of the attack by George Steer, published in the New York Times. The very same day, Picasso created preliminary sketches of a mural that would become one of the great anti-war works of art.

   ["Guernica," a gigantic oil-on-canvas some eleven feet high and twenty-five feet wide, is an abstract rendering of the gruesome firebombing of the city of Guernica.] Beyond these basic facts, art experts have been in sharp disagreement over its content and meaning, a disagreement that Picasso reluctantly weighed in on during his lifetime.

   The painting is rife with representations that have been potent symbols in art for eons: a bull, a horse, an eye, a broken sword. The contorted stance of the bull, often a symbol of aggression, was interpreted by art historian Janet Horowitz to indicate that Picasso believed the bombing would ultimately prove self-defeating for the Germans. This particularity presumes too much, however, as Picasso himself attested. When asked about this interpretation, Picasso did not dismiss it, but claimed that he "paints the objects for what they are" and asserted that any interpretations emerged later, after the image was created.

   P. Johnson asserts it's never a good idea to ask artists their intent. His conclusion is that Picasso left the moral open to interpretation so that an interpretation of either ultimate German defeat or not could be plausible.

BOMBING OF GUERNICA

ATT.

PICASSO STARTS PAINTING

DEF.

EXPERTS DISAGREE ON MEANING

PICASSO ATT.

HOROWITZ CONCLUSION

AUTHOR'S CONCLUSION

PICASSO'S CONCLUSION

P. JOHNSON'S CONCLUSION

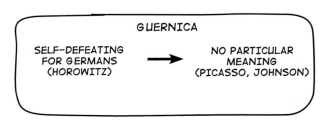

GUERNICA

SELF-DEFEATING FOR GERMANS (HOROWITZ) → NO PARTICULAR MEANING (PICASSO, JOHNSON)

5) There are a lot of proper names here and a lot of facts of which to keep track. It's not until the third paragraph that we get the beginning of the debate that will form the structure of our passage. Horowitz believes *Guernica* demonstrates the bombing would be self-defeating for the Germans. Picasso, in contrast, says that interpretations emerge after the painting is created. This effectively means that the painting itself has no particular meaning. Meaning is formed by what people bring to it. Johnson agrees with this, saying really any interpretation of the paintings, including Horowitz's, could be possible. This means Johnson is aligned with Picasso's point of view.

THE MASTERPIECE

Now that you've had some practice tagging and marking up shorter passages, it's time to try a real one. Below is a full-length Reading Comprehension passage from June 2013. Try your hand at tagging and marking up the passage, including completing the primary structure. Once you're finished, compare it to our markup and see how you've done. There's also a PDF markup on your MyBlueprint account that discusses the passage and how to mark it up correctly.

Then, using your tagged passage as a guide, answer the questions in black. The questions that require you to understand concepts that have yet to be addressed in this book are greyed out, and you needn't be able to answer them correctly at this point. However, the markup will help you with those as well, should you choose to attempt them.

We're excited for you! Get to it.

Calvaria major is a rare but once-abundant tree found on the island of Mauritius, which was also home to the dodo, a large flightless bird that became extinct about three centuries ago. In 1977 Stanley Temple,
(5) an ecologist whose investigation of *Calvaria major* was a sidelight to his research on endangered birds of Mauritius, proposed that the population decline of *Calvaria major* was linked to the demise of the dodo, a hypothesis that subsequently gained considerable
(10) currency. Temple had found only thirteen *Calvaria major* trees on Mauritius, all overmature and dying, and all estimated by foresters at over 300 years old. These trees produced fruits that appeared fertile but that Temple assumed could no longer germinate,
(15) given his failure to find younger trees.
    The temporal coincidence between the extinction of the dodo and what Temple considered the last evidence of natural germination of *Calvaria major* seeds led him to posit a causal connection. Specifically,
(20) he hypothesized that the fruit of *Calvaria major* had developed its extremely thick-walled pit as an evolutionary response to the dodo's habitual consumption of those fruits, a trait enabling the pits to withstand the abrasive forces exerted on them in
(25) the birds' digestive tracts. This defensive thickness, though, ultimately prevented the seeds within the pits from germinating without the thinning caused by abrasion in the dodo's gizzard. What had once been adaptive, Temple maintained, became a lethal
(30) imprisonment for the seeds after the dodo vanished.
    Although direct proof was unattainable, Temple did offer some additional findings in support of his hypothesis, which lent his argument a semblance of rigor. From studies of other birds, he estimated the
(35) abrasive force generated within a dodo's gizzard. Based on this estimate and on test results determining the crush-resistant strength of *Calvaria major* pits, he concluded that the pits could probably have withstood a cycle through a dodo's gizzard. He also fed *Calvaria*
(40) *major* pits to turkeys, and though many of the pits were destroyed, ten emerged, abraded yet intact. Three of these sprouted when planted, which he saw as vindicating his hypothesis.
    Though many scientists found this dramatic and
(45) intriguing hypothesis plausible, Temple's proposals have been strongly challenged by leading specialists in the field. Where Temple had found only thirteen specimens of *Calvaria major*, Wendy Strahm, the foremost expert on the plant ecology of Mauritius,
(50) has identified hundreds, many far younger than three centuries. So *Calvaria major* seeds have in fact germinated, and the tree's reproductive cycle has thus continued, since the dodo's disappearance. Additional counterevidence comes from horticultural
(55) research by Anthony Speke, which shows that while only a minority of unabraded *Calvaria major* seeds germinate, the number is still probably sufficient to keep this species from becoming extinct. The population decline, while clearly acute, could easily
(60) be due to other factors, including disease and damage done by certain nonindigenous animals introduced onto Mauritius in the past few centuries.

22. Which one of the following most accurately expresses the main point of the passage?

    (A) *Calvaria major* germination, though rare, is probably adequate to avoid extinction of the species.
    (B) The appeal of Temple's hypothesis notwithstanding, the scarcity of *Calvaria major* is probably not due to the extinction of the dodo.
    (C) Temple's experimentation with *Calvaria major* pits, though methodologically unsound, nevertheless led to a probable solution to the mystery of the tree's decline.
    (D) Temple's dramatic but speculative hypothesis, though presented without sufficient supporting research, may nevertheless be correct.
    (E) *Calvaria major* would probably still be scarce today even if the dodo had not become extinct.

23. The author indicates that Temple's research on birds of the island of Mauritius

    (A) was largely concerned with species facing the threat of extinction
    (B) furnished him with the basis for his highly accurate estimates of the crush-resistant strength of *Calvaria major* pits
    (C) provided experimental evidence that some modern birds' gizzards exert roughly the same amount of abrasive force on their contents as did dodo gizzards
    (D) was comprehensive in scope and conducted with methodological precision
    (E) was originally inspired by his observation that apparently fertile *Calvaria major* pits were nevertheless no longer able to germinate

June 2013 Passage 4

24. In saying that Temple's supporting evidence lent his argument a "semblance of rigor" (lines 33–34), the author most likely intends to indicate that

   (A) despite his attempts to use strict scientific methodology, Temple's experimental findings regarding *Calvaria major* pits were not carefully derived and thus merely appeared to support his hypothesis
   (B) direct proof of a hypothesis of the sort Temple was investigating is virtually impossible to obtain, even with the most exact measurements and observations
   (C) in contrast to Temple's secondhand information concerning the age of the thirteen overmature *Calvaria major* trees he found, his experiments with turkeys and other birds represented careful and accurate firsthand research
   (D) in his experimentation on *Calvaria major* pits, Temple produced quantitative experimental results that superficially appeared to bolster the scientific credibility of his hypothesis
   (E) although the consensus among experts is that Temple's overall conclusion is mistaken, the scientific precision and the creativity of Temple's experimentation remain admirable

25. The passage indicates which one of the following about the abrasion of *Calvaria major* pit walls?

   (A) Thinning through abrasion is not necessary for germination of *Calvaria major* seeds.
   (B) In Temple's experiment, the abrasion caused by the digestive tracts of turkeys always released *Calvaria major* seeds, undamaged, from their hard coverings.
   (C) Temple was mistaken in believing that the abrasion caused by dodos would have been sufficient to thin the pit walls to any significant degree.
   (D) Abrasion of *Calvaria major* pit walls by the digestive tracts of animals occurred commonly in past centuries but rarely occurs in nature today.
   (E) Temple overlooked the fact that other natural environmental forces have been abrading *Calvaria major* pit walls since the dodo ceased to fulfill this role.

26. It can be most logically inferred from the passage that the author regards Temple's hypothesis that the extinction of the dodo was the cause of *Calvaria major*'s seeming loss of the ability to reproduce as which one of the following?

   (A) essentially correct, but containing some inaccurate details
   (B) initially implausible, but vindicated by his empirical findings
   (C) an example of a valuable scientific achievement outside a researcher's primary area of expertise
   (D) laudable for its precise formulation and its attention to historical detail
   (E) an attempt to explain a state of affairs that did not in fact exist

27. Based on the passage, it can be inferred that the author would be likely to agree with each of the following statements about *Calvaria major* EXCEPT:

   (A) The causes of the evolution of the tree's particularly durable pit wall have not been definitively identified by Temple's critics.
   (B) The notion that the thickness of the pit wall in the tree's fruit has been a factor contributing to the decline of the tree has not been definitively discredited.
   (C) In light of the current rate of germination of seeds of the species, it is surprising that the tree has not been abundant since the dodo's disappearance.
   (D) There is good reason to believe that the tree is not threatened with imminent extinction.
   (E) *Calvaria major* seeds can germinate even if they do not first pass through a bird's digestive system.

Calvaria major is a rare but once-abundant tree found on the island of Mauritius, which was also home to the dodo, a large flightless bird that became extinct about three centuries ago. In 1977 Stanley Temple, (5) an ecologist whose investigation of *Calvaria major* was a sidelight to his research on endangered birds of Mauritius, proposed that the population decline of *Calvaria major* was linked to the demise of the dodo, a hypothesis that subsequently gained considerable (10) currency. Temple had found only thirteen *Calvaria major* trees on Mauritius, all overmature and dying, and all estimated by foresters at over 300 years old. These trees produced fruits that appeared fertile but that Temple assumed could no longer germinate, (15) given his failure to find younger trees.

    The temporal coincidence between the extinction of the dodo and what Temple considered the last evidence of natural germination of *Calvaria major* seeds led him to posit a causal connection. Specifically, (20) he hypothesized that the fruit of *Calvaria major* had developed its extremely thick-walled pit as an evolutionary response to the dodo's habitual consumption of those fruits, a trait enabling the pits to withstand the abrasive forces exerted on them in (25) the birds' digestive tracts. This defensive thickness, though, ultimately prevented the seeds within the pits from germinating without the thinning caused by abrasion in the dodo's gizzard. What had once been adaptive, Temple maintained, became a lethal (30) imprisonment for the seeds after the dodo vanished.

    Although direct proof was unattainable, Temple did offer some additional findings in support of his hypothesis, which lent his argument a semblance of rigor. From studies of other birds, he estimated the (35) abrasive force generated within a dodo's gizzard. Based on this estimate and on test results determining the crush-resistant strength of *Calvaria major* pits, he concluded that the pits could probably have withstood a cycle through a dodo's gizzard. He also fed *Calvaria* (40) *major* pits to turkeys, and though many of the pits were destroyed, ten emerged, abraded yet intact. Three of these sprouted when planted, which he saw as vindicating his hypothesis.

    Though many scientists found this dramatic and (45) intriguing hypothesis plausible, Temple's proposals have been strongly challenged by leading specialists in the field. Where Temple had found only thirteen specimens of *Calvaria major*, Wendy Strahm, the foremost expert on the plant ecology of Mauritius, (50) has identified hundreds, many far younger than three centuries. So *Calvaria major* seeds have in fact germinated, and the tree's reproductive cycle has thus continued, since the dodo's disappearance. Additional counterevidence comes from horticultural (55) research by Anthony Speke, which shows that while only a minority of unabraded *Calvaria major* seeds germinate, the number is still probably sufficient to keep this species from becoming extinct. The population decline, while clearly acute, could easily (60) be due to other factors, including disease and damage done by certain nonindigenous animals introduced onto Mauritius in the past few centuries.

DEF.

HYP.

SUPPORT FOR HYP.

ASS.

TEMPLE'S CONCLUSION:
DODO EXTINCTION → DECLINE IN TREE POPULATION

ATT.

ADDITIONAL SUPPORT FOR TEMPLE'S CONCLUSION

SPECIALISTS' CONCLUSION

RES.

AUTHOR'S CONCLUSION:
OTHER FACTORS → DECLINE IN TREE POPULATION

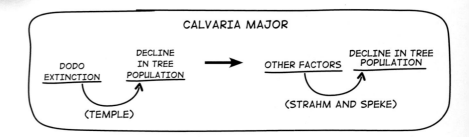

CALVARIA MAJOR: DODO EXTINCTION → DECLINE IN TREE POPULATION (TEMPLE) → OTHER FACTORS → DECLINE IN TREE POPULATION (STRAHM AND SPEKE)

PASSAGE SUMMARY

Frankly, it's a little surprising it took the freaks at LSAC until 2013 to do a passage on bird poop. You knew—just KNEW!—it was coming.

Paragraph one gives us some background on *Calvaria Major* trees, and we are also introduced to Stanley Temple. Temple's a bird expert, so this whole tree thing is not his area of expertise. He notes a correlation—dodo extinction seems to have happened right around the time the last of these trees started growing. He has a hypothesis that these two events are linked (lines 4-10). Remember to mark hypotheses as they often turn into conclusions. This particular hypothesis is a strongly implied causal relationship. The paragraph concludes with Temple's support for his hypothesis, that the only *Calvaria Major* trees were dying.

Paragraph two elaborates on the hypothesis, turning it into a full-blown causal relationship: the extinction of the dodo caused the decline in tree population. The rest of this paragraph supports that idea, so let's get it into our diagram as the Thesis position. The support offered is a plausible explanation of the mechanism that would tie the cause to the effect. Specifically, the tree evolved in response to the dodo eating its seeds by making really thick seedpods. Those seedpods could survive a trip through the dodo's, well, you know what (lines 19-25). Once the dodo disappeared, Temple reasoned, the seedpods were too thick to germinate without passing through a dodo (lines 25-30), and the tree population declined.

Paragraph three is an experiment that Temple performed to test his conclusion. The author peeks his head in here talking about how Temple's experiment had the "semblance of rigor" (lines 33-34). That's a fancy way of saying the experiment was not scientific, and that's negative author's attitude toward the experiment. To sum up, Temple fed the seeds to turkeys. Ten of them weren't destroyed, and three of those sprouted.

In paragraph four, we get some scientists arguing against Temple, which should make it into our diagram as the Antithesis position. Wendy Strahm found a bunch of trees that had sprouted after the dodo went extinct, which is pretty strong evidence that the trees don't need the dodo to reproduce (lines 47-51). (You'd think the tree expert could find these trees. Get it together, Temple!) We've also got some research by Anthony Speke showing that seeds can sprout without the dodo (lines 54-58). Finally, the author comes in at the last sentence, adopting the Antithesis position, saying that the tree decline "could easily be due to other factors."

In sum, a cause and effect relationship is proposed and supported with an experiment, and that cause and effect relationship is challenged by scientists and the author.

The following is an explanation of the important features of the passage that we picked up by tagging correctly. This process of assessing the passage before attacking the questions is vitally important, and we will discuss it at length in subsequent chapters.

PRIMARY STRUCTURE: ANTITHESIS

Stanley Temple's argument is that the extinction of the dodo caused the decline in the tree population. Wendy Strahm, Anthony Speke and the author all believe that it was due to other factors.

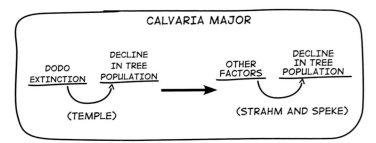

PASSAGE OVERVIEW

MAIN POINT

When the author adopts a point of view, as he does here, that point of view is the main point of the passage. In other words, the main point of the passage is that factors other than the extinction of the dodo were responsible for the decline of the *Calvaria Major* tree population.

PRIMARY PURPOSE

The author wrote the passage to show that other factors were responsible for the decline in tree population.

AUTHORS ATTITUDE

The strongest example of attitude is when the author describes Temple's experiments as having only a "semblance of rigor" (lines 33-34).

QUESTION ANTICIPATION

You are likely to get multiple questions on the Cause and Effect relationship. There was also strong author's attitude and a number of experiments that are likely to appear in the questions.

AND NOW, ON TO THE QUESTIONS

QUESTION 22: MAIN POINT

We predicted the ever-loving heck out of this question, so it's a gimme. Answer choice (B) says that it was other factors, not the dodo extinction, that caused the decline of the trees. (Anyone else here having flashbacks to *The Lorax* and the truffala trees?)

- (A) This answer choice refers only to the results of Speke's experiment (lines 54-58). That's exactly one sentence in the passage, which, of course, is far too narrow to be the main point.
- (C) This is extremely wrong. The author's opinion is the main point of a passage, and this is the opposite of that opinion.
- (D) This is just a weaker version of (C), and it's wrong for the same reason.
- (E) While the author doesn't think the extinction was responsible for the decline, he never ventures a guess as to this hypothetical situation. This is called a counterfactual—speculation about what would've happened if everything in the passage *hadn't happened*. Such an answer choice is, by definition, not supported by the passage. Steer clear of these.

QUESTION 24: AUTHORS ATTITUDE

Here's the question we were anticipating about the author's attitude. When you see something like this—the author turning up his nose at something he doesn't like—you are almost guaranteed a question. (D) is the right answer, talking about how superficial the experiments were. Superficial people are garbage, and so are superficial experiments. Eat it, Temple!

- (A) The problem with the experiment was not that Temple screwed up the implementation. It's that the theoretical basis was bad.
- (B) This experiment stinks. That in no way means all experiments on the subject would stink.
- (C) No, no, no! These experiments stink!
- (E) Not admirable. Crappy.

QUESTION 25: SPECIFIC REFERENCE

This question is a bit open ended, but, when they're asking about what the passage indicates, it means they want the author's take on things. When we're talking about this abrasion—what happens when the seed takes a wild adventure through the digestive tract of a bird—the author thinks that it doesn't matter. The dodo and this abrasion, according to the author, are irrelevant to the tree sprouting. That's answer choice (A).

- (B) No. Many of them were destroyed (lines 40-41).
- (C) Just like (B), this mischaracterizes the results of the experiment. They were abraded and thinned.
- (D) Occurred commonly? The author says that this experiment produced flawed results. An inference like this is not mentioned in the passage and presumes that the author thinks this experiment produced credible results. It didn't.
- (E) There's no indication anywhere in the passage that anything else abraded these pits.

QUESTION 26: AUTHORS ATTITUDE

This is asking us the author's opinion of the Thesis position. The author thinks that position is wrong. That's why (E) is correct. Before we get to the other answers, since we know the author disagrees with the Thesis, anything treating it positively is just wrong and can be easily eliminated.

- (A) No. The Thesis is essentially incorrect. Focus.
- (B) Again, this is saying the Thesis is right. The author thinks it's wrong.
- (C) Wrong-wrong-wrongitty-wrong. It's not valuable. It's a failure.
- (D) If the word were "laughable," we might be on to something here. Laudable means deserving of praise. No. Temple screwed up. Meta point: Primary Structure diagram showing author's opinion allows you to dispense with four wrong answers easily.

ANSWER KEY
22. b, 23. a, 24. d, 25. a, 26. e, 27. c

Congratulations! Your first foray into tagging and marking up the passage is done. Now let's learn some more useful stuff...

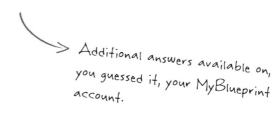

Additional answers available on, you guessed it, your MyBlueprint account.

15/SECONDARYstructures

SECONDARY STRUCTURES, DECONSTRUCTED

After reading every single Reading Comprehension passage ever released (what a hoot that was), we noticed that certain structures cropped up again and again. These structures are distinct from viewpoints so we call them secondary structures. Like primary structures, they prove to be extraordinarily helpful in breaking down passages as well as anticipating questions likely to be asked.

Recognizing secondary structures will not only allow you to answer more questions correctly, it will also save you time as they minimize or obviate entirely the need to re-read parts of the passage. With four passages to read and twenty-seven or so questions to answer in thirty-five minutes, each second is precious. Don't thank us now; thank us when you crush the Reading Comprehension section into a fine powder—which you must not, under any circumstances, snort or place in an envelope and mail to a government official.

THE BREAKDOWN

[Handwritten note: cause & effect + question & answer } secondary structure is part of the conclusion]

The four secondary structures are as follows:

- Cause and Effect
- Example
- Question and Answer
- Classification

[Handwritten note: example and classification } secondary structure part of the premise that support the conclusion]

EXTENSIVE SECONDARY STRUCTURES

When you read a passage and a particular secondary structure is discussed in detail throughout the passage, you are dealing with an extensive secondary structure. In such a case, the secondary structure forms an important part of the primary structure and should be reflected in your primary structure diagram.

Let's think back to earlier chapters where we discussed primary structure. You learned that, in order to determine the primary structure of a passage, you must identify each argument—a conclusion that is supported by premises—and note who is making the argument.

Secondary structures constitute crucial components of the views that you note in your primary structure diagram. In the case of Cause and Effect and Question and Answer secondary structures, the secondary structure is part of the *conclusion* of an argument. In the case of Example and Classification secondary structures, the secondary structure is part of the *premises* that support the conclusion.

Conclusions

Let's take an example to see how an extensive secondary structure might operate as a conclusion.

Imagine a passage in which the author asserts that smoking causes cancer. Now, further imagine that the author uses the rest of the passage to support the idea that smoking causes cancer, talking variously about studies that show higher cancer rates among smokers, the harmful processes that go on in the body when a person smokes, etc.

Here, the main point of the passage—the author's main conclusion—is that smoking causes cancer. You should tag it when you see it, and your primary structure diagram ought to reflect that, as shown below.

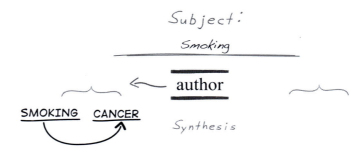

Expect two or more questions about the Cause and Effect relationship, including Main Point, Primary Purpose, and, quite often, Author's Attitude questions. If you can see that the passage is all about the causal relationship, you can anticipate the questions coming your way and cut through them like a hot knife through Dora the Explorer—er, butter. Yes, butter. Sorry.

Premises

Now let's see how a secondary structure might function as a premise.

Imagine a passage where the author's main point is that land claims brought by Native American tribes in U.S. courts have been unfairly decided. This is a value judgment, and value judgments are often conclusions.

Imagine that the rest of the passage describes a 1989 court case involving the Hopi tribe. In the court case, members of the Hopi tribe tried to prove in court that they owned a particular piece of property in Arizona, but, even though they'd lived there longer than anyone could remember, the court kicked them off the land because they didn't have a written deed to the property. Unfair, right?

It should be abundantly clear that this particular court case about the Hopi tribe is being used as an example to support the main point. When the author makes a general claim, an example illustrating that claim provides support. In this case, the primary structure diagram would look something like this:

Subject: Native American land claims

Thesis ← author — Antithesis

Hopi tribe shows courts make unfair decisions

As with our first example, you should expect multiple questions about this secondary structure as it is likely to show up in the Main Point, Primary Purpose, and Author's Attitude questions.

LOCALIZED SECONDARY STRUCTURES

Sometimes one or more secondary structures will appear in a passage, but they won't be the main focus of the passage. Instead, they're confined to one or two sentences. We call these localized secondary structures. Identifying a localized secondary structure is still very helpful because, even though it might not enter into the main point of the passage, you're still quite likely to get a question about it. Tag all localized secondary structures, and when the question pops up, you'll be ready.

The following are examples of extensive and localized secondary structures taken from real Reading Comprehension passages.

EXTENSIVE CAUSE AND EFFECT
SECONDARY STRUCTURE

Over the past 50 years, expansive, low-density communities have proliferated at the edges of many cities in the United States and Canada, creating a phenomenon known as suburban sprawl. Andres
(5) Duany, Elizabeth Plater-Zyberk, and Jeff Speck, a group of prominent town planners belonging to a movement called New Urbanism, contend that suburban sprawl contributes to the decline of civic life and civility.
(10) Current zoning and subdivision regulations, they argue, dictate that suburban homes, stores, businesses, and schools be built in separate areas, and this separation robs people of communal space where they can interact and get to know one another. It is as difficult
(15) to imagine the concept of community without a town square or local pub, these town planners contend, as it is to imagine the concept of family independent of the home.

Suburban housing subdivisions, Duany
(20) and his colleagues add, usually contain homes identical not only in appearance but also in price, resulting in a de facto economic segregation of residential neighborhoods. Children growing up in these neighborhoods, whatever their economic
(25) circumstances, are certain to be ill prepared for life in a diverse society. Moreover, because the widely separated suburban homes and businesses are connected only by "collector roads," residents are forced to drive, often in heavy traffic, in order to
(30) perform many daily tasks. Time that would in a town center involve social interaction within a physical public realm is now spent inside the automobile, where people cease to be community members and instead become motorists, competing for road space,
(35) often acting antisocially. Pedestrians rarely act in this manner toward one another. Duany and his colleagues advocate development based on early-twentieth-century urban neighborhoods that mix housing of different prices and offer residents a "gratifying public
(40) realm" that includes narrow, tree-lined streets, parks, corner grocery stores, cafes, small neighborhood schools, all within walking distance. Such developments, they believe, would give people of diverse backgrounds and lifestyles an opportunity to interact and thus
(45) develop mutual respect.

Opponents of New Urbanism claim that migration to sprawling suburbs is an expression of people's legitimate desire to secure the enjoyment and personal mobility provided by the automobile and the
(50) lifestyle that it makes possible. However, the New Urbanists do not question people's right to their own values; instead, they suggest that we should take a more critical view of these values and of the sprawl-conducive zoning and subdivision policies that reflect
(55) them. New Urbanists are fundamentally concerned with the long-term social costs of the now-prevailing attitude that individual mobility, consumption, and wealth should be valued absolutely, regardless of their impact on community life.

June 2010 Passage 1

1. Which one of the following most accurately expresses the main point of the passage?

   (A) In their critique of policies that promote suburban sprawl, the New Urbanists neglect to consider the interests and values of those who prefer suburban lifestyles.

   (B) The New Urbanists hold that suburban sprawl inhibits social interaction among people of diverse economic circumstances, and they advocate specific reforms of zoning laws as a solution to this problem.

   (C) The New Urbanists argue that most people find that life in small urban neighborhoods is generally more gratifying than life in a suburban environment.

   (D) The New Urbanists hold that suburban sprawl has a corrosive effect on community life, and as an alternative they advocate development modeled on small urban neighborhoods.

   (E) The New Urbanists analyze suburban sprawl as a phenomenon that results from short-sighted traffic policies and advocate changes to these traffic policies as a means of reducing the negative effects of sprawl.

LOCALIZED EXAMPLE SECONDARY STRUCTURE

In certain fields of human endeavor, such as music, chess, and some athletic activities, the performance of the best practitioners is so outstanding, so superior even to the performance of other highly experienced individuals in the field, that some people believe some
(5) notion of innate talent must be invoked to account for this highest level of performance. Certain psychologists have supported this view with data concerning the performance of prodigies and the apparent heritability of relevant traits. They have noted, for example, that
(10) most outstanding musicians are discovered by the age of six, and they have found evidence that some of the qualities necessary for exceptional athletic performance, including superior motor coordination, speed of reflexes, and hand-eye coordination, can be
(15) inborn.

Until recently, however, little systematic research was done on the topic of superior performance, and previous estimates of the heritability of traits relevant to performance were based almost exclusively on
(20) random samples of the general population rather than on studies of highly trained superior performers as compared with the general population. Recent research in different domains of excellence suggests that exceptional performance arises predominantly from
(25) acquired comp[lex skills] rather than fro[m ...] been found tha[t ...] a systematic a[dvantage ...] discrimination [...]
(30) performance, [...] these factors. S[imilarly, superior] exceptional m[emory ...] but only if tho[se configurations are typical of chess] games.

(For example, it has been found that the most accomplished athletes show a systematic advantage in reaction time or perceptual discrimination only in their particular fields of performance, not in more general laboratory tests for these factors. Similarly, superior chess players have exceptional memory for configurations of chess pieces, but only if those configurations are typical of chess games.

(35) The vast majority of exceptional adult performers were not exceptional as children, but started instruction early and improved their performance through sustained high-level training. Only extremely rarely is outstanding performance achieved without at least
(40) ten years of intensive, deliberate practice. With such intensive training, chess players who may not have superior innate capacities can acquire skills that circumvent basic limits on such factors as memory and the ability to process information. Recent research shows that, with the clear exception of some traits such as height, a surprisingly large number of anatomical
(45) characteristics, including aerobic capacity and the percentage of muscle fibers, show specific changes that develop from extended intense training.

The evidence does not, therefore, support the claim that a notion of innate talent must be invoked
(50) in order to account for the difference between good and outstanding performance, since it suggests instead that extended intense training, together with that level of talent common to all reasonably competent performers, may suffice to account for this difference.
(55) Since sustained intense training usually depends on an appropriate level of interest and desire, and since those who eventually become superior performers more often show early signs of exceptional interest than early evidence of unusual ability, motivational factors
(60) are more likely to be effective predictors of superior performance than is innate talent.

---

19. The passage says that superior chess players do not have exceptional memory for which one of the following?

(A) some sequences of moves that are typical of games other than chess
(B) some types of complex sequences without spatial components
(C) some chess games that have not been especially challenging
(D) some kinds of arrangements of chess pieces
(E) some types of factors requiring logical analysis in the absence of competition

See the localized example that correlates to a question!

December 2013 Passage 3

184 / Chapter 15

Reading Comprehension passages aren't supposed to test your knowledge of any subject matter. In fact, we spend the entirety of this book teaching you how to read for structure, rather than topic. But if there were knowledge of one thing that might help you in Reading Comprehension, it would be LSAC's beloved icon: Thurgood Marshall.

He's the only person to have been the topic of at least three Reading Comprehension passages. From Brown v. Board of Education to the first African-American Supreme Court justice, his general awesomeness has been celebrated and documented. Wiki the guy. He's a boss.

16/CAUSEandEFFECT

One thing leads to another

We discuss Cause and Effect secondary structures in detail first for several reasons. First, they are quite common. 14.19% of all Reading Comprehension passages have a Cause and Effect secondary structure. Second, cause and effect shows up all over the Logical Reasoning sections of the exam as well. What you learn here, therefore, can also be applied to the two Logical Reasoning sections on the test. Bonus!

Ditz: Like getting a free makeup bag when you purchase Designer Imposter Body sprays.

That's right, Ditz. Remember, if you like Calvin Klein Obsession™, you'll love Confess™!

WHAT IS CAUSE AND EFFECT

We discussed cause and effect a bit in the last chapter, but let's backtrack to make sure you understand the notion of causation. A cause brings about an effect. You see it everywhere, every day: pushing the gas pedal causes your car to move forward; spinning around in a circle causes you to be dizzy; eating too much causes weight gain, then bariatric surgery, then weight loss, then gaining it all back plus ten pounds. You get the idea.

We symbolize causal relationships by writing the cause first, followed by an arrow leading to the effect. So if we were to posit that watching too much reality television erodes dignity and self worth, we would symbolize it in the following manner:

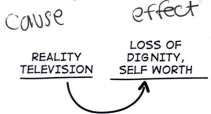

WHY CAUSE AND EFFECT IS IMPORTANT IN READING COMPREHENSION

As we discussed in previous chapters, a cause and effect relationship is often a conclusion, and finding conclusions is one of your main tasks in addressing Reading Comprehension passages. Therefore, finding Cause and Effect secondary structures typically has a payoff in the main idea (which is the main conclusion of the passage).

Take the example of the dinosaur. The makers of the LSAT have an affection for dinosaurs: whether a stegosaur, velociraptor, or improbably mauve[1], they love them. Let's say there's an LSAT passage devoted to a theory of what killed the dinosaurs. The author of the passage might come to the *conclusion* that a giant asteroid impacted the Earth and wiped out the dinosaurs. To be clear, in this case, there is an *effect*—dinosaur extinction—and the author of the passage is concluding that the *cause* is a giant asteroid impact.

By identifying the causal relationship, you've also identified the main idea of the passage.

Ninja: We tried to count how many dinosaur references there are in the history of the LSAT, but even an LSAT ninja cannot count that high.

Even if the causal relationship you identify isn't the main idea of the passage, there's often a specific question asked about the relationship, so it still provides a payoff in terms of points earned on the test.

And don't forget that cause and effect relationships abound in Logical Reasoning, as well. Among others, Strengthen questions will often ask you to make a weak argument better by shoring up the causal connection, Flaw questions will have you identify when a correlation is being confused with causation, and Weaken questions will ask you to identify another cause that could explain an effect[2].

---

[1] See the June 2009 LSAT. Mauve dinosaurs proved to be the undoing on the Games section for the hapless students who sat for this particular exam.

[2] You don't need to know any of these skills for Reading Comprehension, but understanding the basics of cause and effect will provide a foundation for learning these advanced skills in Logical Reasoning, later.

IDENTIFYING CAUSE AND EFFECT RELATIONSHIPS

Now that we know how important causal relationships are, how do we know how to identify them? There are many ways that the makers of the LSAT signal a cause and effect relationship, and you need to be able to pick up on them when reading passages. The following table contains words and phrases that signal causal relationships. Memorize them and be on the lookout for them, and variations on them, when you are reading a passage!

> The first step in identifying a causal relationship is identifying a correlation
> - If 2 things often show up together → correlation
> - If one seems to lead the other → causation & causal relationship

Key Words

"...causes..."
"...leads to..."
"...brings about..."
"...results in..."
"...has the effect..."
"...produces..."
"...is responsible for..."
"...affected..."
"...contributes to..."
"...generates..."
"...is due to..."

BP Minotaur: This is not an exhaustive list, and there is other language that might signal a Cause and Effect secondary structure. When in doubt, remember that the first step in showing causation is correlation. If two things often show up together, you have a correlation. If one seems to lead to the other, it's likely you have a causal relationship.

Remember the *Calvaria Major* trees on the island of Mauritius? Temple thought he had a causal relationship because two things—the extinction of the dodo and the decline in trees—were correlated. Without any causal language, you could have known he was positing a causal relationship.

(handwritten top): effect → result/outcome
affect → influence something, to act on, or produce a change

WHAT IT LOOKS LIKE IN READING COMPREHENSION

(handwritten): affect → comes first in action and has to occur before you can have a result (effect)

Let's see how the makers of the LSAT do it. The following are excerpts from real LSAT Reading Comprehension passages that demonstrate causal relationships.

(handwritten): effect → the something that was influenced

...the union cause was championed by an unprecedented coalition of Korean American groups and (deeply affected) the Korean American community...

...suburban sprawl (contributes) to the decline of civic life and civility...

...large earthquakes (generate) numerous rockfalls in mountain ranges that are sensitive to seismic shaking...

(handwritten): effect → result of a cause
affect → influences
first thing causes an effect on second thing

Ninja: Keep 'effect' and 'affect' straight. An effect is the result of a cause. Attaining ninja status is an effect of training. Training affects combat ability. If something affects something else, the first thing is causing an effect in the second thing. Training affects combat ability but the effect of ninja training is awesomeness.

EXTENSIVE CAUSE AND EFFECT SECONDARY STRUCTURES

If a particular cause and effect relationship is mentioned multiple times in the passage and/or a significant portion of the passage is devoted to providing support for that cause and effect relationship, it is an extensive Cause and Effect secondary structure.

Remember that a cause and effect statement is a conclusion, and, when you have an extensive Cause and Effect secondary structure, it is the Main Point of the passage.

Take a look at this real, live, honest-to-goodness LSAT passage, the associated markup, and the Main Point question. We'll talk about it after you're done.

Leading questions—[questions worded in such a way as to suggest a particular answer]—can yield unreliable testimony either by design, as when a lawyer tries to trick a witness into affirming a particular version of the evidence of a case, or by accident, when a questioner unintentionally prejudices the witness's response. For this reason, a judge can disallow such questions in the courtroom interrogation of witnesses. But their exclusion from the courtroom by no means eliminates the remote effects of earlier leading questions on eyewitness testimony. Alarmingly, the beliefs about an event that a witness brings to the courtroom may often be adulterated by the effects of leading questions that were introduced intentionally or unintentionally by lawyers, police investigators, reporters, or others with whom the witness has already interacted.

(20) [Studies have shown how this layering] process occurs and, perhaps, of the conditions that make for greater risks that an eyewitness's memories have been tainted by leading questions. These studies suggest that not all details of our experiences become
(25) clearly or stably stored in memory—only those to which we give adequate attention. Moreover, experimental evidence indicates that if subtly introduced new data involving remembered events do not actively conflict with our stored memory data, we
(30) tend to process such new data similarly whether they correspond to details as we remember them, or to gaps in those details. In the former case, we often retain the new data as a reinforcement of the corresponding aspect of the memory, and in the latter case, we often
(35) retain them as a construction to fill the corresponding gap. An eyewitness who is asked, prior to courtroom testimony, "How fast was the car going when it passed the stop sign?" may respond to the query about speed without addressing the question of the stop sign.
(40) But the "stop sign" datum has now been introduced, and when later recalled, perhaps during courtroom testimony, it may be processed as belonging to the original memory even if the witness actually saw no stop sign.
(45) The farther removed from the event, the greater the chance of a vague or incomplete recollection and the greater the likelihood of newly suggested information blending with original memories. Since we can be more easily misled with respect to fainter
(50) and more uncertain memories, tangential details are more apt to become constructed out of subsequently introduced information than are more central details. But what is tangential to a witness's original experience of an event may nevertheless be crucial to
(55) the courtroom issues that the witness's memories are supposed to resolve. For example, a perpetrator's shirt color or hairstyle might be tangential to one's shocked observance of an armed robbery, but later those factors might be crucial to establishing the identity of the
(60) perpetrator.

20. Which one of the following most accurately expresses the main point of the passage?

(A) The unreliability of memories about incidental aspects of observed events makes eyewitness testimony especially questionable in cases in which the witness was not directly involved.
(B) Because of the nature of human memory storage and retrieval, the courtroom testimony of eyewitnesses may contain crucial inaccuracies due to leading questions asked prior to the courtroom appearance.
(C) Researchers are surprised to find that courtroom testimony is often dependent on suggestion to fill gaps left by insufficient attention to detail at the time that the incident in question occurred.
(D) Although judges can disallow leading questions from the courtroom, it is virtually impossible to prevent them from being used elsewhere, to the detriment of many cases.
(E) Stricter regulation should be placed on lawyers whose leading questions can corrupt witnesses' testimony by introducing inaccurate data prior to the witnesses' appearance in the courtroom.

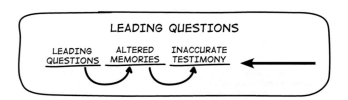

June 2003 Passage 4

The passage is devoted to explaining that leading questions in courtroom testimony *cause* inaccurate testimony. Because the rest of the passage is devoted to supporting that conclusion, the passage contains an extensive Cause and Effect secondary relationship, and the primary structure diagram reflects that. Note that the answer to the Main Point question identifies the causal relationship.

What do I do when I find an extensive Cause and Effect secondary structure?

Every time you see a cause and effect relationship, tag the passage with a diagram—cause on the left, effect on the right, with a loopy arrow connecting the two. You may not be able to determine the moment you read it that the particular causal statement is the Main Point of the passage, and therefore an extensive secondary structure. You would therefore tag it and keep reading. Imagine that the following excerpt appeared at the beginning of a passage:

"Recently, scientists have found a correlation between a particular gene—prevalent in Great Britain—and horrible teeth. These scientists argue that this gene is the cause of the socially crippling condition known as The British Smile."

The moment you read this assertion, you tag it like so:

Suppose that the rest of the passage provides evidence for the claim that this gene is responsible for bad teeth. The passage asserts that there is a strong correlation between the gene and bad teeth; experiments show that replacing the gene in embryos with another produces great smiles in the offspring born to parents with horrendous dentition; the particular gene resides in a portion of the DNA known to control the development of the teeth, etc.

Having read all this, you would then know that the causal statement you tagged at the top of the paragraph is indeed the Main Point of the passage. The tag will therefore make its way into your Primary Structure diagram as follows:

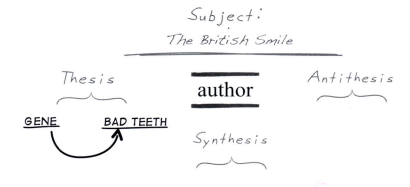

How does this help me answer questions?

Once you've got a diagram like the one above, you have the Main Point and Primary Purpose questions locked up. The correct answer to the Main Point is exactly what is in the diagram. In this case, the right answer to the Main Point question is "There is a gene that causes bad teeth."

The Primary Purpose question asks *why* the author bothered to write the passage. Where the author is present, the Primary Purpose is to argue for his or her point of view. When the author is absent, the Primary Purpose is to present or describe a particular point of view. Assuming a present author, the correct answer to a Primary Purpose question would look something like, "To argue that a particular gene is responsible for a particular dental condition."

If there is a present author—and especially if the author has a strong opinion on the subject—you are likely to get an Author's Attitude question about the causal relationship. Here, for example, if the author implies that he or she believes the evidence supporting the conclusion is strong, the answer to the Author's Attitude question asking about the evidence might look something like, "Satisfied that the evidence supports the causal relationship between the gene and bad teeth."

In this way, finding the Cause and Effect secondary structure helps get you points on the LSAT.

LOCALIZED CAUSE AND EFFECT SECONDARY STRUCTURES

If a Cause and Effect secondary structure is mentioned once, in just a sentence or two, it is a localized Cause and Effect secondary structure. Tag it with a Cause and Effect diagram, but it should not be part of your primary structure diagram. Take a look at the following example:

Primary purpose questions...
- *ask why the passage was written*
- *present author → argue their viewpoint (most likely followed by an attitude question)*
- *absent author → present/describe a viewpoint*

[The United States government agency responsible for overseeing television and radio broadcasting,] the Federal Communications Commission (FCC), had an early history of addressing only the concerns of
(5) parties with an economic interest in broadcasting—chiefly broadcasting companies. The rights of viewers and listeners were not recognized by the FCC, which regarded them merely as members of the public. Unless citizens' groups were applying for broadcasting
(10) licenses, citizens did not have the standing necessary to voice their views at an FCC hearing. Consequently, the FCC appeared to be exclusively at the service of the broadcasting industry.

A landmark case changed the course of that history.
(15) In 1964, a local television station in Jackson, Mississippi was applying for a renewal of its broadcasting license. The United Church of Christ, representing Jackson's African American population, petitioned the FCC for a hearing about the broadcasting policies of that station.
(20) The church charged that the station advocated racial segregation to the point of excluding news and programs supporting integration. Arguing that the church lacked the level of economic interest required for a hearing, the FCC rejected the petition, though it attempted to mollify
(25) the church by granting only a short-term, probationary renewal to the station. Further, the FCC claimed that since it accepted the church's contentions with regard to misconduct on the part of the broadcasters, no hearing was necessary. However, that decision raised a question:
(30) If the contentions concerning the station were accepted, why was its license renewed at all? The real reason for denying the church a hearing was more likely the prospect that citizens' groups representing community preferences would begin to enter the closed worlds of
(35) government and industry.

The church appealed the FCC's decision in court, and in 1967 was granted the right to a public hearing on the station's request for a long-term license. The hearing was to little avail: the FCC dismissed much of
(40) the public input and granted a full renewal to the station. The church appealed again, and this time the judge took the unprecedented step of revoking the station's license without remand to the FCC, ruling that the church members were performing a public service in voicing
(45) the legitimate concerns of the community and, as such, should be accorded the right to challenge the renewal of the station's broadcasting license.

The case established a formidable precedent for opening up to the public the world of broadcasting.
(50) Subsequent rulings have supported the right of the public to question the performance of radio and television licensees before the FCC at renewal time every three years. Along with racial issues, a range of other matters—from the quality of children's programming and the portrayal of violence
(55) to equal time for opposing political viewpoints—are now discussed at licensing proceedings because of the church's intervention.

DEF.

TRADITIONAL
FCC STANCE

ATT.

BACKGROUND OF
CASE: CHURCH
DENIED HEARING

COURT GRANTS
HEARING

ATT.

COURT REVOKES
LICENSE

AUTHOR'S
CONCLUSION

2. The author mentions some additional topics now discussed at FCC hearings (lines 54–59) primarily in order to

(A) support the author's claim that the case helped to open up to the public the world of broadcasting
(B) suggest the level of vigilance that citizens' groups must maintain with regard to broadcasters
(C) provide an explanation of why the public is allowed to question the performance of broadcasters on such a frequent basis
(D) illustrate other areas of misconduct with which the station discussed in the passage was charged
(E) demonstrate that the station discussed in the passage was not the only one to fall short of its obligation to the public

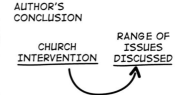

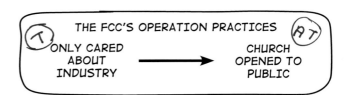

June 2009 Passage 1

The passage is devoted to two points of view, and those are expressed in the primary structure diagram. Specifically, the FCC thinks that the public has no standing to participate in licensing hearings, and the church disagrees. The causal statement at the end of the passage is something else. The church wins the debate over standing, and the causal statement explains the *effects* of them winning the debate. The related question asks directly about this. By tagging the localized Cause and Effect structure, you can readily answer the question and pick up an easy point.

What do I do when I find a Localized Cause and Effect secondary structure?

Always, always, always tag the cause and effect relationship with the standard causal diagram. Make sure that, before you move on to the next sentence, you understand what is the cause and what is the effect and what, if any, support is provided for the statement.

How does this help me answer questions?

In the case of a localized Cause and Effect secondary structure, you will be asked a question other than a Main Point or Primary Purpose question, so anticipating the question is a little less cut and dried. Nevertheless, you are quite likely to be tested on it. The question in the passage you just read is a specific reference question, and it is asking specifically about the cause and effect relationship. If you can see that the "additional topics" are support for the causal claim—the causal *conclusion*—then you don't even need to refer back to the passage to answer the question.

TRY IT OUT FOR YOURSELF

The following is a real LSAT passage with an extensive Cause and Effect secondary structure. Mark up the passage using what you've learned in the previous chapters. Don't forget to fill in your primary structure diagram! Then have at the questions.

For no particular reason, we'd like to stress that a passage could have an extensive Cause and Effect secondary structure *and* have one or more localized Cause and Effect secondary structures, as well. (Just thought we'd mention that here, right before you try this passage.) There's a complete explanation at the end of the chapter for you to check your work.

Since you now have a nearly full arsenal from which to tackle the questions, the training wheels are off and no questions have been greyed out. You will notice that the questions are categorized. Some of these you're already familiar with—those that are closely associated with tracking viewpoints—and others you are not. Each of these question types will be explained in detail later on in the book, so don't let them throw you. Good luck!

Where is this man going on vacation?

(A) Monte Carlo
(B) Tibetan spiritual pilgrimage
(C) The Maldives
(D) His backyard to sit by the above-ground swimming pool

To glass researchers it seems somewhat strange that many people throughout the world share the persistent belief that window glass flows slowly downward like a very viscous liquid. Repeated in
(5) reference books, in science classes, and elsewhere, the idea has often been invoked to explain ripply windows in old houses. The origins of the myth are unclear, but the confusion probably arose partly from a misunderstanding of the fact that the atoms in glass
(10) are not arranged in a fixed crystal structure. In this respect, the structure of liquid glass and the structure of solid glass are very similar, but thermodynamically they are not the same. Glass does not have a precise freezing point; rather, it has what is known as a glass
(15) transition temperature, typically a range of a few hundred degrees Celsius. Cooled below the lower end of this range, molten glass retains an amorphous atomic structure, but it takes on the physical properties of a solid.
(20) However, a new study debunks the persistent belief that stained glass windows in medieval cathedrals are noticeably thicker at the bottom because the glass flows downward. Under the force of gravity, certain solid materials including glass can, in fact, flow
(25) slightly. But Brazilian researcher Edgar Dutra Zanotto has calculated the time needed for viscous flow to change the thickness of different types of glass by a noticeable amount, and, according to his calculations, medieval cathedral glass would require a period well
(30) beyond the age of the universe.

The chemical composition of the glass determines the rate of flow. Even germanium oxide glass, which flows more easily than other types, would take many trillions of years to sag noticeably, Zanotto calculates.
(35) Medieval stained glass contains impurities that could lower the viscosity and speed the flow to some degree, but even a significant difference in this regard would not alter the conclusion, since the cathedrals are only several hundred years old. The study demonstrates
(40) dramatically what many scientists had reasoned earlier based on information such as the fact that for glass to have more than a negligible ability to flow, it would have to be heated to at least 350 degrees Celsius.

The difference in thickness sometimes observed
(45) in antique windows probably results instead from glass manufacturing methods. Until the nineteenth century, the only way to make window glass was to blow molten glass into a large globe and then flatten it into a disk. Whirling the disk introduced ripples and
(50) thickened the edges. To achieve structural stability, it would have made sense to install these panes in such a way that the thick portions were at the bottom. Later, glass was drawn into sheets by pulling it from the melt on a rod, a method that made windows more
(55) uniform. Today, most window glass is made by floating liquid glass on molten tin. This process makes the surface extremely flat.

21. Which one of the following most accurately states the main point of the passage?

    (A) Zanotto's research has proven that the amount of time required for viscous flow to change the thickness of medieval cathedral glass would be greater than the age of the universe.
    (B) The technology of window-glass production has progressed substantially from medieval stained-glass techniques to today's production of very flat and very uniform panes.
    (C) After years of investigation motivated partly by a common misunderstanding about the structure of glass, scientists have developed ways of precisely calculating even extremely slow rates of gravity-induced flow in solids such as glass.
    (D) Recent research provides evidence that although solid glass flows slightly under the influence of gravity, such flow is only one of several factors that have contributed to noticeable differences in thickness between the top and the bottom of some old windows.
    (E) Contrary to a commonly held belief, noticeable differences in thickness between the top and the bottom of some old glass windows are not due to the flowing of solid glass, but probably result instead from old glassworking techniques.

22. The passage most helps to answer which one of the following questions?

    (A) What is one way in which seventeenth-century windowpane manufacturing techniques differ from those commonly used in medieval times?
    (B) What is one way in which nineteenth-century windowpane manufacturing techniques differ from those commonly used today?
    (C) Was glass ever used in windows prior to medieval times?
    (D) Are unevenly thick stained-glass windowpanes ever made of germanium oxide glass?
    (E) How did there come to be impurities in medieval stained glass?

June 2015 Passage 4

23. Which one of the following best summarizes the author's view of the results of Zanotto's study?

    (A) They provide some important quantitative data to support a view that was already held by many scientists.
    (B) They have stimulated important new research regarding an issue that scientists previously thought had been settled.
    (C) They offer a highly plausible explanation of how a mistaken hypothesis came to be widely believed.
    (D) They provide a conceptual basis for reconciling two scientific views that were previously thought to be incompatible.
    (E) They suggest that neither of two hypotheses adequately explains a puzzling phenomenon.

24. The passage suggests that the atomic structure of glass is such that glass will

    (A) behave as a liquid even though it has certain properties of solids
    (B) be noticeably deformed by the force of its own weight over a period of a few millennia
    (C) behave as a solid even when it has reached its glass transition temperature
    (D) flow downward under its own weight if it is heated to its glass transition temperature
    (E) stop flowing only if the atoms are arranged in a fixed crystalline structure

25. The author of the passage attributes the belief that window glass flows noticeably downward over time to the erroneous assumption that

    (A) the atomic structure of solid glass is crystalline rather than amorphous
    (B) the amorphous atomic structure of glass causes it to behave like a very viscous liquid even in its solid form
    (C) methods of glass making in medieval times were similar to the methods used in modern times
    (D) the transition temperature of the glass used in medieval windows is the same as that of the glass used in modern windows
    (E) liquid glass and solid glass are thermodynamically dissimilar

26. Which one of the following is most analogous to the persistent belief about glass described in the passage?

    (A) Most people believe that the tendency of certain fabrics to become wrinkled cannot be corrected during the manufacturing process.
    (B) Most people believe that certain flaws in early pottery were caused by the material used rather than the process used in manufacturing the pottery.
    (C) Most people believe that inadequate knowledge of manufacturing techniques shortens the life span of major appliances.
    (D) Most people believe that modern furniture made on an assembly line is inferior to individually crafted furniture.
    (E) Most people believe that modern buildings are able to withstand earthquakes because they are made from more durable materials than were older buildings.

27. The passage suggests that which one of the following statements accurately characterizes the transition temperature of glass?

    (A) It is higher for medieval glass than for modern glass.
    (B) It has only recently been calculated with precision.
    (C) Its upper extreme is well above 350 degrees Celsius.
    (D) It does not affect the tendency of some kinds of glass to flow downward.
    (E) For some types of glass, it is a specific temperature well below 350 degrees Celsius.

To glass researchers it seems somewhat strange that many people throughout the world share the persistent belief that window glass flows slowly downward like a very viscous liquid. Repeated in (5) reference books, in science classes, and elsewhere, the idea has often been invoked to explain ripply windows in old houses. The origins of the myth are unclear, but the confusion probably arose partly from a misunderstanding of the fact that the atoms in glass (10) are not arranged in a fixed crystal structure. In this respect, the structure of liquid glass and the structure of solid glass are very similar, but thermodynamically they are not the same. Glass does not have a precise freezing point; rather, it has what is known as a glass (15) transition temperature, typically a range of a few hundred degrees Celsius. Cooled below the lower end of this range, molten glass retains an amorphous atomic structure, but it takes on the physical properties of a solid.

(20) However, a new study debunks the persistent belief that stained glass windows in medieval cathedrals are noticeably thicker at the bottom because the glass flows downward. Under the force of gravity, certain solid materials including glass can, in fact, flow (25) slightly. But Brazilian researcher Edgar Dutra Zanotto has calculated the time needed for viscous flow to change the thickness of different types of glass by a noticeable amount, and, according to his calculations, medieval cathedral glass would require a period well (30) beyond the age of the universe.

The chemical composition of the glass determines the rate of flow. Even germanium oxide glass, which flows more easily than other types, would take many trillions of years to sag noticeably, Zanotto calculates. (35) Medieval stained glass contains impurities that could lower the viscosity and speed the flow to some degree, but even a significant difference in this regard would not alter the conclusion, since the cathedrals are only several hundred years old. The study demonstrates (40) dramatically what many scientists had reasoned earlier based on information such as the fact that for glass to have more than a negligible ability to flow, it would have to be heated to at least 350 degrees Celsius.

The difference in thickness sometimes observed (45) in antique windows probably results instead from glass manufacturing methods. Until the nineteenth century, the only way to make window glass was to blow molten glass into a large globe and then flatten it into a disk. Whirling the disk introduced ripples and (50) thickened the edges. To achieve structural stability, it would have made sense to install these panes in such a way that the thick portions were at the bottom. Later, glass was drawn into sheets by pulling it from the melt on a rod, a method that made windows more (55) uniform. Today, most window glass is made by floating liquid glass on molten tin. This process makes the surface extremely flat.

ATT.
Q: WHY IS GLASS RIPPLED?
A: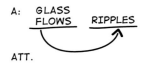
ATT.

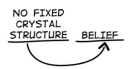

STUDY: BELIEFS WRONG

EX.

ATT.

A: MANUFACTURING METHOD → RIPPLES

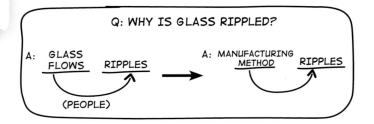

PASSAGE SUMMARY

The appearance of glass flowing downward is caused by the way it was manufactured, and, to think, all along you thought it was just all the hallucinogens you took back in the 60's!

The passage begins with a bit of negative attitude, although not the author's. Researchers think the belief that glass flows downward is "strange." Hot on its heels comes the answer to an implied question: why is old glass rippled? The explanation is causal—the ripples are caused by glass flowing slowly downward. We'll learn more about Question and Answer structures in a bit. For now it's enough for you to know that we tag the questions and its answer, putting it into our causal diagram.

Note that the author uses terms like "myth" and "confusion" (lines 6-7). That's negative author's attitude, so it's clear our author doesn't agree with this explanation of what causes glass to ripple. The paragraph then gives us a second Cause and Effect structure that explains why people believe the first Cause and Effect structure. The misunderstanding is caused by the fact that atoms in glass aren't arranged in a fixed crystal structure. Tag this localized Cause and Effect structure, too.

Because the first answer has support, it's a point of view and should be placed in the primary structure diagram.

Paragraph two introduces a study that debunks this point of view. And, as everyone knows, something that has been debunked can never be rebunked. No rebunking! Flowing can't be the cause of these ripples because, according to this Zinotto character, it would take billions of years to happen. A study is a premise that supports a point of view so we know that the author is going to side with a different point of view. Let's wait and see what it is.

Paragraph three is an example (we love examples!) that provides yet more support that the point of view in paragraph one is wrong. Zanotto did a study (we love studies!) showing that the flowiest glass around would take trillions – not millions, not billions, but trillions – of years to flow (lines 32-39). The author displays strongly positive attitude here, calling it dramatic (line 40).

We get our Antithesis in paragraph four. The real cause of the ripples? Before the 19th century, people sucked at making glass, and they put the thicker part of the glass where it should be, at the bottom, hence the appearance that it flows downward. This is

> **BP Minotaur:** We know this is a localized Cause and Effect structure because it supports the other Cause and Effect structure. People think glass flows slowly downward because of the fact that its structure isn't fixed. If you try it the other way—people think the structure isn't fixed because glass flows down—it doesn't work because it distorts the facts in the passage. This, dear reader, is how you separate primary from subsidiary conclusions.

another answer to the question couched in, again, causal language. Accordingly, we tag it and place it in our primary structure diagram.

To sum up, a question is asked, one answer is provided and shown to be false and a second answer is put forth.

PRIMARY STRUCTURE: ANTITHESIS

We have two causal points of view that answer the question of why old glass ripples: ripples are caused by the downward flow of glass, and ripples are caused by the way glass was made in days of yore.

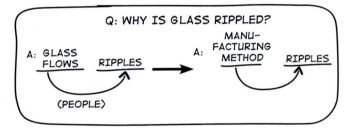

SECONDARY STRUCTURES

The passage is an extensive Question and Answer and Cause and Effect passage, with a localized Cause and Effect structure in the first paragraph, and a localized Example structure in the third paragraph. Whew! That's a lot of secondary structures.

PASSAGE OVERVIEW

MAIN POINT

The author's point of view is that the correct answer to the question of why glass ripples is the old glass manufacturing process. You'll find out soon that the answer to the question in a Question and Answer structure is the main idea. It's also the point of view our author espouses so we know it's the main point for sure.

PRIMARY PURPOSE

The author is primarily concerned with dispelling an incorrect belief and announcing the correct one.

AUTHORS ATTITUDE

Lots of attitude here. The author has a strongly negative attitude toward the Thesis point of view – "myth," "confusion" – and strongly positive attitude toward the study in the third paragraph (line 40).

QUESTION ANTICIPATION

The localized Cause and Effect and Example secondary structures will each likely get a question. The extensive Cause and Effect structure will probably get several questions.

AND NOW, ON TO THE QUESTIONS

QUESTION 21: MAIN POINT

The main point of this passage is that the real cause of ripples and thickness is the manufacturing process. Answer choice (E) says just that. Note how both the Thesis and Antithesis are mentioned and the extended Cause and Effect is invoked with the words "due" and "result."

(A) This is true as far as it goes, but there's an easy way to get rid of this. A study or experiment is almost always a premise supporting a point of view, not a point of view itself. With a present author, the main point of a passage is always a point of view.

(B) This makes up one tiny portion of the last paragraph, ignoring the important issues of flow and people's beliefs, which are also known as points of view. Remember, if the author is present, if it's not a point of view, it's not the main point.

(C) Precisely? All we know is that Zanotto calculated that it would take "many trillions of years" (lines 33-34). That doesn't sound very precise. Is that 4 trillion? 400 trillion? This is not supported by the passage.

(D) This mischaracterizes the passage. Flow is actually debunked as the cause of rippled glass and it certainly isn't "one of several factors."

QUESTION 22: INFERENCE

Here's where the extended Question and Answer structure makes an appearance! Don't worry, you'll learn more about this in a bit. For now, it's enough to know that the question was: why does older glass ripple? and the answer the author sides with is: because of old manufacturing methods. That brings us straight to (B) like a glassmaker on the trail of perfect, glass-making sand.

(A) The passage tells us what happens when the nineteenth century rolls around (lines 46-49), but we don't know about changes before then.

(C) This, like answer choice (A), is testing your ability to understand the timeline. The whole passage is about medieval glass until we get to the last paragraph about modern glass. We don't know anything about what happened before medieval times.

(D) The way to get the answer choice here is to make sure you slow down and absorb material when you find important stuff, and studies are important. Zanotto chose that glass because, if any glass were going to flow, that'd be the one. But the passage doesn't tell us if germanium oxide glass was actually used or not.

(E) Nothing in the passage about this. An indication of what caused the impurities would be a Cause and Effect structure, which we would've noted, but it's never mentioned.

QUESTION 23: AUTHORS ATTITUDE

We were all over the author's attitude about the study when it popped up, and here's the obligatory question about it. The author thinks the study "dramatically" shows that the mistaken belief in paragraph one is wrong. Like, super duper wrong. Another way to put that is answer choice (A).

(B) New research? Never saw that anywhere.

(C) We can get rid of this because the explanation referred to here is in the first paragraph which houses our localized Cause and Effect structure, but we're talking about the study in paragraph three.

(D) The views aren't reconciled. That would be a Synthesis passage. The first view (Thesis) is wrong; the second one (Antithesis) is right.

(E) While we have two answers to the question, one is favored over the other. It is definitely not the case that neither answer the question.

QUESTION 24: INFERENCE

This one's pretty tough. The passage tells us that, below a certain range of temperatures, glass "takes on the physical properties of a solid" (lines 18-19), which strongly implies that it's not a solid above that. Liquids flow, so answer choice (D) is our guy.

(A) No. The whole point of the passage is that glass really behaves like a solid, even though people think it flows.

(B) Again, this is the opposite of what the passage says. It would take trillions of years for the glass to flow noticeably.
(C) Glass is a solid below the transition temperature, not at or above.
(E) Again, again, again... this is the opposite of what the passage says. Cooled glass doesn't flow even though it's *not* crystalline.

QUESTION 25: SPECIFIC REFERENCE

This question asks us about our localized Cause and Effect structure. Hurray! What causes people to believe mistakenly that cool glass flows? The fact that it's not crystalline – or, more to the point, it's amorphous – when it's cool. That's answer choice (B).

(A) This is not the erroneous belief. Everyone knows that glass is amorphous. Duh. It's just that some people have drawn the wrong conclusion from that fact.
(C) No. They're different. That's, like, the whole point of paragraph four.
(D) All we know is what's *different* about old and modern windows. There are zero similarities discussed in the passage.
(E) This is true according to the passage (lines 13-14), but it's not the *cause* of the belief. This is where drawing out our nifty little cause and effect diagram blows an answer choice out of the water. Bye-bye answer choice (E).

QUESTION 26: PARALLEL

So many questions about our Cause and Effect structures! People believed an inherent property (amorphous structure) caused a certain effect (ripples), but it was actually the way it was made. Answer choice (B) is the same exact thing, but with pottery instead.

(A) If you noted that the belief was a cause and effect relationship, you can get rid of this because it doesn't make a claim about something causing something else.
(C) This might be tempting, because it talks about a cause and effect relationship, but it's just a belief that a cause and effect relationship exists when in fact it might not.
(D) This is a judgment about quality, and not a cause and effect relationship. It's out.
(E) This also is not a belief about what caused an observed effect. It's just a belief that something will happen if a particular event occurs.

QUESTION 27: INFERENCE

This question is a little tricky because the transition temperature of glass is discussed in the first paragraph, and yet the answer to this question is found in paragraph three. The minimum temperature that glass has to be to flow is 350 degrees (lines 39-43). Since the range is a few hundred degrees (lines 15-16), its upper end must be significantly higher than 350. That's answer choice (C).

(A) Sometimes it's just as important to know what you don't know as it is to know what you know, y'know? The only comparison between medieval glass and modern glass is in how they're manufactured. Temperature isn't addressed.
(B) There's just nothing in the passage that tells us when we figured out the transition temperature. It could be nine thousand years ago or before lunch today.
(D) It most certainly *does* affect the tendency of glass to flow. Above it, glass flows. Below it, glass doesn't flow.
(E) No, it's a range. That's different than a specific temperature.

Did you know Scotland's national animal is the unicorn? Second only to Wales', which is the supremely awesome dragon.

17/EXAMPLE

HERE'S AN EXAMPLE

We discuss Example secondary structures here because, while they are not quite as prevalent in Reading Comprehension as Cause and Effect secondary structures, they still show up quite a bit (9.46% of all Reading Comprehension passages have an Example secondary structure). Also, as with cause and effect, Example secondary structures show up regularly in the Logical Reasoning sections of the LSAT, and they have the same function there as they do in Reading Comprehension. So pay close attention, and you will be richly rewarded.

WHAT ARE EXAMPLES

An example is an instance that serves to illustrate. A brush is an example of a hair care product. Oatmeal is an example of breakfast food. The Kardashians are an example of the gluttonous appetite of the American media machine to monetize worthless celebrity idols. You get the idea.

WHY EXAMPLES ARE IMPORTANT IN READING COMPREHENSION

In Reading Comprehension, examples are particularly noteworthy because they provide support for conclusions. A specific example thus becomes a premise for a general statement. Take the following example:

> The coffee craze in this country has really gotten out of control. *For example*, in my neighborhood, they just opened a Starbucks™ inside a Starbucks™ next to a Starbucks™!

The grumpy coffee hater here has an opinion. His opinion (and the conclusion of the argument) is that the coffee craze is out of control. To support that statement, he gives a specific, real world example: a bunch of coffee shops right on top of one another in his neighborhood.

By identifying the example in the above argument, you've also identified the support for the main idea, or conclusion.

Even if the example you identify isn't the support for the main idea of the passage, there's often a specific question asked about the example, so it still provides a payoff in terms of points earned on the test.

Moreover, examples proliferate in Logical Reasoning. Among others, Flaw questions will ask you to identify whether or not an example properly supports a conclusion, Parallel questions will ask you to replicate arguments that draw upon examples for premises, and Role questions will ask you to describe how an example fits into an argument.

IDENTIFYING EXAMPLE STRUCTURES

There are many ways the makers of the LSAT will indicate that an example is coming your way. The key words and phrases below should tip you off that you're dealing with an Example secondary structure.

Key Words

"…for example…"
"…in one instance…"
"…as shown by…"
"…demonstrates…"
"…such as…"
"…e.g.,…"

BP Minotaur: Be aware that a particular passage may contain an Example secondary structure using other key words and phrases, or even none at all. So you should be actively on the lookout for examples. If there is a general statement and then a real world situation that conforms to that statement, you have an example.

<u>Flaw questions</u>
- Identify wheather or not an example properly supports a conclusion

<u>Parallel questions</u>
- replicate arguments that draw upon examples for premises

<u>Role questions</u>
- describe how an example fits into an argument

> • Examples give you the premise so if you ask yourself what the example is providing support for you'll have your main points

WHAT IT LOOKS LIKE IN READING COMPREHENSION

Let's see what examples look like on the exam. The following are excerpts from real Reading Comprehension passages that demonstrate examples.

> …the clay tablets that contain the laws of ancient Mesopotamia, *for example*, are still displayed in museums around the world…

> "…while the quickest way to restore heavily fertilized land is to remove and replace the topsoil, this is impractical on a large scale *such as* the European effort…

> …scientists like to think that what mirrors do should be explainable without reference to what the observer does (*e.g.*, rotating a field of sight)…

Cleetus: What does e.g. mean?

Good question, Cleetus. E.g. is Latin for "exempli gratia" and means "for example." So any time you see it on the LSAT, you know you're dealing with an example.

EXTENSIVE EXAMPLE SECONDARY STRUCTURES

If a single example provides support for the primary conclusion of the passage, you have an extensive Example secondary structure. You can also often locate an extensive Example secondary structure by the amount of real estate it takes up: an example that spans more than one paragraph is almost certainly extensive.

If you're having trouble spotting the Main Point of the passage, extensive Example secondary structures can point you in the right direction. Just ask yourself what the example is providing support for, and you'll have the main idea of the passage.

Because an extensive Example is providing support for the Main Point of the passage, the primary structure diagram should include both the example and the main idea.

Take a look at this real, live, honest-to-goodness LSAT passage, the associated primary structure diagram, and the Main Point question. We'll talk about it after you're done.

206 / CHAPTER 17

Personal names are generally regarded by European thinkers in two major ways, both of which deny that names have any significant semantic content. In philosophy and linguistics, John Stuart
(5) Mill's formulation that "proper names are meaningless marks set upon...persons to distinguish them from one another" retains currency; in anthropology, Claude Lévi-Strauss's characterization of names as being primarily instruments of social classification has
(10) been very influential. Consequently, interpretation of personal names in societies where names have other functions and meanings has been neglected. Among the Hopi of the southwestern United States, names often refer to historical or ritual events in order both
(15) to place individuals within society and to confer an identity upon them. Furthermore, the images used to evoke these events suggest that Hopi names can be seen as a type of poetic composition.

Throughout life, Hopis receive several names in
(20) a sequence of ritual initiations. Birth, entry into one of the ritual societies during childhood, and puberty are among the name-giving occasions. Names are conferred by an adult member of a clan other than the child's clan, and names refer to that name giver's clan,
(25) sometimes combining characteristics of the clan's totem animal with the child's characteristics. Thus, a name might translate to something as simple as "little rabbit," which reflects both the child's size and the representative animal.
(30) More often, though, the name giver has in mind a specific event that is not apparent in a name's literal translation. One Lizard clan member from the village of Oraibi is named Lomayayva, "beautifully ascended." This translation, however, tells nothing
(35) about either the event referred to—who or what ascended—or the name giver's clan. The name giver in this case is from Badger clan. Badger clan is responsible for an annual ceremony featuring a procession in which masked representations of spirits
(40) climb the mesa on which Oraibi sits. Combining the name giver's clan association with the receiver's home village, "beautifully ascended" refers to the splendid colors and movements of the procession up the mesa. The condensed image this name evokes—a
(45) typical feature of Hopi personal names—displays the same quality of Western Apache place names that led one commentator to call them "tiny imagist poems."

Hopi personal names do several things simultaneously. They indicate social relationships—
(50) but only i[ndirectly]... Equally i[mportant,] in a sense produce a[n identity.] is thus op[posed...]
(55) names are [...] Lévi-Strau[ss's...] Interprete[rs must understand Hopi clan structures and] linguistic practices in order to discern the beauty and significance of Hopi names.

This view of Hopi names is thus opposed not only to Mill's claim that personal names are without inherent meaning but also to Lévi-Strauss's purely functional characterization. Interpreters must understand Hopi clan structures and linguistic practices in order to discern the beauty and significance of Hopi names.

8. Which one of the following statements most accurately summarizes the passage's main point?

(A) Unlike European names, which are used exclusively for identification or exclusively for social classification, Hopi names perform both these functions simultaneously.
(B) Unlike European names, Hopi names tend to neglect the functions of identification and social classification in favor of a concentration on compression and poetic effects.
(C) Lacking knowledge of the intricacies of Hopi linguistic and tribal structures, European thinkers have so far been unable to discern the deeper significance of Hopi names.
(D) Although some Hopi names may seem difficult to interpret, they all conform to a formula whereby a reference to the name giver's clan is combined with a reference to the person named.
(E) While performing the functions ascribed to names by European thinkers, Hopi names also possess a significant aesthetic quality that these thinkers have not adequately recognized.

December 1998 Passage 2

Here the Main Point of the passage is the conclusion that names can do more than just distinguish people from one another and place them in a particular social class. The Hopi tribe functions as an extended example *supporting* that conclusion. Although the example itself is not the Main Point of the passage, it provides the bulk of the support for the Main Point, and that's why it is both represented in the primary structure diagram as well as the language of the correct answer to the Main Point question.

What do I do when I find an extensive Example secondary structure?

Any time you see an example in the passage, tag it with "Ex." It is of great importance that you identify the general statement for which the example is offered as support. The statement supported by the example may come before or after the example, so think critically. To determine whether the structure is extensive or localized, you may need to read on for a bit before making that determination. Let's say a passage begins like this:

> As everyone knows, modern bestselling books are garbage. For example, *Fifty Shades of Grey* spent nearly a year at the top of the New York Times Bestseller List.

You would tag the second sentence with an: "Ex:" If the rest of the passage focuses on just how bad *Fifty Shades of Grey* is, you have an extensive Example secondary structure. While the example is not the Main Point of the passage, your primary structure diagram will still include it, noting that it provides extensive support for the Main Point of the passage:

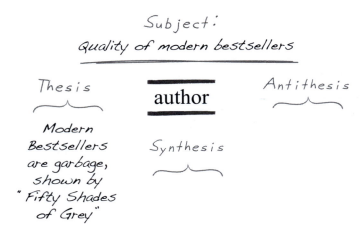

How does this help me answer questions?

The primary structure diagram is a roadmap to answering Main Point and Primary Purpose questions. Given the example above, the right answer to the Main Point question would look something like, "As exemplified by *Fifty Shades of Grey*, modern bestsellers are garbage."

The Primary Purpose question asks why the author expended the energy to write the passage in the first place. With a present author, the Primary Purpose of the passage is to argue for the author's conclusion. Here, the answer to the Primary Purpose question would look something like, "To show that modern bestsellers, like *Fifty Shades of Grey*, are garbage." Our apologies to all of the *Fifty Shades of Grey* lovers out there. It's only an example, not a reflection of our real feelings toward *Twilight* fans writing racy knock-offs and peddling them to the mass market like snake oil in the 1800's.

It is quite possible that other questions about the example will crop up as well. Here, the author feels very strongly about the subject matter. The author might complain about the stilted dialogue or the wooden characters or the hackneyed plot of the book, and the answer to a question about the Author's Attitude on the book might look something like, "Convinced that it is lacking in literary merit."

LOCALIZED EXAMPLE SECONDARY STRUCTURES

If an example shows up in a single paragraph, taking up only a sentence or two, it is a localized secondary structure. Tag it with an "Ex.," and find the statement for which it provides support. Remember, the statement for which the example provides support may come before or after the example. It may also be in a different part of the passage altogether. Take a look at the following passage:

Until recently, biologists were unable to
explain the fact that pathogens—[disease-causing
parasites]— have evolved to incapacitate, and
often overwhelm, their hosts. Such behavior is
(5) at odds with the prevailing view of host-parasite
relations—that, in general, host and parasite
ultimately develop a benign coexistence. This
view is based on the idea that parasites that do not
harm their hosts have the best chance for long-term
(10) survival: they thrive because their hosts thrive. Some
biologists, however, recently have suggested that if
a pathogen reproduced so extensively as to cause its
host to become gravely sick, it could still achieve
evolutionary success if its replication led to a level
(15) of transmission into new hosts that exceeded the loss
of pathogens resulting from the host's incapacitation.
This scenario suggests that even death-causing
pathogens can achieve evolutionary success.

One implication of this perspective is that a
(20) pathogen's virulence—[its capacity to overcome a
host's defenses and incapacitate it]—is a function of
its mode of transmission. For example, rhinoviruses,
which cause the common cold, require physical
proximity for transmission to occur. If a rhinovirus
(25) reproduces so extensively in a solitary host that
the host is too unwell to leave home for a day, the
thousands of new rhinoviruses produced that day
will die before they can be transmitted. So, because
it is transmitted directly, the common cold is
(30) unlikely to disable its victims.

The opposite can occur when pathogens are
transported by a vector—[an organism that can carry
and transmit an infectious agent.] If, for example, a
pathogen capable of being transported by a mosquito
(35) reproduces so extensively that its human host is
immobilized, it can still pass along its genes if a
mosquito bites the host and transmits this dose to
the next human it bites. In such circumstances the
virulence is likely to be more severe, because the
(40) pathogen has reproduced to such concentrations in
the host [...]

While medical literature generally supports the
hypothesis that vector-borne pathogens tend to be
more virulent than directly transmitted pathogens—
witness the lethal nature of malaria, yellow fever,
typhus, and sleeping sickness, all carried by biting
insects—a few directly transmitted pathogens such
as diphtheria and tuberculosis bacteria can be just as
lethal. Scientists call these "sit and wait" pathogens,
because they are able to remain alive outside
their hosts until a new host comes along, without
relying on a vector. Indeed, the endurance of these
pathogens, many of which can survive externally
for weeks or months before transmission into a
new host—compared, for instance, to an average
rhinovirus life span of hours—makes them among
the most dangerous of all pathogens.

DEF.

PREVAILING VIEW

NEW VIEW

DEF.
EX. TRANSMISSION

A. PROXIMITY
(LESS SEVERE)

DEF.
EX.

B. VECTOR
(MORE SEVERE)

EX.

EXCEPTIONS

22. The examples of diphtheria and tuberculosis bacteria
provide the most support for which one of the following
conclusions about the dangerousness of pathogens?

(A) The most dangerous pathogens are those with the
shortest life spans outside a host.
(B) Those pathogens with the greatest endurance outside
a host are among the most dangerous.
(C) Those pathogens transported by vectors are always
the most dangerous.
(D) The least dangerous pathogens are among those with
the longest life spans outside a host.
(E) Those pathogens transmitted directly are always
least dangerous.

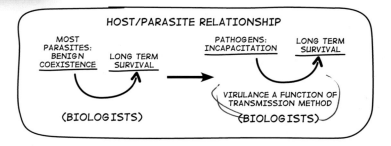

HOST/PARASITE RELATIONSHIP

MOST PARASITES: BENIGN COEXISTENCE → LONG TERM SURVIVAL (BIOLOGISTS)

PATHOGENS: INCAPACITATION → LONG TERM SURVIVAL
VIRULANCE A FUNCTION OF TRANSMISSION METHOD (BIOLOGISTS)

October 2005 Passage 4

The passage is dedicated to explaining how pathogens succeed in reproducing even though they kill their hosts. There are several examples, but Question 22 focuses specifically on one in the final paragraph. The passage distinguishes between pathogens that are transmitted directly and those transmitted by a vector, the latter generally being more deadly. The examples given—diphtheria and tuberculosis—support the idea that there are exceptions. In other words, those pathogens are directly transmitted, but they are quite deadly because they can survive outside the body for long periods of time.

Ditz: I don't like the science passages because of all the scientific terminology.

That's a common sentiment, Ditz. But remember, the passage will either define the word explicitly (as it does with "pathogens" in the first paragraph) or define it through context clues. Either way, it will have the information you need. Trust this: read carefully to pick up the definitions, and you'll be fine. This does not, however, get you out of looking up unfamiliar words now! While scientific terminology will be defined in passaged if necessary, the LSAT assumes a fairly robust vocabulary for all the passages. In the words of a famous 90s rapper: look your words up, yo.

What do I do when I find a Localized Example secondary structure?

You must tag the example, as well as identify the statement for which it provides support. Before getting to the questions, you must understand for what the example is providing support. In the passage above, the example supports the idea that there are exceptions to the general rule that vector-borne pathogens are more dangerous than directly transmitted pathogens.

How does this help me answer questions?

It's often the case that a localized Example secondary structure will correlate to a question. If you make sure that you know what the example is supporting, it's likely you won't need to go back to the passage to answer the question. Even if you do need to go back to the passage, the fact that the example is tagged will save you time in finding it and answering the question correctly.

A GOOD EXAMPLE OF AN EXTENSIVE EXAMPLE SECONDARY STRUCTURE

The following passage is yours to conquer. It contains an extensive Example secondary structure. Mark up the passage, and fill in your primary structure diagram on your way. There is a full explanation at the end of the chapter.

Advances in scientific understanding often do not build directly or smoothly in response to the data that are amassed, and in retrospect, after a major revision of theory, it may seem strange that a crucial hypothesis
(5) was long overlooked. A case in point is the discovery of a means by which the nuclei of atoms can be split. Between 1934, when a group of Italian physicists including Enrico Fermi first bombarded uranium with neutrons, and 1939, when exiled Austrian physicist
(10) Lise Meitner provided the crucial theoretical connection, scientists compiled increasing evidence that nuclear fission had been achieved, without, however, recognizing what they were witnessing.

Earlier, even before the neutron and proton
(15) composition of atomic nuclei had been experimentally demonstrated, some theoretical physicists had produced calculations indicating that in principle it should be possible to break atoms apart. But the neutron-bombardment experiments were not aimed
(20) at achieving such a result, and researchers were not even receptive to the possibility that it might happen in that context. A common view was that a neutron's breaking apart a uranium nucleus would be analogous to a pebble, thrown through a window, causing a house
(25) to collapse.

In Berlin, Meitner pursued research related to that of the Italians, discovering a puzzling group of radioactive substances produced by neutron bombardment of uranium. Fermi and others achieved
(30) numerous similar results. These products remained unidentified partly because precise chemical analyses were hampered by the minute quantities of the substances produced and the dangers of working with highly radioactive materials, but more significantly
(35) because of the expectation that they would all be elements close to uranium in nuclear composition. In 1938 Meitner escaped from Nazi Germany and undertook related research in Sweden, but her research partner Otto Hahn kept her informed of his continuing
(40) experimentation. Late in that year he wrote to her of a surprising result: one of the substances resulting from the neutron bombardment of uranium had been conclusively identified as barium, an element whose structure would have made it impossible to produce
(45) through any mechanism he envisaged as being involved in the experiments. Hahn even remarked that, despite the clear chemical evidence of what had occurred, it went "against all previous experiences of nuclear physics," but he also noted that together the
(50) number of protons and neutrons in the nuclei of barium and technetium, the accompanying product of the experiment, added up to the number of such particles that compose a uranium nucleus.

It was Meitner who finally recognized the
(55) significance of the data in relation to underlying theoretical considerations: the researchers had actually been splitting uranium atoms. Coining the term "nuclear fission," she quickly submitted her conclusion for publication in a paper coauthored with physicist
(60) Otto Frisch. When scientists in Europe and North America rushed to corroborate the findings, it became clear that the relevant evidence had been present for some time, lacking mainly the right conceptual link.

23. The author's primary aim in the passage is to

(A) criticize a traditional view of scientific progress and advocate a replacement
(B) illustrate the often erratic way in which a scientific community achieves progress
(C) judge the relative importance of theory and experimentation in science
(D) take issue with the idea that scientists make slow, steady progress
(E) display the way in which intellectual arrogance sometimes hinders scientific progress

24. The most likely reason that the theoretical physicists in line 16 would have been pleased about Meitner's insight regarding the neutron bombardment experiments is that her insight

(A) was dependent upon the calculations that they had produced
(B) paved the way for work in theoretical physics to become more acceptable abroad
(C) proved that the nuclei of atoms were generally unstable
(D) confirmed their earlier work indicating that atoms could be split
(E) came after years of analyzing the data from experiments conducted between 1934 and 1938

25. Which one of the following is most nearly equivalent to what the author means by "the relevant evidence" (line 62)?

(A) the results of experiments in neutron bombardment of uranium conducted by the physics community between 1934 and 1939
(B) the results of related experiments in neutron bombardment of uranium conducted by Meitner in 1938
(C) the clear chemical evidence that Hahn had found of barium's being produced by neutron bombardment of uranium
(D) the fact that the sum of the number of protons and neutrons in the nuclei of barium and technetium was the same as the number of these particles in a uranium nucleus
(E) the fact that radioactive products of neutron bombardment of uranium went unidentified for so long

June 2012 Passage 4

26. Given the information in the passage, which one of the following, if true, would have been most likely to reduce the amount of time it took for physicists to realize that atoms were being split?

(A) The physicists conducting the experiments in neutron bombardment of uranium were all using the same research techniques.
(B) The physicists conducting the experiments in neutron bombardment of uranium did not have particular expectations regarding the likely nuclear composition of the by-products.
(C) The physicists conducting the experiments in neutron bombardment of uranium had not been aware of the calculations indicating that in principle it was possible to split atoms.
(D) More physicists concentrated on obtaining experimental results from the neutron bombardment of uranium.
(E) Physicists conducted experiments in the neutron bombardment of some substance other than uranium.

27. According to the passage, which one of the following was true of the physics community during the 1930s?

(A) It neglected earlier theoretical developments.
(B) It reevaluated calculations indicating that atoms could be split.
(C) It never identified the by-products of neutron bombardment of uranium.
(D) It showed that uranium atoms were the easiest to split.
(E) It recognized the dangers of working with radioactive substances.

Advances in scientific understanding often do not build directly or smoothly in response to the data that are amassed, and in retrospect, after a major revision of theory, it may seem strange that a crucial hypothesis (5) was long overlooked. A case in point is the discovery of a means by which the nuclei of atoms can be split. Between 1934, when a group of Italian physicists including Enrico Fermi first bombarded uranium with neutrons, and 1939, when exiled Austrian physicist (10) Lise Meitner provided the crucial theoretical connection, scientists compiled increasing evidence that nuclear fission had been achieved, without, however, recognizing what they were witnessing.

Earlier, even before the neutron and proton (15) composition of atomic nuclei had been experimentally demonstrated, some theoretical physicists had produced calculations indicating that in principle it should be possible to break atoms apart. But the neutron-bombardment experiments were not aimed (20) at achieving such a result, and researchers were not even receptive to the possibility that it might happen in that context. A common view was that a neutron's breaking apart a uranium nucleus would be analogous to a pebble, thrown through a window, causing a house (25) to collapse.

In Berlin, Meitner pursued research related to that of the Italians, discovering a puzzling group of radioactive substances produced by neutron bombardment of uranium. Fermi and others achieved (30) numerous similar results. These products remained unidentified partly because precise chemical analyses were hampered by the minute quantities of the substances produced and the dangers of working with highly radioactive materials, but more significantly (35) because of the expectation that they would all be elements close to uranium in nuclear composition. In 1938 Meitner escaped from Nazi Germany and undertook related research in Sweden, but her research partner Otto Hahn kept her informed of his continuing (40) experimentation. Late in that year he wrote to her of a surprising result: one of the substances resulting from the neutron bombardment of uranium had been conclusively identified as barium, an element whose structure would have made it impossible to produce (45) through any mechanism he envisaged as being involved in the experiments. Hahn even remarked that, despite the clear chemical evidence of what had occurred, it went "against all previous experiences of nuclear physics," but he also noted that together the (50) number of protons and neutrons in the nuclei of barium and technetium, the accompanying product of the experiment, added up to the number of such particles that compose a uranium nucleus.

It was Meitner who finally recognized the (55) significance of the data in relation to underlying theoretical considerations: the researchers had actually been splitting uranium atoms. Coining the term "nuclear fission," she quickly submitted her conclusion for publication in a paper coauthored with physicist (60) Otto Frisch. When scientists in Europe and North America rushed to corroborate the findings, it became clear that the relevant evidence had been present for some time, lacking mainly the right conceptual link.

AUTHOR'S CONCLUSION

EX.

EARLY RESEARCH

PRE-MEITNER VIEW

RESEARCH

REASONS FOR FAILURE TO IDENTIFY SUBSTANCES

RESULTS OF HAHN'S EXPERIMENTS

MEITNER EXPLAINS RESULTS WITH A NEW HYPOTHESIS

SCIENTIFIC PROGRESS

SOMETIMES YOU DON'T RECOGNIZE WHAT YOU'RE SEEING AS SHOWN BY FISSION

PASSAGE SUMMARY

What a bunch of dopes! Anyone with half a brain should know that barium and technetium are the products of uranium atom fission. Duh.

The linchpin of paragraph one is the phrase "[a] case in point" (line 5), which is just another way of saying "for example." Examples support conclusions, so when you see an example, figure out what it's there to support. This example illustrates the passage's first sentence, which more or less says that sometimes you don't understand what you're looking at the first time you see it. In other words, the evidence for something might sit around for a while before anyone realizes what it really means. In this particular instance, no one realized that atoms were being split (that's the definition of "fission," by the way) until five years after the initial experiments, when Meitner figured it out.

Paragraph two continues discussing the example, supplying background about the state of affairs when the experiments began in 1934. In principle, some physicists thought that it would be possible to break atoms apart. But the experiments we're talking about weren't intended to split atoms, and no one thought it would be possible to split atoms that way. It would be like knocking down a house with a pebble, or in other words, pretty darn unlikely. This is another point of view, but we don't know if it's going to be developed, so let's hold off on putting it into the diagram.

By the time we get to the third paragraph, it's pretty apparent that the focus of the passage is the example in paragraph one. This indicates that the conclusion in paragraph one is the Thesis position supported by an extensive example. Let's put that in our diagram. We also know the view introduced at the end of the second paragraph isn't developed, so unless another one is introduced, this is going to be a Thesis passage.

The example continues in detail in paragraphs three and four. At first, it was impossible to determine the products of the neutron bombardment experiment because there was so little to work with, the stuff was dangerous, and the expectation that the product would look like uranium (lines 30-36). Then the products were identified as barium and technetium, but nobody realized the significance (lines 40-54).

Finally, Meitner figured out what those products meant. Barium and technetium were there because the Uranium atom had been split into two. Nice work, Meitner!

In summary, a conclusion is offered and supported by an example.

PRIMARY STRUCTURE: THESIS

The passage begins with a conclusion—sometimes you don't know what you're seeing the first time you see it—that's supported by the example that takes up the rest of the passage. Although the example contains various ideas about nuclear physics, they're all there to illustrate that initial conclusion. So this is a Thesis passage, and since the conclusion comes straight from the author, we have a present author.

SCIENTIFIC PROGRESS

SOMETIMES YOU DON'T RECOGNIZE WHAT YOU'RE SEEING AS SHOWN BY FISSION ←

SECONDARY STRUCTURES

The whole passage is one big ol' extensive Example structure.

PASSAGE OVERVIEW

MAIN POINT

Whenever there's an extensive Example structure, the main point is whatever the example is there to illustrate. In this passage, the example illustrates the claim in the very first sentence, which is that sometimes you don't know what you're seeing when you first see it. That's the main point.

PRIMARY PURPOSE

The author wrote the passage in order to provide an example showing that scientific progress is sometimes neither direct nor smooth.

AUTHORS ATTITUDE

The author doesn't express strong attitudes (the familiar scholarly neutral attitude) in the passage, but she does endorse the main point of the passage.

QUESTION ANTICIPATION

Expect several questions on the extensive Example structure. There is also a good chance that there will be questions on the details of the experiments described in the passage as well as the previously held point of view identified in paragraph two.

AND NOW, ON TO THE QUESTIONS...

QUESTION 23: PRIMARY PURPOSE

It's not a Main Point question, but we should still be happy with a straightforward primary purpose. As we anticipated, the passage uses an example to illustrate how scientific progress isn't necessarily direct or smooth. The right answer is (B). Note that the word "illustrate" is just another way of saying "describe with an example." When there's an extensive Example structure, expect it to be reflected in the primary purpose.

(A) The only other view in the passage is the pre-Meitner view which isn't about scientific progress; it's about an experiment. Moreover, the author doesn't criticize it. This is wrong in at least two ways.
(C) Both theory and experimentation are discussed in detail in the passage, but the author never ventures an opinion on whether one is more important than the other.
(D) This answer choice has the same problem as choice (A). It's trying to get you to infer that the scientist is arguing with a traditional view of scientific progress, but that's just not the case.
(E) Arrogance? If anything, everyone in the passage is confused until the end. This answer choice mischaracterizes the passage.

QUESTION 24: VIEWPOINT

This question asks us about the scientists in paragraph two, who believed that atoms could be split. Meitner confirmed from later experimental data that atoms could indeed be split (lines 54-57). It's reasonable to infer that these scientists would be happy to know they were right, and that's answer choice (D).

(A) Meitner's insight relied on the experiments by Fermi and others (lines 26-30), but there's just no support for the idea that Meitner used the theoretical physicists' calculations or even knew about them.

(B) This answer choice is very broad. There's no indication in the passage that theoretical physics was not widely acceptable before Meitner came along (even though we Americans do enjoy beating up a science nerd or two every once in a while).

(C) This answer is also very broad. We know something about a few atoms (uranium, barium, technetium), but we have no idea whether atoms in general are unstable.

(E) There's actually no indication that it took Meitner years to come up with her hypothesis, and who would be pleased with the fact that it took years of analysis? That's like being pleased that the Novocain didn't work when you had a root canal. Just to be clear, the scientists we are talking about in this question did not conduct the experiments that Meitner studied.

QUESTION 25: SPECIFIC REFERENCE

The "relevant evidence" that had been sitting around "for some time" (line 63) is the evidence of nuclear fission. That came from the neutron bombardment experiments performed by Fermi and others. Answer choice (A) is right on the money since it mentions the results of those experiments. This question just asks you to connect the dots between two parts of the extensive Example structure.

(B) Wrong. Meitner did research on radioactive substances (lines 26-29), but there's no indication anywhere that she actually performed experiments.

(C) This answer choice can be dismissed because Hahn's discovery had not "been present for some time" (lines 62-63); it came right before Meitner's big breakthrough. Also, at the beginning of the paragraph, the author identifies Meitner's big insight: "the researchers had actually been splitting uranium atoms." This refers to Fermi and others, not just Hahn.

(D) This information was already known before the experiments, and it was not a result of the experiments. It was merely information that helped sort out the results of the experiments.

(E) The fact that something was unidentified is not relevant evidence for anything, because it is a lack of information. This is very, very wrong.

QUESTION 26: INFERENCE

This question asks for something that would have made it easier for the scientists to recognize that they were actually splitting uranium atoms in their experiments. The relevant part of the passage is in the third paragraph, which we tagged "reasons for failure to identify substances." The main reason they didn't correctly identify the results of the bombardment is that they expected the products to be elements similar to uranium (lines 34-36). If they didn't have that preconceived notion, they might have figured things out sooner. That's answer choice (B).

(A) It's hard to see how a bunch of scientists using the same research techniques would speed anything up.

(C) It's not clear how a lack of awareness that splitting the atom was possible would speed things up. If anything, knowing that would seem to make things move faster and ignorance of that information would slow things down. Wrong.

(D) The problem was not obtaining experimental results (there was plenty of this), but in interpreting their significance. Not our guy.

(E) There's no way to know what experiments on other elements would have revealed, if anything.

QUESTION 27: SPECIFIC REFERENCE

This question is unusually unhelpful for a specific reference question. The third paragraph is the place to look for information about the physics community, but the answer could be just about anything the paragraph states about that community. Choice (E) is correct, since we know that the "dangers of working with highly radioactive materials" (lines 33-34) "hampered" (line 32) their research.

(A) Though there was previous theoretical work showing that atoms could be split, there's no indication that these scientists ignored their work. They just didn't think their particular experiments would split any atoms.
(B) These calculations ended up being accurate, so there's no reason to believe that they were reevaluated at any time.
(C) Wrong. The by-products were identified in 1938 (lines 40-53), which by our calculations is still in the 1930s.
(D) Uranium could be split, as demonstrated by experiments dealing only with uranium. There is no basis to make this comparison with other elements. Maybe you can split oxygen just by squeezing it really hard between your thumb and forefinger. Go ahead, give it a try!

Nice work! Hopefully you found tagging and marking up this passage to be slightly easier than achieving nuclear fission...

18/QUESTIONandANSWER

EVERY QUESTION DESERVES AN ANSWER

As everyone knows, there are no stupid questions...

Touché, Cleetus. At any rate, the Question and Answer secondary structure is less prevalent than Cause and Effect, but comes in just as prevalent as Example, with 9.46% of passages containing a Question and Answer secondary structure.* Moreover, this structure is LSAT gold. This is because Question and Answer structures provide the easiest way to find main ideas in all of Reading Comprehension. Yep. More on this in a minute.

WHAT IS QUESTION AND ANSWER

How long do you plan on studying for the LSAT? Where are you going to law school? Why is Nicolas Cage still making movies? Just like it sounds, the Question and Answer secondary structure revolves around a question posed and answered. We symbolize the Question and Answer relationship by placing a "Q:" followed by the question. Underneath it is the answer introduced by "A:" and followed by the answer to the question. So if we were to ask why you're reading this book and the answer is that it will help your performance on the LSAT, we would symbolize it in the following manner:

    Q: WHY READ BOOK?
    A: BETTER PERFORMANCE.

---

* It's kind of crazy that over the course of over 100 Reading Comprehension passages, there are the exact same percentage of these two secondary structures. Weird.

WHAT IT LOOKS LIKE IN READING COMPREHENSION

Let's take a look at a few examples of what Question and Answer structures look like on real LSATs.

> …is 'loot' acquired in a game taxable, as a prize or award is?…

> …improvements in the general understanding of these mechanisms have turned some biologists' attention to the question of *why* kin recognition occurs at all…

> …law enforcement agencies can effectively nullify particular laws, or particular applications of law, simply by declining to prosecute violators. This power appears to be exercised frequently and I attempt here to explain *why*…

EXTENSIVE QUESTION AND ANSWER SECONDARY STRUCTURES

When a Reading Comprehension passage is primarily devoted to answering a question, you have an extensive Question and Answer secondary structure. Remember that Question and Answer structures are *conclusions*, and the answer part of an extensive Question and Answer secondary structure is the Main Point of the passage. Check out the following passage, associated markup, and Main Point question. We'll discuss it afterward.

- Question and answer structures are <u>conclusions</u> and the answer part is the <u>main</u> point of the passage!

Many literary scholars believe that Zora Neale Hurston's *Their Eyes Were Watching God* (1937) has been the primary influence on some of the most accomplished Black women writing in the United States
(5) today. Indeed, Alice Walker, the author of the prize winning novel *The Color Purple*, has said of *Their Eyes*, "There is no book more important to me than this one." Thus, it seems necessary to ask why *Their Eyes*, a work now viewed by a multitude of readers as remarkably
(10) successful in its complex depiction of a Black woman's search for self and community, was ever relegated to the margins of the literary canon.

The details of the novel's initial reception help answer this question. Unlike the recently rediscovered
(15) and reexamined work of Harriet Wilson, *Their Eyes* was not totally ignored by book reviewers upon its publication. In fact, it received a mixture of positive and negative reviews both from White book reviewers working for prominent periodicals and from important
(20) figures within Black literary circles. In the *Saturday Review of Literature*, George Stevens wrote that "the narration is exactly right, because most of it is dialogue and the dialogue gives us a constant sense of character in action." The negative criticism was partially a
(25) result of Hurston's ideological differences with other members of the Black literary community about the depiction of Black Americans in literature. Black writers of the 1940s believed that the Black artist's primary responsibility was to create protest fiction that explored
(30) the negative effects of racism in the United States. For example, Richard Wright, the author of the much acclaimed *Native Son* (1940), wrote that *Their Eyes* had "no theme" and "no message." Most critics' and readers' expectations of Black literature rendered them unable to
(35) appreciate Hurston's subtle delineation of the life of an ordinary Black woman.

Recent acclaim for *Their Eyes* results from the emergence of feminist literary criticism and the development of standards of evaluation specific to
(40) the work of Black writers; these kinds of criticism changed readers' expectations of art and enabled them to appreciate Hurston's novel. The emergence of feminist literary criticism was crucial because such criticism brought new attention to neglected works such as
(45) Hurston's and alerted readers to Hurston's exploration of women's issues in her fiction. The Afrocentric standards of evaluation were equally important to the rediscovery of *Their Eyes*, for such standards provided readers with the tools to recognize and appreciate the Black folklore
(50) and oral storytelling traditions Hurston incorporated within her work. In one of the most illuminating discussions of the novel to date, Henry Louis Gates, states that "Hurston's strategy seems to concern itself
(55) with the possibilities of representation of the speaking Black voice in writing."

3. Which one of the following best states the main idea of the passage?

(A) Hurston's *Their Eyes Were Watching God* had little in common with novels written by Black authors during the 1940s.
(B) Feminist critics and authors such as Alice Walker were instrumental in establishing Hurston's *Their Eyes Were Watching God* as an important part of the American literary canon.
(C) Critics and readers were unable to appreciate fully Hurston's *Their Eyes Were Watching God* until critics applied new standards of evaluation to the novel.
(D) Hurston's *Their Eyes Were Watching God* was an important influence on the protest fiction written by Black writers in the mid twentieth century.
(E) Afrocentric strategies of analysis have brought attention to the use of oral storytelling traditions in novels written by Black Americans, such as Hurston's *Their Eyes Were Watching God*.

December 1995 Passage 1

The passage above asks why *Their Eyes Were Watching God* was not recognized as an important work when it was published, given that it is recognized as such now. The rest of the passage is devoted to answering that question, first waffling between its good and bad reception, then settling on the ultimate answer in the final paragraph, where the author states that it was necessary to develop feminist and Afrocentric models of criticism to appropriately analyze the book. The primary structure diagram shows that this is the author's Main Point.

What do I do when I find an Extensive Question and Answer secondary structure?

Be on the lookout for questions (either explicit or implied) as you read a passage, and, just as importantly, be sure you have located *all* proposed answers to the question. There could quite possibly be more than one (as we just saw).

If a passage poses a question to which all or the majority of the passage is devoted to answering, then you're dealing with an Extensive Question and Answer secondary structure. As shown below, the question will be the subject of the passage, and the answer(s) will comprise the point(s) of view in the passage.

Imagine a passage that poses a question in the first paragraph such as, "What is the meaning of life?" One set of theologians might answer, "The meaning of life is to contribute productively to society." The author might disagree, and instead say, "The meaning of life is to eat pizza and play video games." In such a case, your primary structure diagram should read thusly:

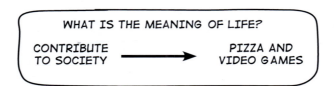

How does this help me answer questions?

By now you know that the Primary Structure diagram will reveal the right answer to the Main Point and Primary Purpose questions. Here, the right answer to the Main Point question would look something like, "Although some theologians believe that the meaning of life is to contribute productively to society, it is actually to eat pizza and play video games."

The Primary Purpose answer choice would say something like, "Dispute a particular theory about the meaning of life and present an alternative to it."

As always, be on the lookout for other questions that draw upon the extensive Question and Answer secondary structure. If, for instance, the author treats the theologians' point of view with disdain, you might get an Author's Attitude question on that particular answer to the question.

LOCALIZED QUESTION AND ANSWER SECONDARY STRUCTURES

If there is a question in the passage that gets answered in a sentence or two, you have a localized Question and Answer secondary structure. Tag it with a "Q:" and an "A:," but understand that it will not be part of your primary structure diagram although there is likely to be a question about it. Check out the following passage.

The paintings of Romare Bearden (1914-1988) represent a double triumph. At the same time that Bearden's work reflects a lifelong commitment to perfecting the innovative painting techniques he
(5) pioneered, it also reveals an artist engaged in a search for ways to explore the varieties of African-American experience.
By presenting scene, character, and atmosphere using a unique layered and fragmented style that
(10) combines elements of painting with elements of collage, Bearden suggested some of the ways in which commonplace subjects could be forced to undergo a metamorphosis when filtered through the techniques available to the resourceful artist. Bearden knew that
(15) regardless of individual painters' personal histories, tastes, or points of view, they must pay their craft the respect of approaching it through an acute awareness of the resources and limitations of the form to which they have dedicated their creative energies.
(20) But how did Bearden, so passionately dedicated to solving the more advanced problems of his painting technique, also succeed so well at portraying the realities of African-American life? During the Great Depression of the 1930's, Bearden painted scenes of
(25) the hardships of the period; the work was powerful, the scenes grim and brooding. Through his depiction of the unemployed in New York's Harlem he was able to move beyond the usual "protest painting" of the period to reveal instances of individual human suffering. His
(30) human figures, presented in their familiar urban settings, managed to express the complex social reality lying beyond the borders of the canvas without compromising their integrity as elements in an artistic composition. Another important element of
(35) Bearden's compositions was his use of muted colors, such as dark blues and purples, to suggest moods of melancholy or despair. While functioning as part of the overall design, these colors also served as symbols of the psychological effects of debilitating social processes.
(40) During the same period, he also painted happier scenes—depictions of religious ceremony, musical performance, and family life—and instilled them with the same vividness that he applied to his scenes of suffering. Bearden sought in his work to reveal in all its
(45) fullness a world long hidden by the clichés of sociology and rendered cloudy by the simplifications of journalism and documentary photography. Where any number of painters have tried to project the "prose" of Harlem, Bearden concentrated on releasing its poetry—its family
(50) rituals and its ceremonies of affirmation and celebration. His work insists that we truly see the African-American experience in depth, using the fresh light of his creative vision. Through an act of artistic will, he created strange visual harmonies out of the mosaic of the African-
(55) American experience, and in doing so reflected the multiple rhythms, textures, and mysteries of life.

9. As it is used in the passage, the phrase "protest painting" (line 28) appears to refer to painting that

(A) depicted general scenes of social hardship and group suffering
(B) portrayed solitary figures in abstract surroundings
(C) challenged the traditional techniques employed by painters
(D) emphasized the experiences of African Americans during the Great Depression
(E) used innovative techniques to suggest the effects of social circumstances on individuals

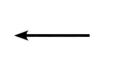

October 2001 Passage 2

The Main Point of the passage is that Romare Bearden was successful as a painter both in technique and in representation of the African-American experience. The question posed in the second paragraph asks how he was able to represent the African-American experience so successfully. The answer is twofold. First, Bearden was able to express the individuality of his subjects. Second, he used colors to evoke negative psychological states. Question nine tests our knowledge of the first part of the view: we should know how Bearden's approach contrasted with his peers.

What do I do when I find a localized Question and Answer secondary structure?

Every time you see a question, tag it with a "Q:" followed by the question, then go and find every proposed answer to that question. In the example above, the question has a two-part answer, and both parts should be tagged with an "A:" and the answer they put forth.

How does this help me answer questions?

There's typically (though not always) at least one question associated with a localized Question and Answer secondary structure. It won't be the Main Point or Primary Purpose question since it's a localized structure, but rather an Inference or Specific Reference (we'll learn more about these question types, later). Since the answer is a conclusion, it is important to note any support provided for it since that may be asked about as well.

A GOOD EXAMPLE OF AN EXTENSIVE QUESTION AND ANSWER SECONDARY STRUCTURE

> Q: CAN YOU DO IT ON YOUR OWN?
> A: YES!

Now it's your turn. Next is a complete passage with an extensive Question and Answer secondary structure. Mark up the passage as only you can, making sure to get the question and its answer into your primary structure diagram. Answer the questions. A full explanation awaits you at the end of the chapter. Tally ho! Sally forth! Some other verb that means move forward with vigor!

It is commonly assumed that even if some forgeries have aesthetic merit, no forgery has as much as an original by the imitated artist would. Yet even the most prominent art specialists can be duped
(5) by a talented artist turned forger into mistaking an almost perfect forgery for an original. For instance, artist Han van Meegeren's *The Disciples at Emmaus* (1937)—painted under the forged signature of the acclaimed Dutch master Jan Vermeer (1632–
(10) 1675)—attracted lavish praise from experts as one of Vermeer's finest works. The painting hung in a Rotterdam museum until 1945, when, to the great embarrassment of the critics, van Meegeren revealed its origin. Astonishingly, there was at least one highly
(15) reputed critic who persisted in believing it to be a Vermeer even after van Meegeren's confession.

Given the experts' initial enthusiasm, some philosophers argue that van Meegeren's painting must have possessed aesthetic characteristics that,
(20) in a Vermeer original, would have justified the critics' plaudits. Van Meegeren's *Emmaus* thus raises difficult questions regarding the status of superbly executed forgeries. Is a forgery inherently inferior as art? How are we justified, if indeed we are, in
(25) revising downwards our critical assessment of a work unmasked as a forgery? Philosopher of art Alfred Lessing proposes convincing answers to these questions.

A forged work is indeed inferior as art, Lessing
(30) argues, but not because of a shortfall in aesthetic qualities strictly defined, that is to say, in the qualities perceptible on the picture's surface. For example, in its composition, its technique, and its brilliant use of color, van Meegeren's work is flawless, even
(35) beautiful. Lessing argues instead that the deficiency lies in what might be called the painting's intangible qualities. All art, explains Lessing, involves technique, but not all art involves origination of a new vision, and originality of vision is one of the
(40) fundamental qualities by which artistic, as opposed to purely aesthetic, accomplishment is measured. Thus Vermeer is acclaimed for having inaugurated, in the seventeenth century, a new way of seeing, and for pioneering techniques for embodying this new way
(45) of seeing through distinctive treatment of light, color, and form.

Even if we grant that van Meegeren, with his undoubted mastery of Vermeer's innovative techniques, produced an aesthetically superior
(50) painting, he did so about three centuries after Vermeer developed the techniques in question. Whereas Vermeer's origination of these techniques in the seventeenth century represents a truly impressive and historic achievement, van Meegeren's production of
(55) *The Disciples at Emmaus* in the twentieth century presents nothing new or creative to the history of art. Van Meegeren's forgery therefore, for all its aesthetic merits, lacks the historical significance that makes Vermeer's work artistically great.

7. Which one of the following most accurately expresses the main point of the passage?

(A) *The Disciples at Emmaus*, van Meegeren's forgery of a Vermeer, was a failure in both aesthetic and artistic terms.
(B) The aesthetic value of a work of art is less dependent on the work's visible characteristics than on certain intangible characteristics.
(C) Forged artworks are artistically inferior to originals because artistic value depends in large part on originality of vision.
(D) The most skilled forgers can deceive even highly qualified art experts into accepting their work as original.
(E) Art critics tend to be unreliable judges of the aesthetic and artistic quality of works of art.

8. The passage provides the strongest support for inferring that Lessing holds which one of the following views?

(A) The judgments of critics who pronounced *The Disciples at Emmaus* to be aesthetically superb were not invalidated by the revelation that the painting is a forgery.
(B) The financial value of a work of art depends more on its purely aesthetic qualities than on its originality.
(C) Museum curators would be better off not taking art critics' opinions into account when attempting to determine whether a work of art is authentic.
(D) Because it is such a skilled imitation of Vermeer, *The Disciples at Emmaus* is as artistically successful as are original paintings by artists who are less significant than Vermeer.
(E) Works of art that have little or no aesthetic value can still be said to be great achievements in artistic terms.

9. In the first paragraph, the author refers to a highly reputed critic's persistence in believing van Meegeren's forgery to be a genuine Vermeer primarily in order to

(A) argue that many art critics are inflexible in their judgments
(B) indicate that the critics who initially praised *The Disciples at Emmaus* were not as knowledgeable as they appeared
(C) suggest that the painting may yet turn out to be a genuine Vermeer
(D) emphasize that the concept of forgery itself is internally incoherent
(E) illustrate the difficulties that skillfully executed forgeries can pose for art critics

October 2010 Passage 2

10. The reaction described in which one of the following scenarios is most analogous to the reaction of the art critics mentioned in line 13?

    (A) lovers of a musical group contemptuously reject a tribute album recorded by various other musicians as a second-rate imitation
    (B) art historians extol the work of a little-known painter as innovative until it is discovered that the painter lived much more recently than was originally thought
    (C) diners at a famous restaurant effusively praise the food as delicious until they learn that the master chef is away for the night
    (D) literary critics enthusiastically applaud a new novel until its author reveals that its central symbols are intended to represent political views that the critics dislike
    (E) movie fans evaluate a particular movie more favorably than they otherwise might have because their favorite actor plays the lead role

11. The passage provides the strongest support for inferring that Lessing holds which one of the following views?

    (A) It is probable that many paintings currently hanging in important museums are actually forgeries.
    (B) The historical circumstances surrounding the creation of a work are important in assessing the artistic value of that work.
    (C) The greatness of an innovative artist depends on how much influence he or she has on other artists.
    (D) The standards according to which a work is judged to be a forgery tend to vary from one historical period to another.
    (E) An artist who makes use of techniques developed by others cannot be said to be innovative.

12. The passage most strongly supports which one of the following statements?

    (A) In any historical period, the criteria by which a work is classified as a forgery can be a matter of considerable debate.
    (B) An artist who uses techniques that others have developed is most likely a forger.
    (C) A successful forger must originate a new artistic vision.
    (D) Works of art created early in the career of a great artist are more likely than those created later to embody historic innovations.
    (E) A painting can be a forgery even if it is not a copy of a particular original work of art.

13. Which one of the following, if true, would most strengthen Lessing's contention that a painting can display aesthetic excellence without possessing an equally high degree of artistic value?

    (A) Many of the most accomplished art forgers have had moderately successful careers as painters of original works.
    (B) Reproductions painted by talented young artists whose traditional training consisted in the copying of masterpieces were often seen as beautiful, but never regarded as great art.
    (C) While experts can detect most forgeries, they can be duped by a talented forger who knows exactly what characteristics experts expect to find in the work of a particular painter.
    (D) Most attempts at art forgery are ultimately unsuccessful because the forger has not mastered the necessary techniques.
    (E) The criteria by which aesthetic excellence is judged change significantly from one century to another and from one culture to another.

It is commonly assumed that even if some forgeries have aesthetic merit, no forgery has as much as an original by the imitated artist would. Yet even the most prominent art specialists can be duped (5) by a talented artist turned forger into mistaking an almost perfect forgery for an original. For instance, artist Han van Meegeren's *The Disciples at Emmaus* (1937)—painted under the forged signature of the acclaimed Dutch master Jan Vermeer (1632– (10) 1675)—attracted lavish praise from experts as one of Vermeer's finest works. The painting hung in a Rotterdam museum until 1945, when, to the great embarrassment of the critics, van Meegeren revealed its origin. Astonishingly, there was at least one highly (15) reputed critic who persisted in believing it to be a Vermeer even after van Meegeren's confession.

Given the experts' initial enthusiasm, some philosophers argue that van Meegeren's painting must have possessed aesthetic characteristics that, (20) in a Vermeer original, would have justified the critics' plaudits. Van Meegeren's *Emmaus* thus raises difficult questions regarding the status of superbly executed forgeries. Is a forgery inherently inferior as art? How are we justified, if indeed we are, in (25) revising downwards our critical assessment of a work unmasked as a forgery? Philosopher of art Alfred Lessing proposes convincing answers to these questions.

A forged work is indeed inferior as art, Lessing (30) argues, but not because of a shortfall in aesthetic qualities strictly defined, that is to say, in the qualities perceptible on the picture's surface. For example, in its composition, its technique, and its brilliant use of color, van Meegeren's work is flawless, even (35) beautiful. Lessing argues instead that the deficiency lies in what might be called the painting's intangible qualities. All art, explains Lessing, involves technique, but not all art involves origination of a new vision, and originality of vision is one of the (40) fundamental qualities by which artistic, as opposed to purely aesthetic, accomplishment is measured. Thus Vermeer is acclaimed for having inaugurated, in the seventeenth century, a new way of seeing, and for pioneering techniques for embodying this new way (45) of seeing through distinctive treatment of light, color, and form.

Even if we grant that van Meegeren, with his undoubted mastery of Vermeer's innovative techniques, produced an aesthetically superior (50) painting, he did so about three centuries after Vermeer developed the techniques in question. Whereas Vermeer's origination of these techniques in the seventeenth century represents a truly impressive and historic achievement, van Meegeren's production of (55) *The Disciples at Emmaus* in the twentieth century presents nothing new or creative to the history of art. Van Meegeren's forgery therefore, for all its aesthetic merits, lacks the historical significance that makes Vermeer's work artistically great.

EX. EMMAUS

FORGERIES CAN BE CONVINCING

ATT.

Q: IS A FORGERY INHERENTLY INFERIOR?

A: YES.

EX.

FORGERY ISN'T ORIGINAL

ATT.

ATT.

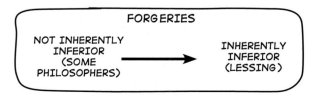

PASSAGE SUMMARY

So we have a point of view right off the bat: most people believe that a forgery could never have the aesthetic merit of (be as pretty as) one by the original artist. The painting by van Meegeren is offered as a counterexample. It fooled even the experts. So, aesthetically speaking, it's hard to say that it's inferior (lines 3-6). The author is astonished that some critic continued thinking it was real (lines 14-16) even after the forgery was revealed. That's author's attitude.

Paragraph two continues to talk about the example in paragraph one, so it's starting to seem like this might be an extensive Example structure. There is a point of view here that, at least in one particular way, a forgery is as good as the original. Because this has now been mentioned in two paragraphs, let's get that into our diagram as the Thesis position. Then we get a question: is a forgery inherently inferior? Let's ask Alfred Lessing.

The answer to that question is yes, and both Lessing and the author adopt that position. We continue with our van Meegeren example. Even though a painting might be aesthetically just as good as the original, it necessarily lacks the creative spark of the original artist (lines 37-41). This is the Antithesis position. Because the question is answered at length, we know this is a Question and Answer secondary structure with two answers. Accordingly, let's put it in our diagram.

In the fourth paragraph, Lessing's analysis is applied to the example of Van Meegeren's forgery of Vermeer. The painting is aesthetically pleasing, but it doesn't have the artistic vision to be considered great like a real Vermeer. There's a lot of author's attitude at the bottom. Vermeer's work is "truly impressive" and a "historic achievement" (lines 53-54), whereas Van Meegeren's art is neither "new" nor "creative" (line 56).

In sum, a point of view is addressed and a counterexample offered in the first paragraph, and then a question is asked and answered in two ways, with the author approving of the latter.

PRIMARY STRUCTURE: ANTITHESIS

There are two points of view in this passage, and it is therefore an Antithesis passage. The author is present, so the main point is the author's point of view.

The Thesis point of view is that forgery can be as good as an original (lines 17-21). The Antithesis point of view is that forgery is inherently inferior (line 29).

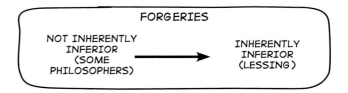

SECONDARY STRUCTURE

There is an extensive Example structure introduced in the first paragraph at lines 6-11, which continues to be discussed throughout the passage. There is an extensive Question and Answer structure at lines 23-24. It is extensive because the Thesis and Antithesis points of view are both answers to the question.

PASSAGE OVERVIEW

MAIN POINT

When the author is present, the author's point of view is the main point of the passage. In this case, that point of view is that a forgery is inherently inferior to the work of the original artist.

PRIMARY PURPOSE

The author wrote the passage to answer the question of whether forgery is inherently inferior.

AUTHORS ATTITUDE

There are several instances of strong author's attitude in paragraph one and paragraph four.

QUESTION ANTICIPATION

The two extensive structures—Example and Question and Answer—are bound to have multiple associated questions. The examples of attitude will likely also be tested.

AND NOW, ON TO THE QUESTIONS...

QUESTION 7: MAIN POINT

As usual, the first question is a Main Point question. As mentioned above, the main point is that a forgery is inherently inferior. That's answer choice (C).

- (A) The author never disagrees that *Emmaus* is aesthetically successful, knocking out (A).
- (B) The aesthetic value of art is indeed visible (it's just that great art is original), so (B) is wrong.
- (D) Answer choice (D) describes just part of paragraph one, and doesn't get in any of the arguments on either side. Too narrow.
- (E) *Some* art critics screwed up in one particular instance. That in no way means that *all* art critics generally are incompetent, like (E) asserts.

QUESTION 8: VIEWPOINT

Lessing is on board with the idea that a painting can be aesthetically wonderful but still not great art (lines 29-32), so (A) is correct.

- (B) There's no indication anywhere in the passage of what anyone, Lessing or others, thinks about financial value, so (B) cannot be inferred from the passage.
- (C) Art critics screwed up in one instance. We don't know that they aren't great every other time, and so we don't know that curators should just ignore them like (C) recommends.
- (D) We can only compare Vermeer and Van Meegeren here. We don't know anything about some other painters, so get rid of answer choice (D).
- (E) Lessing believes that aesthetic merit is not sufficient to be a great achievement. However, it still might be a necessary component to being great, so we don't know that (E) is correct.

QUESTION 9: ROLE

Although this is a Role question, tracking the Author's Attitude helps us answer it. In the first paragraph, the author is astonished that a critic continued to believe Van Meegeren's forgery was correct despite his confession. This leads us to answer choice (E).

- (A) *One* guy is never going to show that *many* art critics are inflexible, so this is wrong.

(B) Well, this guy makes the other critics who revised their opinions look smart in comparison, so it's not clear how he is going to make the others look dumb.

(C) Remember how the author was astonished (!) at the dumb critic? He certainly wasn't suggesting that the forgery might turn out to be real, so toss this one.

(D) This is something the makers of the LSAT love to throw at you, trying to make you think there's something illogical going on. Forgery is a real thing; it's not incoherent.

Pro tip: sometimes students choose answer choices because they contain words they don't know. This is why you should be looking up words like "incoherent" (unclear, disconnected), now. But even if you didn't know the meaning of the word on test day, don't choose it just because you don't. (E) is the clear winner here so you could still discard answer choice (D).

QUESTION 10: PARALLEL

The critics were so sure this thing was real that they hung it in a museum. But it was a fake. Then they were totally embarrassed. That's why answer choice (C) is right. These diners think they're eating Gordon Ramsay but it turns out it's Guy Fieri. Yuck!

(A) Let's get rid of this answer choice because it lacks the element of surprise (it's a fake?!) that the critics suffered.

(B) This answer choice has similar subject matter, which is a red flag for a Parallel question, and the fact that this guy lived more recently doesn't necessarily mean that his work was less innovative.

(D) This is tempting, but it's not talking about a fake; it's talking about hidden political views.

(E) We can eliminate this answer choice for the same reason we eliminated (A).

QUESTION 11: VIEWPOINT

Before diving into this question, let's ask ourselves what we know about Lessing. Well, he's the Antithesis position and thinks that forgeries are inherently inferior because they aren't the origin of important techniques (lines 50-51). This leads us straight to answer choice (B).

(A) We only know that one painting that hung in the museum was a forgery from the passage, so we can't infer that there are other forgeries in museums.

(C) This answer choice is wrong because it is originality of vision that Lessing prizes (lines 36-40), not influence.

(D) There's no mention of how we determine something is a forgery, and Lessing never comments on that either, so this answer choice is wrong.

(E) So very, very tempting, but do not be fooled! An artist might use old techniques, but as long as he combines them with original ones, it might still be great art.

QUESTION 12: INFERENCE

The only indication we have of why Emmaus is a forgery is that it was "painted under the forged signature of the acclaimed Dutch master Jan Vermeer" (lines 8-10). This, it would seem, is enough to make something a forgery, and answer choice (E) gets at that.

(A) This is trying to get us to infer something about other time periods. We know that Emmaus is a forgery by modern standards. There's no way to know if they were ever different.

(B) This makes it seem like most of the art in the world would qualify as forgery. Regardless of how unoriginal the artwork is, if you sign it with your own name, it's not forgery.

(C) No. If it's original, it's not a forgery.

(D) There's just no indication in the passage of when in life artists make their great innovations, so this is wrong.

QUESTION 13: OPERATION

Lessing says that aesthetic value is not the same as art, and we need something that strengthens this connection. Answer choice (B) gives us a scenario outside the forgery context where paintings have aesthetic value but aren't art, strengthening the connection between the two.

- (A) This answer choice talks about what forgers are doing in their spare time, but if that stuff shows originality, it's irrelevant to the divide between great aesthetics and great art.
- (C) It really doesn't matter to that divide whether anyone can detect the forgery, so this answer choice is out.
- (D) This answer choice is talking about art that is both unoriginal and not aesthetically pleasing (stick figures, anyone?), so it can't help us determine that art that is aesthetically pleasing can't be great art.
- (E) The LSAT makers are just being lazy. We've already determined in multiple questions that there's no information to tell us whether these standards have changed. WRONG.

19/CLASSIFICATION

WHERE DOES THIS THING BELONG?

Classification secondary structures are the rarest of the secondary structures, and so we address them last. They are present 5.07% of the time on the test, which is barely statistically significant. However, they crop up enough that we want you to know how to deal with one, should it appear on your LSAT.

WHAT IS CLASSIFICATION

Science fiction movies always contain elements of the improbable: black holes, self-aware robots, highly attractive female aliens. One of the best ways of managing information is to put it into a broader category. Categorizing things—classifying them—is very important on the LSAT, in law school, and in your legal career. After all, you need to know to what group a particular thing or action belongs in order to understand under what legal statute it falls. We symbolize the Classification structure listing the topic of the items in a series, followed by what they are. The above example would be symbolized in the following manner:

SCIENCE FICTION:
1. BLACK HOLES
2. SELF AWARE ROBOTS
3. CUTE FEMALE ALIENS

WHY CLASSIFICATION STRUCTURES ARE IMPORTANT IN READING COMPREHENSION

As with Example secondary structures, Classification structures identify premises. The author will enumerate a list of examples to demonstrate support for a conclusion. Take the following example:

> Many people don't believe that fair food (edibles found at carnivals such as caramel apples and cotton candy) can rise to the level of gourmet, but gastronomes say differently. Pointing to the Oklahoma funnel cake, the deep-fried twinkie, and the blooming onion, these foodologists contend that, despite their humble beginnings, such foods are served in fine dining establishments around the world, albeit in slightly different forms.

Cleetus: Ain't a gastronome one of them farting elfs?

Cleetus, a gastronome is a connoisseur of food, an epicure. A farting elf is, well, a farting elf.

The conclusion here, found in opposition to "many people" is that fair food can rise to the level of gourmet. Support is found in the three kinds of fair food that are served in fine dining establishments around the world. By locating the Classification structure, you've located the support for the main idea of the paragraph.

IDENTIFYING CLASSIFICATION STRUCTURES

A Classification secondary structure consists of three or more things that fall into a category. When you stumble upon three or more things in a Reading Comprehension passage that share certain attributes, you may be dealing with a Classification secondary structure. Sometimes the category will be explicitly identified, making it clear what items in the passage fall into that category. Be aware, however, that it is not necessarily the case that all of the items in the category will be listed immediately after the category is identified – they may be listed lines or even paragraphs later.

Ninja: It is also sometimes the case that the category will not be explicitly identified at all, but a number of items in the passage logically fall into a particular classification nonetheless. In such a case, you must formulate the category in your own words.

These structures can be a little harder to see than the other three secondary structures. Unlike a causal structure that may be tipped off by "result" so you identify it immediately, or an example structure that is introduced with "for example," you won't realize you're dealing with a Classification secondary structure until you've come to the second or third item that falls into a category. Therefore, tagging Classification structures will always occur after the fact, rather than in the moment.

BP Minotaur: We'd love to give you another list of key words, but there really aren't any. So, it's particularly important for you to be actively searching for Classification secondary structures.

WHAT IT LOOKS LIKE IN READING COMPREHENSION

Let's take a look at a few examples of what Classification structures as taken from real, live, LSATs.

> ...I gathered much of the background material for my study of Tucker's life through research in special collections of the New York and Los Angeles public libraries, including microfilmed correspondence, photographs, programs, and newspapers. Also examined...were the ten still available films in which Tucker appeared...

> ...on the verge of a filmless, digital revolution, photography is moving forward into its past. In addition to reviving the tintype process, photographers are polishing daguerreotype plates, coating paper with egg whites, making pinhole cameras, and mixing emulsions from nineteenth-century recipes in order to coax new expressive effects from old photographic techniques...

> ...plants contain two categories of chemical substances: primary and secondary. The primary substances, such as proteins, carbohydrates, vitamins, and hormones, are required for growth and proper functioning and are found in all plants. The secondary substances are a diverse and multitudinous array of chemicals that have no known role in the internal chemical processes of plants' growth or metabolism....

EXTENSIVE CLASSIFICATION SECONDARY STRUCTURES

If the items that fall into the category are sprinkled throughout the passage, or the particular category forms the support for the Main Point of the passage, you're dealing with an extensive Classification secondary structure. Whatever statement or idea is supported by the extensive Classification secondary structure is the Main Point of the passage, and that idea should be in your primary structure diagram. Peruse the following passage, markup, and Main Point question ripped from the pages of a real LSAT and we'll discuss it afterward.

When the same habitat types (forests, oceans, grasslands, etc.) in regions of different latitudes are compared, it becomes apparent that the overall number of species increases from pole to equator. This
(5) latitudinal gradient is probably even more pronounced than current records indicate, since researchers believe that most undiscovered species live in the tropics.

One hypothesis to explain this phenomenon, the "time theory," holds that diverse species adapted
(10) to today's climatic conditions have had more time to emerge in the tropical regions, which, unlike the temperate and arctic zones, have been unaffected by a succession of ice ages. However, ice ages have caused less disruption in some temperate regions than in
(15) others and have not interrupted arctic conditions.

Alternatively, the species energy hypothesis proposes the following positive correlations: incoming energy from the Sun correlated with rates of growth and reproduction; rates of growth and reproduction
(20) with the amount of living matter (biomass) at a given moment; and the amount of biomass with number of species. However, since organisms may die rapidly, high production rates can exist with low biomass. And high biomass can exist with few species. Moreover, the
(25) mechanism proposed—greater energy influx leading to bigger populations, thereby lowering the probability of local extinction—remains untested.

A third hypothesis centers on the tropics' climatic stability, which provides a more reliable supply of
(30) resources. Species can thus survive even with few types of food, and competing species can tolerate greater overlap between their respective niches. Both capabilities enable more species to exist on the same resources. However, the ecology of local
(35) communities cannot account for the origin of the latitudinal gradient. Localized ecological processes such as competition do not generate regional pools of species, and it is the total number of species available regionally for colonizing any particular area that
(40) makes the difference between for example, a forest at the equator and one at a higher latitude. A fourth and most plausible hypothesis focuses on regional speciation, and in particular on rates of speciation and extinction. According to this hypothesis, if speciation
(45) rates become higher toward the tropics, and are not negated by extinction rates, then the latitudinal gradient would result—and become increasingly steep.

The mechanism for this rate of speciation hypothesis is that most new animal species, and
(50) perhaps plant species, arise because a population subgroup becomes isolated. This subgroup evolves differently and eventually cannot interbreed with members of the original population. The uneven spread of a species over a large geographic area promotes this
(55) mechanism: at the edges, small populations spread out and form isolated groups. Since subgroups in an arctic environment are more likely to face extinction than those in the tropics, the latter are more likely to survive long enough to adapt to local conditions and
(60) ultimately become new species.

15. Which one of the following most accurately expresses the main idea of the passage?

(A) At present, no single hypothesis explaining the latitudinal gradient in numbers of species is more widely accepted than any other.
(B) The tropical climate is more conducive to promoting species diversity than are arctic or temperate climates.
(C) Several explanations have been suggested for global patterns in species distribution, but a hypothesis involving rates of speciation seems most promising.
(D) Despite their differences, the various hypotheses regarding a latitudinal gradient in species diversity concur in predicting that the gradient can be expected to increase.
(E) In distinguishing among the current hypotheses for distribution of species, the most important criterion is whether a hypothesis proposes a mechanism that can be tested and validated.

June 1996 Passage 3

The passage is dedicated to explaining why there are more and more species the closer one gets to the equator. It discusses the relative merits of four hypotheses explaining that phenomenon, and eventually endorses one of them. To be clear, the overarching category here is hypotheses explaining a phenomenon, and each of the four theories falls into that category. As you can see, the Classification secondary structure is represented in the primary structure diagram and is implicated in the correct answer to the Main Point question.

What do I do when I find an Extensive Classification secondary structure?

When you find a Classification secondary structure in a passage, you should identify the particular category and tag each item that falls into the category, regardless of where it is in the passage. You may need to define the category in your own words if the passage doesn't do it for you. You should also number the items that fall into the category as they are mentioned.

Imagine a Reading Comprehension passage started off in the following manner:

> There is more than one way to skin a cat.

You might wonder why the passage would say something like that, and you probably would not automatically think extensive Classification secondary structure. However, if the next three paragraphs each introduced a different strategy for cat-skinning: "...filet knives are particularly useful...in-home cat-skinning services have become increasingly popular...if you scare a cat sufficiently, it will spontaneously skin itself..." At that point you would tag the margins in the following way.

```
CAT-SKINNING:
1. FILET
2. IN-HOME
3. SCARE
```

To be clear, you wouldn't know this was a Classification structure until the third way to skin a cat, at which point you would go back to the passage, label the category, and number each instance of it.

To properly fill in your primary structure diagram, you must understand what the classification is supporting. Remember, Classification structures function like premises, providing support for a conclusion. In the case of the above example, your primary structure diagram ought to look like the following:

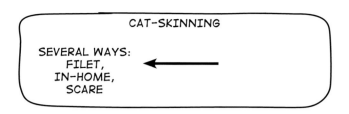

How does this help me answer questions?

By now you know that the primary structure diagram is a road map to the correct answers for Main Point and Primary Purpose questions. Keep in mind, with extensive Classification secondary structures, the answer choice can be fairly weak. The right answer to the Main Point question for the above example would look something like, "There are several ways to skin a cat."

The Primary Purpose of the passage in a case like this would look something like, "...presenting information on cat-skinning."

As ever, there may be other questions that draw upon the Classification structure. Identifying the Author's Attitude toward the category or any of the items in the category, to the extent the author takes a position, is useful. Make sure you understand what the criteria are for being a part of the category, and you'll be able to recognize other things that should or should not fall within it.

LOCALIZED CLASSIFICATION SECONDARY STRUCTURES

If the items in the category only support a subsidiary conclusion, you're dealing with a localized Classification secondary structure. As such, it is not part of the Main Point of the passage, and your diagram will not include it. Be sure to identify the category and tag each item that falls into the category with a number as there is likely to be a question asked about it. Take a look at the following passage.

Painter Frida Kahlo (1910-1954) often used harrowing images derived from her Mexican heritage to express suffering caused by a disabling accident and a stormy marriage. Suggesting much personal and
(5) emotional content, her works—many of them self-portraits—have been exhaustively psychoanalyzed, while their political content has been less studied. Yet Kahlo was an ardent political activist who in her art sought not only to explore her own roots, but also
(10) to champion Mexico's struggle for an independent political and cultural identity.
   Kahlo was influenced by Marxism, which appealed to many intellectuals in the 1920s and 1930s, and by Mexican nationalism. Interest in Mexico's culture and
(15) history had revived in the nineteenth century, and by the early 1900s, Mexican indigenista tendencies ranged from a violently anti-Spanish idealization of Aztec Mexico to an emphasis on contemporary Mexican Indians as the key to authentic Mexican culture.
(20) Mexican nationalism, reacting against contemporary United States political intervention in labor disputes as well as against past domination by Spain, identified the Aztecs as the last independent rulers of an indigenous political unit. Kahlo's form of Mexicanidad, a romantic
(25) nationalism that focused upon traditional art uniting all indigenistas, revered the Aztecs as a powerful pre-Columbian society that had united a large area of the Middle Americas and that was thought to have been based on communal labor, the Marxist ideal.
(30)   In her paintings, Kahlo repeatedly employed Aztec symbols, such as skeletons or bleeding hearts, that were traditionally related to the emanation of life from death and light from darkness. These images of destruction coupled with creation speak not only to
(35) Kahlo's personal battle for life, but also to the Mexican struggle to emerge as a nation—by implication, to emerge with the political and cultural strength admired in the Aztec civilization. *Self Portrait on the Border between Mexico and the United States* (1932), for
(40) example, shows Kahlo wearing a bone necklace, holding a Mexican flag, and standing between a highly industrialized United States and an agricultural, preindustrial Mexico. On the United States side are mechanistic and modern images such as smokestacks,
(45) light bulbs, and robots. In contrast, the organic and ancient symbols on the Mexican side—a blood-drenched Sun, lush vegetation, an Aztec sculpture, a pre-Columbian temple, and a skull alluding to those that lined the walls of Aztec temples emphasize the
(50) interrelation of life, death, the earth, and the cosmos.
   Kahlo portrayed Aztec images in the folkloric style of traditional Mexican paintings, thereby heightening the clash between modern materialism and indigenous tradition; similarly, she favored planned
(55) economic development, but not at the expense of cultural identity. Her use of familiar symbols in a readily accessible style also served her goal of being popularly understood; in turn, Kahlo is viewed by some Mexicans as a mythic figure representative of
(60) nationalism itself.

5. The passage mentions each of the following as an Aztec symbol or image found in Kahlo's paintings EXCEPT a

(A) skeleton
(B) sculpture
(C) serpent
(D) skull
(E) bleeding heart

The passage is devoted to arguing that the works of Mexican artist Frida Kahlo must be analyzed for their political and cultural significance, not just as a reflection of Kahlo's personal life. To support that idea, the author provides a category—Aztec symbols—and enumerates among them skeletons, bleeding hearts, Aztec sculpture, etc. Question number five asks about that Classification structure, and we can simply eliminate all of the wrong answers by referring back to that structure in the passage.

Cleetus: Hoooeee! Look at all the time I saved by not having to return to the whole durn passage again!

What do I do when I find a localized Classification secondary structure?

When you find a localized Classification secondary structure, tag the category and list each item that falls into the category with a number. If the category is not stated explicitly, write it out in your own words.

How does this help me answer questions?

If you find a localized Classification secondary structure, anticipate at least one question other than Primary Purpose or Main Point associated with the structure. If there is a logical order to the items—maybe they come in chronological order, or they are of increasing size—you may be tested on your knowledge of that order.

A GOOD EXAMPLE OF AN EXTENSIVE CLASSIFICATION SECONDARY STRUCTURE

Stay classy, LSAT.

Here's a real live passage from a real live LSAT that contains a real live extensive Classification secondary structure. Mark up the passage, and make sure the Classification secondary structure makes it into your primary structure diagram. Answer all of the questions. There's a full explanation at the end of the chapter. Best of luck!

The prevailing trend in agriculture toward massive and highly mechanized production, with its heavy dependence on debt and credit as a means of raising capital, has been linked to the growing problem of
(5) bankruptcy among small farms. African American horticulturalist Booker T. Whatley has proposed a comprehensive approach to small farming that runs counter to this trend. Whatley maintains that small farms can operate profitably despite these economic
(10) obstacles, and he provides guidelines that he believes will bring about such profitability when combined with smart management and hard work.

Whatley emphasizes that small farms must generate year-round cash flow. To this end, he
(15) recommends growing at least ten different crops, which would alleviate financial problems should one crop fail completely. To minimize the need to seek hard-to-obtain loans, the market for the farm products should be developed via a "clientele membership club"
(20) (CMC), whereby clients pay in advance for the right to go to the farm and harvest what they require. To help guarantee small farmers a market for all of their crops, Whatley encourages them to grow only crops that clients ask for, and to comply with client requests
(25) regarding the use of chemicals.

Whatley stresses that this "pick-your-own" farming is crucial for profitability because 50 percent of a farmer's production cost is tied up with harvesting, and using clients as harvesters allows the farmer to
(30) charge 60 percent of what supermarkets charge and still operate the farm at a profit. Whatley's plan also affords farmers the advantage of selling directly to consumers, thus eliminating distribution costs. To realize profits on a 25-acre farm, for example,
(35) Whatley suggests that a CMC of about 1,000 people is needed. The CMC would consist primarily of people from metropolitan areas who value fresh produce.

The success of this plan, Whatley cautions, depends in large part on a farm's location: the farm
(40) should be situated on a hard-surfaced road within 40 miles of a population center of at least 50,000 people, as studies suggest that people are less inclined to travel any greater distances for food. In this way, Whatley reverses the traditional view of hard-surfaced
(45) roads as farm-to-market roads, calling them instead "city-to-farm" roads. The farm should also have well-drained soil and a ready water source for irrigation, since inevitably certain preferred crops will not be drought resistant. Lastly, Whatley recommends
(50) carrying liability insurance upwards of $1 million to cover anyone injured on the farm. Adhering to this plan, Whatley contends, will allow small farms to exist as a viable alternative to sprawling corporate farms while providing top-quality agricultural goods
(55) to consumers in most urban areas.

1. Which one of the following most accurately states the main point of the passage?

(A) In reaction to dominant trends in agriculture, Booker T. Whatley has advanced a set of recommendations he claims will enable small farms to thrive.
(B) Booker T. Whatley's approach to farming is sensitive to the demands of the consumer, unlike the dominant approach to farming that focuses on massive and efficient production and depends on debt and credit.
(C) As part of a general critique of the trend in agriculture toward massive production, Booker T. Whatley assesses the ability of small farms to compete against large corporate farms.
(D) While CMCs are not the only key to successful small farming, Booker T. Whatley shows that without them small farms risk failure even with a diversity of crops and a good location.
(E) The adoption of Booker T. Whatley's methods of small farming will eventually threaten the dominance of large-scale production and reliance on debt and credit that mark corporate farming.

2. Based on the information in the passage, which one of the following would Whatley be most likely to view as facilitating adherence to an aspect of his plan for operating a small farm?

   (A) a farmer's planting a relatively unknown crop to test the market for that crop
   (B) a farmer's leaving large lanes between plots of each crop to allow people easy access at harvest time
   (C) a farmer's traveling into the city two afternoons a week to sell fresh produce at a farmer's market
   (D) a farmer's using an honor system whereby produce is displayed on tables in view of the road and passersby can buy produce and leave their money in a box
   (E) a farmer's deciding that for environmental reasons chemicals will no longer be used on the farm to increase yields

3. According to the passage, "pick-your-own" farming is seen by Whatley as necessary to the operation of small farms for which one of the following reasons?

   (A) Customers are given the chance to experience firsthand where their produce comes from.
   (B) It guarantees a substantial year-round cash flow for the farm.
   (C) It allows farmers to maintain profits while charging less for produce than what supermarkets charge.
   (D) Only those varieties of crops that have been specifically selected by clients within the CMC will be grown by the farmer.
   (E) Consumers who are willing to drive to farms to harvest their own food comprise a strong potential market for farmers.

4. The author of the passage is primarily concerned with

   (A) summarizing the main points of an innovative solution to a serious problem
   (B) examining contemporary trends and isolating their strengths and weaknesses
   (C) criticizing widely accepted practices within a key sector of the economy
   (D) demonstrating the advantages and disadvantages of a new strategy within an industry
   (E) analyzing the impact of a new idea on a tradition-driven industry

5. The passage provides the most support for inferring which one of the following statements?

   (A) A corporate farm is more likely to need a loan than a small farm is.
   (B) If small farms charged what supermarkets charge for produce that is fresher than that sold by supermarkets, then small farms would see higher profits in the long term.
   (C) Consumers who live in rural areas are generally less inclined than those who live in metropolitan areas to join a CMC.
   (D) If a CMC requests fewer than ten different crops to be grown, then at least one of Whatley's recommendations will not be followed.
   (E) Distribution costs are accounted for in the budget of a small farm with a CMC and are paid directly by customers.

6. According to the passage, Whatley advocates which one of the following actions because it would help to guarantee that small farms have buyers for all of their produce?

   (A) growing at least ten different crops
   (B) charging 60 percent of what supermarkets charge for the same produce
   (C) recruiting only clients who value fresh produce
   (D) honoring the crop requests and chemical-use preferences of clients
   (E) irrigating crops that are susceptible to drought

7. Which one of the following inferences is most supported by the information in the passage?

   (A) The advance payment to the farmer by CMC members guarantees that members will get the produce they want.
   (B) Hard-surfaced roads are traditionally the means by which some farmers transport their produce to their customers in cities.
   (C) A typical population center of 50,000 should be able to support CMCs on at least fifty 25-acre farms.
   (D) Consumers prefer hard-surfaced roads to other roads because the former cause less wear and tear on their vehicles.
   (E) Most roads with hard surfaces were originally given these surfaces primarily for the sake of farmers.

The prevailing trend in agriculture toward massive and highly mechanized production, with its heavy dependence on debt and credit as a means of raising capital, has been linked to the growing problem of
(5) bankruptcy among small farms. African American horticulturalist Booker T. Whatley has proposed a comprehensive approach to small farming that runs counter to this trend. Whatley maintains that small farms can operate profitably despite these economic
(10) obstacles, and he provides guidelines that he believes will bring about such profitability when combined with smart management and hard work.
   Whatley emphasizes that small farms must generate year-round cash flow. To this end, he
(15) recommends growing at least ten different crops, which would alleviate financial problems should one crop fail completely. To minimize the need to seek hard-to-obtain loans, the market for the farm products should be developed via a "clientele membership club"
(20) (CMC), whereby clients pay in advance for the right to go to the farm and harvest what they require. To help guarantee small farmers a market for all of their crops, Whatley encourages them to grow only crops that clients ask for, and to comply with client requests
(25) regarding the use of chemicals.
   Whatley stresses that this "pick-your-own" farming is crucial for profitability because 50 percent of a farmer's production cost is tied up with harvesting, and using clients as harvesters allows the farmer to
(30) charge 60 percent of what supermarkets charge and still operate the farm at a profit. Whatley's plan also affords farmers the advantage of selling directly to consumers, thus eliminating distribution costs. To realize profits on a 25-acre farm, for example,
(35) Whatley suggests that a CMC of about 1,000 people is needed. The CMC would consist primarily of people from metropolitan areas who value fresh produce.
   The success of this plan, Whatley cautions, depends in large part on a farm's location: the farm
(40) should be situated on a hard-surfaced road within 40 miles of a population center of at least 50,000 people, as studies suggest that people are less inclined to travel any greater distances for food. In this way, Whatley reverses the traditional view of hard-surfaced
(45) roads as farm-to-market roads, calling them instead "city-to-farm" roads. The farm should also have well-drained soil and a ready water source for irrigation, since inevitably certain preferred crops will not be drought resistant. Lastly, Whatley recommends
(50) carrying liability insurance upwards of $1 million to cover anyone injured on the farm. Adhering to this plan, Whatley contends, will allow small farms to exist as a viable alternative to sprawling corporate farms while providing top-quality agricultural goods
(55) to consumers in most urban areas.

DEBT ⌒ BANKRUPTCY

WHATLEY'S CONCLUSION

GUIDELINES:
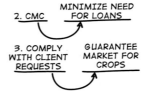

ATT.

WHY WHATLEY THINKS PLAN WILL WORK

EX.

WHO CUSTOMERS WOULD BE

4. HARD-SURFACED ROAD AT MOST 40 MILES FROM AT LEAST 50,000 PEOPLE

5. DRAINAGE AND IRRIGATION

6. INSURANCE

REITERATION OF CONCLUSION

SMALL FARMS

FARMS CAN AVOID BANKRUPTCY WITH PLAN (WHATLEY)

June 2013 Passage 1

PASSAGE SUMMARY

Who needs to become a lawyer when turning profit on a small farm is so easy!

Paragraph one hits us with a Cause and Effect structure (lines 1-5). The effect is bankruptcy among small farms, and the cause is the prevailing trend in agriculture, which basically amounts to borrowing a bunch of money. Our buddy Booker T. Whatley has a plan for small farms to avoid bankruptcy. Whatley makes a prediction —candidate for a conclusion!— that small farms can avoid bankruptcy by sticking to his recommendations and being smart and working hard (lines 10-12).

The second paragraph begins by telling us about all the various guidelines that comprise Whatley's plan. At this point, not only do we know that our candidate for the conclusion is the main conclusion (because the remainder of the passage is devoted to supporting it), but also that we have a Classification secondary structure. This is because Whatley gives us more than two guidelines for how to make a small farm profitable. We keep track of these because it's likely they'll be asked about in the questions.

The first guideline is that farmers should grow a bunch of different crops to mitigate the risks of crop failure and ensure year-round cash flow. That's more cause and effect, in case you were wondering.

You might also wonder who's going to buy all those vegetables, and Whatley's next recommendation addresses that very question. City dwellers will pay for memberships (CMC's) that entitle them to go out to the farm and pick their own produce. Yes, you read that right. We're not talking about the Saturday morning farmer's market here. There's more cause and effect, too; a CMC will help farmers reduce the need for loans.

So that farmers can ensure that they have a market for their crops (yep, more cause and effect), they should listen to their customers and grow only what the customers request, using only chemicals they're okay with.

Paragraph three explains just why Whatley thinks his plan is "crucial" (note the strong attitude) to small farmers' goals of profitability. The plan will give farmers huge savings on harvesting and distribution costs, and they'll be able to pass those savings on to their customers and still make a profit. Then, lo and behold, here comes an example: to make profit on a 25-acre farm, you need at least 1,000 members (lines 35-37).

Don't look now, but we've got yet another element of the plan in paragraph four: be sure to locate your farm on a hard-surfaced road 40 miles or less from a city with at least 50,000 people (lines 39-41). Next up are some more elements of the plan: have drainage and irrigation, and carry $1 million liability insurance policy (lines 45-51). We get a reiteration of the prediction—the Thesis position— as the last sentence, i.e. the conclusion (lines 52-55).

In summary, paragraph one identifies a problem and a proposed plan to address the problem. The rest of the passage is devoted to explaining the elements of the plan. Easy peasy!

PRIMARY STRUCTURE: THESIS

This passage is devoted to explaining a particular plan to address the problem of small farm bankruptcy. That this plan will succeed is the Thesis position. The author of the passage just describes Whatley's plan, so she is not present in our primary structure diagram.

```
┌─────────────────────────────────────┐
│           SMALL FARMS               │
│                                     │
│      FARMS CAN AVOID                │
│   BANKRUPTCY WITH PLAN              │
│          (WHATLEY)                  │
└─────────────────────────────────────┘
```

SECONDARY STRUCTURES

Lots! There is a localized Cause and Effect structure in paragraph one (lines 1-5), and an extensive Classification structure. Some of the elements of the Classification structure are also localized Cause and Effect relationships. There's also a localized example in lines 35-37 illustrating the membership requirements of a CMC.

PASSAGE OVERVIEW

MAIN POINT

There is only one point of view present. Whatley outlines a plan that he believes will help small farms avoid bankruptcy.

PRIMARY PURPOSE

The passage was written to explain the details of Whatley's plan to solve a particular problem.

AUTHOR'S ATTITUDE

The author is absent so there's no author's attitude but Whatley thinks "pick-your-own" is crucial (line 27) for profitability.

QUESTION ANTICIPATION

The multiple Cause and Effect and Example localized structures may get questions. Expect several questions about the extensive Classification structure that details the elements of Whatley's plan.

AND NOW, ON TO THE QUESTIONS...

QUESTION 1: MAIN POINT

The main point, as expressed in lines 8-12 and 51-55, is that Whatley thinks his plan will help small farms turn a profit. Answer choice (A) says that. It is even worded in a manner that indicates that the author is absent ("he claims").

(B) Whatley's approach is sensitive to the demands of the consumer, but there's no information in the passage suggesting that the debt-heavy approach is not. Also, we don't really know if the dominant trend is efficient. It could very well be that the dominant trend destroys a city-sized swath of land to produce one artichoke. (Although a delicious artichoke pizza might be worth environmental catastrophe.)

(C) There's no general critique of massive production in agriculture described in the passage, so this can't be the main idea.

D) This answer choice focuses on a very small part of the passage: the CMC. It's much too narrow to be the main idea.

(E) This answer choice is way too strong. While he thinks his plan will help small farmers thrive, Whatley never says they're going to take over the world. (Though that would be amazing.)

QUESTION 2: VIEWPOINT

We identified each element in Whatley's plan as part of the Classification structure, so we just have to find an answer that would help a farmer enact one of the elements. Answer choice (B) suggests leaving wide lanes for easy access, which would make it easier for clients to come pick their own vegetables (line 21).

- (A) Answer choice (A) goes against Whatley's guidelines. Plant what people request (line 24), not what you hope there might be a market for. (Here, try this revolting looking root! Buy as many as you can carry! Sure, it smells like rotting flesh, but it's on sale today!)
- (C) This sounds sensible in, you know, the real world, but this also goes against the plan by increasing distribution costs instead of letting consumers come to the farm.
- (D) Hope that people pay for what they take? Because Whatley's plan outlines a CMC where clients "pay in advance" (line 20), it's clear Whatley wouldn't agree with this one.
- (E) Whatley suggests complying with client requests about chemicals (line 25), but that doesn't mean getting rid of chemicals altogether. Next.

QUESTION 3: SPECIFIC REFERENCE

This question asks why Whatley thinks pick-your-own farming is necessary. Fortunately, we tagged the attitude in paragraph 3 ("crucial" at line 27), and the answer is right there. Getting people to pick their own vegetables reduces farmers' costs, so they can charge less for vegetables and still make a profit. That's answer choice (C).

- (A) This is nice, but this firsthand experience stuff is never discussed in the passage. Next.
- (B) Guarantees? We know such cash-flow is necessary (lines 13-14), but there's no indication that even Whatley believes his plan is foolproof.
- (D) This answer choice equivocates between different meanings of the word "picking." In pick-your-own, "picking" is synonymous with "harvesting." This answer choice equates it with "selecting," which is a different part of the passage.
- (E) The passage doesn't discuss how strong this market is. Whatley seems optimistic, but never directly addresses how many customers there would actually be. Kick this one to the compost heap of incorrect answers.

QUESTION 4: PRIMARY PURPOSE

When the author is absent, the primary purpose of a passage is generally to present or describe a particular point of view. The Classification structure is also important; the author identifies numerous elements of Whatley's plan to address the growing problem of small-farm bankruptcy. Answer choice (A) fits perfectly on both counts.

- (B) The author discusses contemporary trends in passing in paragraph one, but the passage is devoted to one answer to those trends.
- (C) This answer completely misses the part of the passage about Whatley's plan (oh, only about 95% of the passage). The problems with the widely accepted practices are mentioned only in passing, at the beginning. Note also that "criticizing" implies a very present author, which we don't have.
- (D) Answer choice (D) is incorrect because there is no discussion of disadvantages to Whatley's plan.
- (E) There's no indication that this industry is driven by tradition. We just know what the prevailing trend is (lines 1-5).

However, that trend could be fairly new for all we know. Additionally, "analyzing" this idea would require a much more present author.

QUESTION 5: INFERENCE

This question is very annoyingly open-ended. The answer could be just about anything, as long as it's supported by the passage. So keep the primary structure and (lack of) author's attitude in mind, and scan through the answers to eliminate incorrect answer choices quickly.

Answer choice (D) tests our knowledge of the Classification structure. Sure enough, fewer than ten different crops *does* violate Whatley's guidelines (line 15 and our first-numbered Classification guideline). Answer choice (D) is our answer. Hurray!

- (A) This answer choice can be easily eliminated because it discusses loans for corporate firms, a topic about which we know nothing from the passage.
- (B) This can be eliminated for the same reason as (A): we have no idea what would happen if small farms charged what supermarkets charge. We see a pattern developing!
- (C) Again, not covered in the passage and so cannot be the correct answer.
- (E) We can kick this answer choice to the curb because it does precisely what all of the previous wrong answers did. Namely, it describes a phenomenon not in the passage and so is something for which the passage cannot provide support.

QUESTION 6: SPECIFIC REFERENCE

Here's yet another question about the Classification structure. This one references one of the causal relationships in paragraph two. To guarantee a market for all their crops, farmers should comply with their clients' requests about what to grow and what chemicals to use. That's almost exactly what choice (D) says. Having the cause and effect tagged is a big help since so many of the wrong answers identify other elements of Whatley's plan.

- (A) The reason for this diversification is to guard against crop failure (lines 14-17), not to ensure buyers. If you grow ten disgusting, tasteless vegetables that smell awful (we're looking at you, broccoli!), you probably aren't guaranteeing buyers for your produce.
- (B) It's great to pay less, but that doesn't guarantee that people will buy all of the produce, especially if it's all produce that the clients hate.
- (C) People who value fresh produce are the ones who will likely sign up (lines 36-37), but it's unclear how weeding out clients who don't value fresh produce would help these farms. That would just leave the farms with fewer customers.
- (E) This one is tricky since it mentions our fifth guideline of irrigating crops. Irrigation won't, however, bring in the customers if the crops aren't what they want to buy, so it's not the correct answer.

QUESTION 7: INFERENCE

Another open-ended question. Once again, keep the big picture in mind and look to eliminate wrong answers. Answer choice (B) is the right answer because it pretty much says the same thing the passage does at lines 43-44, when it discusses the "traditional view of hard-surfaced roads as farm-to-market roads."

- (A) This answer choice is way too strong. What if you pay, and then a tornado destroys the farm ten minutes later?

There are no guarantees in small farming, or in life. That's an important lesson, kids.

(C) The passage states that a 25-acre farm needs 1,000 members. So, for a city of 50,000 to support fifty of these farms, every single resident, from nursery to nursing home, would have to be a member. That seems like a dangerous assumption.

(D) This is tempting, but it's asking you to bring your own view into the test. We have no information supporting this or any other explanation for why consumers would be more likely to use hard-surfaced roads.

(E) We have no idea why these roads were built. It could be that they were built to facilitate long haul trucking or for a Boy Scout jamboree or for no other reason than there was a bunch of money lying around.

So there you go. A fun-fest passage packed with Classification joy and broccoli rabe love. Let us know if you decide to step off the legal career path and become a small farmer: we'll be sure to join your CMC! (But only if you're on a hard-surfaced road no more than 40 miles from the Blueprint office.)

20/REVIEW QUIZ

Congratulations on learning all the secondary structures! Between the primary and secondary structures, you've learned all the relevant categories for typing Reading Comprehension passages. You now are well on your way to seeing through the topic of the passage to the structure underneath—the hallmark of a Reading Comprehension master.

It also means you're ready to take a quiz to see how well you've retained the concepts. If you miss a question, review the relevant chapter to make sure you understand all the information about structure before moving on. Circle all correct answers. Keep in mind there may be more than one.

1. Which of the following secondary structures is the most common?
    (A) Example
    (B) Question and Answer
    (C) Classification
    (D) Cause and Effect

2. In a passage with an extensive Question and Answer structure, what is the Main Point of the passage?
    (A) The author's main conclusion
    (B) The answer to the question
    (C) The question
    (D) The primary viewpoint

3. What is the minimum number of items within a category for it to qualify as a Classification secondary structure?
    (A) one
    (B) two
    (C) three
    (D) four

4. Which of the following secondary structures act as premises?
    (A) Cause and Effect
    (B) Example
    (C) Question and Answer
    (D) Classification

5. Which of the following secondary structures are conclusions?
    (A) Cause and Effect
    (B) Example ✗
    (C) Question and Answer
    (D) Classification

6. Which of the following types of questions can be informed by an extensive secondary structure?
    (A) Main Point
    (B) Primary Purpose
    (C) Author's Attitude
    (D) Specific Reference

ANSWER KEY
1. d, 2. [a, b, d], 3. c, 4. [b, d], 5. [a, c], 6. [a, b, c, d]

Wilt Chamberlain scored the highest number of points (100) in a single basketball game. In so doing, he also made 28 out of 32 free throws, a happy anomaly for the career 51.1% free throw shooter.

21/STRUCTURE

A NOTE ON STRUCTURE

Understanding the structure of a passage is important. By passage structure, we are talking about the organization of the passage as well as the strategies the author uses to make his or her point. Before heading into the questions, you must understand how the passage is structured. In many ways, understanding the structure of the passage is the ultimate test on Reading Comprehension, since it looks beyond topic to the arguments being made.

Before you move to the questions, you'll want to summarize the passage in one sentence. This could be something like "Two arguments are made, a criticism is made of the first, and the author sides with second."

Ninja: When you understand a passage on such a conceptual level, you're truly a Reading Comprehension ninja.

Here are some examples of Organization questions that test your knowledge of the passage's structure.

Organization

- Which one of the following most accurately describes the organization of the passage?

- Which one of the following most accurately characterizes the relationship between the two passages?

- Which one of the following best describes the organization of the last paragraph?

- Which one of the following sequences most accurately and completely corresponds to the presentation of the material in the passage?

Not only is it important to understand the structure of the passage as a whole, you'll also be tested on your understanding of particular sentences or paragraphs and how they fit into the structure of the passage. The following are some examples of Role questions that test your knowledge on how particular sentences or paragraphs function in a paragraph or passage.

Role

> Which one of the following most accurately represents the primary function of the author's mention of marketing devices (line 43)?

> The primary function of the third paragraph of the passage in relation to the second paragraph is to

> In the last sentence of the second paragraph, the author mentions "experts in dance" primarily in order to

> Which one of the following pairs most accurately describes why the authors of passage A and passage B, respectively, mention the study by Solnick and Hemenway?

> The author's use of the phrase "no special magic" (line 43) is most likely meant primarily to convey that notions like "voluntary" and "involuntary"

The tagging that you do at the end of each paragraph will help you formulate the passage's structure in your own words. Generally speaking, there are only three types of statements in passages:

- **Conclusion:** A statement that is supported by other statements. This concept has been covered in depth in this book, but to sum up, a conclusion is whatever the author or a party in a passage is trying to prove.

- **Premise:** A statement that provides support for a conclusion.

- **Background:** A statement that is neither a conclusion nor a premise, but provides information that helps you understand the argument. This could be an explanation of a problem the author is trying to solve, the general history of the circumstances relevant to the passage's subject matter, or an undeveloped point of view the author wishes to dispute.

You can arrive at the appropriate tags by asking yourself if there are any conclusions in the paragraph. If so, how are those conclusions supported? If there aren't any conclusions, is the paragraph supporting a conclusion in another paragraph? If not, you are dealing with background, and you must determine how that background serves the passage as a whole. Very often the first paragraph or some portion of the first paragraph is background, so be on the lookout.

Structure is a little more complicated with Comparative Reading passages. Even though there are two passages, there is a structure that encompasses both, meaning that you have to think about how each passage relates to the other. For instance, there could be information in passage B that provides support for a conclusion in passage A. You must note that. We'll talk more about this in our chapter that specifically explores Comparative Reading.

Not only will understanding structure allow you to better understand the passage overall, it will also allow you to anticipate the answer to Organization questions and Role questions like those we listed earlier. These questions will be discussed in more detail in a later chapter.

To practice honing your skills on reading for structure, tackle the following exercise. Remember, you've got to wax on/wax off, paint the fence, sand the floor, etc. before you can beat up the insecure blond guy whose girlfriend you stole. (It's a Karate Kid reference. Go watch it. The original. Not the version with Will Smith's spawn).

STRUCTURE EXERCISE

Read each of the passages below and summarize their structure in one sentence in the space provided. Remember to couch your sentence in terms of arguments. What are the points of view? What is the support for that point of view? And be sure to keep the author's role in mind. Good luck!

Question #1

There's a theory known as "Behavioral Sink." No, this is not the place mom takes you to wash your filthy mouth out with soap. The results of an experiment are illuminating. John B. Calhoun (not to be confused John C. Calhoun, former Senator, Vice President, and all-around jerk) performed an experiment in which he built a mouse paradise with plenty of food and places to create nests, and he introduced eight mice into this little slice of rodent heaven. Within two years, the population had exploded to over two thousand mice. Even though there were still enough resources, mouse society fell to pieces: females retreated to nesting spots, becoming tiny, adorable shut-ins; certain males took to eating, sleeping, grooming, and doing nothing else; the rest of mouse society devolved into cannibalism and unspeakable acts of cute-as-a-button violence.

So, what does this experiment have to do with us? Calhoun, and others like him, believe that we humans are on our way to a similar fate. The similarities between mice and humans are well documented, and, in many ways, our societies function similarly. The examples of human events mirroring the mouse events that occurred in the experiment are chilling. I'll take one of those things: males that eat, sleep, groom, and do nothing else. The rise of the hipster—males who groom their beards obsessively, provide nothing of value to society, and insist on artisan everything—perfectly matches that phenomenon. I could go on, but I need not. It is quite clear that Calhoun is right, and we are on our way to whiskered, buck-toothed oblivion.

ANSWER: _____
_____
_____
_____
_____

Question #2

Honore de Balzac was a corpulent man who looked like Jack Black with a push-broom mustache. This state-of-affairs, in and of itself, is surely enough to secure his place in history. In addition, Balzac – yes, yes, it's really hard not to giggle – had the chutzpah to write two books on marriage before he even got married.

These appalling factoids notwithstanding, many critics praise Balzac as the father of French realism and the greatest literary artist of his day. The work most often cited as an example of his genius is *La Comedie Humaine*, or *The Human Comedy*. The book is a collection of ninety-one finished works and forty-six unfinished works, encompassing stories, analytical essays, and even complete novels.

In *La Comedie*, themes and characters recur from time to time, but what makes the work a breathtaking whole rather than the sum of its parts is its comprehensive realism. Balzac sought to describe things and events in detail, allowing them to tell their own story. *La Comedie* represents a world-view in stories and essays, with subjects as diverse as manners, money, philosophy, poverty, and different careers. It is the coherent worldview presented that sets Balzac apart from his contemporaries. Gustave Flaubert, one of Balzac's most important intellectual heirs, praised this even though he was unimpressed with Balzac's writing style, saying, "What a man he would have been had he known how to write!"

ANSWER: _____

Question #3

In 1991, with the fall of the Berlin Wall, Capitalism triumphed in the Capitalism vs. Communism Cold War Smackdown Extravaganza. Goodbye, Valdimir Lenin; hello, Ronald McDonald! Just so we're clear on what we're talking about: Capitalism is the economic system wherein the means of production are privately owned, and the revenue generated by a business goes to the owners, who pay laborers. Communism, on the other hand, is the economic system in which the people, in the form of the government, own the means of production, and the revenue goes to the people. So, does the fact that Capitalism came out victorious in the Cold War mean that it's the best economic system around?

Communist theorists argue that, regardless of the outcome of the Cold War, Communism is the better, fairer system. Capitalism leaves the vulnerable at the mercy of the powerful, creating intolerable inequality and senseless suffering. The collapse of Communism, these theorists argue, was a problem of implementation, not one of substance. Far from being a true Communist country, the USSR was nothing more than a corrupt kleptocracy masquerading as Communism.

Capitalist theorists, on the other hand, argue that the grotesque abuses of the Soviet regime are no accident, but a necessary feature of Communism. Human nature requires a top-down command structure, and, where property owners don't fill that need, corrupt bureaucrats will. That Capitalism is the best system, these theorists argue, is self-evident from its supremacy in the aftermath of the Cold War and the huge wealth that it's generated. The garish inequality and grinding poverty of the lower classes are unfortunate side effects of economic reality.

In truth, neither of these systems is ideal. There is, however, an economic system that strikes a balance between these two positions: Syndicalism. In Syndicalism, the workers in a particular business own the means of production, and the wealth accrues to them. The benefits of Capitalistic competition are captured in the fact that each syndicate has an incentive to outcompete another syndicate in the same industry. In addition, the unfairness that Communism purported to solve is actually solved with Syndicalism. Since workers share in the company profits proportionally, it's impossible to misuse labor by, among other things, paying starvation wages as happens so often when the means of production are privately owned. Syndicalism, in the final analysis, is the optimal, although still imperfect, economic system.

ANSWER: _____
_____
_____
_____
_____
_____

Question #4

Fairy tales are unambiguously designed for consumption by children. Nobody would call *Hansel and Gretel* or *Little Red Riding Hood* adult material. And yet, these stories are often abhorrent, gruesome affairs. Hansel and Gretel are abandoned by their stepmother and ultimately burn a witch to death in an oven. Little Red Riding Hood's grandmother is eaten by a wolf. *Struwwelpeter*, a collection of German fairy tales published in 1845 by Heinrich Hoffman, recounts stories of children being burned alive and having limbs hacked off.

The most common explanation for this state of affairs is that fairy tales are cautionary tales adults use to shape the behavior of children. *Goldilocks and the Three Bears* is instructive. Goldilocks breaks into a house, eats the food, sleeps in the bed, etc. She's run off by three angry bears when they come home. The moral of the story? No breaking and entering.

However, misbehavior like that of Goldilocks is absent from many of the most terrifying tales. Hansel and Gretel, through no fault of their own, are abandoned by their stepmother in the forest. Why, then, must they go through the terrifying ordeal of being captured by a witch? Why do they have to burn her to death to make their escape? The cautionary tale explanation cannot answer those questions.

In his 1976 book, *The Uses of Enchantment: The Meaning and Importance of Fairy Tales*, Bruno Bettelheim offers an explanation that encompasses all fairy tales, even those without misbehaving children. Fairy tales, Bettelheim argues, offer a safe, hypothetical environment for children to grapple with their fears. All too adult topics like death and abandonment are dealt with in a simple way that children can wrap their minds around. Thus, when one of life's inevitable crises strikes – the death of a friend or family member, a natural disaster, abandonment by a compatriot or a loved one – the child has a frame of reference through which to process the crisis.

ANSWER: _____

Question #5

Slang is a window into the collective consciousness of a particular society, a way to see into the hive mind of a people. Let's take a look at common slang terms and phrases from the Victorian era to see what we can determine about that society.

First off we have "bag o' mystery." Sounds like a fun magic trick, right? Nope. That's slang for sausage. And "doing the bear?" No, no. It's not about sexy time, although it could lead to that kind of thing. It means courting that involves hugging.

It keeps going. How about these: "not up to dick," "mutton shunter," or "poked up?" It would seem that all of these are just dirty. Not so. In actuality, they mean "not feeling well," "police officer," and "embarrassed," respectively. Victorians also called the mouth a "sauce box," and drinking absinthe neat was referred to as "smothering a parrot."

The upshot here is that the British, as strange as they are now, were even stranger back in the Victorian era. In case you thought it was just a lingo thing, consider the outfits and grooming habits: top hats, handlebar mustaches, corsets, and bloomers. Weird, weird, weird.

ANSWER: _____
_____
_____
_____
_____

Question #6

Although a perfect definition of irony eludes us, the Internet (yes, the Internet, that trustworthy repository of conspiracy theories and videos of cats engaged in cuteness) defines irony as, "a state of affairs or an event that seems deliberately contrary to what one expects and is often amusing as a result." This is still pretty vague, but let's look at some indisputable examples of irony and see if the definition holds up.

In 1985, a man drowned at a pool party that was being thrown by New Orleans lifeguards to celebrate a year in which there were no drownings. Indisputably contrary to what one expects. Is it amusing? Depends on how funny drowning is to you, but it passes muster. Here's another: Gary Kremen, the founder of Match.com, lost his wife to a man she met on Match.com. Seems ironic, but, to me at least, it doesn't seem directly contrary to what you'd expect. If Match.com is a good website, then you'd expect anyone, including this guy's wife, to find a better match than they'd found without it. We're one for two, so far.

How about this? There were zero ponies involved in The Pony Express. Seems ironic, maybe, but nobody really thinks that cowboys were riding baby horses. They were riding full-sized horses. The Pony Express was just a cute name for something that was not nearly so cute. So, this bit of irony clearly doesn't fit the definition above. One might come to the conclusion that the definition of irony is flawed, but that would be a mistake. The definition of irony above is as close as one can get to a concept that can't be defined. Irony touches something deep, and sometimes dark, inside of us that doesn't fit neatly into words.

ANSWER: _____
_____
_____
_____
_____
_____

Question #7

Everybody talks about dinosaur extinction, but things like trilobites and placoderms, which also went out with a bang – or maybe a freeze or a flood, who knows? – get no love. However, the extinction events surrounding the swan songs of these strange creatures are fascinating.

The placoderm, an armored prehistoric fish, went extinct in the Devonian event, which actually encompassed a number of mass die-offs between 380 million and 360 million years ago. While the cause is unclear, and there may have been multiple causes, one of the hypotheses regarding the cause is intriguing. During the Devonian event, land plants went from a maximum height of 30 centimeters to a maximum height of 30 meters, a hundred-fold increase.

This had two effects that, in turn, may have caused die-offs. First, larger plants have deeper roots, which turn over soil that would otherwise remain undisturbed. This process likely broke down rocks and released ions into rivers, which in turn nourish algae when they run off into the ocean. An algal bloom can starve the water of oxygen, thereby suffocating other species. The explosion of plant mass on land also released millions of tons of CO_2 into the atmosphere, which would cloud out the sun and create a much colder climate. Warm water creatures couldn't cope.

The trilobite, a little sea dweller resembling the modern day man o' war couldn't make it past the Permian-Triassic extinction, even though it survived the Devonian event. The P-Tr extinction, as it's known to scholars, was by far the most devastating mass extinction in Earth's history. Fully 96% of marine species and 70% of terrestrial vertebrate species died out. Notably, this is the only mass extinction of insects, including the largest insects that ever lived. Anything that could kill off a giant cockroach must've been bad. Again, it's unclear what the causes of the extinction were, and, like the Denovian event, it was likely a confluence of factors, each of which wouldn't have been independently sufficient to cause the die-off.

The most interesting proposed cause of the P-TR extinction is the formation of the supercontinent Pangaea, a process that was completed around the end of the Permian and beginning of the Triassic periods. As the continents slammed into one another, the nutrient rich inner seas between continents disappeared, killing off the species that lived there. This consolidation also erased thousands of miles of shoreline along which land dwellers lived. Not only did these species lose their habitat, invasive species that were once separated by oceans were unleashed on native species that had no natural defenses against them.

ANSWER: _____

Question #8

Is emoji a new language? It certainly is used as a primary texting language by tweens and teens. Perhaps some background is needed for the textually-challenged. Emoji are little pictures that can be added to text messages, and they range from faces displaying various emotions to cars, picnic baskets, medical devices, and hands giving the thumbs up or praying or punching. The original intent of these was to convey the attitude of the sender in a way that's impossible with text only. However, some linguists have taken the position that, as these emoji are used, they are themselves a new language.

Dr. Barnabus Zechariah Twitty, chair of the linguistics department at Northwest Arkansas Junior College, has made this precise claim in his recent book, *Emoji: Happyface of the Future*? Although Dr. Twitty admits that emoji is a pidgin language – in other words, the nascent progenitor of a full language that lacks necessary concepts and modifiers – he argues that emoji will develop into a real language, with new emoji being added to fill in the gaps. He cites numerous examples of coherent, emoji-only messages sent through text as well as the emerging social consensus on fixed meaning of certain emoji.

As persuasive as Dr. Twitty's argument appears on the surface, it ignores two crucial points that fatally undermine his thesis. First, it's impossible to see how emoji could evolve into a spoken language, which means that to classify emoji as a language would require radically redefining what language is. Even if people were to start "speaking emoji" to one another, it would likely just be people using the words of their native language that approximate the picture. This might be slang, but it does not constitute a new language. Secondly, to the extent that emoji are anything new, they're a step backward. It's possible to look at emoji as a new writing system, rather than a language but they take us back to the era of the pictogram, the stuff of hieroglyphics. We evolved out of the constraints of that system because it was too rigid and required unnecessary memorization.

In the final analysis, emoji is useful as a texting aid, but it will never move beyond that, and the use of emoji to communicate beyond this function is a fad that will soon fade as its substantial limitations become clear.

ANSWER: _____
_____
_____
_____
_____
_____

Question #9

Invasive species are species that are not native to a particular ecosystem and that, when introduced into an ecosystem, alter the ecosystem significantly by presenting new challenges to native species. The problem of invasive species has been around for a long time, but with the proliferation of modern modes of travel, few locales on earth are free of this problem. However, recently developed methods of species eradication have proven particularly effective in addressing one of the most frequent offenders: the feral goat.

Dr. Elizabeth Mason, a goat expert at the Goat Institute of El Segundo, developed a detailed plan for eradicating invasive goats in the ecologically important Galapagos Islands. The Galapagos are the islands that inspired Charles Darwin's development of the Theory of Natural Selection, and they are a historical treasure as well as an ecological one. To put the problem in perspective, the largest island, Isabela, was plagued with more than 100,000 feral goats even though the island itself is less than two square miles in size.

Classic hunting methods were effective up to a point, but tracking the goats in the thickly forested interior proved nearly impossible. If even one mating pair remained at the end of the project, the goats could quickly repopulate. Of all the innovative techniques Dr. Mason used, the most ingenious technique was the use of so-called "Judas goats." Sterilized goats were equipped with radio transmitters and released on the island. Since goats are social animals, the Judas goats would join up with herds, allowing the hunters to easily find and eliminate the feral goats by tracking the radio signals. The goats were eradicated from Isabela in a little over a year.

Dr. Mason believes that techniques such as the Judas goat initiative, along with more pedestrian techniques like better data management and streamlined supply chains, can lead to replication of this project to eradicate many different invasive species in many different types of ecosystems.

ANSWER: _____
_____
_____
_____
_____

Question #10

Great Flood mythology – the story of Noah is the flood myth with which westerners are most familiar – appears in the folklore of numerous civilizations over the course of history. A version of the Atlantis story, a city beneath the waves, is similarly prevalent. It is quite likely that the two are related, and that there is a substantial nugget of historical truth behind these stories.

Today, a narrow strip of water, the Bosporus Strait, links the Mediterranean Sea with the Black Sea. Historical theorists, however, believe that this was not the case until around ten thousand years ago, and, more importantly, the Black Sea was not a sea, but a vast valley. According to these theorists, as the last ice age came to an end, sea levels, including that of the Mediterranean, rose drastically and rapidly. The result was that the low-lying area just north of modern-day Istanbul, was rapidly inundated, and the residents of that area were wiped out in a stunning deluge.

This theory finds support across various academic disciplines. Classicists point to the writings of Aristotle and Strabus, both of whom wrote extensively about the City of Atlantis and gave geographical indicators that point to a location in what is now the Black Sea. Marine ecologists have found traces in certain locations of chemical compounds that point to human activity of the kind engaged in during ancient times in large quantities and in places they wouldn't expect. Archaeologists have found a number of structures that appear to be roads leading into what is now the Black Sea.

Until an indisputable Atlantean artifact is found, this theory remains just a theory. However, there are efforts currently underway to send unmanned vessels to the bottom of the Black Sea in the most promising locations, and it is hoped that they will turn up concrete evidence of civilization, if not the very ruins of that civilization.

ANSWER: _____
_____
_____
_____
_____
_____

ANSWER KEY

1. Paragraph one describes an experiment in detail, which, along with an example in the second paragraph, supports the predictive conclusion, which the author endorses, in that paragraph.

2. Paragraph one provides background on an author, an opinion is announced in paragraph two, and supported with an example in that paragraph and in paragraph three.

3. A question is posed in the first paragraph, two answers to the question are posed and discarded, and a third answer that incorporates features of the first two answers is proposed and endorsed by the author.

4. A strange circumstance is presented in the first paragraph, an explanation is proposed in the second paragraph and criticized in the third paragraph, and an alternate explanation is proposed and adopted in the fourth paragraph.

5. Paragraph one provides background about a phenomenon, examples of that phenomenon are given in paragraphs two and three, which support the conclusion in paragraph four.

6. A definition is provided in paragraph one, some information for and against the relevance of the definition is considered in paragraph two, and the author concludes the definition is relevant in paragraph three.

7. A conclusion is announced in paragraph one and supported with details in paragraphs two through five.

8. A question is posed. Background of the subject matter of the question is offered in paragraph one, an answer to the question is proposed in paragraph two and disputed by the author in paragraph three, and a prediction is made in paragraph four.

9. A general problem is identified in the first paragraph, a claim about the effectiveness of a solution to one specific type of the problem is made in that paragraph and supported with details in paragraphs two and three. A prediction is made in paragraph four.

10. A claim is made in the first paragraph that two phenomena are related, an explanation of how they might be related is explained in the second paragraph and supported in the third, and a qualification of the explanation is made in the fourth paragraph.

Now that you've had a chance to practice, it's time to try your newfound structural skills on real Reading Comprehension passages. Tag the following passages for structure, identifying what role each paragraph plays in the overall argument structure. When you finish the passage, write a one sentence summary of the entire organization, then tackle the questions. All questions that don't pertain to structure have been greyed out to allow you to focus on developing this important skill.

Which of the following are names or nicknames for Spider-Man?
1. Your Friendly Neighborhood Spider-Man
2. Peter Parker
3. Wall-Crawler
4. The Webbed Wonder
5. Spidey

Answer: all of the above

EXERCISE 1: OCT. 2011 PASSAGE 1

Determining the most effective way to deter deliberate crimes, such as fraud, as opposed to impulsive crimes, such as crimes of passion, is a problem currently being debated in the legal community. On one side of
(5) the debate are those scholars who believe that deliberate crimes are a product of the influence of societal norms and institutions on individuals. These scholars suggest that changing people's beliefs about crime, increasing the access of the most economically alienated
(10) individuals to economic institutions, and rehabilitating those convicted of this type of crime will reduce the crime rate. On the other side are those legal scholars who believe that the decision to commit a deliberate crime is primarily the result of individual choice. They
(15) suggest that increasing the fines and penalties associated with criminal activity, along with efficacious law enforcement, is the best deterrence method. However, some recent legal scholarship has changed the nature of this debate by introducing an economic principle
(20) that shows that these two positions, far from being antithetical, are surprisingly complementary.

The economic principle that reconciles the two positions is that of utility maximization, which holds that, given a choice of actions, rational individuals will
(25) choose the action that maximizes their anticipated overall satisfaction, or expected utility. The expected utility of an action is ascertained by determining the utilities of the possible outcomes of that action, weighing them according to the likelihood of each
(30) outcome's coming to pass, and then adding up those weighted utilities. Using this economic framework, an individual's decision to commit a crime can be analyzed as a rational economic choice.

According to the utility maximization principle a
(35) person who responds rationally to economic incentives or disincentives will commit a crime if the expected utility from doing so, given the chance of getting caught, exceeds the expected utility from activity that is lawful. Within this framework the two crime-deterrence
(40) methods have the same overall effect. For instance, the recommendations on one side of the crime deterrence debate to increase penalties for crimes and strengthen law enforcement result in an increased likelihood of detection and punishment and impose an increased
(45) cost to the individual if detected and punished. This lowers the expected utility from criminal activity, thereby making a person less likely to choose to commit a deliberate crime. The recommendations on the other side of the debate, such as increasing the
(50) economic opportunities of individuals most alienated from economic institutions, also affect the utility equation. All else being equal, enacting these types of policies will effectively increase the expected utility from lawful activity. This economic
(55) analysis demonstrates that the two positions are not fundamentally in conflict, and that the optimal approach to crime deterrence would include elements of both deterrence strategies.

2. The author mentions "crimes of passion" in line 3 primarily in order to

    (A) give an example of a kind of deliberate crime
    (B) provide a contrast that helps to define a deliberate crime
    (C) demonstrate that not all crimes can be deterred
    (D) help illustrate one side of the current debate in the legal community
    (E) mention a crime that is a product of the influence of societal norms

5. Which one of the following most accurately describes the organization of the passage?

    (A) Two sides of a debate are described and a general principle is used to resolve the conflict between them.
    (B) Two sides of a debate are described and an economic principle is applied to decide between them.
    (C) Two beliefs are described and a principle is introduced to discredit them.
    (D) A general principle is described and instantiated by two different ways of solving a problem.
    (E) A general principle is described and used to highlight the differences between two sides in a debate.

STRUCTURE / 271

PASSAGE SUMMARY

Paragraph one begins with a description of a debate currently raging over how to deter deliberate crimes. Each side of the debate is explained with one side attributing it to social norms and the other to individual choice. The paragraph concludes with "recent" scholarship that shows the two positions can be reconciled. Synthesis anyone?

In paragraph two, the author describes the economic principle that reconciles the debate: utility maximization. Since this view is supported, we know it's the main conclusion of the passage.

The third paragraph applies the theory explained in paragraph two, showing how each of the approaches identified in paragraph one are effective. That is a premise, providing support for the prescriptive statement at the end of the paragraph that "the optimal approach to crime deterrence would include elements of both deterrence strategies."

To sum up: A problem is identified, and two seemingly contradictory solutions to the problem are presented. The solutions are shown not to contradict, and a combination of those solutions is recommended.

BP Minotaur: You should practice summarizing every passage in one or two sentences. And by "should" I mean "will."

Question #2

This is a Role question, and it asks about the background to the debate we identified at the beginning of the passage: the debate about deliberate crime. "Crimes of passion" are examples of impulsive crimes whereas fraud is an example of a deliberate crime. That's answer choice (B).

(A) This answer choice mischaracterizes the passage. Crimes of passion are NOT deliberate crimes.
(C) The passage never tells us how or whether other crimes can be deterred. All we know is that *deliberate* crimes can be deterred.
(D) The two sides of the debate are the conclusions mentioned later on in paragraph one, neither of which relate to crimes of passion.

2. The author mentions "crimes of passion" in line 3 primarily in order to

   (A) give an example of a kind of deliberate crime
   (B) provide a contrast that helps to define a deliberate crime
   (C) demonstrate that not all crimes can be deterred
   (D) help illustrate one side of the current debate in the legal community
   (E) mention a crime that is a product of the influence of societal norms

(E) Again, this is referring to the first of the two views in paragraph one.

Question #5

This is the Organization question we were anticipating. By summarizing the progression of the passage before hitting the questions, we know its answer. Answer choice (A) identifies the background and opposing views in paragraph one and the author's conclusion at the end of the paragraph that synthesizes both views.

> 5. Which one of the following most accurately describes the organization of the passage?
>
>   (A) Two sides of a debate are described and a general principle is used to resolve the conflict between them.
>   (B) Two sides of a debate are described and an economic principle is applied to decide between them.
>   (C) Two beliefs are described and a principle is introduced to discredit them.
>   (D) A general principle is described and instantiated by two different ways of solving a problem.
>   (E) A general principle is described and used to highlight the differences between two sides in a debate.

(B) The author never decides between the sides of the debate. Instead, the author says they should be put together.
(C) The author does not discredit these beliefs. They are both viable aspects of an overall solution.
(D) This has the passage backward. The principle comes after the ways of solving the problem. Also, the author says that these are not so much two different ways of solving a problem as they are two parts of an overall solution to the problem.
(E) This leaves out the idea that these methods are reconcilable, which is the main point of the passage.

Ditz: Like, okay, but like how do I put this in my markup?

Good question, Ditz. By focusing on role-oriented (rather than subject-oriented) tags, organizational tags should just become part of your natural tagging process. It's when you focus on the subject of a paragraph rather than the function it serves in the overall passage that you'll miss organizational tags.

ANSWER KEY

1. d, 2. b, 3. e, 4. b, 5. a, 6. c

Interested in the explanations to the other questions? Okay, okay, you can check the full markup in your *MyBlueprint* account.

EXERCISE 2: DEC. 2011 PASSAGE 4

As part of an international effort to address environmental problems resulting from agricultural overproduction, hundreds of thousands of acres of surplus farmland throughout Europe will be taken out
(5) of production in coming years. Restoring a natural balance of flora to this land will be difficult, however, because the nutrients in soil that has been in constant agricultural use are depleted. Moreover, much of this land has been heavily fertilized, and when such
(10) land is left unplanted, problem weeds like thistles often proliferate, preventing many native plants from establishing themselves. While the quickest way to restore heavily fertilized land is to remove and replace the topsoil, this is impractical on a large scale such as
(15) that of the European effort. And while it is generally believed that damaged ecological systems will restore themselves very gradually over time, a study underway in the Netherlands is investigating the possibility of artificially accelerating the processes through
(20) which nature slowly reestablishes plant diversity on previously farmed land.

In the study, a former cornfield was raked to get rid of cornstalks and weeds, then divided into 20 plots of roughly equal size. Control plots were replanted with
(25) corn or sown with nothing at all. The remaining plots were divided into two groups: plots in one group were sown with a mixture of native grasses and herbs; those in the other group received the same mixture of grasses and herbs together with clover and toadflax. After three
(30) years, thistles have been forced out of the plots where the broadest variety of species was sown and have also disappeared from mats of grass in the plots sown with fewer seed varieties. On the control plots that were left untouched, thistles have become dominant.

(35) On some of the plots sown with seeds of native plant species, soil from nearby land that had been taken out of production 20 years earlier was scattered to see what effect introducing nematodes, fungi, and other beneficial microorganisms associated with later stages
(40) of natural soil development might have on the process of native plant repopulation. The seeds sown on these enriched plots have fared better than seeds sown on the unenriched plots, but still not as well as those growing naturally on the nearby land. Researchers have
(45) concluded that this is because fields farmed for many years are overrun with aggressive disease organisms, while, for example, beneficial mycorrhiza—fungi that live symbiotically on plant roots and strengthen them against the effects of disease organisms—are lacking.
(50) These preliminary results suggest that restoring natural plant diversity to overfarmed land hinges on restoring a natural balance of microorganisms in the soil. In other words, diversity underground fosters diversity aboveground. Researchers now believe that both
(55) kinds of diversity can be restored more quickly to damaged land if beneficial microorganisms are "sown" systematically into the soil along with a wide variety of native plant seeds.

21. Which one of the following most accurately describes the organization of the passage?

(A) A study is described, the results of the study are scrutinized, and the results are judged to be inconclusive but promising.
(B) A hypothesis is presented, evidence both supporting and undermining the hypothesis is given, and a modification of the hypothesis is argued for.
(C) A study is evaluated, a plan of action based on the study's findings is suggested, and conclusions are drawn concerning the likely effectiveness of the plan.
(D) A goal is stated, studies are discussed that argue for modifying the goal's objectives, and a methodology is detailed to achieve the revised goal.
(E) A problem is presented, a study addressing the problem is described, and a course of action based on the study's findings is given.

24. The author's reference to the belief that "damaged ecological systems will restore themselves very gradually over time" (lines 16–17) primarily serves to

(A) introduce a long-held belief that the Netherlands study is attempting to discredit
(B) cite the justification generally used by people favoring intense agricultural production
(C) suggest that the consequences of agricultural overproduction are not as dire as people generally believe
(D) present the most common perception of why agricultural overproduction is problematic
(E) describe the circumstances surrounding and motivating the Netherlands study

PASSAGE SUMMARY

By now, paragraph one ought to look familiar to you. We've got a problem! Specifically, it's really hard to quickly restore old farmland to its natural state. This, future lawyer, is background. How much you wanna bet we're going to hear something about a solution to the problem?

Paragraph two is a study. A study is generally a premise that provides support for a conclusion. This one supports the conclusion at the end of paragraph three that we can solve the problem by sowing native plants and microorganisms into the soil. Specifically, the study supports the idea that sowing native plants helps.

Paragraph three continues to talk about the study. This provides support for the second part of the conclusion—we need to sow fields with microorganisms—by showing that the patches sown without microorganisms don't do as well as natural plots that have such microorganisms.

In sum, a problem is presented, and a study is used to support the use of a two-part solution.

Question #21

We answered this question in our heads (yes, we have numerous heads), and came up with something quite similar to answer choice (E). Background, then premise, then conclusion. Yup!

(A) This answer choice leaves out the first paragraph entirely. This also mischaracterizes the passage; the author never judges the results of the study to be lacking in any way.

(B) There is no hypothesis identified early on in the passage, as this answer choice claims, which also rules out a modification of that hypothesis.

(C) This answer choice, as with (A) conveniently ignores the first paragraph. (Poor paragraph one!) Moreover, there are not any conclusions about whether or not the plan will be effective.

(D) This is wrong because there's no indication in the passage that the goal of restoring farmland quickly should be modified.

21. Which one of the following most accurately describes the organization of the passage?

(A) A study is described, the results of the study are scrutinized, and the results are judged to be inconclusive but promising.
(B) A hypothesis is presented, evidence both supporting and undermining the hypothesis is given, and a modification of the hypothesis is argued for.
(C) A study is evaluated, a plan of action based on the study's findings is suggested, and conclusions are drawn concerning the likely effectiveness of the plan.
(D) A goal is stated, studies are discussed that argue for modifying the goal's objectives, and a methodology is detailed to achieve the revised goal.
(E) A problem is presented, a study addressing the problem is described, and a course of action based on the study's findings is given.

Question #24

We identified the whole first paragraph, including this statement, as background, and the phrase "describe the circumstances" in answer choice (E) says that quite beautifully. Or at least accurately.

> 24. The author's reference to the belief that "damaged ecological systems will restore themselves very gradually over time" (lines 16–17) primarily serves to
>
> (A) introduce a long-held belief that the Netherlands study is attempting to discredit
> (B) cite the justification generally used by people favoring intense agricultural production
> (C) suggest that the consequences of agricultural overproduction are not as dire as people generally believe
> (D) present the most common perception of why agricultural overproduction is problematic
> (E) describe the circumstances surrounding and motivating the Netherlands study

(A) The study does nothing to disconfirm this statement. Instead, it shows that this situation can be sped up.
(B) Huh? The passage never mentions anyone who believes that we ought to just farm land until it turns to barren wasteland.
(C) The passage never discusses how upset people are about overproduction or whether those beliefs are rational. This mischaracterizes the passage.
(D) The most common perception? And what are the other perceptions? No, this is never mentioned, and there is no basis to make a comparison like this.

ANSWER KEY
20. a, 21. e, 22. b, 23. d, 24. e, 25. b, 26. c, 27. b

Dying for the explanations for the remaining questions? You know where to go, grasshopper. It begins with an "m" and rhymes with "MySchmueprint account."

EXERCISE 3: DEC. 2009 PASSAGE 1

Passage A

Recent studies have shown that sophisticated computer models of the oceans and atmosphere are capable of simulating large-scale climate trends with remarkable accuracy. But these models make use
(5) of large numbers of variables, many of which have wide ranges of possible values. Because even small differences in those values can have a significant impact on what the simulations predict, it is important to determine the impact when values differ even
(10) slightly.

Since the interactions between the many variables in climate simulations are highly complex, there is no alternative to a "brute force" exploration of all possible combinations of their values if predictions
(15) are to be reliable. This method requires very large numbers of calculations and simulation runs. For example, exhaustive examination of five values for each of only nine variables would require 2 million calculation-intensive simulation runs. Currently
(20) available individual computers are completely inadequate for such a task.

However, the continuing increase in computing capacity of the average desktop computer means that climate simulations can now be run on privately
(25) owned desktop machines connected to one another via the Internet. The calculations are divided among the individual desktop computers, which work simultaneously on their share of the overall problem. Some public resource computing projects of this kind
(30) have already been successful, although only when they captured the public's interest sufficiently to secure widespread participation.

Passage B

Researchers are now learning that many problems in nature, human society, science, and
(35) engineering are naturally "parallel"; that is, that they can be effectively solved by using methods that work simultaneously in parallel. These problems share the common characteristic of involving a large number of similar elements such as molecules, animals, even
(40) people, whose individual actions are governed by simple rules but, taken collectively, function as a highly complex system.

An example is the method used by ants to forage for food. As Lewis Thomas observed, a solitary ant
(45) is little more than a few neurons strung together by fibers. Its behavior follows a few simple rules. But when one sees a dense mass of thousands of ants, crowded together around their anthill retrieving food or repelling an intruder, a more complex picture
(50) emerges; it is as if the whole is thinking, planning, calculating. It is an intelligence, a kind of live computer, with crawling bits for wits.

We are now living through a great paradigm shift in the field of computing, a shift from sequential
(55) computing (performing one calculation at a time) to massive parallel computing, which employs thousands of computers working simultaneously to solve one computation-intensive problem. Since many computation-intensive problems are inherently
(60) parallel, it only makes sense to use a computing model that exploits that parallelism. A computing model that resembles the inherently parallel problem it is trying to solve will perform best. The old paradigm, in contrast, is subject to the speed limits imposed by purely sequential
(65) computing.

4. The author of passage A mentions public participation (lines 30–32) primarily in order to

(A) encourage public engagement in the sort of computing model discussed in the passage
(B) identify a factor affecting the feasibility of the computing model advocated in the passage
(C) indicate that government support of large-scale computing efforts is needed
(D) demonstrate that adequate support for the type of approach described in the passage already exists
(E) suggest that a computing model like that proposed in the passage is infeasible because of forces beyond the designers' control

5. Passage B relates to passage A in which one of the following ways?

(A) The argument in passage B has little bearing on the issues discussed in passage A.
(B) The explanation offered in passage B shows why the plan proposed in passage A is unlikely to be implemented.
(C) The ideas advanced in passage B provide a rationale for the solution proposed in passage A.
(D) The example given in passage B illustrates the need for the "brute force" exploration mentioned in passage A.
(E) The discussion in passage B conflicts with the assumptions about individual computers made in passage A.

This is a Comparative Reading passage but don't let that throw you off. Just use your newly-honed organization-spotting skills as usual. We'll talk more about the best way to tackle Comparative Reading passages in detail, later. For now just focus on the organizational beats in each passage.

PASSAGE SUMMARY

Paragraph one of passage A gives a brief description of how climate models function. Paragraph two describes a problem with those models: they take more computing power than a single computer can muster. Paragraph three describes a solution to that problem. The solution is that we use a bunch of computers working together to solve the problem. The solution to a problem is a conclusion.

Passage B starts off with a description about how certain problems are solved. We already have a similarity here. Passage A discussed a problem and its solution. It's not yet clear whether these problems are similar, but we will find out that they are. Specifically, here the solution to a problem is to use simple methods working in parallel to solve complex problems. Paragraph two gives an example of parallel problem solving in nature: ants.

Finally, paragraph three of passage B ties the two passages together. It shows that the computing solution described in passage A—using a bunch of computers at once—is a specific instance of parallel problem solving discussed generally in passage B.

To sum up, in passage A, a problem is detailed and a solution to the problem is identified. In passage B, how that solution functions is discussed in detail.

Question #4

The statement this question refers to is part of the paragraph describing the solution to the climate-modeling problem. This is a qualification that puts a limit on the effectiveness of that solution. In other words, it limits the scope of the conclusion that this solution is effective. It's only effective when people jump on board with the idea. That's answer choice (B).

4. The author of passage A mentions public participation (lines 30–32) primarily in order to

   (A) encourage public engagement in the sort of computing model discussed in the passage
   (B) identify a factor affecting the feasibility of the computing model advocated in the passage
   (C) indicate that government support of large-scale computing efforts is needed
   (D) demonstrate that adequate support for the type of approach described in the passage already exists
   (E) suggest that a computing model like that proposed in the passage is infeasible because of forces beyond the designers' control

(A) For this to be the right answer, the author would have needed to claim that more needed to be done.
(C) We're talking about the public here. There is no mention of the government, so this mischaracterizes the passage.

(D) The author says that this has worked only when there is public support, not that the support already exists.

(E) There is a limitation here, but that's a far cry from the idea that this thing just won't work. The passage never says that.

Question #5

We already determined that passage B explains how the solution in passage A works. That's answer choice (C).

(A) If you think the passages are unrelated, you're not paying attention. The passages in comparative reading are always related in some way. This probably will never be the right answer.
(B) The only fact in either passage that related to how likely this solution is to be implemented is in passage A, not passage B. Moreover, passage A doesn't say that the plan is unlikely to be implemented, only that the solution needs public support to be successful.
(D) The portion of passage A that focuses on brute force describes brute force as an unworkable solution. It's never mentioned again in either passage.
(E) While comparative reading passages sometimes conflict with one another, that's not the case here. These passages are complementary.

> 5. Passage B relates to passage A in which one of the following ways?
>
>   (A) The argument in passage B has little bearing on the issues discussed in passage A.
>   (B) The explanation offered in passage B shows why the plan proposed in passage A is unlikely to be implemented.
>   (C) The ideas advanced in passage B provide a rationale for the solution proposed in passage A.
>   (D) The example given in passage B illustrates the need for the "brute force" exploration mentioned in passage A.
>   (E) The discussion in passage B conflicts with the assumptions about individual computers made in passage A.

ANSWER KEY

1. c, 2. c, 3. e, 4. b, 5. c, 6. b, 7. a, 8. e

Insert whiny voice: "But mooommmm, I want to see the explanations for questions 1, 2, 3, 6, 7, and 8!"

Insert mom voice: "Johnny, you know they're on your *MyBlueprint* account!"

22/PUTTINGitallTOGETHER

Take wing, take wing, and soar like a bird!

You (yes, you) are now ready to launch a full frontal assault on any Reading Comprehension passage out there[1]. A passage on Navajo weaving with two points of view and an extensive Example secondary structure? Yes, please! A Thesis passage exploring the intricacies of lichen DNA, replete with localized Cause and Effect secondary structures? Don't mind if you do!

PUTTING IT ALL TOGETHER

It's time to put together all of the skills that you have learned into a smooth, seamless whole. So, let's talk a little bit about how to do that.

As you read a passage, you should be doing the following:

- *Marking up the passage (underlining, bracketing, etc.) in the manner described in Chapter 14.*
- *Tagging the passage as described in Chapter 14 (summarizing each paragraph with a few words, marking examples, attitude, etc.)*
- *Filling in your primary structure diagram.*
- *Identifying and tagging secondary structures.*

After you finish reading the passage, but before attacking the questions, you should:

- *Anticipate the correct answers to these questions:*
  - *Main Point*
  - *Primary Purpose*
  - *Author's Attitude*
  - *Anything the passage lends itself to. For instance, if you have found a localized Cause and Effect secondary structure, anticipate a question about it.*
- *Summarize in a sentence or two the structure of the passage, leaving out the subject matter as much as possible.*

---

[1] Well, except Comparative Reading. But you get the idea.

Ditz: Ummm, that, like, sounds like a lot.

Cleetus: Heck yeah! Ain't nobody got time for that @#$%! They's catfish to catch, and moonshine to make, and Yankees to hornswoggle!

Calm down, you two. Blueprint Ninja, can you allay our friends' fears?

Ninja: Right now, you are learning how to approach a Reading Comprehension passage comprehensively and methodically. With practice, these skills—and the deeper understanding of the test they help you to achieve—will become second nature. You will not be doing every single one of these things on test day, but you must do them now. As my ninja master often said, "To build a dojo, scaffolding must first be erected."

We should also add that, on average, there are about three Main Point questions, one Primary Purpose question, and five Author's Attitude questions per test. That adds up to almost a third of the questions for which you are automatically anticipating the correct answer. If you dive into the questions knowing what you are looking for ahead of time, you can save precious minutes on each passage. In other words, time spent up front translates to time saved in the questions.

PRACTICE MAKES PERFECT, AND PERFECT MAKES A RICH LAWYER

We've given you three passages to practice your newfound techniques, and you should address the passages consistent with the Blueprint method. At the end of the chapter, there are markups of these passages utilizing the Blueprint Reading Method™, which will explain how the passage should have been addressed and the moment you should know when to do what.

A few points before we turn you loose. In our Logic Games book (available online and in a bookstore near you!)*, your setup should look precisely like the official setup, but Reading Comprehension isn't as precise an activity as Logic Games. Your markup should look reasonably similar to the official markup at the end of the chapter, but a point-by-point match is not required. The particular way you characterize a conclusion or a secondary structure, for example, probably won't match the official markup precisely, but your markup *should* in some way tag these items.

So while your markup might say "support" instead of "study supports," that's not an issue. But if the support provided is on the topic of, say, elephants, and your markup says "elephants" instead of "support," that's a problem. Using subject tags instead of role tags means you're not getting at the structure of the passage which is what you need to do to truly master Reading Comprehension.

So, read the passage and create your markup, but check the official markup **before** you attack the questions. If your markup deviates materially from the official markup, figure out why before you get to the questions. Did you read too quickly? Miss something? Mistake a Classification secondary structure for an Example secondary structure? If you don't understand why your markup is different, there is an in-depth explanation accompanying each official markup to provide help.

One more thing. You might anticipate a question and find that the particular concept is not tested. That's not a problem! It's still good practice for test day.

Good luck!

---

* No, really. blueprintLSAT.com/lsat/books

Three classic legal movies you should watch:

To Kill a Mockingbird (1962)
12 Angry Men (1957)
Inherit the Wind (1960)

Fairy tales address themselves to two communities, each with its own interests and each in periodic conflict with the other: parents and children. Nearly every study of fairy tales has taken the perspective of the
(5) parent, constructing the meaning of the tales by using the reading strategies of an adult bent on identifying universally valid tenets of moral instruction for children.

For example, the plot of "Hansel and Gretel" is set in motion by hard-hearted parents who abandon
(10) their children in the woods, but for psychologist Bruno Bettelheim the tale is really about children who learn to give up their unhealthy dependency on their parents. According to Bettelheim, this story-in which the children ultimately overpower a witch who has taken
(15) them prisoner for the crime of attempting to eat the witch's gingerbread house-forces its young audience to recognize the dangers of unrestrained greed. As dependent children, Bettelheim argues, Hansel and Gretel had been a burden to their parents, but on their
(20) return home with the witch's jewels, they become the family's support. Thus, says Bettelheim, does the story train its young listeners to become "mature children."

There are two ways of interpreting a story: one is a "superficial" reading that focuses on the tale's manifest
(25) content, and the other is a "deeper" reading that looks for latent meanings. Many adults who read fairy tales are drawn to this second kind of interpretation in order to avoid facing the unpleasant truths that can emerge from the tales when adults-even parents-are portrayed
(30) as capable of acting out of selfish motives themselves. What makes fairy tales attractive to Bettelheim and other psychologists is that they can be used as scenarios that position the child as a transgressor whose deserved punishment provides a lesson for unruly children.
(35) Stories that run counter to such orthodoxies about child-rearing are, to a large extent, suppressed by Bettelheim or "rewritten" through reinterpretation. Once we examine his interpretations closely, we see that his readings produce meanings that are very different from
(40) those constructed by readers with different cultural assumptions and expectations, who, unlike Bettelheim, do not find inflexible tenets of moral instruction in the tales.

Bettelheim interprets all fairy tales as driven by children's fantasies of desire and revenge, and in doing so suppresses the true nature of parental behavior
(45) ranging from abuse to indulgence. Fortunately, these characterizations of selfish children and innocent adults have been discredited to some extent by recent psychoanalytic literature. The need to deny adult evil has been a pervasive feature of our society, leading us to
(50) position children not only as the sole agents of evil but also as the objects of unending moral instruction, hence the idea that a literature targeted for them must stand in the service of pragmatic instrumentality rather than foster an unproductive form of playful pleasure.

9. Which one of the following most accurately states the main idea of the passage?

(A) While originally written for children, fairy tales also contain a deeper significance for adults that psychologists such as Bettelheim have shown to be their true meaning.
(B) The "superficial" reading of a fairy tale, which deals only with the tale's content, is actually more enlightening for children than the "deeper" reading preferred by psychologists such as Bettelheim.
(C) Because the content of fairy tales has historically run counter to prevailing orthodoxies about child-rearing, psychologists such as Bettelheim sometimes reinterpret them to suit their own pedagogical needs.
(D) The pervasive need to deny adult evil has led psychologists such as Bettelheim to erroneously view fairy tales solely as instruments of moral instruction for children.
(E) Although dismissed as unproductive by psychologists such as Bettelheim, fairy tales offer children imaginative experiences that help them grow into morally responsible adults.

10. Based on the passage, which one of the following elements of "Hansel and Gretel" would most likely be de-emphasized in Bettelheim's interpretation of the tale?

(A) Hansel and Gretel are abandoned by their hard-hearted parents.
(B) Hansel and Gretel are imprisoned by the witch.
(C) Hansel and Gretel overpower the witch.
(D) Hansel and Gretel take the witch's jewels.
(E) Hansel and Gretel bring the witch's jewels home to their parents.

11. Which one of the following is the most accurate description of the author's attitude toward Bettelheim's view of fairy tales?

    (A) concern that the view will undermine the ability of fairy tales to provide moral instruction
    (B) scorn toward the view's supposition that moral tenets can be universally valid
    (C) disapproval of the view's depiction of children as selfish and adults as innocent
    (D) anger toward the view's claim that children often improve as a result of deserved punishment
    (E) disappointment with the view's emphasis on the manifest content of a tale

12. The author of the passage would be most likely to agree with which one of the following statements?

    (A) Children who never attempt to look for the deeper meanings in fairy tales will miss out on one of the principal pleasures of reading such tales.
    (B) It is better if children discover fairy tales on their own than for an adult to suggest that they read the tales.
    (C) A child who is unruly will behave better after reading a fairy tale if the tale is suggested to them by another child.
    (D) Most children are too young to comprehend the deeper meanings contained in fairy tales.
    (E) Children should be allowed to enjoy literature that has no instructive purpose.

13. Which one of the following principles most likely underlies the author's characterization of literary interpretation?

    (A) Only those trained in literary interpretation can detect the latent meanings in stories.
    (B) Only adults are psychologically mature enough to find the latent meanings in stories.
    (C) Only one of the various meanings readers may find in a story is truly correct.
    (D) The meanings we see in stories are influenced by the assumptions and expectations we bring to the story.
    (E) The latent meanings a story contains are deliberately placed there by the author.

14. According to the author, recent psychoanalytic literature suggests that

    (A) the moral instruction children receive from fairy tales is detrimental to their emotional development
    (B) fewer adults are guilty of improper child-rearing than had once been thought
    (C) the need to deny adult evil is a pervasive feature of all modern societies
    (D) the plots of many fairy tales are similar to children's revenge fantasies
    (E) the idea that children are typically selfish and adults innocent is of questionable validity

15. It can be inferred from the passage that Bettelheim believes that children are

    (A) uninterested in inflexible tenets of moral instruction
    (B) unfairly subjected to the moral beliefs of their parents
    (C) often aware of inappropriate parental behavior
    (D) capable of shedding undesirable personal qualities
    (E) basically playful and carefree

16. Which one of the following statements is least compatible with Bettelheim's views, as those views are described in the passage?

    (A) The imaginations of children do not draw clear distinctions between inanimate objects and living things.
    (B) Children must learn that their own needs and feelings are to be valued, even when these differ from those of their parents.
    (C) As their minds mature, children tend to experience the world in terms of the dynamics of the family into which they were born.
    (D) The more secure that children feel within the world, the less they need to hold onto infantile notions.
    (E) Children's ability to distinguish between stories and reality is not fully developed until puberty.

DEC. 2002 PASSAGE 2 MARKUP

       Fairy tales address themselves to two communities, each with its own interests and each in periodic conflict with the other: parents and children. Nearly every study of fairy tales has taken the perspective of the
(5) parent, constructing the meaning of the tales by using the reading strategies of an adult bent on identifying universally valid tenets of moral instruction for children.
       For example, the plot of "Hansel and Gretel" is set in motion by hard-hearted parents who abandon
(10) their children in the woods, but for psychologist [Bruno Bettelheim] the tale is really about children who learn to give up their unhealthy dependency on their parents. According to Bettelheim, this story-in which the children ultimately overpower a witch who has taken
(15) them prisoner for the crime of attempting to eat the witch's gingerbread house-forces its young audience to recognize the dangers of unrestrained greed. As dependent children, Bettelheim argues, Hansel and Gretel had been a burden to their parents, but on their
(20) return home with the witch's jewels, they become the family's support. Thus, says Bettelheim, does the story train its young listeners to become "mature children."
       There are two ways of interpreting a story: one is a "superficial" reading that focuses on the tale's manifest
(25) content, and the other is a "deeper" reading that looks for latent meanings. Many adults who read fairy tales are drawn to this second kind of interpretation in order to avoid facing the <u>unpleasant</u> truths that can emerge from the tales when adults-even parents-are portrayed
(30) as capable of acting out of selfish motives themselves. What makes fairy tales attractive to Bettelheim and other psychologists is that they can be used as scenarios that position the child as a transgressor whose deserved punishment provides a lesson for unruly children.
(35) Stories that run counter to such orthodoxies about child-rearing are, to a large extent, <u>suppressed by Bettelheim</u> or "rewritten" through reinterpretation. Once we examine his interpretations closely, we see that his readings produce meanings that are very different from
(40) those constructed by readers with different cultural assumptions and expectations, who, unlike Bettelheim, do not find inflexible tenets of moral instruction in the tales.
       Bettelheim interprets all fairy tales as driven by
(45) children's fantasies of desire and revenge, and in doing so <u>suppresses</u> the true nature of parental behavior ranging from abuse to indulgence. Fortunately, these characterizations of selfish children and innocent adults have been discredited to some extent by recent
(50) psychoanalytic literature. The need to deny adult evil has been a pervasive feature of our society, leading us to position children not only as the sole agents of evil but also as the objects of unending moral instruction, hence the idea that a literature targeted for them must stand
(55) in the service of pragmatic instrumentality rather than foster an unproductive form of playful pleasure.

STUDIES FOCUS ON MORAL INSTRUCTION FOR CHILDREN

EX.

BETTELHEIM SUPPORTS

SUPERFICIAL VS. DEEPER INTERPRETATION

ATT.

BETTELHEIM IS SUPERFICIAL

ATT.

ALTERNATE VIEW

DEEPER READING SHOWS PARENTAL SHORTCOMINGS

ATT.

AUTHOR'S CONCLUSION

FAIRY TALES

MORAL INSTRUCTION OF CHILDREN → PARENTAL BEHAVIOR CAN ALSO BE BAD

(BETTELHEIM STUDIES)

PASSAGE SUMMARY

This is a fairly difficult passage for most students, as it is about a familiar topic (we've all read fairy tales), but in an unfamiliar light with difficult language. Fortunately, it also discusses Hansel and Gretel, so you can get your gingerbread house reading quota out of the way for the day.

The first paragraph starts by giving some background information about fairy tales. The author says there are two communities in fairy tales: adults and children. The author states that these two perspectives are periodically in conflict but that nearly every study of fairy tales takes the parent's perspective. Although not a bright flashing red light that this is going to be an Antithesis passage, it does give us a nice hint that this will be an Antithesis or Synthesis passage. If there are two perspectives possible and everyone takes the first perspective, as a good LSAT student you should anticipate that there will probably be a viewpoint in the passage that emphasizes the child's perspective.

The second paragraph begins with an example of Hansel and Gretel and how interpreters have focused on the children and ignored the cruelty of the parents. This paragraph also introduces Bettelheim, who acts as a stand-in for the adult perspective view from the first paragraph. The author states the story is not about two kids abandoned by their deadbeat parents but instead about children learning to become mature adults to ease the burden on their progenitors.

The third paragraph starts out with a distinction between superficial readings and deeper readings. A superficial reading focuses on the "manifest content" (taking the story literally), while the deeper reading looks for "latent meanings" (looking for the lesson behind the story). The author then tells us that while most adults read fairy tales using the second reading, Bettelheim uses the tales as "moral scenarios" for children, indicating Bettelheim is closer to the superficial view. About two thirds of the way through the paragraph we get the first clear attitude indications. "Suppressed" and "rewritten" tell us that our author doesn't particularly like it that Bettelheim ignores elements in fairy tales that go against his view of parents being wonderful and children being nasty little brutes who need to learn lessons. The author also indicates at the very end that many readers get completely different interpretations than Bettelheim's.

Lastly, the author gives us her opinion; Bettelheim is wrong. The author writes that "the need to deny adult evil has been a pervasive feature of our society" and that fairy tales don't have to have a moral purpose but can instead just be "playful pleasure."

In summary, the author tells us what Bettelheim's view is, explains why it is problematic, then gives her own view in return.

PRIMARY STRUCTURE: ANTITHESIS

There are two clear points of view in the passage which means it's an Antithesis. The first view we see is Bettelheim's: fairy tales are instruments of moral instruction that should be read to emphasize the badness of the children and how they need to grow. The second view is the author's: fairy tales don't have to be interpreted in rigid, moralistic ways and they can exist merely for the enjoyment of children.

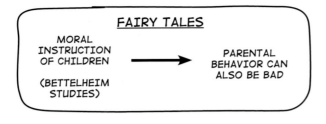

SECONDARY STRUCTURES

There are no secondary structures in this passage.

PASSAGE OVERVIEW

MAIN IDEA

In an Antithesis passage, we're looking for a main idea that encapsulates both points of view but that sides with the author's conclusion, provided the author is present. Our author definitely is (we know this from the interjection of her opinion in paragraph three), and she sides with the children rather than the parents. So the main idea is going to be that, contrary to Bettelheim's view, fairy tales can exist outside of moral instruction for children. In case you had any doubt, our author thoughtfully places her conclusion at the end of the passage, a common place for a conclusion to appear.

PRIMARY PURPOSE

This passage was written to show that Bettelheim, and studies like his, are wrong and to propose an alternate way of reading fairy tales.

AUTHOR'S ATTITUDE

This passage is relatively unusual for a reading comprehension passage in that the author has a pronounced negative tone toward Bettelheim.

QUESTION ANTICIPATION

Given the strong tone we should expect a fair number of questions regarding the author's attitude. Because it is an Antithesis passage, we should expect questions that will ask about the relationship between the two views or that focus on one view in particular.

AND NOW, ONTO THE QUESTIONS...

QUESTION 9: MAIN POINT

Surprisingly, we start with a Main Point question. Actually that's not surprising at all—most passages begin with a Main Point question. We should be careful of answer choices that give us Bettelheim's view only, and that capitalize on sloppy readers who don't notice that there are two points of view, rather than one. Answer choice (D) fits our criteria as it mentions both positions and clearly aligns with the author's view. Although it doesn't mention Bettelheim by name, it does talk about "the need to deny adult evil" which Bettelheim clearly identifies with. It also states that the view erroneously treats fairy tales as instruments of moral instruction which is a direct match for our author's conclusion at the end of the passage.

(A) This answer choice focuses on Bettelheim and neglects our author's point of view. Next!
(B) Close but no cigar. This answer choice gives an Antithesis, but it's the wrong Antithesis. Our author doesn't say that superficial or deep readings are wrong, just that Bettelheim is wrong.
(C) As with (A), this answer choice focuses only on Bettelheim and misses the author's view.
(E) This answer choice may seem attractive, as it gives us Bettelheim's view and then an "although" that would seem to introduce the author's view. However, the second point of view presented,

that fairy tales help children "grow into morally responsible adults" is just a reiteration of Bettelheim's view. This is the third answer choice that focuses solely on Bettelheim so recognizing this passage as an Antithesis really helped us mow through incorrect answer choices.

QUESTION 10: VIEWPOINT

This question is asking us what Bettelheim would de-emphasize about Hansel and Gretel. Since we are excellent Blueprint students and tagged our passage well, we know from our "Att." tag in paragraph four that Bettelheim suppresses examples of parental misbehavior. Answer choice (A) is perfect in this regard, as it is a clear example of parents behaving badly.

(B) This answer choice is somewhat attractive since it appears that Bettelheim de-emphasizes evil actions by parents. However, the witch is not Hansel and Gretel's *parent* so this is not the right answer.

(C) This answer misses the mark, as children misbehaving is exactly the type of thing Bettelheim would emphasize. This question is asking for the opposite.

(D) Similar to (C), this answer choice focuses on the bad actions of children (which Bettelheim loves) and neglects parental behavior.

(E) This answer choice can trick people who don't read the question clearly. In this case the kids are overcoming an obstacle and helping their parents. This element would probably be emphasized by Bettelheim. Always make sure you read the question carefully!

QUESTION 11: AUTHOR'S ATTITUDE

Here's the author's attitude question we've been anticipating. We know the author doesn't particularly care for Bettelheim so we want to find an answer choice that is strongly negative. We should eliminate anything positive and be careful about answer choices that are too extremely negative or are negative for the wrong reasons. Answer choice (C)'s use of "disapproval" gets the right tone, and the author disapproves precisely because Bettelheim glosses over adult evil.

(A) This answer choice has two major problems. First is that "concern" is not negative enough for our author's tone. Second, it mixes up Bettelheim's view with the author's view. Bettelheim, not the author, views fairy tales as instruments of moral instruction for children.

(B) This answer choice starts off wonderfully as "scorn" is a pretty darn good match for the tone we want. Unfortunately, there's more to an answer choice than just the first word, and after "scorn" this answer choice has a major problem. Our author dislikes Bettelheim because she thinks kids should be able to enjoy fairy tales without them being morality plays for children. Nowhere in the passage does the author state she dislikes Bettelheim because he holds moral truths to be universal. Remember in author's attitude questions to get the right tone but also the correct reason for the tone.

(D) This answer choice starts with "anger," which is a bit too strong. Our author isn't fond of Bettelheim but she doesn't appear to be taking it personally. Moreover, she never sides one way or another on whether using fairy tales as moral instruction actually makes children behave any better.

(E) As with (D), "disappointment" isn't a great fit to start. Our author thinks Bettelheim is wrong, but doesn't state clearly that she is disappointed in him. Also, our author doesn't take a particularly strong stand on superficial versus deeper readings.

QUESTION 12: AUTHOR'S ATTITUDE

This can be a tough question because it doesn't tell us in the passage where the answer can be found. However, this question asks us what the author would agree with, so our right answer is likely to be something that is a match for those points in the passage where the author is clearly present. These include lines 28, 37, 44, and her conclusion at the end of the passage. The best way to tackle such a question is to skim the answer choices looking for something that accords with the attitude articulated in one of these instances. In this case answer choice (E) is a direct match for the last sentence of the passage. Hurray.

(A) This answer choice is a bit of a mouthful, but when it's untangled, it means that one of the pleasures of reading fairy tales revolves around their deeper meanings. This contradicts our author's main point that fairy tales don't have to be solely instruments of moral instruction, so we can eliminate it.

(B) This answer choice is not stated clearly in the passage, which means our author isn't going to agree with it. The passage talks about parents' perspectives versus children's perspectives in the first paragraph, but that's not the same thing as a fairy tale that is suggested by a parent.

(C) This answer choice has the same problem as (B) in that it is never discussed in the passage. Moreover, it espouses Bettelheim's view that children can become better from learning about fairy tales, a view with which the author disagrees. Wrong on two counts.

(D) This answer choice has a huge problem right from the beginning. "Most" is far too strong to be justified. Nothing in the passage has strong enough language to say whether over half of the children in the world are unable to comprehend fairy tales.

QUESTION 13: AUTHOR'S ATTITUDE

We know from our tagging that "literary interpretation" occurs in paragraph three. Sure enough, at the end of paragraph three the author talks about interpretation and states that different readers from different backgrounds come up with completely different interpretations of the tales. If people from different backgrounds have different interpretations, we can safely assume that these backgrounds are influencing their interpretations in some way. This matches up pretty well with (D): that the assumptions we bring to a story influence the meaning we draw from it.

(A) Our author believes that literary interpretations can be produced from readers with "different cultural assumptions and expectations" (lines 42 and 43) and not only those trained in literary interpretation. Next.

(B) As with (A), this answer choice is far too restrictive given our author's view to be the principle underlying her characterization of literary interpretation.

(C) LSAC must have really liked (A) and (B) because they're recycling this for the third time. The author says that different people come up with different interpretations but that does not mean that only one is correct.

(E) Our author doesn't discuss whether or not latent meanings are deliberately placed in a story by the author – only that they exist. More importantly, this principle doesn't strengthen her characterization of literary interpretation.

QUESTION 14: AUTHOR'S ATTITUDE

Although our tag doesn't specifically mention psychoanalytic literature, it does mention deeper readings, which takes us to paragraph four. About halfway through the paragraph the author states that recent psychoanalytic literature has partially discredited the idea of innocent adults and evil children. (E) describes adult evil as being of "questionable validity," making it the correct answer choice.

- (A) This answer choice can be tempting at first, but goes too far. The passage states that fairy tales don't have to be solely about moral instruction, but our author never goes so far as to say that moral instruction is bad.
- (B) Our passage never mentions anything about improper child rearing, so it certainly isn't suggested by psychoanalytic literature or a view espoused by our author.
- (C) This answer choice is extremely tempting. It seems like a perfect match for the language in line 52, but that little "all" at the end makes it waaaay too strong. Line 53 makes it clear that our author thinks denying adult evil has been "a pervasive feature of our society," not all societies. Nice try, LSAT.
- (D) This answer choice certainly could be true, but there's no clear support for it in the passage so it's not clear that our author would agree with it. As with (B), always be careful of answer choices that could be true but aren't supported explicitly by the passage.

QUESTION 15: VIEWPOINT

This question is somewhat difficult in that there's no reference regarding where we will find the answer to the question. In these cases we should be mindful of our main point and our tagging. Given that we have a view point question, we should also be on the lookout for incorrect answers that are not supported explicitly by the passage. In this case the end of paragraph 2 states that "the story trains its young listeners to become 'mature children'" (lines 22-23). This indicates that Bettelheim believes children can learn valuable lessons from fairy tales and become better children. This leads us to answer choice (D).

- (A) This answer choice might be alluring because moral instruction seems really boring and you probably weren't super excited when you were young and learning moral lessons. Don't fall into the LSAT's trap though; leave your prior information at the testing room door and recognize that there's never an indication one way or another in the passage regarding whether or not children are interested in moral instruction. Therefore, it can't be the correct answer.
- (B) You should be able to eliminate this answer choice fairly easily as it is almost the opposite of what we are looking for. Remember that Bettelheim denies adult evil, so he certainly wouldn't believe that their moral beliefs would be unfair.
- (C) This answer choice has the same problem that (B) has and can be eliminated as readily. Bettelheim denies adult evil and wouldn't describe parental behavior as inappropriate.
- (E) This answer is closer to the author's view than to Bettelheim's. Bettelheim views children as needing moral instruction from fairy tales, not as playful and carefree. Next!

QUESTION 16: VIEWPOINT

This is a difficult question because it asks us to find the answer choice that contradicts Bettelheim's view. This requires us to 1. Locate Bettelheim's view and 2. Find what isn't compatible with it. We start by reiterating what we know about Bettelheim; he denies adult evil, he thinks children can change, and he views fairy tales as moral instruction. Next we find the answer choice that doesn't lie down with this. In this case answer (B) is almost a direct contradiction with Bettelheim's view. He always sides with the parents and thinks children need moral instruction. Therefore he would be relatively unlikely to think that children should value their needs when they differ from their parents'.

(A) This answer could possibly be true, but the passage never states anything definite about drawing lines between living things and inanimate objects so we don't know whether or not it is compatible with Bettelheim's views. Next!

(C) The passage doesn't discuss children experiencing the world in terms of the dynamics of the family into which they were born. Nor does it discuss their maturing minds (don't be thrown off by the reference to "mature children" in line 24 – that's different than maturing minds). In both cases, we can't possibly know Bettelheim's view of these issues so (C) cannot be correct.

(D) This answer choice is definitely not what we're looking for as it seems like something with which Bettelheim would probably agree. The whole point of fairy tales in his view is to help children become more mature.

(E) This answer is a more extreme version of (A) and (C) in that it is not supported or even mentioned in the passage at all. The passage never talks about distinguishing reality from fiction or puberty.

Fun Fact: All clownfish begin life as males.

Countee Cullen (Countee Leroy Porter, 1903–1946) was one of the foremost poets of the Harlem Renaissance, the movement of African American writers, musicians, and artists centered in the Harlem
(5) section of New York City during the 1920s. Beginning with his university years, Cullen strove to establish himself as an author of romantic poetry on abstract, universal topics such as love and death. Believing poetry should consist of "lofty thoughts beautifully
(10) expressed," Cullen preferred controlled poetic forms. He used European forms such as sonnets and devices such as quatrains, couplets, and conventional rhyme, and he frequently employed classical allusions and Christian religious imagery, which were most likely
(15) the product both of his university education and of his upbringing as the adopted son of a Methodist Episcopal reverend.

Some literary critics have praised Cullen's skill at writing European-style verse, finding, for example,
(20) in "The Ballad of the Brown Girl" an artful use of diction and a rhythm and sonority that allow him to capture the atmosphere typical of the English ballad form of past centuries. Others have found Cullen's use of European verse forms and techniques unsuited
(25) to treating political or racial themes, such as the themes in "Uncle Jim," in which a young man is told by his uncle of the different experiences of African Americans and whites in United States society, or "Incident," which relates the experience of an eight-
(30) year-old child who hears a racial slur. One such critic has complained that Cullen's persona as expressed in his work sometimes seems to vacillate between aesthete and spokesperson for racial issues. But Cullen himself rejected this dichotomy, maintaining that his
(35) interest in romantic poetry was quite compatible with his concern over racial issues. He drew a distinction between poetry of solely political intent and his own work, which he believed reflected his identity as an African American. As the heartfelt expression of
(40) his personality accomplished by means of careful attention to his chosen craft, his work could not help but do so.

Explicit references to racial matters do in fact decline in Cullen's later work, but not because
(45) he felt any less passionately about these matters. Rather, Cullen increasingly focused on the religious dimension of his poetry. In "The Black Christ," in which the poet imagines the death and resurrection of a rural African American, and "Heritage," which
(50) expresses the tension between the poet's identification with Christian traditions and his desire to stay close to his African heritage, Cullen's thoughts on race were subsumed within what he conceived of as broader and more urgent questions about the suffering and
(55) redemption of the soul. Nonetheless, Cullen never abandoned his commitment to the importance of racial issues, reflecting on one occasion that he felt "actuated by a strong sense of race consciousness" that "grows upon me, I find, as I grow older."

7. Which one of the following most accurately states the main point of the passage?

(A) While much of Cullen's poetry deals with racial issues, in his later work he became less concerned with racial matters and increasingly interested in writing poetry with a religious dimension.
(B) While Cullen used European verse forms and his later poems increasingly addressed religious themes, his poetry never abandoned a concern for racial issues.
(C) Though Cullen used European verse forms, he acknowledged that these forms were not very well suited to treating political or racial themes.
(D) Despite the success of Cullen's poetry at dealing with racial issues, Cullen's primary goal was to re-create the atmosphere that characterized the English ballad.
(E) The religious dimension throughout Cullen's poetry complemented his focus on racial issues by providing the context within which these issues could be understood.

8. Given the information in the passage, which one of the following most closely exemplifies Cullen's conception of poetry?

(A) a sonnet written with careful attention to the conventions of the form to re-create the atmosphere of sixteenth-century English poetry
(B) a sonnet written with deliberate disregard for the conventions of the form to illustrate the perils of political change
(C) a sonnet written to explore the aesthetic impact of radical innovations in diction, rhythm, and sonority
(D) a sonnet written with great stylistic freedom to express the emotional upheaval associated with romantic love
(E) a sonnet written with careful attention to the conventions of the form expressing feelings about the inevitability of death

October 2003 Passage 2

9. Which one of the following is NOT identified by the author of the passage as characteristic of Cullen's poetry?

    (A) It often deals with abstract, universal subject matter.
    (B) It often employs rhyme, classical allusions, and religious imagery.
    (C) It avoids traditional poetic forms in favor of formal experimentation.
    (D) It sometimes deals explicitly with racial issues.
    (E) It eventually subsumed racial issues into a discussion of religious issues.

10. The passage suggests which one of the following about Cullen's use of controlled poetic forms?

    (A) Cullen used controlled poetic forms because he believed they provided the best means to beautiful poetic expression.
    (B) Cullen's interest in religious themes naturally led him to use controlled poetic forms.
    (C) Only the most controlled poetic forms allowed Cullen to address racial issues in his poems.
    (D) Cullen had rejected the less controlled poetic forms he was exposed to prior to his university years.
    (E) Less controlled poetic forms are better suited to poetry that addresses racial or political issues.

11. The references to specific poems in the second paragraph are most likely intended to

    (A) contrast some of Cullen's more successful poems with some of his less successful ones
    (B) serve as illustrations of Cullen's poetry relevant to the critics' claims
    (C) demonstrate that Cullen's poetic persona vacillates from poem to poem
    (D) summarize the scope of Cullen's treatment of racial issues in his poetry
    (E) illustrate the themes Cullen used in expressing his concern about racial matters

12. Based on the passage, the literary critics mentioned in line 18 would be most likely to hold which one of the following views of Cullen's poetry?

    (A) It demonstrates that European verse forms can be successfully adapted to different contexts.
    (B) It is most notable for the ways in which its content reflects Cullen's upbringing and education.
    (C) It is more successful when it does not attempt to capture the atmosphere of previous poetic styles.
    (D) Its reliance on European verse forms is best suited to dealing with racial concerns.
    (E) Its focus is divided between aesthetic and racial concerns.

13. Which one of the following most accurately describes the organization of the passage?

    (A) Biographical information about Cullen is outlined, his artistic development is traced through several of his poems, and a critical evaluation of his later work is offered.
    (B) Biographical information about Cullen is outlined, criticism of his use of European verse forms is presented, and the success of this use is evaluated.
    (C) Biographical information about Cullen is outlined, his approach to writing poetry is described, and the relationship between his poetry and his life is discussed.
    (D) Cullen's approach to poetry is described, certain poems are characterized as his most notable, and a claim about the religious focus of his work is made.
    (E) Cullen's approach to poetry is described, differing opinions about the success of his poetry are presented, and thematic developments in his later work are discussed.

OCT. 2003 PASSAGE 2 MARKUP

[Countee Cullen] (Countee Leroy Porter, 1903–1946) was one of the foremost poets of the Harlem Renaissance, the movement of African American writers, musicians, and artists centered in the Harlem
(5) section of New York City during the 1920s. Beginning with his university years, Cullen strove to establish himself as an author of romantic poetry on abstract, universal topics such as love and death. Believing poetry should consist of "lofty thoughts beautifully
(10) expressed," Cullen preferred controlled poetic forms. He used European forms such as sonnets and devices such as quatrains, couplets, and conventional rhyme, and he frequently employed classical allusions and Christian religious imagery, which were most likely
(15) the product both of his university education and of his upbringing as the adopted son of a Methodist Episcopal reverend.

    Some literary critics have praised Cullen's skill at writing European-style verse, finding, for example,
(20) in "The Ballad of the Brown Girl" an artful use of diction and a rhythm and sonority that allow him to capture the atmosphere typical of the English ballad form of past centuries. Others have found Cullen's use of European verse forms and techniques unsuited
(25) to treating political or racial themes, such as the themes in "Uncle Jim," in which a young man is told by his uncle of the different experiences of African Americans and whites in United States society, or "Incident," which relates the experience of an eight-
(30) year-old child who hears a racial slur. One such critic has complained that Cullen's persona as expressed in his work sometimes seems to vacillate between aesthete and spokesperson for racial issues. But Cullen himself rejected this dichotomy, maintaining that his
(35) interest in romantic poetry was quite compatible with his concern over racial issues. He drew a distinction between poetry of solely political intent and his own work, which he believed reflected his identity as an African American. As the heartfelt expression of
(40) his personality accomplished by means of careful attention to his chosen craft, his work could not help but do so.

    Explicit references to racial matters do in fact decline in Cullen's later work, but not because
(45) he felt any less passionately about these matters. Rather, Cullen increasingly focused on the religious dimension of his poetry. In "The Black Christ," in which the poet imagines the death and resurrection of a rural African American, and "Heritage," which
(50) expresses the tension between the poet's identification with Christian traditions and his desire to stay close to his African heritage, Cullen's thoughts on race were subsumed within what he conceived of as broader and more urgent questions about the suffering and
(55) redemption of the soul. Nonetheless, Cullen never abandoned his commitment to the importance of racial issues, reflecting on one occasion that he felt "actuated by a strong sense of race consciousness" that "grows upon me, I find, as I grow older."

DESCRIPTION OF WORK

CRITICS' VIEW: PRAISE FOR EUROPEAN-STYLE VERSE
EX.

2ND VIEW: NOT SUITED TO POLITICS
EX.

EX.

CULLEN'S VIEW

AUTHOR'S CONCLUSION

FOCUS ON RELIGION
EX.

EX.
AUTHOR'S CONC.

NEVER LOST COMMITMENT TO RACE

CULLEN'S POETRY

SKILLFUL USE OF EUROPEAN-STYLE VERSE (CRITICS) → NOT POLITICAL/ RACIAL ENOUGH (CRITICS)

↓

AFRICAN-AMERICAN IDENTITY (CULLEN)

PASSAGE SUMMARY

Ever get the feeling that someone at the LSAC was a English Lit major and really wants to keep the memory of some of these obscure poets alive?

In this passage, we learn about Countee Cullen. "Who's that?" you might ask. Well, the first paragraph talks about his bio then discusses his writing style. That's all it does (background, anyone?) so let's tag it and move to the second paragraph...

...Which starts with the view of some literary critics. We have our first viewpoint, and they "have praised Cullen's skill at writing European-style verse" (lines 18-20). That's a good candidate for the Thesis position. Reading on, they give an example of this work ("The Ballad of the Brown Girl" in line 20), so we should tag that. Since examples are provided to support the critics' view, we can now safely put it in our primary structure diagram as the Thesis.

In the same paragraph we get our second viewpoint. These critics "have found Cullen's use of European verse forms and techniques unsuited to treating political or racial themes" (lines 23-25). So it seems they're not big fans. We get two examples to back up their viewpoint ("Uncle Jim" in line 26 and "Incident" in line 29), so we know this is the Antithesis position.

Then the man himself jumps into the fray. "Cullen himself rejected this dichotomy, maintaining that his interest in romantic poetry was quite compatible with his concern over racial issues" (lines 33-36). So he can please the European-style lovers while silencing the critics, thus bringing the desires of everyone together. Can you say Synthesis? Exciting! The author comes in immediately to champion this vision, so our author is aligned with the Synthesis position.

The final paragraph goes off on a bit of a tangent, but we've left the critics behind. Since the information presented here isn't attributed to anyone else, it must be the author. After discussing the religious focus of Cullen's later work (lines 44-46) and giving a few examples ("The Black Christ" in line 46 and "Heritage" in line 48), the author hops back in. "Nonetheless" is a surefire clue that the author is about to drop some concluding statements on us, and here he states that "Cullen never abandoned his commitment to the importance of racial issues," thus agreeing again with Cullen's own assessment of his work.

In summary we are given background on Cullen's work followed by two different opinions on it. The author sides with Cullen's view and a later development in his work is explained.

PRIMARY STRUCTURE: SYNTHESIS

There are three points of view in the passage, making this a Synthesis passage. The author is present and aligns with the Synthesis, as is almost always the case in Synthesis passages.

The Thesis represents the viewpoint of the critics who praise Cullen's skill at writing European-style verse (lines 18-19). The Antithesis represents the other critics who feel this style is "unsuited to treating political or racial themes" (lines 23-25); they'd prefer his work to use another style to focus on racial issues.

Cullen then comes in as the Synthesis, "maintaining that his interest in romantic poetry was compatible with his concern over racial issues" (lines 33-36). It's the best of both worlds, bringing the desires of both critics together. The author is aligned with Cullen.

```
          CULLEN'S POETRY
    SKILLFUL USE OF      NOT POLITICAL/
    EUROPEAN-STYLE          RACIAL
        VERSE               ENOUGH
       (CRITICS)            (CRITICS)
                  ↓
              AFRICAN-AMERICAN
                  IDENTITY
                  (CULLEN)
```

SECONDARY STRUCTURE

There are no extensive secondary structures but there are a large number of localized Example secondary structures throughout the passage (lines 20, 26, 29, 46, and 48).

PASSAGE OVERVIEW

MAIN POINT

The main point of the passage, given by Cullen and agreed with by the author, is that despite his later focus on religious issues and his European style, the poet was still able to maintain a focus on racial issues. We see Cullen arguing this in lines 33-36 and the author jumping in to agree.

PRIMARY PURPOSE

The author wrote this passage to analyze criticism of a poet.

AUTHOR'S ATTITUDE

As is usually the case in these literature passages, the author ultimately aligns with a positive view of the artist. However, the author does agree that the racial issues weren't always a central feature of the poet's work, so he doesn't dismiss the Antithesis critics completely.

QUESTION ANTICIPATION

Expect a few Viewpoint questions. Also, there were a lot of examples and an entire paragraph about Cullen's style, so expect some questions about these aspects of Cullen's work, as well.

AND NOW, ON TO THE QUESTIONS...

QUESTION 7: MAIN POINT

Anyone else blindsided by this Main Point question? Just kidding. There's almost always a lead-off Main Point question. As stated above, the main point is that Cullen maintained his concern for racial issues despite using European-style verse and a later focus on religious issues. We get that in (B).

- (A) While his later works did focus on religious issues, it wasn't because of a decrease in his concern over racial issues (lines 55-59).
- (C) Straight from Cullen's own mouth, we see him saying these two things are compatible (lines 33-36).
- (D) Primary goal? We never rank his goals, so we can't pick this answer.
- (E) While "Cullen's thoughts on race were subsumed within" the religious dimension in his later works (lines 51-54), we don't know they provided context. This is also just the last paragraph, ignoring the entire viewpoint about his European-style verse.

QUESTION 8: VIEWPOINT

Where did we learn about Cullen's work? That was the first paragraph. Checking back there, we find that Cullen thought "poetry should consist of 'lofty thoughts beautifully expressed'" in controlled poetic forms (lines 9-10). We need an answer choice that matches up with this characterization, and we get it in (E). We have a careful attention to form, lofty thoughts, and beautiful expression.

- (A) While the "attention to the conventions" rings true, the "atmosphere" in the second part is off. While the critics in the second paragraph praise Cullen for the ability to "capture the atmosphere typical of the English ballad form of past centuries" (lines 22-23), the specificity of the 16th century in the answer choice rules it out.

(B) Cullen liked controlled poetic forms, so he wouldn't appreciate something that threw those forms out.

(C) This sounds pretty lofty, but we don't know if it conformed to the relevant poetic form.

(D) Stylistic freedom? No thank you. We, like Cullen, prefer a poem that has a set form. Like a haiku or dirty limerick.

QUESTION 9: SPECIFIC REFERENCE

This question is so open-ended that rather than anticipating the correct answer, it's best to move to the answer choices and rely on our markup to eliminate incorrect answers. Remember, we're looking for something that ISN'T an aspect of Cullen's poetry. Answer choice (A) is tricky since you might think his focus on race would mean he didn't deal with universal subject matter. However, the background from paragraph 1 tells us in lines 7-8 that he specifically did beginning in his university years. This isn't our answer.

Answer choice (B) is an easy dismissal since all of paragraph 3 discusses the focus on his religious work. Answer choice (C) is the correct answer because we know Cullen used poetic forms. This fails to characterize his poetry correctly and so is our answer.

(D) and (E) both cover familiar territory and can be easily dismissed. (D) comes from the Antithesis position where Cullen was critiqued for addressing racial themes and (E) is from the last paragraph that focuses on the religious themes in his later work.

QUESTION 10: INFERENCE

Yet another question about Cullen's poetic stylings, so we should focus on the first paragraph. There, we learn that he focused on controlled poetic forms because of his preference for poetry consisting of "lofty thoughts beautifully expressed" (lines 9-10). If that's why he focused on those forms, he must believe those forms would lead to poetry with those characteristics. We get that in (A).

(B) While Cullen did focus on religious themes, it is never stated that this led to the controlled poetic forms.

(C) Cullen did address racial issues in his poems, and he did use controlled poetic forms, but saying that these forms were the ONLY way to address these issues is too strong.

(D) Our passage starts with his university years (lines 5-6), so we can't say anything about the years prior to that.

(E) While some critics argued this (lines 23-25), Cullen and the author disagreed with this assessment.

QUESTION 11: ROLE

A Role question about our examples? Yes, please. These examples showed up in the first half of the second paragraph, where we were exploring the viewpoints of the critics. The examples provided support for the views, which gives us (B).

(A) While some critics found Cullen's poems more successful than other critics did, we never get a single group listing certain poems as more successful than other poems.

(C) These examples were about the critics' view, so it wasn't about the author demonstrating anything.

(D) The first example was cited by the critics who talked about this European-style verse, not the racial issues in his poetry. So the first example doesn't serve this role. And even the later examples are about how this verse hindered the exploration of racial issues, not the scope of the issues themselves.

(E) Again, this ignores that first example, and it doesn't really capture the second and third ones.

QUESTION 12: VIEWPOINT

Line 18 introduced us to the Thesis view – those critics who found Cullen's use of European-style verse to be skillful. And that's all we learn about their view. We need to find an answer along these lines, and we get it in (A). Cullen was definitely not European, so these critics saying he successfully used their style implies that it can be adapted to other contexts.

(B) Cullen's upbringing and education are brought up by the author in the first paragraph as background info, not by these critics.

(C) These critics praised his skills while stating that he captured the atmosphere of past centuries, so this is the opposite of what they believe.

(D) The first critics did not talk about racial issues.

(E) Again, the first critics didn't bring up the racial issues in his poetry.

QUESTION 13: ORGANIZATION

Nice. A softball Organization question to end this passage. From our summary (don't forget to summarize each passage before moving to the questions!) we see (E) is a perfect fit.

(A) While several poems are given as examples, they don't trace his artistic development. And if you view the move toward religious issues as tracing his development, that comes after the criticism.

(B) This answer choice completely ignores the third paragraph's discussion of his shift in focus to religious issues.

(C) This misses two of the three viewpoints.

(D) Again, we're missing the criticism. This also says the passage picks certain poems as the most notable, whereas the passage just uses them as examples.

And with that, the memory of Countee Cullen lives on!

Spotlight on Uranus

Did you know Uranus:
- is the 7th planet in our solar system?
- rotates the opposite direction of the Earth?
- has a year equivalent to 84 Earth years?
- has 2 sets of outer rings?
- has 3 moons named Oberon, Titania, and Miranda?

As one of the most pervasive and influential popular arts, the movies feed into and off of the rest of the culture in various ways. In the United States, the star system of the mid-1920s–in which actors were
(5) placed under exclusive contract to particular Hollywood film studios–was a consequence of studios' discovery that the public was interested in actor's private lives, and that information about actors could be used to promote their films. Public relations agents fed the information
(10) to gossip columnists, whetting the public's appetite for the films which, audiences usually discovered, had the additional virtue of being created by talented writers, directors, and producers devoted to the art of storytelling. The important feature of this relationship
(15) was not the benefit to Hollywood, but rather to the press; in what amounted to a form of cultural cross-fertilization, the press saw that they could profit from studios' promotion of new films.

Today this arrangement has mushroomed into an
(20) intricately interdependent mass-media entertainment industry. The faith by which this industry sustains itself is the belief that there is always something worth promoting. A vast portion of the mass media–television and radio interviews, magazine articles, even product
(25) advertisements–now does most of the work for Hollywood studios attempting to promote their movies. It does so not out of altruism but because it makes for good business: If you produce a talk show or edit a newspaper, and other media are generating public
(30) curiosity about a studio's forthcoming film, it would be unwise for you not to broadcast or publish something about the film, too, because the audience for your story is already guaranteed.

The problem with this industry is that it has begun
(35) to affect the creation of films as well as their promotion. Choices of subject matter and actors are made more and more frequently by studio executives rather than by producers, writers, or directors. This problem is often referred to simply as an obsession with turning a
(40) profit, but Hollywood movies have almost always been produced to appeal to the largest possible audience. The new danger is that, increasingly, profit comes only from exciting an audience's curiosity about a movie instead of satisfying its desire to have an engaging experience
(45) watching the film. When movies can pull people into theaters instantly on the strength of media publicity rather than relying on the more gradual process of word of mouth among satisfied moviegoers, then the intimate relationship with the audience–on which the vitality of
(50) all popular art depends–is lost. But studios are making more money than ever by using this formula, and for this reason it appears that films whose appeal is due not merely to their publicity value but to their ability to affect audiences emotionally will become increasingly
(55) rare in the U.S. film industry.

22. The passage suggests that the author would be most likely to agree with which one of the following statements?

   (A) The Hollywood films of the mid-1920s were in general more engaging to watch than are Hollywood films produced today.
   (B) The writers, producers, and directors in Hollywood in the mid-1920s were more talented than are their counterparts today.
   (C) The Hollywood film studios of the mid-1920s had a greater level of dependence on the mass-media industry than do Hollywood studios today.
   (D) The publicity generated for Hollywood films in the mid-1920s was more interesting than is the publicity generated for these films today.
   (E) The star system of the mid-1920s accounts for most of the difference in quality between the Hollywood films of that period and Hollywood films today.

23. According to the author, the danger of mass-media promotion of films is that it

   (A) discourages the work of filmmakers who attempt to draw the largest possible audiences to their films
   (B) discourages the critical review of the content of films that have been heavily promoted
   (C) encourages the production of films that excite an audience's curiosity but that do not provide satisfying experiences
   (D) encourages decisions to make the content of films parallel the private lives of the actors that appear in them
   (E) encourages cynicism among potential audience members about the merits of the films publicized

24. The phrase "cultural cross-fertilization" (line 17) is used in the passage to refer to which one of the following?

   (A) competition among different segments of the U.S. mass media
   (B) the interrelationship of Hollywood movies with other types of popular art
   (C) Hollywood film studios' discovery that the press could be used to communicate with the public
   (D) the press's mutually beneficial relationship with Hollywood film studios
   (E) interactions between public relations agents and the press

June 1999 Passage 4

25. Which one of the following most accurately describes the organization of the passage?

    (A) description of the origins of a particular aspect of a popular art; discussion of the present state of this aspect; analysis of a problem associated with this aspect; introduction of a possible solution to the problem
    (B) description of the origins of a particular aspect of a popular art; discussion of the present state of this aspect; analysis of a problem associated with this aspect; suggestion of a likely consequence of the problem
    (C) description of the origins of a particular aspect of a popular art; analysis of a problem associated with this aspect; introduction of a possible solution to the problem; suggestion of a likely consequence of the solution
    (D) summary of the history of a particular aspect of a popular art; discussion of a problem that accompanied the growth of this aspect; suggestion of a likely consequence of the problem; appraisal of the importance of avoiding this consequence
    (E) summary of the history of a particular aspect of a popular art; analysis of factors that contributed to the growth of this aspect; discussion of a problem that accompanied the growth of this aspect; appeal for assistance in solving the problem

26. The author's position in lines 35-47 would be most weakened if which one of the following were true?

    (A) Many Hollywood studio executives do consider a film's ability to satisfy moviegoers emotionally.
    (B) Many Hollywood studio executives achieved their positions as a result of demonstrating talent at writing, producing, or directing films that satisfy audiences emotionally.
    (C) Most writers, producers, and directors in Hollywood continue to have a say in decisions about the casting and content of films despite the influence of studio executives.
    (D) The decisions made by most Hollywood studio executives to improve a film's chances of earning a profit also add to its ability to satisfy moviegoers emotionally.
    (E) Often the U.S. mass media play an indirect role in influencing the content of the films that Hollywood studios make by whetting the public's appetite for certain performers or subjects.

JUNE 1999 PASSAGE 4 MARKUP

As one of the most pervasive and influential popular arts, the movies feed into and off of the rest of the culture in various ways. In the United States, the star system of the mid-1920s–in which actors were
(5) placed under exclusive contract to particular Hollywood film studios–was a consequence of studios' discovery that the public was interested in actor's private lives, and that information about actors could be used to promote their films. Public relations agents fed the information
(10) to gossip columnists, whetting the public's appetite for the films which, audiences usually discovered, had the additional virtue of being created by <u>talented</u> writers, directors, and producers devoted to the art of storytelling. The important feature of this relationship
(15) was not the benefit to Hollywood, but rather to the press; in what amounted to a form of cultural cross-fertilization, the press saw that they could profit from studios' promotion of new films.

Today this arrangement has mushroomed into an
(20) intricately interdependent mass-media entertainment industry. The faith by which this industry sustains itself is the belief that there is always something worth promoting. A vast portion of the mass media– television and radio interviews, magazine articles, even
(25) product advertisements–now does most of the work for Hollywood studios attempting to promote their movies. It does so not out of altruism but because it makes for good business: If you produce a talk show or edit a newspaper, and other media are generating public
(30) curiosity about a studio's forthcoming film, it would be unwise for you not to broadcast or publish something about the film, too, because the audience for your story is already guaranteed.

The <u>problem</u> with this industry is that it has begun
(35) to affect <u>the creation of films</u> as well as their promotion. Choices of subject matter and actors are made more and more frequently by studio executives rather than by producers, writers, or directors. This problem is often referred to simply as an obsession with turning a
(40) profit, but Hollywood movies have almost always been produced to appeal to the largest possible audience. The new <u>danger</u> is that, increasingly, profit comes only from exciting an audience's curiosity about a movie instead of satisfying its desire to have an engaging experience
(45) watching the film. When movies can pull people into theaters instantly on the strength of media publicity rather than relying on the more gradual process of word of mouth among satisfied moviegoers, then the intimate relationship with the audience–on which the vitality of
(50) all popular art depends–is lost. <u>But studios are making more money than ever by using this formula, and for this reason it appears that films whose appeal is due not merely to their publicity value but to their ability to affect audiences emotionally will become increasingly
(55) rare in the U.S. film industry.</u>

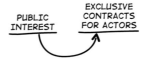

ATT.

HISTORY OF ACTOR/
STUDIO/MEDIA
RELATIONSHIPS

TODAY'S ACTOR/
STUDIO/MEDIA
RELATIONSHIPS

ATT.

PROBLEMS:
EXECS CHOOSE
MOVIES

ATT.

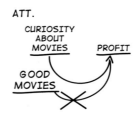

ATT.

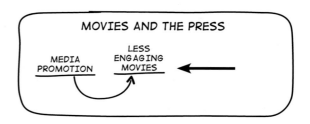

PASSAGE SUMMARY

Charlie Sheen. Tara Reid. Lindsay Lohan. We all know their off-screen antics are going to be more interesting than the movies in which they star (Herbie: Fully Loaded, anyone?). The author of this passage thinks he knows why.

In the first paragraph, we get a bit of history about early Hollywood and its relationship to the press. We should have noticed the localized causal claim at line 6 where we're told that the "star system" was a consequence of the public's interest in the private lives of actors. The author comes out in line 12 to tell us that this promoted films created by "talented" individuals, which clearly demonstrates his opinion of these classic films. Finally, he tells us "the important feature" of this was the benefit to the press. We're not told exactly how the press profited, however, so we should keep an eye out for that.

The second paragraph takes us from the past to the present. Today, there is interdependence between the media and entertainment industries. In another localized causal claim, we're told that the media does most of the promotional legwork for Hollywood because it's just good business (line 28). Hollywood gets their films promoted and the media gains viewers hungry for gossip on the stars.

But like the celebrity marriages on which they report, this relationship has become toxic (a "problem"/"new danger," lines 34 and 42). Today, making a profitable movie is less about creating an engaging experience for the audience and more about creating excitement through media publicity (lines 41-45). If publicity drives ticket sales, why bother making good films? Often when we get a problem in a passage, the author offers us a solution. Alas, this author sees no light at the end of the tunnel, as films lose the relationship with the audience on which their vitality depends (lines 48-50). He ends with a gloomy prediction: Good movies will become increasingly rare.

In summary, the author gives us an overview of the development of the media's relationship with Hollywood (past to present), its negative effects on current films, and a grim prediction for the future.

PRIMARY STRUCTURE: THESIS

We only have one point of view in this passage, making it a Thesis passage. The author is present and aligns with the thesis, as we see in lines 12 ("talented"), 34-35 ("The problem with this industry..."), and 41-45 ("The new danger..."). He also makes a prediction in lines 50-55. The author contends that the relationship between Hollywood and the media has become toxic, resulting in less-engaging movies.

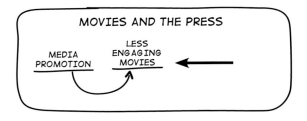

SECONDARY STRUCTURES

We don't have any extended secondary structures, but we did find three localized causal claims in this passage (lines 6, 27, 41-45).

PASSAGE OVERVIEW

MAIN POINT

The main point of this passage is that the focus on media promotion has caused movies to become less engaging. We see this throughout the third paragraph, where the author introduces us to a "problem" with the industry (line 34), and the "new danger" of less engaging films (lines 42, 44) on which the vitality of film depends (lines 49-50). These arguments are put forward without attribution, so they must be the arguments of the author. While the author makes a prediction at the end of the passage (lines 50-55), this is a consequence of his main point and not the main point itself.

PRIMARY PURPOSE

The author's primary purpose in this passage is to explore the development of a problem over time and how it might get worse in the future.

AUTHOR'S ATTITUDE

The author displays an uncharacteristically large amount of attitude in this passage. In the first paragraph, he tells us that those who made movies in the early years of Hollywood were "talented...storytell[ers]" (lines 12-14). And while the second paragraph is him describing a phenomenon, he comes right back in the third paragraph by telling us of a "problem with this industry" (line 34). He clearly believes taking the decisions out of the "talented" hands and putting them on the studio executives has led to a "new danger" (line 42). They are relying on publicity rather than creating "satisfied moviegoers" (line 48). Finally, he offers a dire prediction: Movies that "affect their audiences emotionally will become increasingly rare" (lines 54-55). They just don't make 'em like they used to.

In summary, the author thinks that the film industry of the 1920s was run by talented individuals, but Hollywood has been coopted in recent times by the relationship it has with the media, creating a culture of sensationalism that results in less engaging films.

QUESTION ANTICIPATION

When the author is not just taking sides but throwing words like "talented" and "new danger" around, you should expect to see many questions asking about the author's attitude.

Also, since we spotted several localized causal claims, we'll be ready for any Specific Reference questions related to them.

AND NOW, ON TO THE QUESTIONS...

QUESTION 22: AUTHOR'S ATTITUDE

We don't start with our expected Main Point question, but an Author's Attitude question is a reasonable alternative given his strong presence in the passage. Since we're given nothing to go on other than a viewpoint (the author's), this question is not one for which we can make a great prediction. However, before going into the answer choices, we can refresh ourselves on the author's viewpoint.

Looking back at the passage, we noted that the author thought films were crafted by talented storytellers in the '20s (lines 13-14), but a new danger has focused modern films on publicity rather than engaging storytelling (lines 43-47). Seeing that strong, opinionated language leads us directly to answer choice (A).

> (B) While the author clearly feels the directors, writers, and producers in the '20s were talented (line 13), he doesn't make a comment about the talent of those groups today. We know he doesn't like the modern films, but it's the studio executives who are calling the shots now (lines 37-39). If we picked this answer, we fell for an equivocation and comparison fallacy: Just because they were talented in the past when

they made good movies doesn't mean they lack that talent now that the movies are less engaging.

(C) If anything, the author thinks that modern studios are more dependent on the mass-media industry than they were in the 1920s. Today, studio profits increasingly come only from media promotion (lines 41-43). In the 1920s, studios used both media promotion and good filmmaking to generate profits; they were more diversified.

(D) We don't have any evidence about when media promotion was more "interesting," so we can't figure out how to author would have felt about this claim. This answer choice asks us to commit a similar equivocation fallacy to that of answer choice (B): Just because the author thinks modern publicity is harmful to the industry doesn't mean he finds it less interesting. He might enjoy a good celebrity sex tape as much as the next guy.

(E) The first word we should have noticed in this answer choice is "most" – to back that up, we need an equally strong statement in the passage. Without a complete ranking of the different influences on film quality, we can't say one is more important than another. Even if we missed that, however, we should still have questioned this answer choice because of our understanding of the author's main point and the causal claim made in the first paragraph. The author clearly believes it's the focus on publicity instead of talented storytelling that has created the drop in quality of films between the '20s and today. Also, it was initially this publicity that caused the star system to develop; this answer choice is mixing up an effect of the shift to publicity (the star system) for a cause.

QUESTION 23: AUTHOR'S ATTITUDE

Again, we see a question asking us about the author's attitude. Here, we're looking for a danger of media promotion. Two things should point us to a correct answer. First, we noticed the author call something a "new danger" (line 43). This "new danger" was stated in causal language, another clue that it would show up in a question. Recognizing this, along with our tagging, leads us to look for an answer telling us that studios now focus on "exciting an audience's curiosity about a movie" (lines 44-45) rather than creating an "engaging experience." We find that in (C).

(A) Lines 41-44 tell us that "Hollywood movies have almost always been produced to appeal to the largest possible audience." The new danger isn't that we've stopped doing that; rather, it's how we're doing it (*People Magazine* promos instead of writing *Casablanca*).

(B) The passage doesn't really mention critical review of films at all. In a question asking for you to find something the author specifically mentions, don't pick one that introduces a new concept.

(D) The last time we heard anything about the private lives of the actors was in the first paragraph, and there is never any talk about a push for films to parallel the private lives of modern actors. We get a generic statement that studio executives make decisions on subject matter and actors (lines 37-38), but without specifics, this isn't the answer we're looking for.

(E) We are told that the audience will feel increasingly less "intimate" (line 50) and less satisfied, but cynicism is never mentioned.

QUESTION 24: SPECIFIC REFERENCE

Is it just us, or does "cultural cross-fertilization" sound more fun than it actually is? The first step when dealing with a Specific Reference question is to head back to the denoted lines in the passage. Here, we find ourselves in the first paragraph. Since that paragraph's role was to explore the beginnings of the press's relationship with Hollywood, we know it has something to do with that. Reading lines 14-19 (which include the phrase) lets us know that this mixture of Hollywood and the press is exactly what we're looking for. And (D) it is.

- (A) Competition among different segments of the US mass media is mentioned at the end of the second paragraph (lines 28-33). This question is asking about the end of the first paragraph.
- (B) Before we pick this answer, let's try to put together a list of the other types of popular art with which movies are interrelated in the passage. Can't do it? That's because the popular arts are only mentioned in passing in lines 1-2. Moving on...
- (C) Hollywood "discovers" that the public is interested in the private lives of actors (lines 6-9), not that the media can be used to communicate with the public. The latter doesn't seem like much of a discovery; it's like discovering that the police can be used to capture criminals.
- (E) We're told that public relations agents and the press do interact (lines 9-10), but this is mentioned much earlier than the phrase with which we're concerned. It's important to be aware of the question type, and this Specific Reference question is referring to a very specific portion of the passage.

QUESTION 25: ORGANIZATION

Organization questions are great since they test precisely the skills you're working on: moving past the topic of the passage and reading for structure. Efficiently answering Organization questions relies on either a good summary of the passage or good role tags. Here, our summary doesn't quite get us to the correct answer quickly so we should move to our tags.

Looking at our tags, we see a discussion of the history of a relationship in the first paragraph which moves into the present in the second paragraph. Then, the author introduces a problem stemming from this relationship and a prediction about the future. Answer choice (B) matches our anticipation, point for point.

- (A) This answer choice looks great right up until the last clause where we're told the passage offers a solution. Remember, while the author did give us a problem, he offered no solution.
- (C) There are two things wrong with this answer choice. First, it forgets to mention the second paragraph altogether. Second, as in (A), the author never offers a solution.
- (D) This answer choice, just like (C), fails to mention the second paragraph. Additionally, the author never tells us how important it will be to avoid the consequence. While it is implied by his strong attitude that he feels it is important, he never says it. In a question asking for the actual organization of the passage, we can't stray into assumptions.
- (E) This answer choice looks very attractive until we get to the last clause. The author never asks for help in solving the problem. Remember, there was never any talk about solutions, just a sad prediction about the future of movies.

QUESTION 26: OPERATION

The author's position in lines 35-47 is neatly summed up by the causal relationship we found: Film execs are generating profits by using media publicity instead of by putting out satisfying movies, and this is leading to a loss in the "intimate relationship" (lines 48-49) between films and their audiences. For Operation questions, we should find the problem in the argument and anticipate an answer choice that weakens it. In this case, the author concludes that focusing on publicity will lead to worse movies. Well, we don't know that's true. Maybe they can focus on publicity and create a great movie. These two concepts aren't mutually exclusive, so we have an exclusivity fallacy. Answer choice (D) tells us that these giants-among-men can do both, and so the intimate relationship isn't in jeopardy.

(A) We've all considered many things in our lives. Bungee jumping. Eating fugu. Calling the ex up when you're feeling lonely. Just because we consider something doesn't mean we actually go through with it (except the ex...we've all been there). So just because the studio execs consider emotional satisfaction of their viewers doesn't mean they do anything about it.

(B) At least one exec has some talent in writing, producing, or directing? Big deal. She's an executive now, with new goals and responsibilities. It's not necessarily true that she will be more likely to care about an audience's satisfaction.

(C) So most producers, writers, and directors continue to have "a say" in content and casting decisions. Good for them. Unfortunately, having "a say" doesn't necessarily mean having any influence.

(E) This isn't something that would hurt the author's argument. In fact, this is the kind of thing the author is warning us about. The mass media has too big of a role in Hollywood.

Break time. Go watch some trashy movies and be a part of the problem!

23/comparativeREADING

PARTICULAR PASSAGES PREFER TO BE PAIRED

In the run-up to the June 2007 test—in what could only be described as a particularly lurid episode of Logicians Gone Wild—the makers of the LSAT shook the foundations of the world of standardized testing.

A little background: from the beginning of time (or close to it, anyway), Reading Comprehension consisted of four solo passages, each accompanied by five to eight questions.

Fast forward to early 2007: LSAC announced that one of the four passages would henceforth consist of two smaller, related passages, still accompanied by five to eight questions. Thus, Comparative Reading was born.

Prior to the test, LSAC released exactly one example for test takers to review, much to the chagrin of those test takers. (Quick shout-out for not being in their shoes. Huzzah!)

Since then, many Comparative Reading passages have been released and Blueprint has created a methodology for tackling this particular type of passage. Lucky for you, everything you have learned up until this point applies to Comparative Reading passages, and so the information herein will merely augment your already phenomenal Reading Comprehension capabilities.

Students' reactions to these passages are mixed. Some actually find them easier than single passages. However, some hate them more than finding out the ingredient list for Chicken McNuggets.

Either way, Blueprint will give you all the tools you need to tackle this particular type of Reading Comprehension passage.

HOW TO TACKLE COMPARATIVE READING PASSAGES

In addition to the familiar reading method, you will identify points of agreement and disagreement between the two speakers.

For Passage A:

- Underline and tag all <u>conclusions</u>.   scientists' conc.
- Underline and tag the <u>main conclusion</u>.   author's conc.
- Tag and mark up the passage in the same manner as a long passage.   Ex., Att. etc.
- Pay particular attention to identifying the support for all conclusions when tagging the passage.   evid./support
- Create a primary structure diagram for the passage.

For Passage B:

- Underline and tag all <u>conclusions</u>.   scientists' conc.
- Underline and tag the <u>main conclusion</u>.   author's conc.
- Tag and mark up the passage in the same manner as a long passage.   Ex., Att. etc.
- Pay particular attention to identifying the support for all conclusions when tagging the passage.   evid./support
- Create a primary structure diagram for the passage.
- Identify all areas where the speakers agree or disagree with a (+) or (-).   (+) (−)
- For each area where an agreement or disagreement is noted, make the same notation for Passage A.
- If there are multiple places of agreement or disagreement, number them to keep the points of intersection clear, such as (1+), (2+), etc.
  (1+)   (2−)

comparativeREADING

As discussed in the last chapter, there are three things you must do after finishing the passage but before attacking the questions.

First, you must anticipate questions as well as the correct answers to those questions. You'll still anticipate Main Point, Primary Purpose, and Author's Attitude questions, and such questions could be asked about either passage and possibly about both passages. So anticipate away. You should also be anticipating the answers to questions about the things to which the passage lends itself. For example, if you see a localized Cause and Effect relationship in Passage A, you may very well see a question about it.

On top of that, you must anticipate the right answers to questions that compare and contrast the two passages. This is where the added step of tagging with (+) and (-) pays off. If, for instance, both passages discuss how a particular enzyme is used in photosynthesis, anticipate a question about it. Whether they are in agreement or disagreement about how that enzyme functions, it's important as there is very likely to be a question about it. Take a look at the following prompts taken from real Comparative Reading passages.

> Which one of the following is the central topic of each passage?

> Both passages explicitly mention which one of the following?

> Which one of the following statements is most strongly supported by both passages?

In addition to these steps, you must summarize the structure of the passage in a sentence or two just as you would for a longer passge. In this case, however, you must additionally capture the structural relationship *between the two passages*. It might look something like this: "Passage A presents a question and answers that question. Passage B answers the question in another way." Or maybe: "Passage A describes a particular phenomenon. Passage B poses a causal explanation of that phenomenon." You are quite likely to be asked a question about this relationship. Take a look at the following prompts taken from real Comparative Reading Passages:

> Which one of the following most accurately describes the attitude expressed by the author of passage B toward the overall argument in passage A?

> The relationship between passage A and passage B is most analogous to the relationship in which one of the following?

As you will see in the coming pages, the questions associated with Comparative Reading passages test not only your understanding of each passage, but your understanding of the relationship between the two passages.

PRACTICE, AND THE COMPETITION WILL PALE BY COMPARISON

Read the following passage and mark it up and tag it using the Blueprint methods, including marking points of agreement (+) and disagreement (-). When you're done, check your work against the markup we made, and see where you did well and where you might improve.

Passage A is from a source published in 2004 and passage B is from a source published in 2007.

Passage A

Millions of people worldwide play multiplayer online games. They each pick, say, a medieval character to play, such as a warrior. Then they might band together in quests to slay magical beasts; their
(5) avatars appear as tiny characters striding across a Tolkienesque land.

The economist Edward Castronova noticed something curious about the game he played: it had its own economy, a bustling trade in virtual goods.
(10) Players generate goods as they play, often by killing creatures for their treasure and trading it. The longer they play, the wealthier they get.

Things got even more interesting when Castronova learned about the "player auctions."
(15) Players would sometimes tire of the game and decide to sell off their virtual possessions at online auction sites.

As Castronova stared at the auction listings, he recognized with a shock what he was looking at. It
(20) was a form of currency trading! Each item had a value in the virtual currency traded in the game; when it was sold on the auction site, someone was paying cold hard cash for it. That meant that the virtual currency was worth something in real currency. Moreover, since
(25) players were killing monsters or skinning animals to sell their pelts, they were, in effect, creating wealth.

Passage B

Most multiplayer online games prohibit real-world trade in virtual items, but some actually encourage it, for example, by granting participants
(30) intellectual property rights in their creations.

Although it seems intuitively the case that someone who accepts real money for the transfer of a virtual item should be taxed, what about the player who only accumulates items or virtual currency within
(35) a virtual world? Is "loot" acquired in a game taxable, as a prize or award is? And is the profit in a purely in-game trade or sale for virtual currency taxable? These are important questions, given the tax revenues at stake, and there is pressure on governments to answer
(40) them, given that the economies of some virtual worlds are comparable to those of small countries.

Most people's intuition probably would be that accumulation of assets within a game should not be taxed even though income tax applies even to noncash
(45) accessions to wealth. This article will argue that income tax law and policy support that result. Loot acquisitions in game worlds should not be treated as taxable prizes and awards, but rather should be treated like other property that requires effort to obtain, such
(50) as fish pulled from the ocean, which is taxed only upon sale. Moreover, in-game trades of virtual items should not be treated as taxable barter.

By contrast, tax doctrine and policy counsel taxation of the sale of virtual items for real currency,
(55) and, in games that are intentionally commodified, even of in-world sales for virtual currency, regardless of whether the participant cashes out. This approach would leave entertainment value untaxed without creating a tax shelter for virtual commerce.

7. Which one of the following pairs of titles would be most appropriate for passage A and passage B, respectively?

   (A) "The Economic Theories of Edward Castronova"
   "Intellectual Property Rights in Virtual Worlds"
   (B) "An Economist Discovers New Economic Territory"
   "Taxing Virtual Property"
   (C) "The Surprising Growth of Multiplayer Online Games"
   "Virtual Reality and the Law"
   (D) "How to Make Money Playing Games"
   "Closing Virtual Tax Shelters"
   (E) "A New Economic Paradigm"
   "An Untapped Source of Revenue"

8. Which one of the following most accurately expresses how the use of the phrase "skinning animals" in passage A (line 25) relates to the use of the phrase "fish pulled from the ocean" in passage B (line 50)?

   (A) The former refers to an activity that generates wealth, whereas the latter refers to an activity that does not generate wealth.
   (B) The former refers to an activity in an online game, whereas the latter refers to an analogous activity in the real world.
   (C) The former, unlike the latter, refers to the production of a commodity that the author of passage B thinks should be taxed.
   (D) The latter, unlike the former, refers to the production of a commodity that the author of passage B thinks should be taxed.
   (E) Both are used as examples of activities by which game players generate wealth.

9. With regard to their respective attitudes toward commerce in virtual items, passage A differs from passage B in that passage A is more

   (A) critical and apprehensive
   (B) academic and dismissive
   (C) intrigued and excited
   (D) undecided but curious
   (E) enthusiastic but skeptical

10. Based on what can be inferred from their titles, the relationship between which one of the following pairs of documents is most analogous to the relationship between passage A and passage B?

    (A) "Advances in Artificial Intelligence"
        "Human Psychology Applied to Robots"
    (B) "Internet Retailers Post Good Year"
        "Lawmakers Move to Tax Internet Commerce"
    (C) "New Planet Discovered in Solar System"
        "Planet or Asteroid: Scientists Debate"
    (D) "Biologists Create New Species in Lab"
        "Artificially Created Life: How Patent Law Applies"
    (E) "A Renegade Economist's Views on Taxation"
        "Candidate Runs on Unorthodox Tax Plan"

11. The passages were most likely taken from which one of the following pairs of sources?

    (A) passage A: a magazine article addressed to a general audience
        passage B: a law journal article
    (B) passage A: a technical journal for economists
        passage B: a magazine article addressed to a general audience
    (C) passage A: a science-fiction novel
        passage B: a technical journal for economists
    (D) passage A: a law journal article
        passage B: a speech delivered before a legislative body
    (E) passage A: a speech delivered before a legislative body
        passage B: a science-fiction novel

12. Which one of the following most accurately describes the relationship between the two passages?

    (A) Passage A summarizes a scholar's unanticipated discovery, while passage B proposes solutions to a problem raised by the phenomenon discovered.
    (B) Passage A explains an economic theory, while passage B identifies a practical problem resulting from that theory.
    (C) Passage A reports on a subculture, while passage B discusses the difficulty of policing that subculture.
    (D) Passage A challenges the common interpretation of a phenomenon, while passage B reaffirms that interpretation.
    (E) Passage A states a set of facts, while passage B draws theoretical consequences from those facts.

13. Based on passage B, which one of the following is a characteristic of some "games that are intentionally commodified" (line 55)?

    (A) The game allows selling real items for virtual currency.
    (B) The game allows players to trade avatars with other players.
    (C) Players of the game grow wealthier the longer they play.
    (D) Players of the game own intellectual property rights in their creations.
    (E) Players of the game can exchange one virtual currency for another virtual currency.

DECEMBER 2013 PASSAGE 2 MARKUP

Passage A

Millions of people worldwide play multiplayer online games. They each pick, say, a medieval character to play, such as a warrior. Then they might band together in quests to slay magical beasts; their
(5) avatars appear as tiny characters striding across a Tolkienesque land.

The economist Edward Castronova noticed something curious about the game he played: it had its own economy, a bustling trade in virtual goods.
(10) Players generate goods as they play, often by killing creatures for their treasure and trading it. The longer they play, the wealthier they get.

Things got even more interesting when Castronova learned about the "player auctions."
(15) Players would sometimes tire of the game and decide to sell off their virtual possessions at online auction sites.

As Castronova stared at the auction listings, he recognized with a shock what he was looking at. It
(20) was a form of currency trading! Each item had a value in the virtual currency traded in the game; when it was sold on the auction site, someone was paying cold hard cash for it. That meant that the virtual currency was worth something in real currency. Moreover, since
(25) players were killing monsters or skinning animals to sell their pelts, they were, in effect, creating wealth.

Passage B

Most multiplayer online games prohibit real-world trade in virtual items, but some actually encourage it, for example, by granting participants
(30) intellectual property rights in their creations.

Although it seems intuitively the case that someone who accepts real money for the transfer of a virtual item should be taxed, what about the player who only accumulates items or virtual currency within
(35) a virtual world? Is "loot" acquired in a game taxable, as a prize or award is? And is the profit in a purely in-game trade or sale for virtual currency taxable? These are important questions, given the tax revenues at stake, and there is pressure on governments to answer
(40) them, given that the economies of some virtual worlds are comparable to those of small countries.

Most people's intuition probably would be that accumulation of assets within a game should not be taxed even though income tax applies even to noncash
(45) accessions to wealth. This article will argue that income tax law and policy support that result. Loot acquisitions in game worlds should not be treated as taxable prizes and awards, but rather should be treated like other property that requires effort to obtain, such
(50) as fish pulled from the ocean, which is taxed only upon sale. Moreover, in-game trades of virtual items should not be treated as taxable barter.

By contrast, tax doctrine and policy counsel taxation of the sale of virtual items for real currency,
(55) and, in games that are intentionally commodified, even of in-world sales for virtual currency, regardless of whether the participant cashes out. This approach would leave entertainment value untaxed without creating a tax shelter for virtual commerce.

BACKGROUND

ATT.
(+)

GAME HAS ITS
OWN ECONOMY
ATT.

PLAYERS SELL
VIRTUAL
POSSESSIONS
FOR CASH (+1)

ATT.

VIRTUAL CURRENCY
HAS ACTUAL VALUE

EX. OF HOW
VALUE IS
CREATED (+2)

[VIRTUAL CURRENCY: GAME PLAY CREATES REAL VALUE ←]

EX. OF HOW GAMES
VIEW REAL WORLD
TRADE (+)

Q: IS VIRTUAL
LOOT/CURRENCY
TAXABLE?

A: DON'T TAX
VIRTUAL LOOT/
CURRENCY

EX. LOOT/CURRENCY
SHOULD ONLY BE TAXED
WHEN SOLD FOR CASH (+1)

EX. ILLUSTRATING
WHEN TO TAX (+2)

[Q: IS VIRTUAL CURRENCY TAXABLE?
A: NO, EXCEPT WHEN INTENT IS TO CREATE REAL-WORLD VALUE ←]

WHEN
TO TAX

PASSAGE SUMMARIES

PASSAGE A

Can you believe LSAC actually has a Reading Comprehension passage on World of Warcraft™? What's next? A documentary on Comic Con? An exposé on chess clubs? The mind reels.

The first paragraph provides some background on online games. In paragraph two, we are introduced to economist Edward Castronova, who finds the virtual economy "curious" (line 8). We box Mr. Castronova (clearly a ladies' man) and underline the attitude.

In paragraph three, we find out that there are "player auctions," which the author describes as "even more interesting" (line 13). At this point, you should be aware that there is more attitude in this passage than in most, and it's fairly clear there will be at least one attitude question. In the auctions, players sell the virtual items they've accrued for real money.

The final paragraph culminates with the author getting far more excited about this stuff than he should. (Line 19 contains what may be the only exclamation point to ever have appeared in a Reading Comprehension passage.) What's so exciting? Virtual currency has actual value in cold, hard cash. And by playing the game, players are creating value. Although a main idea is not stated explicitly in the passage, tracking the author's attitude really helps point us in the right direction. The author is most excited about the idea that virtual games can yield real currency exchange. Because the passage leads to this final idea, this is the main point of the passage. You should also note that there are two examples of the creation of wealth at the end of the passage: killing monsters and skinning animals.

In summary, passage A describes an economist's first, exciting brush with multiplayer online games and the fact that they generate virtual trading and actual wealth.

PASSAGE B

Passage B stamps out all the fun we had in passage A by talking about taxes. Wah-wah.

Picking up on the idea of real-world value that appeared in passage A, paragraph one gives an example: intellectual property rights in players' creations. Mark it with a (+) since passage A discussed real-world trade in virtual items, also.

Paragraph two discusses accepting real money for a virtual item—the basis of passage A—and indicates that the general point of view is that such a transfer should be taxed. Slap a (+1) on this and on its passage A counterpart since they both discuss selling stuff for real money. Up next is a series of questions about taxing various virtual assets. Our ears should perk up to a possible Question and Answer secondary structure so look for answers to one or more of the questions in the next paragraph, which might give you the main idea of the passage.

Paragraph three doesn't disappoint, explaining that most people's intuitions are that we don't tax virtual items and that the "article will argue that income tax law and policy will support that." It's very rare for a passage to come out with such an obvious main idea, so thank whatever deity in whom we believe (we're partial to Zeus) and move on. Be sure to note the analogy to fishing, which is an example of when things should be taxed. This, like the example in passage A, talks about how value is accrued in games so put a (+2) on it and its passage A counterpart.

The final paragraph details an exception to the author's argument that virtual transactions shouldn't be taxed. In games that are intentionally commodified—where the intent is to create value that can be traded for real world currency—transactions in the game for virtual currency ought to be taxed.

In summary, passage B asks a question about whether or not virtual items should be taxed, which the author answers "no," with one proviso.

BOTH PASSAGES

Passage A identifies a phenomenon and displays a strongly positive attitude toward that phenomenon while passage B poses and answers a question about the implications of the phenomenon.

PASSAGE A PRIMARY STRUCTURE: THESIS

Passage A only has one point of view: the author is in agreement with Edward Castronova that it's terribly exciting that multiplayer online games contain a form of currency trading.

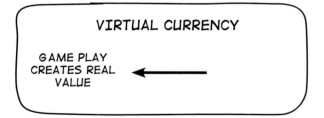

PASSAGE B PRIMARY STRUCTURE: THESIS

Passage B has a Question and Answer secondary structure. Since there's only one answer to the question (no, virtual goods should not be taxed with one small exception), this too is a Thesis passage.

```
Q:   IS VIRTUAL CURRENCY TAXABLE?
A:       NO, EXCEPT WHEN
         INTENT IS TO CREATE    ←
         REAL-WORLD VALUE
```

SECONDARY STRUCTURES

There is a localized example in passage A at lines 24-25. In passage B, there is an extensive Question and Answer secondary structure introduced at lines 30-36, and a localized example at lines 44-50. Don't forget that with Question and Answer secondary structures the answer to the question is the main idea, which is true of passage B.

PASSAGE OVERVIEW

MAIN POINT

Passage A: In the absence of an explicit main point, the main point is the one that best reflects the author's overall opinion about the passage. Here, it's that online multiplayer games create value that can be bought and sold with real money. We can find this conclusion by tracking the thing about which our author feels most strongly.

Passage B: Passage B has perhaps the easiest conclusion to spot in the history of LSAT Reading Comprehension: in-game transactions shouldn't be taxed. This is because it explicity states "This article will argue...." Keep in mind there's a small qualification to that conclusion, which is that, in games that are intended to create value, in-game transactions should be taxed.

PRIMARY PURPOSE

The author of passage A wrote the passage to identify an interesting discovery. The author of passage B wrote the passage to answer a question regarding that discovery.

AUTHOR'S ATTITUDE

Author's attitude in passage A is expressed strongly throughout the passage: "something curious" (line 8), "even more interesting" (line 13), and "recognized with a shock" (line 18). The author's attitude is strongly positive. The author of passage B displays less attitude, but he is convinced that games should not be taxed except under a particular circumstance.

QUESTION ANTICIPATION

In Comparative Reading passages, we should anticipate questions about similarities and differences between the passages. Since there are examples covering the same issue, we should expect one or more questions about them. The intense author's attitude in passage A is also ripe for a question.

AND NOW, ON TO THE QUESTIONS

QUESTION 7: MAIN POINT

Title questions are just Main Point questions in disguise. By referring to our primary structure diagram, it is clear that (B) is the right answer, because each title encompasses the main point of each passage.

(A) Answer choice (A) is wrongy wrong wrong. First, we don't learn anything in passage A about Castronova's theories, just a phenomenon he discovered. Second, while passage B discusses intellectual property, that's just one example of how wealth can be accrued in a game, which is far too narrow to be the main idea.

(C) Answer choice (C) is off the mark because we have no idea from passage A whether or not multiplayer online games are growing or not.

(D) While the first part of answer choice (D) is an amazing title for a book on playing professional poker, it fails to exemplify passage A, which is focusing more on the fact that money is being made, rather than on how to make it. The title for passage B identifies a consideration contained in the last paragraph, but it is far too narrow to be the main point of the passage.

(E) While passage A talks about a surprising economic discovery, it's much too strong to call it a whole new paradigm for all economics. The second title gets passage B wrong because that passage is arguing that, for the most part, online gaming should not be taxed. Next!

QUESTION 8: ROLE

Sure enough, we get a question regarding an example from each passage. Both of these examples are geared toward explaining how games create real-world value. However, the example in passage A is something that happens in the game, while the example in passage B does so with an analogy to fishing, a real-world activity. That's answer choice (B).

(A) Answer choice (A) is incorrect because both of these activities generate wealth.

(C) This choice mischaracterizes the position of the author of passage B who thinks things should be taxed when they are traded for real money.

(D) Answer choice (D) suffers the same problem as answer choice (C) and is an easy dismissal.

(E) This is tempting, but the example of pulling fish from the ocean is a real-world activity, not an online activity and so we can eliminate this answer choice.

QUESTION 9: AUTHOR'S ATTITUDE

This question asks us about the attitude of the author in passage A, which can be summed up as, "OMG! OMG! This is so awesome!" That, of course, is answer choice (C). If we're tracking author's attitude (and of course we are!), this one is a breeze.

- (A) Answer choice (A) is precisely the opposite of how our author is feeling. Good-bye.
- (B) This one misses the mark because the tone is far too ebullient to be academic and the passage certainly isn't dismissive.
- (D) Answer choice (D) might seem alluring with the use of the word "curious," which was used to communicate attitude in line 8. But it is the phenomenon that is curious, not the author. The author is as excited as a small child in a ball pit, and doesn't seem undecided in the least.
- (E) This answer choice is designed to fool the student that fails to read the second adjective. While "enthusiastic" is correct, passage A never once expresses skepticism.

QUESTION 10: PARALLEL

Let's take a step back. As we know from question #7, title questions are the same as Main Point questions. So we're looking for an answer choice that uses a different topic to convey the main point of the passages: the discovery of a phenomenon, and the legal implications of that phenomenon. Answer choice (D) does this with the topic of artificially created life.

- (A) Answer choice (A) discusses a discovery in the first title, which is promising. But the second title discusses the application of human psychology, which is missing the element of the legal implications of the phenomenon.
- (B) Pro tip for answer choice (B): always be wary of similar subject matter in answers to parallel questions. Sure enough, though the subject in answer choice (B) is the internet (at least superficially related to online gaming), a rise in sales, is very different than the discovery of a new phenomenon. Put this answer choice in the garbage along with that leftover Thai from the back of your fridge.
- (C) While the first title in answer choice (C) talks about a discovery, it's not a new phenomenon. Rather, it's just another example of something we've seen many times before. Moreover, passage B does not debate whether or not online gaming really is an economy, but whether we should tax it. Next!
- (E) In answer choice (E) the idea that we should be skeptical of answers with similar subject matter raises its head again. While answer choice (B) picked up on the subject matter of the first passage (online), this answer choice mimics the topic of the second passage (taxation). However, the economist in passage A is not a renegade; he just found a new phenomenon. Moreover, passage B is not the documentation of how a certain person does things, but a discussion of whether we should treat a particular phenomenon a certain way under the law.

QUESTION 11: INFERENCE

The fact that we kept track of the attitude of the authors should help us here. Passage A is very casual in tone with lots of opinion, while passage B is more scholarly. That's why (A) is correct. Passage A would fit right into a newsy-sounding magazine, and passage

(B) specifically says, "[t]his article will argue that income tax law and policy support that result" (lines 44-45).

- (B) Answer choice (B) is incorrect because technical journals are much more staid than passage A.
- (C) While we at Blueprint love a good science fiction novel (*Ender's Game* is amazing), both of the articles discuss real-world discoveries, and anything describing them as fiction, sci-fi or otherwise, is just wrong. Good-bye, (C).
- (D) Answer choice (D) misses the mark because passage A is far too casual to be a law journal article, and passage B is too scholarly to be a political speech.
- (E) Apparently someone at LSAC has sci-fi on the brain because "science-fiction novel" reappears in answer choice (E). While it's still wrong, we really love that this wacky answer choice is used twice. Thanks for the easy elimination, LSAC!

QUESTION 12: ORGANIZATION

This question (very common in Comparative reading passages) tests how well we completed our markup! Since we summarized the passages before attacking the question, so we should be able to find the answer quickly. Remember that passage A discusses a discovery while passage B poses a question about that discovery and answers it. Answer choice (A) precisely covers this.

- (B) Answer choice (B) misses the "discovery" aspect of passage A. Next.
- (C) Answer choice (C) is incorrect because subculture is not the point of passage A: it's the economics of the issue, not the sociology. If we missed the first part, the second clause is also incorrect because taxing and policing are two different governmental functions.
- (D) This answer choice posits that the two passages stand in opposition to one another, when they don't. Moving on.
- (E) Answer choice (E) is incorrect because passage B talks about how we treat the discovery in practical terms; it is not drawing theoretical consequences from it. We could also eliminate this answer choice because while passage A does have facts, it's characterized mostly by the amount of opinion and attitude it contains.

QUESTION 13: SPECIFIC REFERENCE

The key to answering this question lies in understanding the purpose of the example that kicked off passage B in lines 26-29. One way in which games intentionally create value is to grant intellectual property rights (lines 27-30). That's answer choice (D). Like so many questions that reference specific line numbers, the answer lies elsewhere in the passage. However, few lie so far away from the lines specified in the question. You may have found this question took you the longest to answer and, if so, you would not be alone.

- (A) This answer choice gets backward a phenomenon addressed in both passages, which is the sale of virtual items for real currency.
- (B) In answer choice (B), the only time "avatar" appears in the passage is in the background paragraph that starts passage A (lines 1-6). We know that the avatar is a feature of the game, but there's no indication it is ever bought and sold. Kick this answer choice to the curb like a puppy that's not housebroken. (Kidding! Just kick it to the backyard).
- (C) While it's possible that answer choice (C) could happen, it's just as possible that the players might lose all their

value by making a mistake in the game. We don't know from the passage so this is not the correct answer choice.

(E) For answer choice (E), while it's clear that virtual items can be traded for virtual currency (line 55), there's no indication anywhere in the passage that virtual currency can be traded for other virtual currency.

Hurray! You've finished your first Comparative Reading passage armed with all the data you needed to crush it. Celebrate by purchasing some virtual ice cream with Bitcoins!

24/questionT'

ANY QUESTIONS?

Up until this point, our focus has been on the passages, not the questions themselves. Now, however, it is time to focus on particular question types and how to address them.

BP Minotaur: There is a lesson to be learned here. The bulk of this book, (over 2/3), was devoted to analyzing passages, even though points are only available in the questions. This is as it should be. When you are the master of what you have read, the questions often answer themselves. Conversely, if you rush through the passage in order to get to the questions, you will wander aimlessly through them, often choosing wrong answers. While we will talk about timing extensively in a subsequent chapter, understand this: putting work in on the front end pays off on the questions, and that is true of all three sections of the test. Even though it sounds counterintuitive, you will get more points and save time overall by spending more time on the passage, rather than in the questions.

Cleetus: Save time by spending more time? Shoot... Don't think I can wrap my bean around that one.

As long as you abide by the principle, Cleetus, bean wrapping is unnecessary.

After cataloguing every Reading Comprehension question released by LSAC (a highly enjoyable task as we've mentioned previously), Blueprint has identified that there are ten question types. Just ten! Each come with an accompanying strategy we've developed for the best way to deal with them.

Some question types are quite common, and we have already discussed those that crop up the most (Main Point, Primary Purpose, Author's Attitude, Organization, and Role) in detail. Others are less prevalent. However, marking up the passage and tagging it correctly should make answering any of the ten questions much easier.

...ng Comprehension primarily tests your ability to understand the information presented in the ...sage. As such, it should come as no surprise that the first seven types of questions all belong to what we at Blueprint call the Characterization family.

Questions in the Characterization family have answers that are in the passage. If the answer isn't in the passage, it's not the right answer. Even though these questions all reside in the same family, there are still properties specific to each question type. To that end, we've outlined each question in detail, including what the correct answer looks like, what the incorrect answer looks like, and how you can use the Blueprint methods to find the right answer as efficiently as possible.

① Main Point Questions

author present → author's point of view MP
author absent → summary of views MP

> Which one of the following most accurately expresses the main point of the passage?

What they're looking for:
- When the author is present, the Main Point is the author's point of view.
- When the author is absent, the Main Point is a summary of all the points of view.
- Questions that ask you what an appropriate title would be for the passage are also Main Point questions. Address them accordingly.

question/answer → answer main point
cause/effect → causal structure

Pro tip: main point

Don't forget in Question and Answer secondary structures the answer to the question is the main idea. In Cause and Effect secondary structures the main idea will almost always refer to the causal structure.

Criteria for the right answer choice:
Accurate descriptions of the author's opinion or, when the author is absent, all of the opinions, or a summary of the data presented.

Ways to spot wrong answer choices:
- Answers that mischaracterize the passage, even if the mischaracterization is minor.
- Answers that are too narrow. Answers that miss a point or points of view. Answers that focus on only one of two or more relevant issues in the passage.
- Answers that treat another point of view *besides the author's* as the main point. (This, obviously, only pertains to passages where the author is present.)

How your tagging/markup/diagram gets you the answer:
The Main Point is always accurately reflected in your primary structure diagram, and you should have anticipated the right answer before you get to the questions.

Question Types:
1) Main Point
2) Primary Purpose
3) Author's attitude

Primary Purpose Questions

author present → advocate author's view

author absent → describe views

> The primary purpose of the passage is to

What they're looking for:
- When the author is present, the Primary Purpose is to advocate/promote/argue for the author's point of view.
- When the author is absent, the Primary Purpose is to describe/explain the points of view. This will look more or less like a description of the structure of the passage.

Criteria for the right answer choice:
Accurate descriptions of why the passage was written.

Ways to spot wrong answer choices:
- Answers that mischaracterize the passage, even if that mischaracterization is minor.
- Answers that are too narrow. Answers that focus on the purpose of parts of the passage rather than its entirety.

How your tagging/markup/diagram gets you the answer:
The Primary Purpose is always accurately reflected in your primary structure diagram, and you should anticipate the correct answer to this question before you get to the questions.

 Author's Attitude Questions

> Which one of the following most accurately describes the author's attitude toward critics of *Beowolf*?

What they're looking for:
- Whenever the author has a view on something, up to and including the author's point of view that appears in your primary structure diagram, it is possible that there will be an Author's Attitude question about it.

Pro tip:
Watch out for indications that an author has strong feelings—positive or negative—about a certain issue. When that happens, you are almost guaranteed an Author's Attitude question about it.

Criteria for the right answer choice:
The author has a positive or negative view on the particular issue, *and* the answer describes the author's view correctly.

Ways to spot wrong answer choices:
- Answers that mischaracterize the passage.
- Answers that mischaracterize the author's attitude.
- Answers that identify an attitude expressed by a party in the passage other than the author.

How your tagging/markup/diagram gets you the answer:
Author's attitude should be underlined in the passage and tagged with an "Att." to the right of the passage. You should anticipate the correct answer to Author's Attitude questions before you get to the questions.

④ Viewpoint Questions

> The passage suggests that the historians would be most likely to agree with which one of the following statements?

What they're looking for:
- These questions function exactly like Author's Attitude questions; the only difference is that they test your knowledge of the opinions and attitudes of parties in the passage other than the author.

Pro tip:
Watch out for indications that a party has strong feelings—positive or negative—about a certain issue.

Criteria for the right answer choice:
The party identified in the prompt has an opinion on the particular issue, and the answer describes the party's opinion correctly.

Ways to spot wrong answer choices:
- Answers that mischaracterize the passage.
- Answers that mischaracterize the party's opinion.
- Answers that identify an opinion expressed by a party in the passage other than the one identified in the prompt.

How your tagging/markup/diagram gets you the answer:
Underline any attitude in the passage. If it's not the author's, be sure to label it for easy reference.

Question Types

1) Main Point ⎫
2) Primary Purpose ⎬ Characterization questions
3) Author's attitude ⎪
4) Viewpoint ⎪
5) Role ⎪
6) Organization ⎭
7) Parallel
8) Special Reference ⎫ Implication questions
9) Inference ⎭
10) Strengthen/Weaken → Operation question

Examples & Classifications ⇒ premises
Question/answer ⇒ conclusion
Cause/effect ⇒ conclusion

⑤ Role Questions

> The primary function of the last paragraph of the passage is to

What they're looking for:
A correct description of the argumentative purpose of the particular paragraph or sentence being asked about.

Criteria for the right answer choice:
- A statement can play one of three basic roles in an argument:
  - **Background.** Information that is relevant to an argument, but does not provide support for the conclusion. This includes descriptions of the situation in which an argument takes place.
  - **Premise.** A premise is a piece of information that provides support for a conclusion.
  - **Conclusion.** A conclusion is supported by premises.
  - Remember that subsidiary conclusions are supported by premises but also support another conclusion.
- Before answering the question, identify which of these three statement types the sentence or paragraph is, and *how* it is performing that function.

Pro tip:
Remember, Examples and Classification structures act as premises. Cause and Effect and Question and Answer structures are conclusions.

Ways to spot wrong answer choices:
- Answers that identify a role other than the one the sentence or paragraph plays in an argument.
- Answers that mischaracterize exactly how the sentence or paragraph functions. For example, if the answer choice correctly identifies the sentence or paragraph as a premise, but incorrectly identifies the conclusion it is supporting, then it is wrong.

How your tagging/markup/diagram gets you the answer:
The role tags on your markup will get you the answers to these questions.

Statement plays one of three roles
1. *background*
2. *premise — provides information in support of the conclusion*
3. *conclusion — supported by premise(s)*
   ↳ *subsidary conclusions are supported by premises but also support another conclusion*

↳ *to answer a role question... identify which of the three statement types the sentence or paragraph is and how its preforming that function*

Organization Questions

> Which one of the following best describes the organization of the passage?

What they're looking for: An accurate description of the organization **and** argumentative structure of the passage as a whole.

Criteria for the right answer choice: The right answer should describe the passage paragraph by paragraph, correctly identifying how each paragraph fits into the argument(s) contained in the passage.

Ways to spot wrong answer choices:
- Answers that mischaracterize the organization, i.e. number of paragraphs, order of paragraphs, number of conclusions or premises in a particular paragraph or the passage as a whole.
- Answers that mischaracterize exactly how a paragraph functions.

How your tagging/markup/diagram got you the answer: Tagging the passage correctly will help you answer these questions. In addition, while it needn't match word for word, you should have anticipated the correct answer accurately when you summarized the passage structure before moving to the questions.

(7) Parallel Questions

> Which one of the following strategies is most similar to Scheich's experimental strategy as it is described in the passge?

These questions can vary greatly, but they ask you to identify a similar, parallel, or analogous situation to something that occurs in the passage.

What they're looking for:
- A situation that functionally resembles one in the passage, although it takes place in a wholly different context; or
- The correct application of a principle or definition that was applied in the passage to a different situation.

Criteria for the right answer choice:
- Before looking at the answer choices, you must formulate in your own words the situation/principle/definition identified in the prompt, discarding subject matter as much as possible.
- The right answer choice should conform to the situation/principle in all relevant ways without adding anything unnecessary.

Ways to spot wrong answer choices:
- Answers that are missing an important part of the situation/definition/principle.
- Answers that add something unnecessary to the situation/definition/principle.
- SIMILAR SUBJECT MATTER! While it is possible that the correct answer choice will contain similar subject matter, it is a red flag. Be extra skeptical of such answer choices.

How your tagging/markup/diagram got you the answer:
Tagging definitions, research, and studies can often get you the answer to these questions. Make sure you not only tag these things, but understand how they are used. If you do, you will be able to answer the Parallel question, which is almost always a difficult question.

BP Minotaur: Because they require you to analyze five situations that are different than the situation in the passage, Parallel questions tend to be very time consuming. If you are short on time on the test, Parallel questions are good candidates to skip.

questionTYPES / 331

Questions in the Implication family have answers that are based on the passage. The correct answer can be a restatement of information in the passage, but these questions are more likely to ask you to draw a reasonable conclusion based on the information in the passage. As with the Characterization family, we've outlined each question in detail, including what the correct and incorrect answers look like and how you can use your markup to find the right answer as efficiently as possible.

Specific Reference Questions

> The passage says all of the following EXCEPT:

> Which one of the following is most nearly equivalent to what the author means by "the relevant evidence" (line 62)?

Specific Reference questions come in two flavors: Questions that direct you where to look in the passage (e.g. a line number) and questions that ask you about something explicitly stated in the passage. The first are easy to type and the second are less so. Both, however, require answer choices that are fully supported in the passage. In this way they are very similar to Inference questions though they are slightly different, as you will soon see.

What they're looking for:
- Something that was specifically stated in the passage.
- Beware! When the prompt references a particular line in the passage, the answer is generally not found in that line. You must read a few sentences before and a few after for context. Usually the answer will be near the line cited, but it could also be referring to another portion of the passage. Think critically.

Criteria for the right answer choice: Something that accurately describes a statement in the passage.

Ways to spot wrong answer choices: Answers that mischaracterize the passage.

How your tagging/markup/diagram got you the answer: When the question sends you to a particular line or paragraph, check your tags to see the most important feature of the passage in that area. Often this will yield the correct answer.

Specific reference questions either...
① direct you where to look in a passage (line #)
② ask you about something directly stated in the passage
→ both require answer choices fully supported in the passage

332 / Chapter 24

9. Inference Questions

the right answer is a conclusion that has support in the passage
- *look for weak answer choices as they are easier to support*

> It can be inferred from the passage that during patrolling behavior, the platypus is attempting to

Inference questions ask you to infer or conclude information based on the passage. The correct answer can be a restatement of information in the passage but is it more likely to ask you to draw a reasonable conclusion based on information in the passage. These questions belong to what we at Blueprint call the Implication family because you job is to accurately ascertain what it implied by the passage.

What they're looking for: A statement that is supported by information in the passage.

Criteria for the right answer choice: The right answer is a *conclusion* that has support in the passage. In other words, some statement or set of statements provides support for it.

Pro tip: Look for weak answer choices, as a weak claim is easier to support than a strong one.

Ways to spot wrong answer choices: Answers that are not supported by information in the passage. This includes answers that refer to subject matter that is similar to that in the passage but distinct (an answer choice about "most people" when the passage is only discussing one person, for instance).

How your tagging/markup/diagram got you the answer: These questions can touch on a wide range of things in the passage. Your tagging will help you locate the part of the passage where the answer lies. However, if the correct answer isn't immediately apparent, eliminate incorrect answers that you know are not supported by the passage.

> **Ninja:** If you get to the final passage and don't have enough time left to read it, Specific Reference questions are points that can still be picked up. If you read the line referred to, as well as a few lines above and below for context, you can often quickly answer the question.

> **Ninja:** Inference questions, on the other hand, can be a time suck more deadly than an Ashiko foot spike to the throat. If you are running out of time, skip questions like: "The passage provides the most support for which of the following statements?" and "Which of the following can be inferred from the passage?"

Strengthen and Weaken questions belong to what we at Blueprint call the Operation family. This is because the correct answer choice will be added to the passage in order to strengthen it or weaken it. Though prevalent in Logical Reasoning, this type of question is not common in Reading Comprehension. However, they do crop up from time to time so we want you to know how to deal with them.

Strengthen/Weaken Questions

> Which one of the following, if true, would most strengthen the passage's position concerning apes?

What they're looking for: New information which, if added to an argument, would make the conclusion more likely to be true (in the case of a Strengthen question) or less likely to be true (in the case of a Weaken question).

Criteria for the right answer choice:
- If it is a Strengthen question, the new information will partially or completely cure the weakness in the argument.
- If it is a Weaken question, the new information will either identify the weakness in plain terms, or give a reason to believe that the weakness is even worse than previously thought.

Ways to spot wrong answer choices:
- Answers that perform the wrong operation, i.e. an answer to a Strengthen question that weakens, or an answer to a Weaken question that strengthens.
- Answers that strengthen or weaken an argument other than the one identified in the prompt.
- Answers that neither strengthen nor weaken the argument.

How your tagging/markup/diagram got you the answer: If you are tagging criticisms and assumptions, you will head into the questions knowing likely problem areas. It is these areas that will often be the focus on a Strengthen or Weaken question.

If strengthn question...
- the new information will paritally or completly cure the weakness of the argument

If weaken question....
- the new information will either
  ① identify the weakness in plain terms or
  ② give reason to believe that the weakness is even worse than previously thought

QUESTION TYPE DRILL

Handwritten list (top right):
① main point
② primary purpose
③ author's attitude
④ viewpoint
⑤ role
⑥ organization
⑦ parallel
⑧ special reference
⑨ inference
⑩ strengthn/weaken

Read the sample prompts in the following exercise and type each question in the space provided. The answers may be found at the end of the drill.

---

1. Based on the passage, it can be inferred that the author would be likely to agree with which of the following statements?

   TYPE: author's attitude

2. Which one of the following, if true, would cast doubt on the position concerning mammalian reproduction taken in the third paragraph of the passage?

   TYPE: operation

3. Which of the following most accurately describes the relationship between the two passages?

   TYPE: organization

4. Which one of the following is most analogous to the method of experimentation described in the second paragraph of the passage?

   TYPE: parallel

questionTYPES / 335

5. In the context of the third paragraph, the function of the phrase "an exemplary study" is to

TYPE: role

6. Which one of the following statements is most strongly supported by the passage?

TYPE: Inference

7. The author of the passage is primarily concerned with

TYPE: primary purpose

8. Based on the information in the passage, which one of the following best describes Jenkins' view on black holes?

TYPE: viewpoint

9. The passage explicitly states which of the following?

TYPE: specific reference

10. Which one of the following does the author mention as an example of bacterial reproduction?

TYPE: specific reference

11. The author's main purpose in mentioning post modern criticism (lines 13-16) is to

TYPE: __role__

12. Which one of the following most accurately summarizes the passage?

TYPE: __organization__

13. If the passage were to appear in a legal journal, the most fitting title would be which one of the following?

TYPE: __Main point__

14. The author of the passage would be most likely to disagree with which one of the following?

TYPE: __authors attitude__

15. Which one of the following best describes the organization of the passage as a whole?

TYPE: __organization__

16. Which one of the following, if true, would provide the most support for the reasoning in the first paragraph of the passage?

TYPE: __operation__

17. It can be most reasonably inferred that the author would agree with which one of the following statements?

TYPE: author's attitude

18. The authors of the two passages would be most likely to disagree about

TYPE: authors attitude

19. The author's discussion in the third paragraph proceeds in which one of the following ways?

TYPE: organization

20. Each of the following excerpts from the passage exhibits the author's attitude toward the novel *The Fountainhead* EXCEPT:

TYPE: author's attitude

From 1956 to 1975 there was a "Directed Memory/Reading Recall" section of the test where you had 15 minutes to read three passages and answer 30 questions WITHOUT LOOKING BACK AT THE PASSAGE.

And you thought you had it tough.

ANSWER KEY

1. Author's Attitude
2. Operation
3. Organization
4. Parallel
5. Role
6. Inference
7. Primary Purpose
8. Viewpoint
9. Specific Reference
10. Specific Reference
11. Role
12. Organization
13. Main Point
14. Author's Attitude
15. Organization
16. Operation
17. Author's Attitude
18. Author's Attitude
19. Organization
20. Author's Attitude

25/it'sGOtime

WE BELIEVE YOU CAN FLY!

Congratulations! You now possess all of the Blueprint Reading Comprehension wisdom we have to impart regarding making markups. This means that from here on out, you should be able to deal with any passage you encounter. To that end, as was foretold long ago, you must soon meet the LSAT on the field of battle to claim your rightful place among the pantheon of Reading Comprehension gods. In anticipation of that glorious day, we present you a challenge.

In the following pages, you will find all four passages from the December 2014 exam, in the order in which they appeared on the test. This will give you a sense of the mix of difficulty, subject matter, structures, and organization you will see on test day. Please read the passages and address the questions using all you've learned up to this point.

We've included the Blueprint Reading Method™ for each passage to take you through the passage paragraph by paragraph, explaining what you should tag, how you should anticipate questions, how to fill in your primary structure diagram, and how to address each question. More importantly, the Blueprint Reading Method™ will let you know how to know when to do these things so you can see the clues that LSAC lays out to tip you off to important structures.

Ditz: So I should be timing these, right?

No, Ditz. At this point, you should **not** be timing yourself. You're still absorbing and practicing the techniques, so don't apply the pressure of trying to execute new skills quickly before you've had a chance to practice them. Focus on tagging the passage and anticipating questions correctly. Worry about timing later. This means if it takes you an hour and a half to correctly tag a passage, that's fine. Worry about accuracy rather than speed right now.

DECEMBER 2014: PASSAGE 1

Given the amount of time and effort that curators, collectors, dealers, scholars, and critics spend on formulating judgments of taste in relation to oil paintings, it seems odd that so few are prepared to
(5) apply some of the same skills in exploring works of art that stimulate another sense altogether: that of smell. Why is great perfume not taken more seriously? While art professionals are very serious about many branches of literature, architecture, and music, I have
(10) yet to find a curatorial colleague who regularly beats a path to the fragrance counter in search of, say, *Joy Parfum*, the 1930 masterpiece by Henri Alméras.
  And yet, the parallels between what ought to be regarded as sister arts are undeniable. Painters
(15) combine natural and, these days, synthetic pigments with media such as oils and resins, much as the perfumer carefully formulates natural and synthetic chemical compounds. The Old Masters deployed oil paint across the color spectrum, and applied layers on
(20) a determining ground and various kinds of underpainting, slowly building up to the surface, completing their work with thin glazes on top. Thus various types of mashed-up earth and vegetable suspended in linseed or poppy oil are brushed over a
(25) stretch of woven fabric. They begin to dry, and a picture is born. Its appearance changes over time, because the tendency of oil paint is to become gradually more transparent.
  So, too, talented "noses" experiment with
(30) complex configurations of olfactory elements and produce in symphonic combination many small sensations, at times discordant, sweet, bitter, melancholy, or happy, as the case may be. These combinations change and develop in sequence or in
(35) unison as the substance and its constituents evaporate at different rates, some quickly, others slowly, thanks to the warmth of our skin. A brilliant perfumer may thus devise an imaginary world no less powerful, or intimate, than that of a great composer or painter, and
(40) in calling on our capacity to discover there some memory of childhood or of a long-forgotten experience, perfumers are in the same business as the artist who creates the illusion of life on canvas.
  Perhaps one reason that truly great smells are so
(45) often undervalued is that perfumes are today made and distributed under the not particularly watchful gaze of a few large corporations. The cynical bean counters in Paris and Zurich do not hesitate to tamper with old formulas, insisting on the substitution of cheap
(50) chemical compounds that approximately resemble rarer, better ingredients in an effort to increase profits. They do not tell their customers when or how they do this; indeed, they presume their customers won't notice the difference. Consequently, fine perfume is
(55) now hopelessly entangled with the international cosmetic dollar, and ill-served by marketing and public relations.

1. Which one of the following most accurately expresses the main point of the passage?

   (A) Despite their pursuit of profit, corporations that produce and market perfumes value artistic skill.
   (B) A masterpiece perfume evokes reactions that are no less powerful than those evoked by a masterpiece in music or painting.
   (C) The corporate nature of the perfume business is the reason that so few truly great perfumes are now produced.
   (D) Great perfumes are works of art and deserve respect and attention as such.
   (E) Perfume-making and oil painting should be regarded as sister arts, both of which involve the skilled application of complex configurations of ingredients.

2. In which one of the following circumstances would the author of the passage be most likely to believe that a perfume manufacturer is justified in altering the formula of a classic perfume?

   (A) The alteration makes the perfume more closely resemble Joy Parfum.
   (B) The alteration is done to replace an ingredient that is currently very costly.
   (C) The alteration replaces a synthetic chemical compound with a natural chemical compound.
   (D) The alteration is done to make the perfume popular with a wider variety of customers.
   (E) The alteration takes a previously altered perfume closer to its creator's original formula.

342 / Chapter 25

3. The word "noses" (line 29) refers to

   (A) perfumers
   (B) perfume collectors
   (C) particular perfumes
   (D) people with expertise in marketing perfumes
   (E) people with expertise in pricing perfumes

4. The passage provides the most support for which one of the following statements about art?

   (A) A work of art can bring about an aesthetic experience through the memories that it evokes.
   (B) In any work of art, one can detect the harmonious combination of many small sensations.
   (C) A work of art will inevitably fail if it is created for the sake of commercial success.
   (D) The best works of art improve with age.
   (E) Some forms of art are superior to others.

5. The author would be most likely to hold which one of the following opinions about *Joy Parfum* by Henri Alméras?

   (A) As time goes on, its artistry is appreciated more and more.
   (B) As a work of art, it is no less important than a great piece of sculpture.
   (C) It was the foremost accomplishment of its time in perfume making.
   (D) It is a fragrance that is appreciated only by people with refined taste.
   (E) Its original formula is similar to many other perfumes of the 1930s.

6. Which one of the following is most analogous to what the author calls the "cynical bean counters" (line 47)?

   (A) an art museum curator who caters to popular tastes in choosing works for an exhibition
   (B) a movie studio executive who imposes cost-saving production restrictions on a film's director
   (C) a director of an art institute who cuts the annual budget because of projections of declining revenues
   (D) a business executive who convinces her company to invest in art merely for the sake of tax benefits
   (E) an art school dean who slashes the budget of one project in order to increase the budget of his pet project

7. The last paragraph most strongly supports which one of the following statements?

   (A) The names of the world's best perfumes are not known to most customers.
   (B) The profitability of a particular perfume is not a good indicator of its quality.
   (C) Companies that sell perfume pay little attention to what their customers want.
   (D) Perfume makers of the past would never tamper with established formulas.
   (E) Companies that sell perfume make most of their profits on perfumes in the least expensive price ranges.

8. Which one of the following most accurately describes the organization of the passage?

   (A) The first paragraph makes an observation, the middle paragraphs elaborate on that observation while considering one possible explanation for it, and the final paragraph delivers an alternative explanation.
   (B) The first paragraph advances a thesis, the middle paragraphs present a case for that thesis, and the final paragraph considers and rejects one particular challenge to that thesis.
   (C) The first paragraph sets out a challenge to received wisdom, the middle paragraphs present a response to that challenge, and the final paragraph presents a concrete example that supports the response.
   (D) The first paragraph poses a question, the middle paragraphs present a case that helps to justify the posing of that question, and the final paragraph presents a possible answer to the question.
   (E) The first paragraph outlines a problem, the middle paragraphs present two consequences of that problem, and the final paragraph attempts to identify the parties that are responsible for the problem.

Here we are, test day! Yay! (Or at least a simulated test day.) Pretend the proctor has just uttered those momentous words, "You may begin." Time to tackle this passage like Paula Deen taking on a bowl of mashed potatoes.

HOW TO READ THE PASSAGE

Paragraph 1

> Given the amount of time and effort that curators, collectors, dealers, scholars, and critics spend on formulating judgments of taste in relation to oil paintings, it seems odd that so few are prepared to
> (5) apply some of the same skills in exploring works of art that stimulate another sense altogether: that of smell. Why is great perfume not taken more seriously? While art professionals are very serious about many branches of literature, architecture, and music, I have
> (10) yet to find a curatorial colleague who regularly beats a path to the fragrance counter in search of, say, *Joy Parfum*, the 1930 masterpiece by Henri Alméras.

Q: WHY ISN'T PERFUME TAKEN SERIOUSLY?

EX.

CONC.: PERFUME SHOULD BE TAKEN SERIOUSLY

ATT.

Paragraph one starts us off with a question, which we love to see. Oil paintings get a lot of attention from important types of people, so why not perfume (line 7)? Let's tag the passage, "Q: Why isn't perfume taken seriously?" This is a Question and Answer secondary structure, and it is important to tag, as you'll remember, because the answer to a question is a conclusion. Note that we don't have an answer yet.

Ninja: A question stated early on in the passage may indicate an extensive Q&A structure. If the rest of the passage is devoted to answering the question, then those answers, however many there are, will constitute the points of view in the primary structure diagram. In such a case, we must anticipate multiple questions about it. If, on the other hand, it is answered in a line or two elsewhere, it is a localized structure, about which we will likely see only one question.

The author pops his good-smelling mug in at line 9 ("I have yet to find...") which is a rare example of an "I" statement in a passage. This lets us know unequivocally that the author is present. Next up is an example (!) of what the author thinks is a "masterpiece" of perfumery: *Joy Parfum*, formulated by Henri Alméras. Remember, an example is a *premise* that supports another statement. The tricky bit here is that the supported statement is implied: some perfumes should be taken seriously.

Cleetus: I found it! The answer to the question! It took me three-hunnerd and some pages, but I finally did it! "Some perfumes should be taken seriously." 180 here I come!

Well, actually Cleetus, sorry to let you down, but, if we're being precise, this doesn't answer the question. The question is: why don't people take perfume seriously? This statement merely implies that, all things being equal, people *should* take perfume seriously. That offers no solution to the mystery of why people don't take it seriously. However, the good news is that this is a prescriptive statement (a recommendation, if you like). Prescriptive statements are very often conclusions. If we see support for it, we can slap that puppy into the primary structure diagram.

Don't forget to underline and tag the attitude we see in line 12 where the author refers to the example of *Joy Parfum* as a "masterpiece."

Paragraphs 2 and 3

(15) And yet, the parallels between what ought to be regarded as sister arts are undeniable. Painters (combine natural and, these days, synthetic pigments with media such as oils and resins, much as the perfumer carefully formulates natural and synthetic chemical compounds. The Old Masters deployed oil paint across the color spectrum, and applied layers on
(20) a determining ground and various kinds of underpainting, slowly building up to the surface, completing their work with thin glazes on top. Thus various types of mashed-up earth and vegetable suspended in linseed or poppy oil are brushed over a
(25) stretch of woven fabric. They begin to dry, and a picture is born. Its appearance changes over time, because the tendency of oil paint is to become gradually more transparent.
So, too, talented "noses" experiment with
(30) complex configurations of olfactory elements and produce in symphonic combination many small sensations, at times discordant, sweet, bitter, melancholy, or happy, as the case may be. These combinations change and develop in sequence or in
(35) unison as the substance and its constituents evaporate at different rates, some quickly, others slowly, thanks to the warmth of our skin. A brilliant perfumer may thus devise an imaginary world no less powerful, or intimate, than that of a great composer or painter, and
(40) in calling on our capacity to discover there some memory of childhood or of a long-forgotten experience, perfumers are in the same business as the artist who creates the illusion of life on canvas.

SIMILARITIES BETWEEN PAINTING AND PERFUME:

1. NATURAL AND SYNTHETIC COMPOUNDS

2. COMPLEX AND LAYERED

3. CHANGE OVER TIME

4. EVOKE EMOTION AND MEMORY

Paragraph two and three, taken together, are devoted to discussing the similarities between painting, which people do take seriously, and perfume, which they do not. The argument being advanced here is an argument by comparison. The author is pointing out that painting and perfume are similar in a number of ways. Because painting is taken seriously, all of these details provide support for the prescriptive statement in paragraph one: People should take perfume seriously.

BP MINOTAUR: The argument here can be boiled down to this:

Premise: painting and perfume are similar.
Premise: painting is taken seriously.

Conclusion: perfume should also be taken seriously.

We now know we have a conclusion and support for the conclusion from paragraph one, that perfume should be taken seriously. Accordingly, we can place it into our primary structure diagram. The author states this point of view, so let's put our author arrow pointing toward Thesis.

It's important to fully understand the support offered for a point of view. So, before we move on, let's be particular about how painting and perfume are similar. Paintings and perfume both: (1) mix natural and synthetic ingredients (lines 14-18); (2) contain complex, layered combinations (lines 18-22 and 29-33); (3) change over time (lines 25-28 and 33-37); and (4) are able to evoke memory and emotion (lines 37-43).

BP Ninja: This is an extensive Classification structure. As you'll remember, a Classification is a category and a list of at least three items that fall into the category. In this case, (1)-(4) fall into the category "similarities between perfume and painting." This Classification structure is extensive because it acts as premises for the conclusion that perfume should be taken seriously.

Because the main idea is supported by an extensive Classification structure, this should be reflected in your primary structure diagram. Something along the lines of "Perfume should be taken seriously because it's like art" reflects the secondary structure nicely.

Paragraph 4

> (45) Perhaps one reason that truly great smells are so often undervalued is that perfumes are today made and distributed under the not particularly watchful gaze of a few large corporations. The <u>cynical bean counters</u> in Paris and Zurich do not hesitate to tamper with old formulas, insisting on the substitution of cheap
> (50) chemical compounds that approximately resemble rarer, better ingredients in an effort to increase profits. They do not tell their customers when or how they do this; indeed, they presume their customers won't notice the difference. Consequently, fine perfume is
> (55) now <u>hopelessly entangled</u> with the international cosmetic dollar, and <u>ill-served</u> by marketing and public relations.

ATT.

A: COMPANIES USE CHEAP SUBSTITUTES

ATT.

Paragraph four finally gives us an answer to the question posed in paragraph one. The answer, or at least a partial answer, to the question of why perfume isn't taken seriously is that corporations that make perfume are cheap, so the ingredients used by the master perfumers who created a perfume get swapped out for inexpensive, noticeable substitutes. Let's write that next to the paragraph: "A: corporations make cheap perfume." Because this Question and Answer structure isn't the main idea of the paragraph, we know it's a localized structure. However, much more space than just a few lines (nearly two paragraphs) was devoted to it. Remember, in Reading Comprehension passages, the more real estate devoted to a concept, the more likely there is to be a question about it. This local Question and Answer structure is so developed that you can virtually guarantee one question and likely two.

Finally, author's attitude is buzzing around this paragraph like flies on honey: "*cynical* bean counters…*hopelessly* entangled…*ill-served* by marketing and public relations." All in all, it's fair to say that the author does not like the modern perfume industry. Let's underline these moments and label them "Att." in the margin.

The completed markup looks like this:

        Given the amount of time and effort that curators, collectors, dealers, scholars, and critics spend on formulating judgments of taste in relation to oil paintings, it seems odd that so few are prepared to
(5) apply some of the same skills in exploring works of art that stimulate another sense altogether: that of smell. Why is great perfume not taken more seriously? While art professionals are very serious about many branches of literature, architecture, and music, I have
(10) yet to find a curatorial colleague who regularly beats a path to the fragrance counter in search of, say, *Joy Parfum*, the 1930 <u>masterpiece</u> by Henri Alméras.

        And yet, the parallels between what ought to be regarded as sister arts are undeniable. Painters
(15) (combine natural and, these days, synthetic pigments with media such as oils and resins, much as the perfumer carefully formulates natural and synthetic chemical compounds. The Old Masters deployed oil paint across the color spectrum, and applied layers on
(20) a determining ground and various kinds of underpainting, slowly building up to the surface, completing their work with thin glazes on top. Thus various types of mashed-up earth and vegetable suspended in linseed or poppy oil are brushed over a
(25) stretch of woven fabric. They begin to dry, and a picture is born. Its appearance changes over time, because the tendency of oil paint is to become gradually more transparent.

        So, too, talented "noses" experiment with
(30) complex configurations of olfactory elements and produce in symphonic combination many small sensations, at times discordant, sweet, bitter, melancholy, or happy, as the case may be. These combinations change and develop in sequence or in
(35) unison as the substance and its constituents evaporate at different rates, some quickly, others slowly, thanks to the warmth of our skin. A brilliant perfumer may thus devise an imaginary world no less powerful, or intimate, than that of a great composer or painter, and
(40) in calling on our capacity to discover there some memory of childhood or of a long-forgotten experience, perfumers are in the same business as the artist who creates the illusion of life on canvas.

        Perhaps one reason that truly great smells are so
(45) often undervalued is that perfumes are today made and distributed under the not particularly watchful gaze of a few large corporations. The <u>cynical bean counters</u> in Paris and Zurich do not hesitate to tamper with old formulas, insisting on the substitution of cheap
(50) chemical compounds that approximately resemble rarer, ~~better ingredients in~~ an effort to increase profits. They do not tell their ~~customers~~ when or how they do this; indeed, they presume their customers won't notice the difference. Consequently, fine perfume is
(55) now hopelessly entangled with the international cosmetic dollar, and ill-served by marketing and public relations.

Q: WHY ISN'T PERFUME TAKEN SERIOUSLY?

EX.
CONC.: PERFUME SHOULD BE TAKEN SERIOUSLY
ATT.

SIMILARITIES BETWEEN PAINTING AND PERFUME:

1. NATURAL AND SYNTHETIC COMPOUNDS

2. COMPLEX AND LAYERED

3. CHANGE OVER TIME

4. EVOKE EMOTION AND MEMORY

A: COMPANIES USE CHEAP SUBSTITUTES
ATT.

.

ATT.

PERFUME SHOULD BE TAKEN SERIOUSLY BECAUSE IT'S LIKE ART ←

We've read, we've tagged, and we've marked. Now it's time to prepare ourselves for the questions to come. To that end, let's anticipate.

1. Anticipate the main idea

There is exactly one point of view here, i.e. that perfume ought to be taken seriously. Since it's supported by an extended Classification structure, it's likely that will find its way into the correct answer choice. Hence our final main idea is that perfume should be taken seriously because it's like art. The author is clearly present (remember the "I" from line 9) and she never assigns that point of view to another party in the passage, so it is her own point of view. That means the arrow in the primary structure diagram should point to "Thesis."

2. Anticipate the primary purpose

When the author is present, as here, the primary purpose is, generally speaking, to advocate for the author's point of view. So, here, the primary purpose is to argue that perfume ought to be taken seriously.

3. Anticipate the author's attitude

This passage is rife with strong indications of author's attitude. There is very positive attitude in the description of *Joy Parfum* in paragraph one and there is very negative attitude toward the perfume industry in paragraph four. By the way, anyone else look up *Joy Parfum*? Turns out you can own it for just $350 a bottle!

4. Anticipate anything to which the passage lends itself

Ooooohhhh, so much anticipation here. (Did that sound weird? That was kinda weird.) What's really great about this passage is that there is exactly one localized Question and Answer structure (paragraphs one and four), one localized Example structure (paragraph one), and one extended Classification structure (paragraphs two and three). We made sure to tag those, and we're going to tear up their associated questions.

5. Summarize the entire passage in a sentence

Remember, the way to summarize the passage is to track how the argument(s) are made. In this passage, a question is posed in paragraph one, a prescriptive statement is announced in paragraph one and supported in paragraphs two and three, and the question is answered in the fourth paragraph.

NOW FOR THE QUESTIONS

Question #1

Here it is, the main point question that almost invariably starts off the questions. The passage was mostly devoted to supporting the prescriptive statement in the first paragraph that perfume should be taken seriously. It's supported by an extended Classification structure that should be taken seriously because perfume is like art. Answer choice (D) nails it and we are awesome sauce.

A wrong answer to a main point question can generally be discarded either because it mischaracterizes the passage, or it is too narrow, or it talks about something the passage never mentioned, or some combination of those three things. Answer choice (A) mischaracterizes the passage. Corporations make junk perfume (lines 47-51). They certainly don't "value artistic skill," so (A) is out. Answer choice (B) is too narrow. It's more or less a recapitulation of the last sentence of paragraph three. Answer choice (C) mischaracterizes the passage. We aren't talking about the reason why so few great perfumes are actually made. So that's out. Answer choice (E) is too narrow. It focuses on the Classification structure (the premises) of the conclusion, but doesn't include the conclusion itself.

1. Which one of the following most accurately expresses the main point of the passage?

    (A) Despite their pursuit of profit, corporations that produce and market perfumes value artistic skill.
    (B) A masterpiece perfume evokes reactions that are no less powerful than those evoked by a masterpiece in music or painting.
    (C) The corporate nature of the perfume business is the reason that so few truly great perfumes are now produced.
    (D) Great perfumes are works of art and deserve respect and attention as such.
    (E) Perfume-making and oil painting should be regarded as sister arts, both of which involve the skilled application of complex configurations of ingredients.

Question #2

This is an Inference question which specifically cites the manufacturers that the author hated on in paragraph four. We know the author haaaaaaaates it when they make cheap substitutions. So, in asking us what the author would approve of, it's definitely the opposite of what the manufacturers are doing. Answer choice (E) gives us a circumstance that the author likes because it's getting closer to the master perfumer's vision of what it should smell like, the complete opposite of the manufacturers moving away from the original formula.

> 2. In which one of the following circumstances would the author of the passage be most likely to believe that a perfume manufacturer is justified in altering the formula of a classic perfume?
>
> (A) The alteration makes the perfume more closely resemble Joy Parfum.
> (B) The alteration is done to replace an ingredient that is currently very costly.
> (C) The alteration replaces a synthetic chemical compound with a natural chemical compound.
> (D) The alteration is done to make the perfume popular with a wider variety of customers.
> (E) The alteration takes a previously altered perfume closer to its creator's original formula.

Although the author likes *Joy Parfum*, it's not at all clear that she thinks changing any fragrance to be more like that *particular* perfume is a good thing. In fact, that would likely change the perfumer's vision for the perfume, so we can get rid of (A). Answer choice (B) identifies what the author hates about the perfume biz (cynical bean counters!), so he certainly wouldn't find this cost-cutting measure justified. Answer choice (C) is talking about synthetic versus natural ingredients, and the author seems to be fine with either or both (lines 29-34). Since the whole point is to be as close to the perfumer's vision as possible, it's unclear under what circumstances this shift would be justified or not. Finally, answer choice (D) misses the mark in the same way (C) does. It doesn't relate to the perfumer's vision for the piece. If the alteration takes it closer to that, the author would like it; if it were vice versa, the author wouldn't like it. Farewell (D)!

Question #3

This Specific Reference question kindly directs us where to look for the answer in the passage. If you didn't get from the lines following "noses" that it refers to the people making the perfume (they experiment with "olfactory elements" (line 30)), you would arrive at the correct answer by continuing to read to line 37 that begins "A brilliant perfumer thus..." That gives us answer choice (A).

> 3. The word "noses" (line 29) refers to
>
> (A) perfumers
> (B) perfume collectors
> (C) particular perfumes
> (D) people with expertise in marketing perfumes
> (E) people with expertise in pricing perfumes

Perfume collectors don't "experiment with complex configurations of olfactory elements" (lines 29-30), or with anything for that matter. So answer choice (B) is wrong.

Perfumes are the things smelled, not something, like a nose, which does the smelling, so answer choice (C) makes no sense as an answer to this question. Answer choices (D) and (E) both refer to types of people that are never mentioned in the passage, so they are wrong.

Question #4

4. The passage provides the most support for which one of the following statements about art?

   (A) A work of art can bring about an aesthetic experience through the memories that it evokes.
   (B) In any work of art, one can detect the harmonious combination of many small sensations.
   (C) A work of art will inevitably fail if it is created for the sake of commercial success.
   (D) The best works of art improve with age.
   (E) Some forms of art are superior to others.

This is a fairly broad Inference question and your first instinct might be to panic. But don't! Because the best thing to do in such cases is to skim the answer choices and see if you can get the correct answer from your tagging or marks in the passage. Sure enough, answer choice (A) rewards us for recognizing the Classification structure. Huzzah! It's the fourth entry in that structure: art, like perfume and painting, is able to evoke memory and emotion (lines 37-43). So very predictable, LSAT.

Answer choice (B) is very broad and strong. The passage limits itself to painting and perfume, but this answer talks about every single kind of art. There's no support in the passage for sculpture or performance art or sand animation art (yep, it's a thing). Answer choice (C) is tempting because we know that commercializing perfume has screwed it up as art, but that is because it moves away from the perfumer's vision. There's no indication in the passage, however, that *every* type of art would fail in the same way. This answer choice is way too broad. With (D), we're again confronted with a statement about how all art works. Can't go that far. Answer choice (E) is a comparison that is not supported. All we know is that painting and perfume are similar, but we don't know if they're better or worse than each other or anything else.

5. The author would be most likely to hold which one of the following opinions about *Joy Parfum* by Henri Alméras?

   (A) As time goes on, its artistry is appreciated more and more.
   (B) As a work of art, it is no less important than a great piece of sculpture.
   (C) It was the foremost accomplishment of its time in perfume making.
   (D) It is a fragrance that is appreciated only by people with refined taste.
   (E) Its original formula is similar to many other perfumes of the 1930s.

Question #5

This is an Author's Attitude question referring to the very positive attitude we noted in paragraph one. The author describes *Joy Parfum* as an example supporting the idea that perfume ought to be treated as art. Answer choice (B) says exactly that.

Answer choice (A) is at odds with the author's complaint that people don't appreciate perfume, so this is the wrong answer. Answer choice (C) is asking us to compare *Joy Parfum* to every single

it'sGOtime / 353

other perfume of its time. There's no information in the passage that would allow us to do that. There's no indication that the average Joe can't appreciate *Joy* or any other type of perfume, so there's no support for (D). Answer choice (E), like answer choice (C), is asking us to compare *Joy Parfum* to other perfumes of the day, but they're never mentioned. So this is out.

Question #6

6. Which one of the following is most analogous to what the author calls the "cynical bean counters" (line 47)?

   (A) an art museum curator who caters to popular tastes in choosing works for an exhibition
   (B) a movie studio executive who imposes cost-saving production restrictions on a film's director
   (C) a director of an art institute who cuts the annual budget because of projections of declining revenues
   (D) a business executive who convinces her company to invest in art merely for the sake of tax benefits
   (E) an art school dean who slashes the budget of one project in order to increase the budget of his pet project

The previous question asked us about the author's positive attitude toward *Joy*. Later on, we noted negative attitude toward "bean counters." Here we're being asked about them, but as part of a Parallel question. To answer this question, we'll need to summarize what's wrong with the bean counters and find the answer that replicates it in a different scenario.

The bean counters turn great perfume into junk by swapping out high quality ingredients for cheap stuff so they can save a few bucks. Answer choice (B) talks about saving a few bucks, so that's our guy.

Answer choice (A) talks about popular tastes, but that in no way lines up with cheap and cost saving, so it's wrong. Answer choice (C) talks about cutting costs, but it's brought on by financial trouble, which is not mentioned in regard to the perfume manufacturers. Answer choice (D) talks about investing in art, which is the opposite of destroying art like the bean counters do. Finally, answer choice (E) talks about increasing spending on his pet project, something that the cynical bean counters have no intention of doing.

Pro tip: (A), (C), (D), and (E) have art as the subject matter like the passage. Remember to treat the same subject matter with caution. Sure enough, they're all wrong. The only correct answer is the one that *doesn't* discuss art.

Question #7

This Inference question refers us to paragraph four, which does two things. The author answers the question of why perfume is not taken seriously—darn you, cynical bean counters!—and expresses decidedly negative attitude toward what they are doing. Put those two things together, and you get answer choice (B). The author definitely does not think that turning a profit on perfume leads to high quality perfume.

Answer choice (A) talks to us about perfume names and what most customers know. There's no support for this statement anywhere in the passage. Answer choice (C) might be tempting because it describes these companies as disregarding taste, but they disregard the perfumer's vision. There's no indication in the passage of whether or not they cater to customer desires. We don't know what dead perfumers would've done differently, so answer choice (D) can be discarded. Answer choice (E) is making a very specific claim about these companies' business model that is not supported in the passage. Cheap perfume could make up 1% or 99% of perfume company profits for all we know.

Question #8

Were you wondering when the Question and Answer structure was going to pay off? Us too! Well here it is in this Organization question. Answer choice (D) correctly describes the progression of all of the paragraphs. Interestingly, it doesn't mention the actual main idea of the passage within the organization, but the structure it describes is still correct, so it's our boy.

The observation that answer choice (A) describes is that perfume isn't taken seriously. Paragraphs two and three do not provide an explanation

7. The last paragraph most strongly supports which one of the following statements?

   (A) The names of the world's best perfumes are not known to most customers.
   (B) The profitability of a particular perfume is not a good indicator of its quality.
   (C) Companies that sell perfume pay little attention to what their customers want.
   (D) Perfume makers of the past would never tamper with established formulas.
   (E) Companies that sell perfume make most of their profits on perfumes in the least expensive price ranges.

8. Which one of the following most accurately describes the organization of the passage?

   (A) The first paragraph makes an observation, the middle paragraphs elaborate on that observation while considering one possible explanation for it, and the final paragraph delivers an alternative explanation.
   (B) The first paragraph advances a thesis, the middle paragraphs present a case for that thesis, and the final paragraph considers and rejects one particular challenge to that thesis.
   (C) The first paragraph sets out a challenge to received wisdom, the middle paragraphs present a response to that challenge, and the final paragraph presents a concrete example that supports the response.
   (D) The first paragraph poses a question, the middle paragraphs present a case that helps to justify the posing of that question, and the final paragraph presents a possible answer to the question.
   (E) The first paragraph outlines a problem, the middle paragraphs present two consequences of that problem, and the final paragraph attempts to identify the parties that are responsible for the problem.

for that observation. Instead, they provide an explanation for why that observation is troubling. Answer choice (B) is attractive up to a point. There is indeed a thesis in the first paragraph—art should be taken seriously—that is supported in paragraphs two and three. However, the last paragraph doesn't address a challenge to that thesis. It explains why the thesis is not more widespread. Answer choice (C) treats the idea that perfume is not serious as "received wisdom," but the author never says that anyone has ever actually made that observation. Finally, answer choice (E) talks about paragraphs two and three as though the topics described are consequences of a problem, but those paragraphs describe the positive aspects of two things. That's way different. So (E) is out.

So now that we're all perfume experts, let's go and find a scent made out of the essence of 1,000 jasmine blossoms...

Fun Fact: Romans used urine to clean and whiten their teeth.

DECEMBER 2014: PASSAGE 2

"Stealing thunder" is a courtroom strategy that consists in a lawyer's revealing negative information about a client before that information is revealed or elicited by an opposing lawyer. While there is no point
(5) in revealing a weakness that is unknown to one's opponents or that would not be exploited by them, many lawyers believe that if the weakness is likely to be revealed in opposing testimony, it should be volunteered; otherwise, the hostile revelation would
(10) be more damaging.
 Although no empirical research has directly tested the effectiveness of stealing thunder in actual trials, studies involving simulated trial situations have suggested that the technique is, in fact, effective, at
(15) least within a reasonably broad range of applications. Lawyers' commonly held belief in the value of stealing thunder is not only corroborated by those experimental findings; it is also supported by several psychological explanations of why the technique
(20) should work. For one thing, volunteering damaging information early may create an image of credibility. Psychological research suggests that people who reveal information that appears to be against their own best interest are likely to be perceived as more credible
(25) and thus may be more persuasive. Stealing thunder may also provide juries with an impetus for critical assessment by previewing, and thus alerting them to, testimony that the opposition plans to present. In psychological experiments, audiences that were
(30) previously warned of an upcoming attempt at persuasion became more resistant to the persuasive attempt, forming counterarguments based on the warning. Also, the value placed on a persuasive message is probably much like the value placed on any
(35) commodity; the scarcer the commodity, the more valuable it is. A persuasive message will thus increase in value and effectiveness to the extent that it is seen as scarce. In the courtroom, a piece of evidence brought by both the prosecution and the defense, as
(40) when thunder is stolen, may be seen as less scarce—becoming "old news." Thus, unless that evidence is of overriding consequence, it should carry less weight than if it had been included only in hostile testimony.
 Finally, stealing thunder may work because the
(45) lawyer can frame the evidence in his or her own terms and downplay its significance, just as politicians sometimes seek to put their "spin" on potentially damaging information. However, it may therefore be effective only when the negative information can be
(50) framed positively. Jurors, who often initially have little information about a case, are usually eager to solidify their position regarding the case. They can therefore be expected to use the early positive framing to guide their subsequent analysis of the trial information. But
(55) this also suggests limitations on the use of the technique: when information is very damaging, stealing thunder may create an early negative impression that forms a cognitive framework for jurors, who then filter subsequent information through this schema.

9. Which one of the following most accurately expresses the main point of the passage?

(A) Although there are limits to the usefulness of stealing thunder, its effectiveness in actual trials has been demonstrated through research conducted by psychologists and legal scholars.
(B) The commonly practiced courtroom strategy of stealing thunder can have unintended consequences if the lawyers using it do not accurately predict jurors' attitudes.
(C) Lawyers' commonly held belief in the value of stealing thunder is supported by several psychological explanations of how that strategy may influence jurors.
(D) The risks involved in stealing thunder can outweigh the probable benefits when the information to be revealed is too readily available or too negative in its impact.
(E) Research designed to confirm the usefulness of stealing thunder has vindicated lawyers' belief in the value of the technique and has identified the general limitations of the strategy's effectiveness.

10. It can be most reasonably inferred from the passage that which one of the following is an example of stealing thunder?

(A) warning jurors that a client on the opposing side has a serious conflict of interest and cannot be trusted
(B) disclosing in opening statements of a defense against copyright infringement that one's client has in the past been guilty of plagiarism
(C) responding to the opposition's revelation that one's client has a minor criminal background by conceding that this is the case
(D) pointing out to jurors during opening statements the mistaken reasoning in the opposition's case
(E) stressing that one's client, while technically guilty, is believable and that mitigating circumstances should be considered

11. Which one of the following does the author mention as a factor that in some instances probably contributes to the success of stealing thunder?

(A) careful timing of the thunder-stealing message to precede the opposition's similar message by only a short time
(B) some lawyers' superior skill in assessing jurors' probable reactions to a message
(C) the willingness of some lawyers' clients to testify in person about their own past mistakes
(D) jurors' desire to arrive at a firm view regarding the case they are hearing
(E) lawyers' careful screening of prospective jurors prior to the beginning of courtroom proceedings

12. The author discusses the "cognitive framework" that jurors create (line 58) primarily to

    (A) indicate that at least some information mentioned early in a trial can influence the way jurors evaluate information presented later in the trial
    (B) indicate that jurors bring into court with them certain attitudes and biases that at least in part inform their opinions during trials
    (C) suggest that damaging evidence that is framed positively early in a trial will have a greater impact than damaging evidence presented later in a trial
    (D) theorize that stealing thunder is best done as early as possible in a case, before the opposition has an opportunity to solidify jurors' opinions
    (E) speculate that creating credibility in some cases is probably more effective than positively framing very harmful information

13. The author's attitude regarding stealing thunder can most accurately be described as

    (A) concerned that the technique may become so common that lawyers will fail to recognize its drawbacks
    (B) favorable toward its use by lawyers during the opening statements of a case but skeptical of its value otherwise
    (C) concerned that research results supporting it may omit crucial anecdotal evidence indicating pitfalls in its use
    (D) approving of its use on the grounds that its success is experimentally supported and can be psychologically explained
    (E) skeptical of its suitability for use by lawyers without lengthy experience in courtroom strategies

14. The author's characterization of stealing thunder in the passage is based at least partly on both

    (A) informal surveys of lawyers' clients' reactions to stealing thunder and controlled research based on simulated trial situations
    (B) statistical surveys of lawyers who steal thunder and observations of lawyers' tactics in trials
    (C) records of judges' decisions in court cases and the results of studies involving simulated courtroom situations
    (D) informal observations of nontrial uses of techniques analogous to stealing thunder and controlled studies of lawyers' courtroom behavior
    (E) research that was not directly concerned with legal proceedings and research in which subjects participated in simulated trial situations

15. By saying that certain studies have suggested that in some applications, "the technique is, in fact, effective" (line 14), the author most likely means that those studies have given evidence that the technique in question

    (A) inclines juries to regard the clients of those using the technique more favorably than would be the case if the negative information about them were first divulged by the opposition
    (B) is a reliable means, in courtroom settings, of introducing a set of counterarguments that jurors will be able to use in resisting the opposition's subsequent attempts at persuasion
    (C) invariably results in cases being decided in favor of the clients of those using the technique rather than in favor of parties opposing those clients, if it is used broadly
    (D) appears generally to succeed as a means of forcefully capturing jurors' attention and thus leading them to focus more attentively than they would otherwise on the lawyer's message
    (E) more often than not achieves its goal of timing a negative revelation so as to dramatically precede the opposition's revelation of the same information

16. The passage most strongly implies that many lawyers believe which one of the following concerning decisions about whether to steal thunder?

    (A) A lawyer should be concerned with how readily the negative information can be positively framed, especially if the information is very negative.
    (B) A lawyer should take into account, among other things, whether or not the jurors are already familiar with some of the relevant facts of the case prior to the trial.
    (C) The decision should be based on careful deliberations that anticipate both positive and negative reactions of jurors and opposing lawyers.
    (D) The decision should depend on how probable it is that the opposition will try to derive an advantage from mentioning the negative information in question.
    (E) The decision should be based at least partly on a lawyer's knowledge of relevant psychological research findings and legal statistics.

One down, three to go. Remember, tagging and anticipating are the keys to performance. Let's go!

HOW TO READ THE PASSAGE

Paragraph 1

> "Stealing thunder" is a [courtroom strategy that consists in a lawyer's revealing negative information about a client before that information is revealed or elicited by an opposing lawyer.] While there is no point
> (5) in revealing a weakness that is unknown to one's opponents or that would not be exploited by them, many lawyers believe that if the weakness is likely to be revealed in opposing testimony, it should be volunteered; otherwise, the hostile revelation would
> (10) be more damaging.

DEF.

LAWYERS' CONC.

Stealing thunder! Sounds awesome in theory. In practice, meh...

Paragraph one starts us off with a definition, so let's bracket that definition. You are quite likely to get a question that tests your ability to correctly apply a definition to a different set of facts. So what is stealing thunder? Releasing damaging information before your opponent can. A sentence later, we get the opinion of some lawyers on the issue: steal thunder when you can. We label it a conclusion because it's supported by a premise. If you don't steal thunder, the hostile revelation is even worse. This is a candidate for the main idea so let's see if we get more support for it. If so, we'll put it into our primary structure diagram.

Paragraph 2

Although no empirical research has directly tested the effectiveness of stealing thunder in actual trials, studies involving simulated trial situations have suggested that the <u>technique is, in fact, effective,</u> at (15) least within a reasonably broad range of applications. Lawyers' commonly held belief in the value of stealing thunder is not only corroborated by those experimental findings; it is also supported by several psychological explanations of why the technique (20) should work. For one thing, volunteering damaging information early may create an image of credibility. Psychological research suggests that people who reveal information that appears to be against their own best interest are likely to be perceived as more credible (25) and thus may be more persuasive. Stealing thunder may also provide juries with an impetus for critical assessment by previewing, and thus alerting them to, testimony that the opposition plans to present. In psychological experiments, audiences that were (30) previously warned of an upcoming attempt at persuasion became more resistant to the persuasive attempt, forming counterarguments based on the warning. Also, the value placed on a persuasive message is probably much like the value placed on any (35) commodity; the scarcer the commodity, the more valuable it is. A persuasive message will thus increase in value and effectiveness to the extent that it is seen as scarce. In the courtroom, a piece of evidence brought by both the prosecution and the defense, as (40) when thunder is stolen, may be seen as less scarce— becoming "old news." Thus, unless that evidence is of overriding consequence, it should carry less weight than if it had been included only in hostile testimony.	STUDY AUTHOR'S CONC. PSYCHOLOGICAL EXPLANATIONS: 1. CREDIBILITY 2. PREVIEW OPPONENT'S ARGUMENT EXP. 3. MAKES IT OLD NEWS

The first line of paragraph two makes it look like we are going to support the lawyerly point of view revealed in the last paragraph that stealing thunder is a good idea. Some people did some studies (lines 13-15). Remember, a study is a premise that provides support for a conclusion. Here, the conclusion is that stealing thunder works. Since we have a conclusion and some support, let's get that into our diagram as the Thesis position.

We also have our author wading into the fray. She asserts that stealing thunder "is, in fact, effective" (line 14). We know it's the author because it's an opinion not attributed to anyone else. Underline it, label it, and point our author arrow toward the Thesis in our primary structure diagram.

Paragraph two then goes on to provide even more support for the idea that stealing thunder works. Broadly speaking, this paragraph and part of the next, provide a bunch of psychological explanations for why it works. There are four, so we know we're seeing a Classification structure.

it'sGOtime /

Ninja: When three or more things fall into a category, that, as you will remember, is a Classification structure. Here, as usual, the Classification structure functions as a premise that provides support for the conclusion that stealing thunder is an effective technique.

To be clear, the category is psychological explanations for stealing thunder, and the things in this category are as follows: (1) It helps create credibility (lines 22-25); (2) It alerts jurors to the arguments to come from the opposing party (lines 25-28) which, experiments show (tag those experiments!), makes jurors more resistant to the opposing parties' later arguments on the subject (lines 28-33); (3) It makes the evidence less compelling because it's old news by the time the opposing party gets a hold of it (lines 38-41); and (4) It allows a lawyer to put his or her own spin on the topic first (lines 44-46).

Because this category provides support for the idea that stealing thunder is effective, we have an extended Classification structure and our primary structure diagram should reflect that. Accordingly, we should amend the Thesis position from "stealing thunder is effective" to "stealing thunder is effective because of psychological factors."

Paragraph 3

> (45) Finally, stealing thunder may work because the lawyer can frame the evidence in his or her own terms and downplay its significance, just as politicians sometimes seek to put their "spin" on potentially damaging information. However, it may therefore be effective only when the negative information can be
> (50) framed positively. Jurors, who often initially have little information about a case, are usually eager to solidify their position regarding the case. They can therefore be expected to use the early positive framing to guide their subsequent analysis of the trial information. But
> (55) this also suggests limitations on the use of the technique: when information is very damaging, stealing thunder may create an early negative impression that forms a cognitive framework for jurors, who then filter subsequent information through this schema.

4. SPIN

QUALIFICATION

Paragraph three is...

Ditz: Antithesis, right? Thesis was that stealing thunder is good, and this paragraph says stealing thunder is bad.

Well, Ditz, no, you don't have to put it in your diagram. In fact, you shouldn't. Paragraph four mentions a problem with stealing thunder, but this is a qualification, not an opposing point of view.

BP Minotaur: It's important to understand the scope of a conclusion—how broadly it applies—and the qualification here just says the conclusion that stealing thunder works only goes so far. This is a frequent occurrence in the last paragraph of a passage, and it's important to note how exactly the conclusion is limited.

Thanks, Minotaur. Your goatee is looking especially nice this evening.

So, let's be particular about when stealing thunder *doesn't* work: in some cases, where a lawyer can't put a positive spin on the information, releasing it before the opponent does just helps the juror to decide against the lawyer early on in the case (lines 48-52).

The last sentence of the passage, by using the word "limitation" (line 55) makes clear, if it wasn't clear before, that the point of the paragraph is a qualification of the conclusion that stealing thunder works.

You're rip-roarin'-ready to tackle those questions, but let's stick to the method. Remember we need to do five things before we move to the questions.

1. Anticipate the main idea

There is exactly one point of view here, which is that stealing thunder works. This is the view of some lawyers (lines 8-10), and it's a view with which the author agrees (lines 14-15). The author's point of view is always the main idea, and here it's supported by an extended Classification structure so the main idea is "stealing thunder is effective because of psychological factors."

2. Anticipate the primary purpose

The author is present, so the primary purpose is why she wrote the passage. Here, it's to argue that in the majority of cases, stealing thunder is an effective technique for a variety of psychological reasons.

3. Anticipate the author's attitude

Unlike the last passage where the author was bubbling over with positive and negative attitudes toward things, this author is pretty calm. It's clear that she agrees that stealing thunder works, but she doesn't wax rhapsodic about it.

4. Anticipate anything to which the passage lends itself

There are really three things to keep track of here. There's a definition in paragraph one, a Classification structure in paragraphs two and three, and some studies/experiments. We tagged them and will be ready for any questions asked about them.

5. Summarize the entire passage in a sentence

Focus on the arguments when doing this! Here, a point of view was stated in paragraph one, supported with explanations and research in paragraph two, and qualified in paragraph three.

The completed markup looks like this:

	"Stealing thunder" is a courtroom strategy that consists in a lawyer's [revealing negative information about a client before that information is revealed or elicited by an opposing lawyer.] While there is no point	DEF.
(5)	in revealing a weakness that is unknown to one's opponents or that would not be exploited by them, many <u>lawyers believe that if the weakness is likely to be revealed in opposing testimony, it should be volunteered;</u> otherwise, the hostile revelation would	LAWYERS' CONC.
(10)	be more damaging.	
	Although no empirical research has directly tested the effectiveness of stealing thunder in actual trials, studies involving simulated trial situations have suggested that <u>the technique is, in fact, effective,</u> at	STUDY AUTHOR'S CONC.
(15)	least within a reasonably broad range of applications. Lawyers' commonly held belief in the value of stealing thunder is not only corroborated by those experimental findings; it is also supported by several psychological explanations of why the technique	PSYCHOLOGICAL EXPLANATIONS:
(20)	should work. For one thing, volunteering damaging information early may create an image of credibility. Psychological research suggests that people who reveal information that appears to be against their own best interest are likely to be perceived as more credible	1. CREDIBILITY
(25)	and thus may be more persuasive. Stealing thunder may also provide juries with an impetus for critical assessment by previewing, and thus alerting them to, testimony that the opposition plans to present. In psychological experiments, audiences that were	2. PREVIEW OPPONENT'S ARGUMENT
(30)	previously warned of an upcoming attempt at persuasion became more resistant to the persuasive attempt, forming counterarguments based on the warning. Also, the value placed on a persuasive message is probably much like the value placed on any	EXP.
(35)	commodity; the scarcer the commodity, the more valuable it is. A persuasive message will thus increase in value and effectiveness to the extent that it is seen as scarce. In the courtroom, a piece of evidence brought by both the prosecution and the defense, as	3. MAKES IT OLD NEWS
(40)	when thunder is stolen, may be seen as less scarce—becoming "old news." Thus, unless that evidence is of overriding consequence, it should carry less weight than if it had been included only in hostile testimony.	
	Finally, stealing thunder may work because the	
(45)	lawyer can frame the evidence in his or her own terms and downplay its significance, just as politicians sometimes seek to put their "spin" on potentially damaging information. However, it may therefore be effective only when the negative information can be	4. SPIN QUALIFICATION
(50)	framed positively. Jurors, who often initially have little information about a case, are usually eager to solidify their position regarding the case. They can therefore be expected to use the early positive framing to guide their subsequent analysis of the trial information. But	
(55)	this also suggests limitations on the use of the technique: when information is very damaging, stealing thunder may create an early negative impression that forms a cognitive framework for jurors, who then filter subsequent information through this schema.	

STEALING THUNDER

EFFECTIVE BECAUSE OF PSYCHOLOGICAL FACTORS (LAWYERS)

NOW FOR THE QUESTIONS

Question #9

Ah, the Main Point question. Right on time, too. The main idea of the passage, as we've already determined, is that stealing thunder is effective because of psychological factors. Answer choice (C) says precisely that.

Answer choice (A) mischaracterizes the passage in a few ways. First, the passage doesn't talk about how stealing thunder ends up working out in actual trials. There is a study of "simulated trial situations," but not actual trials. Also, the passage uses the expertise of psychologists, but not legal scholars. Answer choice (B) is too narrow, talking only about paragraph three. It also mischaracterizes how a lawyer should know when and when not to use the technique. It's not about predicting juror reactions; it's about determining whether a positive spin is possible (lines 48-50). Answer choice (D) is also too narrow, focusing only on when stealing thunder shouldn't be used, even though the passage mostly focuses on its value. Finally, answer choice (E) is very strong, talking about how the lawyers have been vindicated. While there's some support that it works, "vindication" is far too strong. In addition, even though there's a study at the top of paragraph two, the vast majority of the support is not research; it's theoretical explanations of why the strategy works. Next!

9. Which one of the following most accurately expresses the main point of the passage?

   (A) Although there are limits to the usefulness of stealing thunder, its effectiveness in actual trials has been demonstrated through research conducted by psychologists and legal scholars.
   (B) The commonly practiced courtroom strategy of stealing thunder can have unintended consequences if the lawyers using it do not accurately predict jurors' attitudes.
   (C) Lawyers' commonly held belief in the value of stealing thunder is supported by several psychological explanations of how that strategy may influence jurors.
   (D) The risks involved in stealing thunder can outweigh the probable benefits when the information to be revealed is too readily available or too negative in its impact.
   (E) Research designed to confirm the usefulness of stealing thunder has vindicated lawyers' belief in the value of the technique and has identified the general limitations of the strategy's effectiveness.

10. It can be most reasonably inferred from the passage that which one of the following is an example of stealing thunder?

    (A) warning jurors that a client on the opposing side has a serious conflict of interest and cannot be trusted
    (B) disclosing in opening statements of a defense against copyright infringement that one's client has in the past been guilty of plagiarism
    (C) responding to the opposition's revelation that one's client has a minor criminal background by conceding that this is the case
    (D) pointing out to jurors during opening statements the mistaken reasoning in the opposition's case
    (E) stressing that one's client, while technically guilty, is believable and that mitigating circumstances should be considered

Question #10

Inference questions have the potential to be an open-ended nightmare, but this one makes our life easy by drawing on the definition we bracketed in the first paragraph. All we need to do is define stealing thunder, then search for an instance of it in the answer choices. The definition is: "revealing negative information about a client before that information is revealed or elicited by an opponent." Answer choice (B) is a perfect example. The lawyer gets the bad news about his client's past bad behavior early on.

Answer choice (A) is talking about revealing *the opponent's* damaging information. That's not stealing thunder. That's being a lawyer.

Answer choice (C) is the opposite of stealing thunder. It describes reacting to the revelation of information rather than revealing it oneself. Stealing thunder is supposed to prevent something like that from happening. Answer choice (D), like answer choice (A), talks about attacking the opponent rather than revealing one's own information. And answer choice (E), ha, oh boy... acknowledging your client is guilty is not stealing thunder. It's giving up.

Question #11

Aaaaaaaaannnnddd... here's the question we knew was coming about our Classification structure. In this case, it's a Specific Reference question. The passage gives four different psychological explanations for the success of stealing thunder. The fourth reason is that it allows a lawyer to put his spin on the information up front, and jurors "are usually eager to solidify their positions regarding the case" (lines 51-52). Answer choice (D) says the same thing in different words.

We know that stealing thunder must occur sometime before the opponent

11. Which one of the following does the author mention as a factor that in some instances probably contributes to the success of stealing thunder?

    (A) careful timing of the thunder-stealing message to precede the opposition's similar message by only a short time
    (B) some lawyers' superior skill in assessing jurors' probable reactions to a message
    (C) the willingness of some lawyers' clients to testify in person about their own past mistakes
    (D) jurors' desire to arrive at a firm view regarding the case they are hearing
    (E) lawyers' careful screening of prospective jurors prior to the beginning of courtroom proceedings

would otherwise reveal the damaging information, but answer choice (A) talks about getting the revelation as close in time as possible to the opposition's discussion of that fact, and there's no indication in the passage that such close timing is necessary or even advisable. Answer choice (B) misstates how a lawyer comes to a decision about whether or not to steal thunder. It's not predicting jurors' reaction; it's whether there's a way to spin the fact positively (lines 48-50). Let's get rid of answer choice (C) quickly because there's no support for it anywhere in the passage. Answer choice (E) fails for the same reason; there's nothing about screening jurors in the passage.

Question #12

This is a Role question, which means we're being asked about how a particular statement fits into the argument. The "cognitive framework" refers to the last part of the Classification structure supporting the idea that stealing thunder works. Jurors like to make up their minds early, and that provides support for the idea that stealing thunder works when the lawyer can spin the information positively. Answer choice (A) is just another way of saying that.

12. The author discusses the "cognitive framework" that jurors create (line 58) primarily to

   (A) indicate that at least some information mentioned early in a trial can influence the way jurors evaluate information presented later in the trial
   (B) indicate that jurors bring into court with them certain attitudes and biases that at least in part inform their opinions during trials
   (C) suggest that damaging evidence that is framed positively early in a trial will have a greater impact than damaging evidence presented later in a trial
   (D) theorize that stealing thunder is best done as early as possible in a case, before the opposition has an opportunity to solidify jurors' opinions
   (E) speculate that creating credibility in some cases is probably more effective than positively framing very harmful information

Answer choice (B) is talking about what jurors are doing before trial starts, something the passage never addresses. Answer choice (C) is attractive because jurors want to solidify their opinions early on, but that doesn't necessarily mean the information must be disclosed early on in the trial, just early enough to set in before the other lawyer starts talking about it. Answer choice (D) suffers from the same problem as (C). Answer choice (E) talks about credibility, which is the first item in the Classification structure. However, the cognitive framework refers to the fourth item.

Question #13

Lucky question thirteen! It's the often-asked Author's Attitude question. We've already determined that the author is not overly positive or negative, but she does endorse the conclusion that stealing thunder works. Answer choice (D) says just that. Note that it also gets in the extended Classification structure that provides the evidence for it. Big payoffs for spotting secondary structures, kids!

The author never talks about how often the technique is used now or how often it will be used in the future, so answer choice (A) has no support. Answer choice (B) talks about exactly one phase of trial being the time to steal thunder, but there's no indication in the passage that it can't be used successfully after that. The author likes the study, and there's never any complaint about it, so answer choice (C) mischaracterizes the author's attitude. Lastly, the closest the author gets to skepticism about stealing thunder is when she says that it's probably not useful where there's no good way to spin the information (lines 54-59). However, there's no indication that a relatively new lawyer can't use it successfully.

13. The author's attitude regarding stealing thunder can most accurately be described as

   (A) concerned that the technique may become so common that lawyers will fail to recognize its drawbacks
   (B) favorable toward its use by lawyers during the opening statements of a case but skeptical of its value otherwise
   (C) concerned that research results supporting it may omit crucial anecdotal evidence indicating pitfalls in its use
   (D) approving of its use on the grounds that its success is experimentally supported and can be psychologically explained
   (E) skeptical of its suitability for use by lawyers without lengthy experience in courtroom strategies

Question #14

In order to anticipate the correct answer to this Specific Reference question, we should revisit the author's opinion on stealing thunder. Essentially, her position is that it works, which is the Thesis position. It is based on the study and the psychological explanations in the passage that we tagged. Anything that doesn't identify one of those two things is wrong. Answer choice (E) correctly describes the study mentioned early in paragraph two (lines 11-15). If you tagged the study when you saw it and understood exactly what the study looked like (simulated trials), then it's easy to get the correct answer here.

14. The author's characterization of stealing thunder in the passage is based at least partly on both

   (A) informal surveys of lawyers' clients' reactions to stealing thunder and controlled research based on simulated trial situations
   (B) statistical surveys of lawyers who steal thunder and observations of lawyers' tactics in trials
   (C) records of judges' decisions in court cases and the results of studies involving simulated courtroom situations
   (D) informal observations of nontrial uses of techniques analogous to stealing thunder and controlled studies of lawyers' courtroom behavior
   (E) research that was not directly concerned with legal proceedings and research in which subjects participated in simulated trial situations

There is no mention in the passage of surveys of clients, so (A) is out. Answer choice (B) talks statistics. Nope. And (C)? No talk about judges' decisions anywhere in the passage. As for (D), nontrial uses? Is that like telling your significant other you're cheating before someone else does? Nothing about other uses in this passage, so (D) is out.

Question #15

This Specific Reference directs us to line 14 which is where we tagged the study. The study shows that stealing thunder works, and the whole point of stealing thunder is to make the information less persuasive in jurors' eyes. That's answer choice (A). Circle it! Bubble it! Celebrate it!

Answer choice (B) talks about introducing counterarguments to what is coming from the opposition. While the author talks elsewhere in the passage about spinning the information, that's not necessarily a counterargument, which is a response to another argument. Answer choice (C) says that the technique is 100% guaranteed to get you a win in court. This goes way beyond the idea that stealing thunder can be effective. Answer choice (D) makes it seem like stealing thunder's purpose is to keep the jury from falling asleep. That's not what's going on here. Answer choice (E) talks about timing and drama, which is also not the point of stealing thunder. In fact, some of it is about palliating drama, as when it makes the information "old news" (line 41).

15. By saying that certain studies have suggested that in some applications, "the technique is, in fact, effective" (line 14), the author most likely means that those studies have given evidence that the technique in question

    (A) inclines juries to regard the clients of those using the technique more favorably than would be the case if the negative information about them were first divulged by the opposition
    (B) is a reliable means, in courtroom settings, of introducing a set of counterarguments that jurors will be able to use in resisting the opposition's subsequent attempts at persuasion
    (C) invariably results in cases being decided in favor of the clients of those using the technique rather than in favor of parties opposing those clients, if it is used broadly
    (D) appears generally to succeed as a means of forcefully capturing jurors' attention and thus leading them to focus more attentively than they would otherwise on the lawyer's message
    (E) more often than not achieves its goal of timing a negative revelation so as to dramatically precede the opposition's revelation of the same information

Question #16

Tagging the passage correctly really pays off in this Inference question by saving us time. The lawyers' opinions are discussed in paragraph one, which we tagged as their conclusion. So we know right where to go to answer the question. They believe stealing thunder works, but they also believe that it should be volunteered only if it is "likely to be revealed in opposing testimony." Answer choice (D) points out that this is part of the process in deciding whether or not to steal thunder.

16. The passage most strongly implies that many lawyers believe which one of the following concerning decisions about whether to steal thunder?

    (A) A lawyer should be concerned with how readily the negative information can be positively framed, especially if the information is very negative.
    (B) A lawyer should take into account, among other things, whether or not the jurors are already familiar with some of the relevant facts of the case prior to the trial.
    (C) The decision should be based on careful deliberations that anticipate both positive and negative reactions of jurors and opposing lawyers.
    (D) The decision should depend on how probable it is that the opposition will try to derive an advantage from mentioning the negative information in question.
    (E) The decision should be based at least partly on a lawyer's knowledge of relevant psychological research findings and legal statistics.

Answer choice (A) is attractive because it mentions what the author believes. However, the passage is silent on whether the lawyers agree with the qualification the author stated in the last paragraph. Answer choice (B) talks about prior familiarity with facts of trial. It's possible that stealing thunder would be unnecessary if everyone on the jury already knew the damaging information, but there's no discussion of this anywhere in the passage. Answer choice (C) looks like a few answers to other questions that mischaracterized the passage. The passage never says that lawyers need to read the jurors' minds. They just need to determine whether it's going to come out inevitably. Answer choice (E) makes a connection with using stealing thunder and being familiar with studies about it. There's no discussion anywhere in the passage about whether lawyers need to read studies about stealing thunder before using it as a tactic.

And that's the end of that one! Didn't we get a nice payoff for noting the extended Classification structure. Now if you'll excuse us, we need to preempt some information being leaked to TMZ...

DECEMBER 2014: PASSAGE 3

Passage A

To a neuroscientist, you are your brain; nothing causes your behavior other than the operations of your brain. This viewpoint, together with recent findings in
(5) neuroscience, radically changes the way we think about the law. The official line in the law is that all that matters is whether you are rational, but you can have someone who is totally rational even though their strings are being pulled by something beyond their
(10) control. Indeed, people who believe themselves to be making a free and rational moral choice may really be deluding themselves—a brain scan might show that such a choice correlates with activity in emotional centers in the brain rather than in the region of the
(15) brain associated with deliberative problem solving. This insight suggests that the criminal-justice system should abandon the idea of retribution—the idea that bad people should be punished because of their freely chosen immoral acts—which is now dominant as a
(20) justification of punishment. Instead, the law should focus on deterring future harms. In some cases, this might mean lighter punishments. If it is really true that we do not get any prevention bang from our punishment buck when we punish some person, then it is not worth punishing that person.

Passage B

(25) Neuroscience constantly produces new mechanistic descriptions of how the physical brain causes behavior, adding fuel to the deterministic view that all human action is causally necessitated by events that are independent of the will. It has long been
(30) argued, however, that the concept of free will can coexist with determinism.
In 1954 English philosopher Alfred J. Ayer put forth a theory of "soft determinism." He argued, as the philosopher David Hume had two centuries earlier,
(35) that even in a deterministic world, a person can still act freely. Ayer distinguished between free actions and constrained actions. Free actions are those that are caused by internal sources, by one's own will (unless one is suffering from a disorder). Constrained actions
(40) are those that are caused by external sources, for example, by someone or something forcing you physically or mentally to perform an action, as in hypnosis or in mental disorders such as kleptomania. When someone performs a free action to do A, he or
(45) she could have done B instead, since no external source precluded doing so. When someone performs a constrained action to do A, he or she could have done only A.
Ayer argued that actions are free as long as they
(50) are not constrained. It is not the existence of a cause but the source of the cause that determines whether an action is free. Although Ayer did not explicitly discuss the brain's role, one could make the analogy that those actions—and indeed those wills—that originate from
(55) a disease-free brain are not constrained, and are therefore free, even though they may be determined.

17. Both passages are concerned with answering which one of the following questions?

   (A) Should people be punished for actions that are outside of their control?
   (B) Does scientific research into the brain have implications regarding freedom of the will?
   (C) Can actions that are not free be effectively deterred by the threat of punishment?
   (D) Is the view that retribution is a legitimate justification for punishment compatible with the findings of neuroscience?
   (E) Can an action be free if someone else physically forced the actor to perform it?

18. Which one of the following concepts plays a role in the argument of passage B but not in that of passage A?

   (A) mental disorder
   (B) free choice
   (C) causality
   (D) self-delusion
   (E) moral responsibility

19. One purpose of the reference by the author of passage B to David Hume (line 34) is to

   (A) characterize Ayer as someone who is not an original thinker
   (B) add credence to the theory of soft determinism
   (C) suggest that the theory of soft determinism is primarily of historical importance
   (D) suggest that the theory of soft determinism has been in existence as long as mechanistic descriptions of the brain have
   (E) add intellectual respectability to the view that the brain should not be described mechanistically

20. Passage B differs from passage A in that passage B displays an attitude toward the ideas it discusses that is more

 (A) engaged
 (B) dismissive
 (C) detached
 (D) ironic
 (E) skeptical

21. Which one of the following arguments is most analogous to the argument advanced in passage A?

 (A) Many word processors are packed with nonessential features that only confuse most users and get in the way of important functions. Word processors with fewer features thus enhance productivity.
 (B) Economic models generally presume that actors in an economy are entirely rational. But psychological studies have documented many ways in which people make irrational choices. Thus, economic models, in theory, should not be able to predict human behavior.
 (C) The existing program for teaching mathematics in elementary schools is based on mistaken notions about what sorts of mathematical concepts children can grasp, and it should therefore be replaced.
 (D) Civil disobedience is justified only in those cases in which civil law conflicts with one's sincere moral or religious convictions. Any attempt to justify civil disobedience on something other than moral or religious grounds is therefore illegitimate.
 (E) Being autonomous does not imply having full control over one's behavior. After all, addicted smokers are unable to exercise control over some behaviors but are nevertheless autonomous in the general sense.

Turn the page, and... enter into the mysterious temple deep in the Comparative Reading jungle. Don't forget to be on the lookout for similarities and differences between the passages!

HOW TO READ THE PASSAGE

Paragraph 1 of Passage A

Passage A

To a neuroscientist, you are your brain; nothing causes your behavior other than the operations of your brain. This viewpoint, together with recent findings in neuroscience, radically changes the way we think
(5) about the law. The official line in the law is that all that matters is whether you are rational, but you can have someone who is totally rational even though their strings are being pulled by something beyond their control. Indeed, people who believe themselves to be
(10) making a free and rational moral choice may really be deluding themselves—a brain scan might show that such a choice correlates with activity in emotional centers in the brain rather than in the region of the brain associated with deliberative problem solving.
(15) This insight suggests that the criminal-justice system should abandon the idea of retribution—the idea that bad people should be punished because of their freely chosen immoral acts—which is now dominant as a justification of punishment. Instead, the law should
(20) focus on deterring future harms. In some cases, this might mean lighter punishments. If it is really true that we do not get any prevention bang from our punishment buck when we punish some person, then it is not worth punishing that person.

Margin notes:
- OPERATION OF BRAIN → BEHAVIOR
- ATT. "OFFICIAL" LEGAL VIEW
- RESEARCH
- DEF.
- AUTHOR'S CONC.

Right out of the gate, we get a viewpoint: Neuroscientists think there's nothing more to you than the three pounds of beige Jell-O between your ears.

To be clear, the neuroscientists' viewpoint is a causal relationship; the operations of your brain cause your behavior. Let's draw a darling little causal diagram next to that part of the passage.

A moment later, the author talks about "recent findings," which is telegraphing the fact that there has been some kind of research into the brain (lines 3-5). The author's attitude is on display when he says these findings "radically" change the way we think about... the law? Well, that's a rapid change from science passage to legal passage. We are ninjas, however, so we will adapt to change whenever necessary.

The next line talks about the "official line" in the law. This is a point of view (tag it!) that the author immediately disputes. The author points out that brain scans—research, tag it!—show that a seemingly rational decision can come from the emotional center of the brain (lines 11-14). Research always acts as a premise, which supports a conclusion. The conclusion comes right after, and it's a prescriptive statement: Punishment shouldn't be about retribution. It should instead be about deterring from future harms. We know this is the author's main conclusion, because everything leading up to it supports it. The old system is bad, so let's have a new one. Let's place it in our primary structure diagram as the Thesis.

Despite the "official" view in lines 5-6 about rationality being the only thing that matters, this view doesn't make it into our primary structure diagram because it is not developed. It is only a statement against which the author contrasts his own, supported view. Hence this passage is a Thesis passage.

Cleetus: Dagnabbit! I put it down as Antithesis!

Don't worry, Cleetus. Finding the viewpoint means you're headed in the right direction and it's better to err on the side of thoroughness. Just be sure to ask yourself next time where the support (premises) are for every point of view you tag. If there's no support, it doesn't make it into the diagram.

The author also gives us a definition of retribution, which is "the idea that people should be punished because of their freely chosen immoral acts" (lines 16-18). Be sure to bracket and label that definition.

BP Minotaur: There's something a little odd about this passage. Its tone is more casual than the run-of-the-mill RC passage. The use of the pronoun "you" instead of "one" is out of character for the LSAT. Similarly, the phrase "bang for your buck" is slang, and the author uses a variation on it in the last line. This distinction might seem insignificant to you—yes, "you" you—but it's not to the stuffy old logicians at LSAC. Chances are very good they will test you on it (hint hint).

Now then! On to passage B. Remember, while reading pay close attention to similarities and differences with passage A.

Paragraph 1 of Passage B

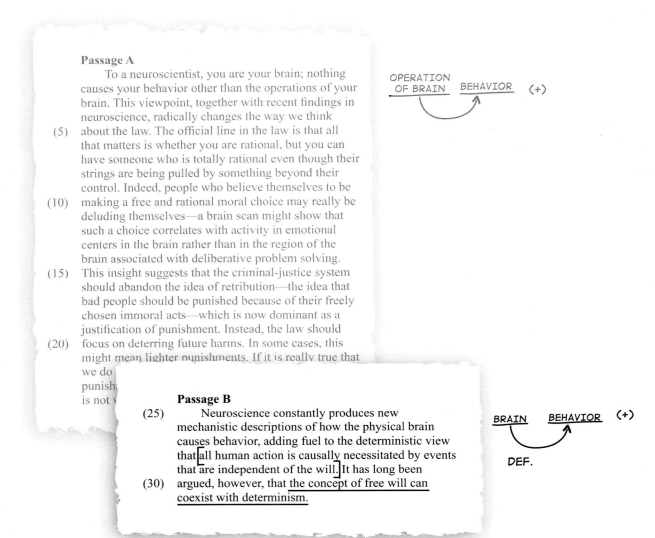

We can't even get through the first sentence without finding a similarity with passage A. The author talks about how, in neuroscience, the "physical brain *causes* behavior," which dovetails with the neuroscientists' opinion in the first sentence of passage A. Let's tag the causal claim and put a (+) next to each. Then we get a definition of determinism, which is the official term for the neuroscientists' claim (that action is caused by something other than rational behavior). Bracket the definition and tag it. But passage B is not going to agree with passage A. We get a "however" (line 30) that lets us know that free will and determinism can coexist. That sounds a lot like a conclusion and if we find support for it, we'll put it in our primary structure diagram.

Paragraph 2 of Passage B

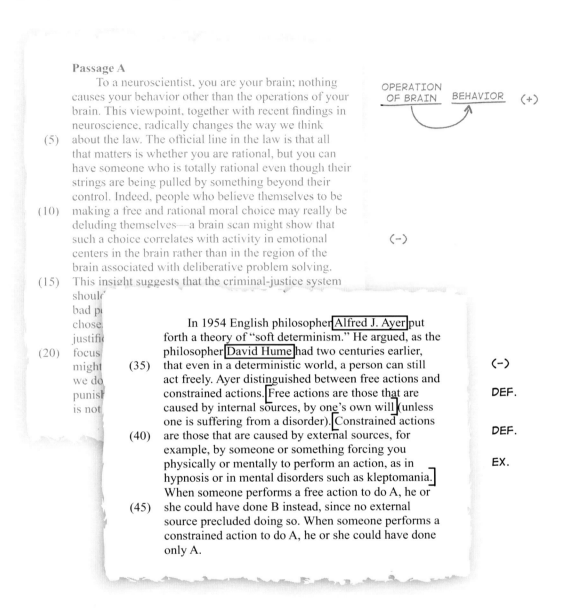

Paragraph two gives us some stuffy old men we can talk about. Both Alfred Ayer and David Hume believe that a person can act freely. We should put our first (-) here with a corresponding (-) at line 12 in passage A because this is different than people not having free choice, as the author of passage A states.

These philosophers are offering support for the view that free will and determinism can coexist, so we know that's the main idea of the passage. Throw it into the primary structure diagram!

There are also definitions of free will and determinism so be sure to bracket and tag that yummy definition goodness. Free actions are caused by internal sources, and constrained actions are caused by external forces (lines 36-40). Let's note here that the author lumps mental disorders in with external forces.

Paragraph 3 of Passage B

Passage A

To a neuroscientist, you are your brain; nothing causes your behavior other than the operations of your brain. This viewpoint, together with recent findings in neuroscience, radically changes the way we think
(5) about the law. The official line in the law is that all that matters is whether you are rational, but you can have someone who is totally rational even though their strings are being pulled by something beyond their control. Indeed, people who believe themselves to be
(10) making a free and rational moral choice may really be deluding themselves—a brain scan might show that such a choice correlates with activity in emotional centers in the brain rather than in the region of the brain associated with deliberative problem solving.
(15) This insight suggests that the criminal-justice system should abandon the idea of retribution—the idea that bad people should be punished because of their freely chosen immoral acts—which is now dominant as a justification of punishment. Instead, the law should
(20) focus on deterring future harms. In some cases, this might r...
we do ...
punishm...
is not v...

OPERATION OF BRAIN → BEHAVIOR   (+)

(-)

Ayer argued that <u>actions are free as long as they
(50) are not constrained.</u> It is not the existence of a cause but the source of the cause that determines whether an action is free. Although Ayer did not explicitly discuss the brain's role, one could make the analogy that those actions—and indeed those wills—that originate from
(55) a disease-free brain are not constrained, and are therefore free, even though they may be determined.

AYER'S CONC.

Let's bring it home! The final paragraph reiterates the conclusion in paragraph one that free will and determinism can go together. Then the author brings it back around to neuroscience. Even if there's a cause of our behavior, it can still be free if the brain is not diseased (lines 52-56).

We know this is a Thesis passage with the author siding with Ayer so make sure your primary structure diagram reflects this.

1. Anticipate the main idea

Two passages, two main ideas. The author of passage A winds his way to the point of view that we should only punish to deter, not to get revenge. That's the only supported point of view, so it's the main point.

The author of passage B devotes his passage to supporting Hume and Ayer's point of view that determinism and freewill are compatible. Since the author espouses this point of view, it's the main point.

2. Anticipate the primary purpose

The primary purpose is tied up with the main point and the author's attitude. Ask yourself, why did the author take the time to write the passage?

With passage A, the author is conversational in tone and yet passionate about the subject matter. So we would characterize the primary purpose as something like, "Advocate for a change in the criminal justice system."

Passage B is more scholarly in tone, although the author does side with Hume and Ayer. This passage's purpose would be: "Argue that two seemingly incompatible ideas are actually compatible."

3. Anticipate the author's attitude

The author in passage A is pretty excited about the "radical" change in thinking (lines 5-6). The author of passage B doesn't really stand out, so there's not a lot of attitude.

4. Anticipate anything to which the passage lends itself

In both passages, there are a number of definitions to keep track of. In passage A, the author discusses scientific research, which is important as support for the conclusion.

With Comparative Reading, the most important things to keep track of are the similarities and differences between the passages. There is one similarity—brain activity causes behavior—and one difference—people really do have free choice.

5. Summarize the entire passage in a sentence

This part is trickier for Comparative Reading than it is for single passages because you must encapsulate the relationship between the two passages. Passage A discusses free choice skeptically in order to advocate for a change in the law, while passage B discusses the same topic, but explains that free choice really exists.

The completed markup looks like this:

Passage A

To a neuroscientist, you are your brain; nothing causes your behavior other than the operations of your brain. This viewpoint, together with recent findings in
(5) neuroscience, radically changes the way we think about the law. The official line in the law is that all that matters is whether you are rational, but you can have someone who is totally rational even though their strings are being pulled by something beyond their
(10) control. Indeed, people who believe themselves to be making a free and rational moral choice may really be deluding themselves—a brain scan might show that such a choice correlates with activity in emotional centers in the brain rather than in the region of the
(15) brain associated with deliberative problem solving. This insight suggests that the criminal-justice system should abandon the idea of retribution—[the idea that bad people should be punished because of their freely chosen immoral acts]—which is now dominant as a
(20) justification of punishment. Instead, the law should focus on deterring future harms. In some cases, this might mean lighter punishments. If it is really true that we do not get any prevention bang from our punishment buck when we punish some person, then it is not worth punishing that person.

Passage B

(25) Neuroscience constantly produces new mechanistic descriptions of how the physical brain causes behavior, adding fuel to the deterministic view that [all human action is causally necessitated by events that are independent of the will]. It has long been
(30) argued, however, that the concept of free will can coexist with determinism.

In 1954 English philosopher Alfred J. Ayer put forth a theory of "soft determinism." He argued, as the philosopher David Hume had two centuries earlier,
(35) that even in a deterministic world, a person can still act freely. Ayer distinguished between free actions and constrained actions. [Free actions are those that are caused by internal sources, by one's own will] (unless one is suffering from a disorder). [Constrained actions
(40) are those that are caused by external sources, for example, by someone or something forcing you physically or mentally to perform an action, as in hypnosis or in mental disorders such as kleptomania.] When someone performs a free action to do A, he or
(45) she could have done B instead, since no external source precluded doing so. When someone performs a constrained action to do A, he or she could have done only A.

Ayer argued that actions are free as long as they
(50) are not constrained. It is not the existence of a cause but the source of the cause that determines whether an action is free. Although Ayer did not explicitly discuss the brain's role, one could make the analogy that those actions—and indeed those wills—that originate from
(55) a disease-free brain are not constrained, and are therefore free, even though they may be determined.

OPERATION OF BRAIN → BEHAVIOR (+)

ATT.
"OFFICIAL" LEGAL VIEW

RES.

(−)

DEF.

AUTHOR'S CONC.

> NEUROSCIENCE AND PUNISHMENT
>
> PUNISH ONLY TO DETER ←

OPERATION OF BRAIN → BEHAVIOR (+)

DEF.

AUTHOR'S CONC.

(−)

DEF.

DEF.

EX.

AYER'S CONC.

> NEUROSCIENCE AND FREE WILL
>
> FREEWILL AND DETERMINISM ARE COMPATIBLE (HUME AND AYER) ←

NOW FOR THE QUESTIONS

Question #17

The questions for Comparative Reading passages quite often ask us to figure out what the authors agree on or disagree on. That's why it's so important to tag similarities and differences. Here, they're asking us for a similarity. There's one big one in the passages, which is that both passages refer to neuroscience and the belief that our actions are the result of brain processes. That's answer choice (B). That's a nice payoff for good tagging, people!

17. Both passages are concerned with answering which one of the following questions?

    (A) Should people be punished for actions that are outside of their control?
    (B) Does scientific research into the brain have implications regarding freedom of the will?
    (C) Can actions that are not free be effectively deterred by the threat of punishment?
    (D) Is the view that retribution is a legitimate justification for punishment compatible with the findings of neuroscience?
    (E) Can an action be free if someone else physically forced the actor to perform it?

Answer choice (A), like several of the other answer choices, talks about punishment. When we determined the structure of these passages, we took note of the fact that only passage A is concerned with the criminal justice system. Because this concern doesn't show up in passage B, this is the wrong answer. Answer choices (C) and (D) can be tossed for the same reason. Answer choice (E) identifies a concern that is only discussed in passage B at lines 39-43. Nothing about this in passage A, so it's out.

Question #18

This Role question is a bit of an ogre. Whereas question #17 was about similarity between the passages, this one is about the difference. Unfortunately, our tagged difference (how the passages differ about free will) only eliminates an answer choice, (B), rather than getting us to the correct answer. This is because though they differ in opinion about free choice, both passages still discuss it. However, it's a start.

18. Which one of the following concepts plays a role in the argument of passage B but not in that of passage A?

    (A) mental disorder
    (B) free choice
    (C) causality
    (D) self-delusion
    (E) moral responsibility

We can eliminate other answer choices based on the passages. (C) can be eliminated because the point of agreement in the passages centers on the brain causing behavior. (D) and (E) can both be eliminated because they're in passage A (lines 10-12) and *not* in B, so they're the opposite of what we're looking for. This brings us to the correct answer choice, (A).

it'sGOtime / 381

Answer choice (A) identifies the discussion of mental disorder, which shows up in line 44. While passage (A) talks about the brain in general, there's no discussion of disorders. So (A) is our guy.

Question #19

19. One purpose of the reference by the author of passage B to David Hume (line 34) is to

    (A) characterize Ayer as someone who is not an original thinker
    (B) add credence to the theory of soft determinism
    (C) suggest that the theory of soft determinism is primarily of historical importance
    (D) suggest that the theory of soft determinism has been in existence as long as mechanistic descriptions of the brain have
    (E) add intellectual respectability to the view that the brain should not be described mechanistically

This is another Role question, asking us what is the point of mentioning some dude who's been dead for a couple of centuries. To put it in LSAT parlance, this is an appeal to authority. When you mention that an intellectual giant just happens to agree with your conclusion—in this case, that free will and determinism are compatible—it's a premise that provides support for your conclusion. Answer choice (B) correctly identifies the role that Hume plays here.

Answer choice (A) makes it sound like the author is attacking Ayer, but the author treats Ayer's argument as credible. We can get rid of (C) because the author expressly talks about how the debate over determinism is playing out in light of recent discoveries in neuroscience (lines 25-31). Answer choice (D) asks us to make a factual determination about how old two different things are, but there's no indication in the passage of how old either is. It leaves open the possibility that one or both goes back to before Hume. Answer choice (E) just misrepresents the argument being made. There's no indication in the passage that there's something wrong with describing the brain mechanistically. Instead, the argument is that, even if it's described that way, free choice is still possible.

Question #20

Our friendly neighborhood Minotaur waved his shiny hoof to let us know this Author's Attitude question was coming. The tone of passage A is remarkably conversational, and the author of the passage displays strong attitude toward the subject matter. Passage B, on the other hand, is scholarly in tone. That's why answer choice (C) is correct. Passage B is certainly more detached from, and analytical about, the material.

20. Passage B differs from passage A in that passage B displays an attitude toward the ideas it discusses that is more

    (A) engaged
    (B) dismissive
    (C) detached
    (D) ironic
    (E) skeptical

Answer choice (A) has it backward. Passage A is far more engaged than passage B. Answer choice (B) is something that is very unlikely to be a correct answer choice here or for any other passage. To be dismissive is to ignore a position. Authors of passages almost always engage in reasoned argumentation. They never just put up a hand and say, "Pssshhh, please." Regarding answer choice (D), both passages are sincere in their discussions of the subject matter, so there's no irony anywhere. Finally, passage A is skeptical of the retribution theory of punishment, but there's no skepticism in passage B, so answer choice (E) has it backward.

Question #21

This is a Parallel question, and we can use our one sentence description of passage structure to get the answer. Passage A said that the basis of the current punishment model is flawed, and that we should adopt a new one. Answer choice (C) says the exact same thing, just about teaching math rather than locking up evildoers.

21. Which one of the following arguments is most analogous to the argument advanced in passage A?

    (A) Many word processors are packed with nonessential features that only confuse most users and get in the way of important functions. Word processors with fewer features thus enhance productivity.
    (B) Economic models generally presume that actors in an economy are entirely rational. But psychological studies have documented many ways in which people make irrational choices. Thus, economic models, in theory, should not be able to predict human behavior.
    (C) The existing program for teaching mathematics in elementary schools is based on mistaken notions about what sorts of mathematical concepts children can grasp, and it should therefore be replaced.
    (D) Civil disobedience is justified only in those cases in which civil law conflicts with one's sincere moral or religious convictions. Any attempt to justify civil disobedience on something other than moral or religious grounds is therefore illegitimate.
    (E) Being autonomous does not imply having full control over one's behavior. After all, addicted smokers are unable to exercise control over some behaviors but are nevertheless autonomous in the general sense.

Since a question like this is very abstract, it's easy to get lost in the details of the answer choices. What's important to note here is that the conclusion of passage A is a prescriptive conclusion. It says that we should make a certain change. Any answer choice that has a different type of conclusion is out. You can get rid of answer choices (A), (D), and (E) on that basis. You can also throw out answer choice (B) because it's talking about the fact that we expect a particular model to fail rather than recommending that a particular course of action be taken.

Ditz: I got rid of (D) and (E) because the subject matter was similar to the passage!

Very good, Ditz. Similar subject matter is a red flag for answers to Parallel questions, and they are nearly always wrong. The makers of the LSAT are testing your ability to see structure independent of subject matter, and such answer choices are designed to trip up the test taker who is focused on topic.

Well, what did you think? Some people love Comparative Reading and some hate it. This was relatively straightforward, though Question #18 was a bear. Just one more passage to go!

In a Rolling Stone reader's choice poll, "Thriller" was the #1 music video of all time.

DECEMBER 2014: PASSAGE 4

This passage is adapted from a review of a 1991 book.

In a recent study, Mario García argues that in the United States between 1930 and 1960 the group of political activists he calls the "Mexican American Generation" was more radical and politically diverse
(5) than earlier historians have recognized. Through analysis of the work of some of the era's most important scholars, García does provide persuasive evidence that in the 1930s and 1940s these activists anticipated many of the reforms proposed by the more
(10) militant Chicanos of the 1960s and 1970s. His study, however, suffers from two flaws.

First, García's analysis of the evidence he provides to demonstrate the Mexican American Generation's political diversity is not entirely
(15) consistent. Indeed, he undermines his primary thesis by emphasizing an underlying consensus among various groups that tends to conceal the full significance of their differences. Groups such as the League of United Latin American Citizens, an
(20) organization that encouraged Mexican Americans to pursue a civil rights strategy of assimilation into the United States political and cultural mainstream, were often diametrically opposed to organizations such as the Congress of Spanish-Speaking People, a coalition
(25) group that advocated bilingual education and equal rights for resident aliens in the United States. García acknowledges these differences but dismisses them as insignificant, given that the goals of groups as disparate as these centered on liberal reform, not
(30) revolution. But one need only note the fierce controversies that occurred during the period over United States immigration policies and the question of assimilation versus cultural maintenance to recognize that Mexican American political history since 1930
(35) has been characterized not by consensus but by intense and lively debate.

Second, García may be exaggerating the degree to which the views of these activists were representative of the ethnic Mexican population residing in the
(40) United States during this period. Noting that by 1930 the proportion of the Mexican American population that had been born in the United States had significantly increased, García argues that between 1930 and 1960 a new generation of Mexican American
(45) leaders appeared, one that was more acculturated and hence more politically active than its predecessor. Influenced by their experience of discrimination and by the inclusive rhetoric of World War II slogans, these leaders, according to García, were determined to
(50) achieve full civil rights for all United States residents of Mexican descent. However, it is not clear how far this outlook extended beyond these activists. Without a better understanding of the political implications of important variables such as patterns of bilingualism
(55) and rates of Mexican immigration and naturalization, and the variations in ethnic consciousness these variables help to create, one cannot assume that an increase in the proportion of Mexican Americans born in the United States necessarily resulted in an increase
(60) in the ethnic Mexican population's political activism.

22. According to the passage, the League of United Latin American Citizens differed from the Congress of Spanish-Speaking People in that the League of United Latin American Citizens

   (A) sought the political goals most popular with other United States citizens
   (B) fought for equal rights for resident aliens in the United States
   (C) favored a more liberal United States immigration policy
   (D) encouraged Mexican Americans to speak Spanish rather than English
   (E) encouraged Mexican Americans to adopt the culture of the United States

23. It can be inferred from the passage that García would most probably agree with which one of the following statements about the Mexican American political activists of the 1930s and 1940s?

   (A) Some of their concerns were similar to those of the Mexican American activists of the 1960s and 1970s.
   (B) They were more politically diverse than the Mexican American activists of the 1960s and 1970s.
   (C) They were as militant as the Mexican American activists of the 1960s and 1970s.
   (D) Most of them advocated bilingual education and equal rights for resident aliens in the United States.
   (E) Most of them were more interested in revolution than in liberal reform.

24. The passage suggests that García assumes which one of the following to have been true of Mexican Americans between 1930 and 1960?

    (A) Increased ethnic consciousness among Mexican Americans accounted for an increase in political activity among them.
    (B) Increased familiarity among Mexican Americans with United States culture accounted for an increase in political activity among them.
    (C) The assimilation of many Mexican Americans into United States culture accounted for Mexican Americans' lack of interest in political activity.
    (D) Many Mexican Americans were moved to political militancy as a means of achieving full civil rights for all United States residents of Mexican descent.
    (E) Many Mexican Americans were moved to political protest by their experience of discrimination and the patronizing rhetoric of World War II slogans.

25. It can be inferred that the author of the passage believes which one of the following about the Mexican American political activists of the 1930s and 1940s?

    (A) Their common goal of liberal reform made them less militant than the Mexican American activists of the 1960s and 1970s.
    (B) Their common goal of liberal reform did not outweigh their political differences.
    (C) Their common goal of liberal reform helped them reach a consensus in spite of their political differences.
    (D) They were more or less evenly divided between those favoring assimilation and those favoring cultural maintenance.
    (E) They did not succeed in fully achieving their political goals because of their disparate political views.

26. The author of the passage expresses uncertainty with regard to which one of the following?

    (A) whether or not one can assume that the increase in the number of Mexican Americans born in the United States led to an increase in Mexican American political activism
    (B) whether or not historians preceding García were correct in their assumptions about Mexican Americans who were politically active between 1930 and 1960
    (C) whether or not there was general consensus among Mexican American political activists between 1930 and 1960
    (D) the extent to which the views of Mexican American activists were shared by the ethnic Mexican population in the United States
    (E) the nature of the relationship between the League of United Latin American Citizens and the Congress of Spanish-Speaking People

26. The passage supports which one of the following statements about ethnic consciousness among Mexican Americans?

    (A) Ethnic consciousness increases when rates of Mexican immigration and naturalization increase.
    (B) Ethnic consciousness increases when the number of Mexican Americans born in the United States increases.
    (C) Ethnic consciousness decreases when the number of Mexican Americans assimilating into the culture of the United States increases.
    (D) Variations in the influence of Mexican American leaders over the Mexican American population at large account in part for variations in ethnic consciousness.
    (E) Variations in rates of Mexican immigration and naturalization account in part for variations in ethnic consciousness.

Almost there! Passage four is usually pretty tough, so stay focused!

HOW TO READ THE PASSAGE

Paragraph 1

This passage is adapted from a review of a 1991 book.

In a recent study, Mario García argues that in the United States between 1930 and 1960 the group of political activists he calls the "Mexican American Generation" was more radical and politically diverse
(5) than earlier historians have recognized. Through analysis of the work of some of the era's most important scholars, García does provide persuasive evidence that in the 1930s and 1940s these activists anticipated many of the reforms proposed by the more
(10) militant Chicanos of the 1960s and 1970s. His study, however, suffers from two flaws.

GARCIA'S CONC.

ATT.

AUTHOR'S CONC.

This paragraph is rife with taggable goodies. First, let's box Mario Garcia as we do for all proper names. The author tells us that Garcia makes an argument. When you argue for something, whatever you're arguing for is your conclusion, so let's underline and tag Garcia's conclusion. To be clear, Garcia thinks that Mexican American activism between 1930 and 1960 was more radical and politically diverse than people think (lines 4-5). The author shows a tiny bit of positive attitude toward Garcia's argument, calling some of the evidence persuasive (tag that attitude!). But then, the author drops the hammer on poor Garcia. Garcia's argument is not just flawed—it's double flawed!

Before we move to the next paragraph, it's important to note that there are two points of view here, Garcia's and the author's, and they are at odds with one another. This is looking like an Antithesis passage, and, if it is, we already have the two points of view that will end up in our primary structure diagram. Let's read on to see if they have support before doing so, however.

Paragraph 2

> First, García's analysis of the evidence he provides to demonstrate the Mexican American Generation's political diversity is not entirely
> (15) consistent. Indeed, he undermines his primary thesis by emphasizing an underlying consensus among various groups that tends to conceal the full significance of their differences. Groups such as the League of United Latin American Citizens, an
> (20) organization that encouraged Mexican Americans to pursue a civil rights strategy of assimilation into the United States political and cultural mainstream, were often diametrically opposed to organizations such as the Congress of Spanish-Speaking People, a coalition
> (25) group that advocated bilingual education and equal rights for resident aliens in the United States. García acknowledges these differences but dismisses them as insignificant, given that the goals of groups as disparate as these centered on liberal reform, not
> (30) revolution. But one need only note the fierce controversies that occurred during the period over United States immigration policies and the question of assimilation versus cultural maintenance to recognize that Mexican American political history since 1930
> (35) has been characterized not by consensus but by intense and lively debate.

FIRST FLAW: GARCIA MISSES DIFFERENCES

ASSIMILATE VS. BILINGUAL AND EQUAL RIGHTS

The author starts this paragraph by attacking the second half of Garcia's argument, that the early Mexican American community was more politically diverse than previously thought.

Ninja: Reading this paragraph, it might seem to you that, instead of attacking Garcia, the author is making Garcia's argument for him. After all, the author talks extensively about how different (politically diverse) the views are between these two groups. Here's where it helps to focus on the scope of the author's conclusion.

The author is not trying to prove that Garcia's conclusion is false. Instead, the author is attacking the way Garcia makes his arguments. So, when the author says that Garcia "undermines his primary thesis," he is saying that Garcia does a substandard job of making his argument.

Thanks, Ninja. The author doesn't like Garcia's argument because Garcia dismisses legitimate differences that would actually support his conclusion. The differences between these two groups seem pretty strong. The League of United Latin American Citizens is all about assimilation whereas the Congress of Spanish-Speaking People is all about maintaining Spanish as a language and obtaining rights for non-citizens (lines 18-26). For some strange reason, though, instead of focusing on this as support for his argument regarding the political diversity of the Mexican American community of the time, Garcia says these differences aren't important because both groups sought reform over revolution (lines 26-30).

To put it mildly, the author thinks Garcia is shooting himself in the foot by dismissing valuable evidence that would support his argument. Get it together, Garcia! We also know at this point that both Garcia's view and the author's view from the first paragraph are developed so we can put them both in the primary structure diagram. Huzzah!

Paragraph 3

> Second, García may be exaggerating the degree to which the views of these activists were representative of the ethnic Mexican population residing in the
> (40) United States during this period. Noting that by 1930 the proportion of the Mexican American population that had been born in the United States had significantly increased, García argues that between 1930 and 1960 a new generation of Mexican American
> (45) leaders appeared, one that was more acculturated and hence more politically active than its predecessor. Influenced by their experience of discrimination and by the inclusive rhetoric of World War II slogans, these leaders, according to García, were determined to
> (50) achieve full civil rights for all United States residents of Mexican descent. However, it is not clear how far this outlook extended beyond these activists. Without a better understanding of the political implications of important variables such as patterns of bilingualism
> (55) and rates of Mexican immigration and naturalization, and the variations in ethnic consciousness these variables help to create, one cannot assume that an increase in the proportion of Mexican Americans born in the United States necessarily resulted in an increase
> (60) in the ethnic Mexican population's political activism.

SECOND FLAW: NOT REPRESENTATIVE

MISSING FACTORS:
1. BILINGUALISM
2. IMMIGRATION AND NATURALIZATION
3. ETHNIC CONSCIOUSNESS

ASS.

In the second paragraph, the author attacked Garcia over the second part of his argument. How much you wanna bet that he's about to do the same regarding the first part of the argument for the third paragraph?

And so it comes to pass...The author lays out the second flaw in Garcia's position in paragraph three. Garcia is exaggerating the idea that the activists' views represented the views of the Mexican population residing in the US as a whole. This makes sense. How representative of the US population are views of activist groups like Earth First! or the Tea Party?

The author goes on to lay out Garcia's argument in full. It becomes clear with words like "influenced" (line 47) that it's a causal argument: the increase in the Mexican American population resulted in new leaders that experienced discrimination and saw inclusive WWII slogans, giving rise to a determination to achieve full rights. Tag this causal argument as there is likely to be a question about it.

After laying out Garcia's argument, the author proceeds to point out its deficiencies. Factors such as bilingualism, immigration and naturalization, and ethnic consciousness must all be taken into account before Garcia can assume the activists are speaking for everyone in the Mexican American community. Because there are three factors supporting a premise, this is a localized Classification structure. Tag it and don't forget to tag the assumption, too.

Now that we've dissected the passage, it's time to anticipate (as always) five important items before moving on to the questions.

1. Anticipate the main idea

This is an Antithesis passage. There is Garcia's point of view, "the Mexican American Generation was more radical and politically diverse" than previously acknowledged (lines 4-5). That's Thesis. Then there is the author's point of view: the study is flawed in two ways. Since the author's point of view is always the main point of a passage, the main point of this passage is that the study is flawed.

2. Anticipate the primary purpose

Why did the author write this thing? To argue that Garcia's study is flawed in two ways.

3. Anticipate the author's attitude

The author displays some positive attitude toward Garcia early on, saying that some of the evidence is "persuasive" (line 7), but, for the most part, the author is solidly unimpressed with Garcia's work.

4. Anticipate anything to which the passage lends itself

It's important to keep in mind the two examples of flawed reasoning in paragraphs two and three. Specifically, in paragraph two Garcia dismisses evidence that would support his conclusion, and in paragraph three Garcia lacks the information to support his conclusion. That lacking information is fleshed out in a localized Classification structure, which we will almost surely get a question about.

5. Summarize the entire passage in a sentence

A study is identified in paragraph one, two criticisms of the study are made in paragraph one and elaborated upon in paragraphs two and three.

This passage is adapted from a review of a 1991 book.

In a recent study, Mario García argues that in the United States between 1930 and 1960 the group of political activists he calls the "Mexican American Generation" was more radical and politically diverse
(5) than earlier historians have recognized. Through analysis of the work of some of the era's most important scholars, García does provide persuasive evidence that in the 1930s and 1940s these activists anticipated many of the reforms proposed by the more
(10) militant Chicanos of the 1960s and 1970s. His study, however, suffers from two flaws.
    First, García's analysis of the evidence he provides to demonstrate the Mexican American Generation's political diversity is not entirely
(15) consistent. Indeed, he undermines his primary thesis by emphasizing an underlying consensus among various groups that tends to conceal the full significance of their differences. Groups such as the League of United Latin American Citizens, an
(20) organization that encouraged Mexican Americans to pursue a civil rights strategy of assimilation into the United States political and cultural mainstream, were often diametrically opposed to organizations such as the Congress of Spanish-Speaking People, a coalition
(25) group that advocated bilingual education and equal rights for resident aliens in the United States. García acknowledges these differences but dismisses them as insignificant, given that the goals of groups as disparate as these centered on liberal reform, not
(30) revolution. But one need only note the fierce controversies that occurred during the period over United States immigration policies and the question of assimilation versus cultural maintenance to recognize that Mexican American political history since 1930
(35) has been characterized not by consensus but by intense and lively debate.
    Second, García may be exaggerating the degree to which the views of these activists were representative of the ethnic Mexican population residing in the
(40) United States during this period. Noting that by 1930 the proportion of the Mexican American population that had been born in the United States had significantly increased, García argues that between 1930 and 1960 a new generation of Mexican American
(45) leaders appeared, one that was more acculturated and hence more politically active than its predecessor. Influenced by their experience of discrimination and by the inclusive rhetoric of World War II slogans, these leaders, according to García, were determined to
(50) achieve full civil rights for all United States residents of Mexican descent. However, it is not clear how far this outlook extended beyond these activists. Without a better understanding of the political implications of important variables such as patterns of bilingualism
(55) and rates of Mexican immigration and naturalization, and the variations in ethnic consciousness these variables help to create, one cannot assume that an increase in the proportion of Mexican Americans born in the United States necessarily resulted in an increase
(60) in the ethnic Mexican population's political activism.

NOW FOR THE QUESTIONS

Question #22

Whhhhhaaaattt??? No main point question? Trying to throw us off balance with a Specific Reference question up first, LSAT? Well, too bad, a ninja always lands on his or her feet. The author mentions the difference between these two groups as support for the idea that the study is flawed. Specifically, we know from our tagging that the League was for assimilation whereas the Congress wasn't (lines 18-26). Answer choice (E) discusses adopting the culture of the U.S. That's assimilation, and that's why (E) is right.

> 22. According to the passage, the League of United Latin American Citizens differed from the Congress of Spanish-Speaking People in that the League of United Latin American Citizens
>
> (A) sought the political goals most popular with other United States citizens
> (B) fought for equal rights for resident aliens in the United States
> (C) favored a more liberal United States immigration policy
> (D) encouraged Mexican Americans to speak Spanish rather than English
> (E) encouraged Mexican Americans to adopt the culture of the United States

Answer choice (A) is talking about other U.S. citizens, but the passage never discusses what's going on with other citizens, so there's no support for this answer. Answer choice (B) is referring to the goals of the Congress, but this question asks us about the goals of the League. Answer choice (C) refers to immigration policy, but the passage does not mention the views of either group on the subject. Answer choice (D) talks about encouraging people not to speak English, which is diametrically opposed to the assimilation goals that the League advocated.

Question #23

This Inference question asks us about Garcia's point of view. The passage is devoted to examining his point of view, so the prompt doesn't really narrow things down. However, answer choice (A) identifies the fact that Garcia presented "persuasive evidence" that these earlier activists anticipated the reforms of later activists (lines 7-10).

> 23. It can be inferred from the passage that García would most probably agree with which one of the following statements about the Mexican American political activists of the 1930s and 1940s?
>
> (A) Some of their concerns were similar to those of the Mexican American activists of the 1960s and 1970s.
> (B) They were more politically diverse than the Mexican American activists of the 1960s and 1970s.
> (C) They were as militant as the Mexican American activists of the 1960s and 1970s.
> (D) Most of them advocated bilingual education and equal rights for resident aliens in the United States.
> (E) Most of them were more interested in revolution than in liberal reform.

Answer choice (B) is tempting because Garcia argues that they were politically diverse, but this comparison is not supported. Garcia believes they were more diverse than historians gave them credit for, but that doesn't mean that they were more diverse than those who came after. Answer choice (C) is wrong for the same reason; this comparison is just not made in the passage. Answer choice (D) is too strong. We know that *some* activists advocated for bilingualism (line 25), but there's no way to know if *most* of them did. Answer choice (E) runs directly counter to the fact that the groups mentioned were more interested in liberal reform than revolution (lines 29-30).

Question #24

Well, here's another Inference question about Garcia's point of view. However, it gives us the dates 1930-1960, which is mentioned twice in the passage. The first is Garcia's conclusion that the Mexican American generation was more radical and diverse than thought (lines 4-6). The second is the developed casual chain in paragraph three. Scanning the answer choices for either of these two yields (B), which is the causal chain from paragraph three. Hurray for localized Cause and Effect structures!

According to the author, one of the problems with Garcia is that he fails to account for variations in ethnic consciousness, and answer choice (A) says the opposite. So that's out. Answer choice (C) talks about a lack of interest among Mexican Americans, which is exactly the opposite of Garcia's point of view, so this is wrong. Answer choice (D) muddles paragraphs two and three. Militancy is discussed in paragraph three, but the information about securing civil rights is discussed in paragraph two which is about diversity of views rather than depth of radicalism. Answer choice (E) uses the word "patronizing" to describe the World War II slogans, but Garcia talks about how those slogans were inclusive (line 48). That's the opposite of patronizing. So this is wrong.

24. The passage suggests that García assumes which one of the following to have been true of Mexican Americans between 1930 and 1960?

   (A) Increased ethnic consciousness among Mexican Americans accounted for an increase in political activity among them.
   (B) Increased familiarity among Mexican Americans with United States culture accounted for an increase in political activity among them.
   (C) The assimilation of many Mexican Americans into United States culture accounted for Mexican Americans' lack of interest in political activity.
   (D) Many Mexican Americans were moved to political militancy as a means of achieving full civil rights for all United States residents of Mexican descent.
   (E) Many Mexican Americans were moved to political protest by their experience of discrimination and the patronizing rhetoric of World War II slogans.

Question #25

We get another Inference question, but this one is about the author. Like the previous question, it directs us to the 1930's and 40's, which is where we were just looking. In both places (paragraphs one and three) the author criticizes Garcia. In paragraph one the author says that Garcia's argument has two flaws. In paragraph three, the author states that Garcia's causal chain suffers from an assumption.

25. It can be inferred that the author of the passage believes which one of the following about the Mexican American political activists of the 1930s and 1940s?

    (A) Their common goal of liberal reform made them less militant than the Mexican American activists of the 1960s and 1970s.
    (B) Their common goal of liberal reform did not outweigh their political differences.
    (C) Their common goal of liberal reform helped them reach a consensus in spite of their political differences.
    (D) They were more or less evenly divided between those favoring assimilation and those favoring cultural maintenance.
    (E) They did not succeed in fully achieving their political goals because of their disparate political views.

Scanning the answer choices for either we find answer choice (B) identifies the first of the two flaws the author finds with Garcia, what we labeled "Garcia misses differences." Boom.

The author never makes a comparison between the earlier and later generations of activists, and so we don't know who he thinks was more militant, so answer choice (A) doesn't work. Answer choice (C) identifies Garcia's take on the differences between these groups, but we're being asked about the author. Answer choice (D) does something that answers often do, which is to ask you for an inference about numbers relating to something discussed in the passage. Was there a 50/50 split between the League and the Congress? No idea. Lastly, Garcia thinks the differences are unimportant, so he certainly does not think that the differences destroyed the movement. That gets rid of answer choice (E).

Question #26

There are three likely candidates for the author's "uncertainty" in this Author's Attitude question: the two criticisms leveled at Garcia, the Classification structure in paragraph three that discusses what Garcia has left out, and the assumption the author says that Garcia is making (also in paragraph three). Answer choice (D) pulls from the Classification structure by identifying the fact that, until we know those three things, we can't know whether Mexican Americans in general shared the radicalism of the activist leaders (lines 51-60).

Answer choice (A) mischaracterizes Garcia's argument. The argument is not that there is an increase in the quantity of political activism, it's that the quality of political activism became more radical. We can get rid of answer choice (B) by focusing on the author's conclusion. The author never says whether the earlier historians are right or wrong. He focuses very closely on how Garcia screwed up in making his argument, regardless of whether his conclusion was good or bad. Regarding answer choice (C), the author is very certain that there was not a consensus (line 35). Answer choice (E) is wrong for the same reason as (C). The author is certain that there was a great deal of disagreement between these groups.

26. The author of the passage expresses uncertainty with regard to which one of the following?

   (A) whether or not one can assume that the increase in the number of Mexican Americans born in the United States led to an increase in Mexican American political activism
   (B) whether or not historians preceding García were correct in their assumptions about Mexican Americans who were politically active between 1930 and 1960
   (C) whether or not there was general consensus among Mexican American political activists between 1930 and 1960
   (D) the extent to which the views of Mexican American activists were shared by the ethnic Mexican population in the United States
   (E) the nature of the relationship between the League of United Latin American Citizens and the Congress of Spanish-Speaking People

Question #27

In this Inference question we know where to look because ethnic consciousness is part of the localized Classification structure at the end of paragraph three. Once we get there we find that sentence says that variations in ethnic consciousness depend at least in part on bilingualism and rates of immigration and naturalization. That's answer choice (E).

Answer choice (A) goes too far. We know that consciousness varies as a result of immigration and naturalization. That leaves open the possibility that it actually goes down when immigration and naturalization increase, rather than increasing. Answer choices (B) and (C) both bring in information from earlier in the passage that the author never links to ethnic consciousness. Answer choice (D) is wrong because it mischaracterizes the relationship between ethnic consciousness and determining how representative of the people's attitudes are the views of leadership. Ethnic consciousness affects this determination, but answer choice (D) says it's the other way around.

27. The passage supports which one of the following statements about ethnic consciousness among Mexican Americans?

    (A) Ethnic consciousness increases when rates of Mexican immigration and naturalization increase.
    (B) Ethnic consciousness increases when the number of Mexican Americans born in the United States increases.
    (C) Ethnic consciousness decreases when the number of Mexican Americans assimilating into the culture of the United States increases.
    (D) Variations in the influence of Mexican American leaders over the Mexican American population at large account in part for variations in ethnic consciousness.
    (E) Variations in rates of Mexican immigration and naturalization account in part for variations in ethnic consciousness.

YOU DID IT!

Congratulations! You just completed a full Reading Comprehension section from a recent LSAT. Did it feel good? Pat yourself on your well-deserving tummy. Feel not so good? Never fear! We've got lots more passages for you to practice on.

26/morePRACTICE

NOW, HOW ABOUT A LITTLE MORE PRACTICE?

You've seen what a full section of Reading Comprehension looks like, but you must practice until you are a deadly weapon of the Reading Comprehension variety. So here are ten more passages taken from real LSATs (as always!) for you to complete.

You know the drill. Read each passage, tagging and marking up the passage as you go, filling in your primary structure diagram, summarizing the passage and anticipating questions. Official explanations for all of these are available online in your *MyBlueprint* account.*

It's still not time to introduce timing into the mix. These exercises are all about getting the methods down, not rushing through techniques. If you rush when you're just learning, you won't learn the methods correctly. We don't care if it takes you an hour or more to do a passage according to the Blueprint Method. That's good! Because attention to detail is what's needed now, not concern over timing. Later, we'll devote a whole chapter to timing.

---

* Haven't accessed your *MyBlueprint* account yet? Follow these steps:
1. Go to blueprintlsat.com
2. Click on "Login" and make a free *MyBlueprint* account if you have not already done so.
3. Enjoy the glory that is the Blueprint explanation for each passage.

If you experience any difficulty (or just want to shower us with praise), feel free to contact us at info@blueprintlsat.com, 888-4BP-PREP.

It is generally believed that while in some cases government should intervene to protect people from risk—by imposing air safety standards, for example—in other cases, such as mountain climbing,
(5) the onus should be on the individual to protect himself or herself. In the eyes of the public at large, the demarcation between the two kinds of cases has mainly to do with whether the risk in question is incurred voluntarily. This distinction between voluntary and
(10) involuntary risk may in fact be the chief difference between lay and expert judgments about risk. Policy experts tend to focus on aggregate lives at stake; laypeople care a great deal whether a risk is undertaken voluntarily. However, judgments about whether
(15) a risk is "involuntary" often stem from confusion and selective attention, and the real reason for such judgments frequently lies in an antecedent judgment of some other kind. They are thus of little utility in guiding policy decisions.
(20) First, it is not easy to determine when a risk is voluntarily incurred. Although voluntariness may be entirely absent in the case of an unforeseeable collision with an asteroid, with most environmental, occupational, and other social risks, it is not an all-
(25) or-nothing matter, but rather one of degree. Risks incurred by airline passengers are typically thought to be involuntary, since passengers have no control over whether a plane is going to crash. But they can choose airlines on the basis of safety records or choose not to
(30) fly. In characterizing the risks as involuntary, people focus on a small part of a complex interaction, not the decision to fly, but the accident when it occurs.
Second, people often characterize risks as "voluntary" when they do not approve of the purpose
(35) for which people run the risks. It is unlikely that people would want to pour enormous taxpayer resources into lowering the risks associated with skydiving, even if the ratio of dollars spent to lives saved were quite good. By contrast, people would probably not object to
(40) spending enormous resources on improving the safety of firefighters, even though the decision to become a firefighter is voluntary. In short, there is no special magic in notions like "voluntary" and "involuntary." Therefore, regulatory policy should be guided by
(45) a better understanding of the factors that underlie judgments about voluntariness.
In general, the government should attempt to save as many lives as it can, subject to the limited public and private resources devoted to risk reduction.
(50) Departures from this principle should be justified not by invoking the allegedly voluntary or involuntary nature of a particular risk, but rather by identifying the more specific considerations for which notions of voluntariness serve as proxies.

21. Which one of the following most accurately expresses the main point of the passage?

    (A) In general, whether people characterize a risk as voluntary or involuntary depends on whether they approve of the purpose for which the risk is taken.
    (B) Decisions about government intervention to protect people from risks should be based primarily on how many lives can be saved rather than on whether the risks are considered voluntary.
    (C) Though laypeople may object, experts should be the ones to determine whether the risk incurred in a particular action is voluntary or involuntary.
    (D) Public-policy decisions related to the protection of society against risk are difficult to make because of the difficulty of distinguishing risks incurred voluntarily from those incurred involuntarily.
    (E) People who make judgments about the voluntary or involuntary character of a risk are usually unaware of the complicated motivations that lead people to take risks.

22. The passage indicates that which one of the following is usually a significant factor in laypeople's willingness to support public funding for specific risk-reduction measures?

    (A) an expectation about the ratio of dollars spent to lives saved
    (B) deference to expert judgments concerning whether the government should intervene
    (C) a belief as to whether the risk is incurred voluntarily or involuntarily
    (D) a judgment as to whether the risk puts a great number of lives at stake
    (E) a consideration of the total resources available for risk reduction

23. According to the passage, which one of the following do laypeople generally consider to involve risk that is not freely assumed?

    (A) traveling in outer space
    (B) participating in skydiving
    (C) serving as a firefighter
    (D) traveling in airplanes
    (E) climbing mountains

October 2013, Passage 4

24. It can be inferred from the passage that the author would be most likely to agree with which one of the following statements?

    (A) People should generally not be protected against the risks incurred through activities, such as skydiving, that are dangerous and serve no socially useful purpose.
    (B) The fact that plane crash victims chose to fly would usually be deemed by policy experts to be largely irrelevant to decisions about the government's role in regulating air safety.
    (C) Both the probability of occurrence and the probability of resulting death or injury are higher for plane crashes than for any other kind of risk incurred by airline passengers.
    (D) For public-policy purposes, a risk should be deemed voluntarily incurred if people are not subject to that risk unless they make a particular choice.
    (E) The main category of risk that is usually incurred completely involuntarily is the risk of natural disaster.

25. The author's use of the phrase "no special magic" (line 43) is most likely meant primarily to convey that notions like "voluntary" and "involuntary"

    (A) do not exhaustively characterize the risks that people commonly face
    (B) have been used to intentionally conceal the factors motivating government efforts to protect people from risks
    (C) have no meaning beyond their literal, dictionary definitions
    (D) are mistakenly believed to be characteristics that inform people's understanding of the consequences of risk
    (E) provide a flawed mechanism for making public policy decisions relating to risk reduction

26. The passage most strongly supports the inference that the author believes which one of the following?

    (A) Whenever an activity involves the risk of loss of human life, the government should intervene to reduce the degree of risk incurred.
    (B) Some environmental risks are voluntary to a greater degree than others are.
    (C) Policy experts are more likely than laypeople to form an accurate judgment about the voluntariness or involuntariness of an activity.
    (D) The government should increase the quantity of resources devoted to protecting people from risk.
    (E) Government policies intended to reduce risk are not justified unless they comport with most people's beliefs.

27. Which one of the following most accurately describes the author's attitude in the passage?

    (A) chagrin at the rampant misunderstanding of the relative risks associated with various activities
    (B) concern that policy guided mainly by laypeople's emphasis on the voluntariness of risk would lead to excessive government regulation
    (C) skepticism about the reliability of laypeople's intuitions as a general guide to deciding government risk-management policy
    (D) conviction that the sole criterion that can justify government intervention to reduce risk is the saving of human lives
    (E) eagerness to persuade the reader that policy experts' analysis of risk is distorted by subtle biases

Passage A

Until recently, conservationists were often complacent about the effect of nonindigenous plant and animal species on the ecosystems they invade. Many shared Charles Elton's view, introduced in
(5) his 1958 book on invasive species, that disturbed habitats are most vulnerable to new arrivals because they contain fewer or less vigorous native species. Now, however, ecologists realize that when humans introduce new species into existing ecosystems, even
(10) pristine, species-rich habitats are threatened. The rapidly increasing conservation problems and high damage and control costs generated by these invasions merit serious concern.

Invasive plants profoundly affect ecosystems
(15) and threaten biodiversity throughout the world. For example, to the untrained eye, the Everglades National Park in Florida appears wild and natural. Yet this and other unique ecosystems are being degraded as surely as if by chemical pollution. In
(20) Florida, forests are growing where none existed before. Traditionally, saw grass dominated large regions of Florida's marshes, providing habitat for unique Everglades wildlife. Although saw grass grows over 9 feet tall, introduced Australian melaleuca
(25) trees, typically 70 feet tall, now outcompete marsh plants for sunlight. As melaleuca trees grow and form dense stands, their leaf litter increases soil elevations, inhibiting normal water flow. Wildlife associated with saw grass marshes declines. Similarly, in Australia,
(30) the introduction of Scotch broom plants led to the disappearance of a diverse set of native reptiles.

Passage B

The real threat posed by so-called invasive species isn't against nature but against humans' ideas of what nature is supposed to be. Species invasion is
(35) not a zero-sum game, with new species replacing old ones at a one-to-one ratio. Rather, and with critical exceptions, it is a positive-sum game, in which ecosystems can accept more and more species. Indeed, in both marine and terrestrial ecosystems, ecologists
(40) have found that invasions often increase biodiversity at the local level: if you add many new species and lose few or no native species, the overall species count goes up.

Invasions don't cause ecosystems to collapse.
(45) Invasions may radically alter the components of an ecosystem, perhaps to a point at which the ecosystem becomes less valuable or engaging to humans. But 50 years of study has failed to identify a clear ecological difference between an ecosystem rich
(50) in native species and one chock-full of introduced species. Unlike ecosystem destruction—clear cutting of forests, for example—invasions don't make ecosystems shrink or disappear. They simply transform them into different ecosystems.

(55) When the issue is phrased as one of ecosystem destruction, the stakes are stark: we choose between nature's life and nature's death. In actuality, introduced species present a continuum. A few species do cause costly damage and tragic extinctions. But most plant
(60) and animal species simply blend in harmlessly. The issue they present for humans is not whether we will be surrounded by nature but rather what kind of nature we will have around us.

15. Both passages are concerned with answering which one of the following questions?

    (A) Why are some ecosystems more vulnerable to introduced species than others?
    (B) What distinguishes introduced species that are harmful from those that are harmless?
    (C) What approach should be taken to protect ecosystems from introduced species?
    (D) How are ecosystems affected by the introduction of new species?
    (E) How are species able to spread beyond their native ecosystems?

16. Passage A, but not passage B, asserts which one of the following regarding ecologists who study introduced species?

    (A) Their research has been limited to studying the economic impact of introduced species.
    (B) They are inconsistent in their use of criteria for determining what defines an ecosystem.
    (C) Most agree that introduced species can cause extinctions.
    (D) Before Elton, most of them were concerned only with preserving biodiversity at the local level.
    (E) They do not share Elton's view that introduced species primarily threaten disturbed habitats.

17. The author of passage B would be most likely to agree with which one of the following statements about the term "natural" as it is used in passage A (line 17)?

    (A) It correctly characterizes a difference between pristine and disturbed environments.
    (B) It contradicts a concept of nature put forth elsewhere in passage A.
    (C) It helps to clarify a difference between the "wild" and the "natural."
    (D) It introduces an unconventional definition of nature.
    (E) It conflates physical nature with an arbitrary ideal of nature.

18. Which one of the following is most analogous to the main point of passage B?

    (A) The loss of a favorite piece of clothing when it starts to fray after many years is not necessarily a meaningful loss.
    (B) The alteration of a culture's folk music by the influence of music from other cultures is not always lamentable.
    (C) The expansion of urban development into previously rural areas is a necessary consequence of progress.
    (D) Cultures can only benefit when they absorb and adapt ideas that originated in other cultures.
    (E) While horticulturalists can create new plant species through hybridization, hybridization also occurs in the wild.

19. Which one of the following most accurately characterizes the relationship between the two passages?

    (A) Passage A presents a hypothesis about the causes of a particular phenomenon, while passage B presents an alternative hypothesis about the causes of that phenomenon.
    (B) Passage A questions a common assumption about a particular phenomenon, while passage B shows why that assumption is well-founded.
    (C) Passage A presents evidence that a particular phenomenon is widely considered to be undesirable, while passage B presents evidence that the same phenomenon is usually considered to be beneficial.
    (D) Passage A warns about the dangers of a particular phenomenon, while passage B argues that the phenomenon should not generally be considered dangerous.
    (E) Passage A proposes a particular course of action, while passage B raises questions about the advisability of that approach.

Can a sovereign have unlimited legal power? If a sovereign does have unlimited legal power, then the sovereign presumably has the legal power to limit or even completely abdicate its own legal power.
(5) But doing so would mean that the sovereign no longer has unlimited legal power, thereby contradicting the initial supposition. This theoretical conundrum is traditionally known as the paradox of omnipotence.

Social scientists have recognized that sovereign
(10) omnipotence can be a source of considerable practical difficulty for sovereigns themselves. Douglass North and Barry Weingast show that English and French monarchies in the seventeenth and eighteenth centuries confronted a practical challenge created by
(15) the paradox of their own omnipotence.

North and Weingast point out that it is often in a sovereign's best interest to make a credible commitment not to perform certain acts. For example, a sovereign with absolute power can refuse to honor
(20) its financial commitments. Yet creditors will not voluntarily lend generous amounts at favorable terms to an absolute monarch who can renege upon debts at will.

In the struggle to expand their empires, the
(25) English and French monarchies required vast amounts of capital. At the outset of the seventeenth century, however, neither regime could credibly commit itself to repay debts or to honor property rights. The absence of limitations upon the legal power of monarchs meant
(30) that there was no law or commitment monarchs could make that they could not also unmake or disregard. Consequently, these monarchs earned a reputation for expropriating wealth, repudiating debts, and reneging upon commitments. Not surprisingly, creditors took
(35) such behavior into account and demanded higher interest rates from monarchs than from the monarchs' wealthy subjects.

North and Weingast argue that the constitutional settlement imposed in England by the Glorious
(40) Revolution of 1688 halted such faithless conduct. Henceforth, Parliament controlled the Crown's purse strings. Parliament, in turn, represented commercial interests that would not tolerate governmental disregard for property rights. The Crown's newfound
(45) inability to dishonor its commitments translated into a newfound ability to borrow: the Crown's borrowing increased and interest rates fell, because lenders concluded that the Crown would honor its debts.

Thanks to North, Weingast, and others writing
(50) in the same vein, it is now conventional to hold that constitutional arrangements benefit sovereigns by limiting their power. But such scholars neglect the extent to which constitutions can fail in this regard. For example, the constitutional settlement imposed
(55) by the Glorious Revolution did not solve the paradox of omnipotence but just relocated the problem from one branch of government to another: whereas it was once the Crown that lacked the power to bind itself, it is now Parliament that lacks this power. The
(60) doctrine of parliamentary sovereignty is a pillar of England's unwritten constitution, and it provides that Parliament lacks legal power over the extent of its own legal power.

20. Which one of the following most accurately expresses the main point of the passage?

(A) The paradox of omnipotence poses a practical problem for governments, which is not necessarily solved by constitutional arrangements.
(B) Abstract theoretical paradoxes often have practical analogues in the political sphere.
(C) The paradox of omnipotence ceased to be an acute practical problem for English monarchs after the Glorious Revolution.
(D) Contrary to what many social scientists believe, the Glorious Revolution did not solve the practical problem of sovereign omnipotence faced by English monarchs.
(E) The supposition that a sovereign has unlimited legal power leads to a logical contradiction.

21. The passage most strongly supports the claim that creditors in England and France in the years before 1688 held which one of the following views about wealthy subjects in those countries?

(A) They did not contribute their fair share to the cost of expanding the empires.
(B) They focused on short-term gains at the expense of their own credibility.
(C) They were trying to establish a government that would respect property rights.
(D) They clearly understood the paradox of sovereign omnipotence.
(E) They were more likely than their monarchs to honor financial commitments.

October 2012, Passage 4

22. Based on the passage, which one of the following considerations would be most important for an English creditor after the Glorious Revolution who is deciding whether to lend money to the Crown at a relatively low interest rate?

    (A) whether most members of Parliament are aware of the paradox of sovereign omnipotence
    (B) whether Parliament can be depended on to adequately represent commercial interests
    (C) when the most recent Parliamentary elections were held
    (D) how many new laws Parliament has enacted in the past year
    (E) whether the Crown's borrowing has increased in recent years

23. Which one of the following principles underlies the author's argument in the last paragraph of the passage?

    (A) The adequacy of a solution to a political problem should be judged in terms of practical consequences rather than theoretical considerations.
    (B) A genuine solution to a political problem must eliminate the problem's fundamental cause rather than just its effects.
    (C) A problem inherent in a certain form of government can be solved only if that form of government is completely abandoned.
    (D) In terms of practical consequences, it is preferable for unlimited legal power to rest with an elected body rather than an unelected monarch.
    (E) A country's constitution should explicitly specify the powers of each branch of government.

24. According to the passage, which one of the following was a consequence of the absence of limitations on the legal power of English and French monarchs in the seventeenth and eighteenth centuries?

    (A) It was difficult for those monarchs to finance the expansion of their empires.
    (B) Those monarchs enacted new laws to specify the obligations of creditors.
    (C) It became increasingly easy for wealthy subjects in England and France to borrow money.
    (D) Those monarchs borrowed more money than they would have if their power had been restricted.
    (E) Those monarchs were forced to demonstrate a willingness to respect property rights.

25. The author mentions the English and French monarchies' need for capital (lines 24–26) primarily in order to

    (A) cast doubt on the claim that it is in a sovereign's interest to make a commitment not to perform certain acts
    (B) illustrate the low opinion that creditors had of monarchs
    (C) emphasize the unlimited nature of the legal power of monarchs
    (D) help explain why the paradox of omnipotence was an acute practical problem for those monarchies
    (E) reinforce the claim that sovereigns have historically broken their commitments for short-term gain

26. Suppose the Parliament in England makes a commitment to become a permanent member of a multinational body. It can be inferred from the passage that

    (A) the commitment will undermine Parliament's ability to obtain credit on favorable terms
    (B) lenders will become more confident that Parliament will honor its debts
    (C) Parliament has the legal authority to end the commitment at any time
    (D) the commercial interests represented by Parliament will disapprove of the commitment
    (E) the commitment will increase Parliament's legal power

27. Which one of the following claims would be accepted by North and Weingast but not by the author of the passage?

    (A) After 1688, commercial interests in England trusted Parliament to protect their property rights.
    (B) The paradox of omnipotence is no longer a practical problem for any actual government.
    (C) In England, the Crown was able to borrow money at lower interest rates after the Glorious Revolution than before.
    (D) In the seventeenth century, English and French monarchs had a reputation for failing to uphold financial commitments.
    (E) The constitutional settlement imposed by the Glorious Revolution solved the problem of sovereign omnipotence.

David Warsh's book describes a great contradiction inherent in economic theory since 1776, when Adam Smith published *The Wealth of Nations*. Warsh calls it the struggle between the Pin Factory and
(5) the Invisible Hand.

Using the example of a pin factory, Smith emphasized the huge increases in efficiency that could be achieved through increased size. The pin factory's employees, by specializing on narrow tasks, produce
(10) far more than they could if each worked independently. Also, Smith was the first to recognize how a market economy can harness self-interest to the common good, leading each individual as though "by an invisible hand to promote an end which was no part of
(15) his intention." For example, businesses sell products that people want, at reasonable prices, not because the business owners inherently want to please people but because doing so enables them to make money in a competitive marketplace.

(20) These two concepts, however, are opposed to each other. The parable of the pin factory says that there are increasing returns to scale—the bigger the pin factory, the more specialized its workers can be, and therefore the more pins the factory can produce per worker. But
(25) increasing returns create a natural tendency toward monopoly, because a large business can achieve larger scale and hence lower costs than a small business. So given increasing returns, bigger firms tend to drive smaller firms out of business, until each industry is
(30) dominated by just a few players. But for the invisible hand to work properly, there must be many competitors in each industry, so that nobody can exert monopoly power. Therefore, the idea that free markets always get it right depends on the assumption that returns to scale
(35) are diminishing, not increasing.

For almost two centuries, the assumption of diminishing returns dominated economic theory, with the Pin Factory de-emphasized. Why? As Warsh explains, it wasn't about ideology; it was about
(40) following the line of least mathematical resistance. Economics has always had scientific aspirations; economists have always sought the rigor and clarity that comes from representing their ideas using numbers and equations. And the economics of diminishing
(45) returns lend themselves readily to elegant formalism, while those of increasing returns—the Pin Factory— are notoriously hard to represent mathematically.

Many economists tried repeatedly to bring the Pin Factory into the mainstream of economic thought
(50) to reflect the fact that increasing returns obviously characterized many enterprises, such as railroads. Yet they repeatedly failed because they could not state their ideas rigorously enough. Only since the late 1970s has this "underground river"—a term used to
(55) describe the role of increasing returns in economic thought—surfaced into the mainstream of economic thought. By then, economists had finally found ways to describe the Pin Factory with the rigor needed to make it respectable.

15. Which one of the following most accurately expresses the main point of the passage?

(A) Mainstream economists have always assumed that returns to scale are generally increasing rather than decreasing.
(B) The functioning of the Invisible Hand is accepted primarily because diminishing returns can be described with mathematical rigor.
(C) Recent developments in mathematics have enabled the Pin Factory to be modeled even more rigorously than the Invisible Hand.
(D) Adam Smith was the first economist to understand how a market economy can enable individual self-interest to serve the common good.
(E) Economists have, until somewhat recently, failed to account for the increasing returns to scale common in many industries.

16. The author's attitude towards the idea that the Pin Factory model should be part of the mainstream of economic thought could most accurately be described as one of

(A) hostility
(B) uncertainty
(C) curiosity
(D) indifference
(E) receptivity

17. The main purpose of the fourth paragraph is to

(A) critique a theory purporting to resolve the tensions between two economic assumptions
(B) explain a difficulty associated with modeling a particular economic assumption
(C) outline the intuitions supporting a particular economic assumption
(D) describe the tensions resulting from attempts to model two competing economic assumptions
(E) refute an argument against a particular economic assumption

December 2012, Passage 3

18. It can be inferred from the passage that the Pin Factory model would continue to be an "underground river" (line 54) were it not for

    (A) the fact that economics has always been a discipline with scientific aspirations
    (B) David Warsh's analysis of the work of Adam Smith
    (C) economists' success in representing the Pin Factory model with mathematical rigor
    (D) a sudden increase in the tendency of some industries toward monopoly
    (E) a lowering of the standards used by economists to assess economic models

19. The reference to railroads (line 51) serves to

    (A) resolve an ambiguity inherent in the metaphor of the Invisible Hand
    (B) illustrate the difficulty of stating the concept of the Pin Factory with mathematical rigor
    (C) call attention to the increasing prevalence of industries that have characteristics of the Pin Factory
    (D) point to an industry that illustrates the shortcomings of economists' emphasis on the Invisible Hand
    (E) present an example of the high levels of competition achieved in transportation industries

20. Which one of the following best illustrates the concept of increasing returns to scale described in the second paragraph of the passage?

    (A) A publishing house is able to greatly improve the productivity of its editors by relaxing the standards to which those editors must adhere. This allows the publishing house to employ many fewer editors.
    (B) A large bee colony is able to use some bees solely to guard its nectar sources. This enables the colony to collect more nectar, which can feed a larger colony that can better divide up the work of processing the nectar.
    (C) A school district increases the total number of students that can be accommodated in a single building by switching to year-round operation, with a different quarter of its student body on vacation at any given time.
    (D) The lobster industry as a whole is able to catch substantially more lobsters a day with the same number of traps because advances in technology make the doors to the traps easier for lobsters to get through.
    (E) A large ant colony divides and produces two competing colonies that each eventually grow large and prosperous enough to divide into more colonies. These colonies together contain more ants than could have existed in one colony.

21. The passage states which one of the following?

    (A) The only way that increasing returns to scale could occur is through increases in the specialization of workers.
    (B) Economics fails in its quest to be scientific because its models lack mathematical rigor.
    (C) The Pin Factory model's long-standing failure to gain prominence among economists was not a problem of ideology.
    (D) Under the Pin Factory model no one is in a position to exert monopoly power.
    (E) Adam Smith did not recognize any tension between the Pin Factory model and the Invisible Hand model.

22. Which one of the following, if true, would most undermine the connection that the author draws between increased size and monopoly power?

    (A) In some industries, there are businesses that are able to exert monopoly power in one geographical region even though there are larger businesses in the same industry in other regions.
    (B) As the tasks workers focus on become narrower, the workers are not able to command as high a salary as when they were performing a greater variety of tasks.
    (C) When an industry is dominated by only a few players, these businesses often collude in order to set prices as high as a true monopoly would.
    (D) The size that a business must reach in order to begin to achieve increasing returns to scale varies widely from industry to industry.
    (E) If a business has very specialized workers, any gains in productivity achieved by making workers even more specialized are offset by other factors such as higher training costs and increased turnover.

An organism is considered to have an infection when a disease-causing agent, called a pathogen, establishes a viable presence in the organism. This can occur only if the pathogenic agent is able to reproduce
(5) itself in the host organism. The only agents believed until recently to be responsible for infections—viruses, bacteria, fungi, and parasites—reproduce and regulate their other life processes by means of genetic material, composed of nucleic acid (DNA or RNA). It was thus
(10) widely assumed that all pathogens contain such genetic material in their cellular structure.

This assumption has been challenged, however, by scientists seeking to identify the pathogen that causes Creutzfeldt-Jakob disease (CJD), a degenerative
(15) form of dementia in humans. CJD causes the brain to become riddled with tiny holes, like a sponge (evidence of extensive nerve cell death). Its symptoms include impaired muscle control, loss of mental acuity, memory loss, and chronic insomnia. Extensive experiments
(20) aimed at identifying the pathogen responsible for CJD have led surprisingly to the isolation of a disease agent lacking nucleic acid and consisting mainly, if not exclusively, of protein. Researchers coined the term "prion" for this new type of protein pathogen.

(25) Upon further study, scientists discovered that prions normally exist as harmless cellular proteins in many of the body's tissues, including white blood cells and nerve cells in the brain; however, they possess the capability of converting their structures into a dangerous abnormal
(30) shape. Prions exhibiting this abnormal conformation were found to have infectious properties and the ability to reproduce themselves in an unexpected way, by initiating a chain reaction that induces normally shaped prions to transform themselves on contact, one after
(35) another, into the abnormal, pathogenic conformation. This cascade of transformations produces a plaque, consisting of thread-like structures, that collects in the brain and ultimately destroys nerve cells. Because prions, unlike other pathogens, occur naturally in the
(40) body as proteins, the body does not produce an immune response when they are present. And in the absence of any effective therapy for preventing the cascade process by which affected prions reproduce themselves, CJD is inevitably fatal, though there are wide variations in pre-
(45) symptomatic incubation times and in how aggressively the disease progresses.

Although the discovery of the link between prions and CJD was initially received with great skepticism in the scientific community, subsequent research has
(50) supported the conclusion that prions are an entirely new class of infectious pathogens. Furthermore, it is now believed that a similar process of protein malformation may be involved in other, more common degenerative neurological conditions such as Alzheimer's disease
(55) and Parkinson's disease. This possibility has yet to be fully explored, however, and the exact mechanisms by which prions reproduce themselves and cause cellular destruction have yet to be completely understood.

1. Which one of the following most accurately expresses the main point of the passage?

    (A) Although most organisms are known to produce several kinds of proteins, the mechanism by which isolated protein molecules such as prions reproduce themselves is not yet known in detail.
    (B) Research into the cause of CJD has uncovered a deadly class of protein pathogens uniquely capable of reproducing themselves without genetic material.
    (C) Recent research suggests that prions may be responsible not only for CJD, but for most other degenerative neurological conditions as well.
    (D) The assertion that prions cause CJD has been received with great skepticism in the scientific community because it undermines a firmly entrenched view about the nature of pathogens.
    (E) Even though prions contain no genetic material, it has become clear that they are somehow capable of reproducing themselves.

October 2013, Passage 1

2. Which one of the following is most strongly supported by the passage?

   (A) Understanding the cause of CJD has required scientists to reconsider their traditional beliefs about the causes of infection.
   (B) CJD is contagious, though not highly so.
   (C) The prevention of CJD would be most efficiently achieved by the prevention of certain genetic abnormalities.
   (D) Although patients with CJD exhibit different incubation times, the disease progresses at about the same rate in all patients once symptoms are manifested.
   (E) The prion theory of infection has weak support within the scientific community.

3. If the hypothesis that CJD is caused by prions is correct, finding the answer to which one of the following questions would tend most to help a physician in deciding whether a patient has CJD?

   (A) Has the patient suffered a severe blow to the skull recently?
   (B) Does the patient experience occasional bouts of insomnia?
   (C) Has the patient been exposed to any forms of radiation that have a known tendency to cause certain kinds of genetic damage?
   (D) Has any member of the patient's immediate family ever had a brain disease?
   (E) Does the patient's brain tissue exhibit the presence of any abnormal thread-like structures?

4. Which one of the following is most strongly supported by the passage?

   (A) The only way in which CJD can be transmitted is through the injection of abnormally shaped prions from an infected individual into an uninfected individual.
   (B) Most infectious diseases previously thought to be caused by other pathogens are now thought to be caused by prions.
   (C) If they were unable to reproduce themselves, abnormally shaped prions would not cause CJD.
   (D) Alzheimer's disease and Parkinson's disease are caused by different conformations of the same prion pathogen that causes CJD.
   (E) Prion diseases generally progress more aggressively than diseases caused by other known pathogens.

5. It can be inferred from the passage that the author would be LEAST likely to agree with which one of the following?

   (A) The presence of certain abnormally shaped prions in brain tissue is a sign of neurological disease.
   (B) Some patients currently infected with CJD will recover from the disease.
   (C) Prions do not require nucleic acid for their reproduction.
   (D) The body has no natural defense against CJD.
   (E) Scientists have only a partial understanding of the mechanism by which prions reproduce.

6. Given the manner in which the term "pathogen" is used in the passage, and assuming that the prion theory of infection is correct, which one of the following statements must be false?

   (A) Nothing that lacks nucleic acid is a pathogen.
   (B) Prions are a relatively newly discovered type of pathogen.
   (C) All pathogens can cause infection.
   (D) Pathogens contribute in some manner to the occurrence of CJD.
   (E) There are other pathogens besides viruses, bacteria, fungi, and parasites.

7. Which one of the following, if true, would most undermine the claim that prions cause CJD?

   (A) Several symptoms closely resembling those of CJD have been experienced by patients known to have a specific viral infection.
   (B) None of the therapies currently available for treating neurological diseases is designed to block the chain reaction by which abnormal prions are believed to reproduce.
   (C) Research undertaken subsequent to the studies on CJD has linked prions to degenerative conditions not affecting the brain or the central nervous system.
   (D) Epidemiological studies carried out on a large population have failed to show any hereditary predisposition to CJD.
   (E) A newly developed antibacterial drug currently undergoing clinical trials is proving to be effective in reversing the onset of CJD.

Taking the explication of experience as its object as well as its method, Marjorie Shostak's *Nisa: The Life and Words of a !Kung Woman* weaves together three narrative strands, and in doing
(5) so challenges the ethnographer's penchant for the general and the anonymous. The first strand, the autobiographical details of a 50-year-old woman's life among the seminomadic !Kung hunter-gatherers of Botswana, adds to the ethnographical literature
(10) on the !Kung. The second presents Nisa's story as a metaphor for woman's experience, a story that reflects many of the experiences and dilemmas addressed in recent feminist writing. The third tells the story of an intercultural encounter in which the distinction
(15) between ethnographer and subject becomes blurred.

Nisa explains Nisa's personality in terms of !Kung ways and, for the general reader, corrects and qualifies a number of received attitudes about "simple" societies. Michel Leiris' warning that "We are all too
(20) inclined to consider a people happy if considering them makes us happy" applies particularly to the !Kung, whose seemingly uncomplicated way of life, enlightened attitudes toward child rearing, and undeniable charm make them prime candidates for
(25) Western appreciation. But Nisa's answer to Shostak's question, "What is it to be a !Kung woman?" makes us feel the force of ugly facts we might otherwise skim over. Only 54 percent of !Kung children live to marry; Nisa loses all four of her children and a cherished
(30) husband. Nisa's memories of sibling rivalries, of her terrible rages when denied her mother, of nasty fights over food undermine the idyllic vision Westerners cherish of childhoods lived in such "simple" circumstances.

(35) Woven into Nisa's autobiography are allusions to Shostak's personal engagement with issues of gender. Nisa's response to "What is it to be a !Kung woman?" also seems to answer another question, "What is it to be a woman?" In fact, Nisa's answers illuminate not
(40) just one woman's experience, but women's experience in general. It is a salutary shock to realize how much ethnographic literature omits the perspective of women about women.

Nisa's story is interwoven with Shostak's
(45) presentation of their encounter; at times each seems to exist primarily in response to the other. Nisa's autobiography is a distinct narrative in a particular voice, but it is manifestly the product of a collaboration. Indeed, by casting *Nisa* in the shape of
(50) a "life," Shostak employs a potent Western literary convention. Real lives, in fact, do not easily arrange themselves as stories that have recognizable shapes: Nisa, for example, often says "We lived in that place, eating things. Then we left and went somewhere
(55) else." It is in the process of the dialogue between Nisa and Shostak that a shaped story emerges from this seemingly featureless background.

8. Shostak's approach to ethnography differs from the approach of most ethnographers in which one of the following ways?

   (A) She observes the culture of one group in order to infer the cultural characteristics of other, similar groups.
   (B) She studies the life experiences of individuals apart from the cultural practices of a group.
   (C) She contrasts individuals' personal histories with information about the individuals' culture.
   (D) She exemplifies her general hypotheses about a culture by accumulating illustrative empirical data.
   (E) She emphasizes the importance of the personal and the individual.

9. Which one of the following best expresses the author's opinion of the way most ethnographic literature deals with women's views of women?

   (A) It is admirable that many ethnographic studies avoid the narrow focus of some recent feminist thought as it deals with women's views of women.
   (B) It is encouraging that most women ethnographers have begun to study and report the views of women in the groups they study.
   (C) It is unfortunate that most ethnographic literature does not deal with women's views of women at all.
   (D) It is surprising that more ethnographic studies of women do not use the information available through individual interviews of women about women.
   (E) It is disappointing that most ethnographic studies of women's views about women fail to connect individual experiences with larger women's issues.

October 2012, Passage 2

10. It can be inferred that which one of the following best exemplifies the "received attitudes" mentioned in line 18?

    (A) The !Kung are people of undeniable charm.
    (B) Considering the !Kung makes Western observers happy.
    (C) People who live seminomadic lives have few serious problems.
    (D) A large percentage of !Kung children die before reaching adulthood.
    (E) The experience of seminomadic women is much like that of other women.

11. Which one of the following would most clearly support the author's contention that Nisa's experience as a !Kung woman illuminates women's experience in general?

    (A) A systematic survey of a representative sample of Western women indicates that these women sympathize with Nisa's tragedies.
    (B) The use of the explication of experience as both a subject and a method becomes an extremely fruitful technique for ethnographers studying issues facing both men and women in non-Western cultures.
    (C) Critics of feminist writers applaud the use of Shostak's dialogue technique in the study of women's issues.
    (D) Another ethnographer explores the experiences of individual women in a culture quite different from that of the !Kung and finds many issues that are common to both cultures.
    (E) Ethnographers studying the !Kung interview !Kung women other than Nisa and find that most of them report experiences similar to those of Nisa.

12. It can be inferred that the "potent Western literary convention" mentioned in lines 50-51 is most probably which one of the following?

    (A) personal revelation
    (B) dramatic emphasis
    (C) expository comparison
    (D) poetic metaphor
    (E) novelistic storytelling

13. The approach of which one of the following is most similar to Shostak's approach as her approach is described in the passage?

    (A) The producer of a documentary film interacts on film with the film's subject to reveal insights about the subject's life.
    (B) A work presented as an athlete's autobiography is actually ghostwritten by a famous biographer.
    (C) An ethnographer describes the day-to-day life of an individual in order to exemplify the way of life of a group of desert dwellers.
    (D) A writer illustrates her views of women's experience by recounting stories from her own childhood.
    (E) The developer of a series of textbooks uses anecdotes based on the experiences of people of many cultures to highlight important points in the text.

14. It can be inferred that the author of the passage believes that the quotation in lines 53-55 best exemplifies which one of the following?

    (A) the cultural values of seminomadic peoples such as the !Kung
    (B) the amorphous nature of the accounts people give of their lives
    (C) the less-than-idyllic nature of the lives of nomadic people
    (D) an autobiographical account that has a recognizable story
    (E) a distinction between ethnographer and subject

Passage A

Research concerning happiness and wealth reveals a paradox: at any one time richer people report higher levels of happiness than poorer people in the same society report, and yet over time advanced societies
(5) have not grown happier as they have grown richer. Apparently, people are comparing their income with some norm, and that norm must be rising along with actual income. Two phenomena—habituation and rivalry—push up the norm.
(10) When our living standards increase, we love it initially but then we adjust and it makes little difference. For example, if we ask people with different incomes what income they consider sufficient, the "required income" correlates strongly with their actual
(15) income: a rise in actual income causes a roughly equivalent rise in required income. We can also look at reported happiness over time. Job satisfaction depends little on the absolute level of wages but rises if wages rapidly increase.
(20) We do not have the same experience with other aspects of our lives. We do not foresee how we adjust to material possessions, so we overinvest in acquiring them, at the expense of leisure.
Now consider the phenomenon of rivalry. In a
(25) study conducted by Solnick and Hemenway, people were asked to choose between two options, with all prices held constant:
A. You earn $50,000 a year while everyone else earns $25,000;
(30) B. You earn $100,000 a year while others make $200,000.
The majority chose the first. They were happy to be poorer, provided their relative position improved.
And indeed, how people compare to their
(35) "reference group"—those most like them—is crucial for happiness. In East Germany, for example, living standards have soared since 1990, but the level of happiness has plummeted because people now compare themselves with West Germans, rather than with people
(40) in other Soviet bloc countries.

Passage B

Does the Solnick and Hemenway study mean that we care most about one-upmanship? Perhaps out of our primeval past comes the urge to demonstrate our superiority in order to help ensure mating prospects,
(45) keeping our genetic lines going. Still programmed like this, we get unexplainable pleasure from having a bigger house than our neighbors.
This theory may sound good and is commonly heard, but it is not the explanation best supported by
(50) the evidence. Rather, the data show that earning more makes people happier because relative prosperity makes them feel that they are successful, that they have created value.
If two people feel equally successful, they will
(55) be equally happy even if their incomes differ greatly. Of course, people who earn more generally view themselves as successful. But it is the success—not the money per se—that provides the happiness. We use material wealth to show not just that we are
(60) prosperous, but that we are prosperous because we create value.
What scholars often portray as an ignoble tendency—wanting to have more than others—is really evidence of a desire to create value. Wanting to
(65) create value benefits society. It is a bonus that it also brings happiness.

15. Both passages are primarily concerned with explaining which one of the following?

(A) the human desire to create value
(B) the relationship between income and happiness
(C) the biological basis of people's attitudes toward wealth
(D) the human propensity to become habituated to wealth
(E) the concept of "required income"

16. The author of passage B would be most likely to agree with which one of the following statements?

(A) The desire to demonstrate that one is wealthier than others is a remnant of human beings' primeval past.
(B) Very few people would be willing to accept a lower standard of living in return for greater relative wealth.
(C) Being wealthier than other people would not make one happier if one believed that one's wealth was due merely to luck.
(D) Gradual increases in employees' wages do not increase their job satisfaction.
(E) The overall level of happiness in a society usually increases as the society becomes wealthier.

17. The author of passage B would be most likely to regard the conclusion that the Solnick and Hemenway study points to the existence of a "phenomenon of rivalry" (line 24) as

   (A) ungenerous in its view of human nature and mistaken in its interpretation of the evidence
   (B) flattering in its implications about human nature but only weakly supported by the available evidence
   (C) plausible in its account of human nature but based largely upon ambiguous evidence
   (D) unflattering in its implications about human nature but more or less valid in the conclusions drawn from the evidence
   (E) accurate concerning human nature and strongly supported by the evidence

18. Which one of the following pairs most accurately describes why the authors of passage A and passage B, respectively, mention the study by Solnick and Hemenway?

   (A) to present a view that will be argued against
   to present a view for which additional evidence will be provided
   (B) to present a view that will be argued against
   to provide evidence for one explanation of a phenomenon
   (C) to provide evidence for one explanation of a phenomenon
   to present a view for which additional evidence will be provided
   (D) to provide evidence for one explanation of a phenomenon
   to introduce the main topic to be discussed
   (E) to introduce the main topic to be discussed
   to present a view that will be argued against

19. Which one of the following pairs of terms would most likely be used by the authors of passage A and passage B, respectively, to describe a person who wants to make more money than his or her neighbors?

   (A) insular, cosmopolitan
   (B) altruistic, egocentric
   (C) happy, miserable
   (D) misguided, admirable
   (E) lucky, primitive

20. In arguing for their respective positions, the author of passage A and the author of passage B both do which one of the following?

   (A) explain a phenomenon by pointing to its biological origins
   (B) endorse a claim simply because it is widely believed
   (C) accept a claim for the sake of argument
   (D) attempt to resolve an apparent paradox
   (E) assert that their positions are supported by data

With his first published works in the 1950s, Amos Tutuola became the first Nigerian writer to receive wide international recognition. Written in a mix of standard English, idiomatic Nigerian English, and literal translation of his native language, Yoruba, Tutuola's works were quick to be praised by many literary critics as fresh, inventive approaches to the form of the novel. Others, however, dismissed his works as simple retellings of local tales, full of unwelcome liberties taken with the details of the well-known story lines. However, to estimate properly Tutuola's rightful position in world literature, it is essential to be clear about the genre in which he wrote; literary critics have assumed too facilely that he wrote novels.

No matter how flexible a definition of the novel one uses, establishing a set of criteria that enable Tutuola's works to be described as such applies to his works a body of assumptions the works are not designed to satisfy. Tutuola is not a novelist but a teller of folktales. Many of his critics are right to suggest that Tutuola's subjects are not strikingly original, but it is important to bear in mind that whereas realism and originality are expected of the novel, the teller of folktales is expected to derive subjects and frameworks from the corpus of traditional lore. The most useful approach to Tutuola's works, then, is one that regards him as working within the African oral tradition.

Within this tradition, a folktale is common property, an expression of a people's culture and social circumstances. The teller of folktales knows that the basic story is already known to most listeners and, equally, that the teller's reputation depends on the inventiveness with which the tale is modified and embellished, for what the audience anticipates is not an accurate retelling of the story but effective improvisation and delivery. Thus, within the framework of the basic story, the teller is allowed considerable room to maneuver—in fact, the most brilliant tellers of folktales transform them into unique works.

Tutuola's adherence to this tradition is clear: specific episodes, for example, are often repeated for emphasis, and he embellishes familiar tales with personal interpretations or by transferring them to modern settings. The blend of English with local idiom and Yoruba grammatical constructs, in which adjectives and verbs are often interchangeable, re-creates the folktales in singular ways. And, perhaps most revealingly, in the majority of Tutuola's works, the traditional accents and techniques of the teller of folktales are clearly discernible, for example in the adoption of an omniscient, summarizing voice at the end of his narratives, a device that is generally recognized as being employed to conclude most folktales.

1. Which one of the following most accurately expresses the main point of the passage?

    (A) Amos Tutuola is an internationally acclaimed writer of folktales whose unique writing style blends together aspects of Yoruba, Nigerian English, and standard English.
    (B) Amos Tutuola's literary works should be evaluated not as novels but as unique and inventively crafted retellings of folktales.
    (C) Amos Tutuola is an important author because he is able to incorporate the traditions of an oral art form into his novels.
    (D) Critics are divided as to whether Amos Tutuola's literary works should be regarded as novels or folktales.
    (E) The folktale is a valuable African literary genre that finds singular expression in the works of Amos Tutuola.

2. Tutuola's approach to writing folktales would be most clearly exemplified by a modern-day Irish author who

    (A) applied conventions of the modern novel to the retelling of Irish folktales
    (B) re-created important elements of the Irish literary style within a purely oral art form
    (C) combined characters from English and Irish folktales to tell a story of modern life
    (D) transplanted traditional Irish folktales from their original setting to contemporary Irish life
    (E) utilized an omniscient narrator in telling original stories about contemporary Irish life

December 2008, Passage 1

3. Which one of the following most accurately characterizes the author's attitude toward Tutuola's position in world literature?

(A) convinced that Tutuola's works should be viewed within the context of the African oral tradition
(B) certain that Tutuola's works will generate a renewed interest in the study of oral traditions
(C) pleased at the reception that Tutuola's works have received from literary critics
(D) confident that the original integrity of Tutuola's works will be preserved despite numerous translations
(E) optimistic that Tutuola's works reflect what will become a growing new trend in literature

4. According to the passage, some critics have criticized Tutuola's work on the ground that

(A) his literary works do not exhibit enough similarities to the African oral tradition from which they are drawn
(B) his mixture of languages is not entirely effective as a vehicle for either traditional folktales or contemporary novels
(C) his attempt to fuse elements of traditional storytelling style with the format of the novel is detrimental to his artistic purposes
(D) his writing borrows substantially from well-known story lines and at the same time alters their details
(E) his unique works are not actually novels, even though he characterizes them as such

5. The author attributes each of the following to Tutuola EXCEPT:

(A) repetition of elements in his stories for emphasis
(B) relocation of traditional stories to modern settings
(C) attainment of international recognition
(D) use of an omniscient narrator in his works
(E) transformation of Yoruba folktales into modern novels

6. The author refers to the "corpus of traditional lore" (lines 26–27) as part of an attempt to

(A) distinguish expectations that apply to one literary genre from those that apply to another literary genre
(B) argue that two sharply differing literary genres are both equally valuable
(C) challenge critics who ascribe little merit to innovative ways of blending two distinct literary genres
(D) elucidate those characteristics of one literary genre that have direct counterparts in another, largely dissimilar genre
(E) argue for a new, more precise analysis of two literary genres whose distinguishing characteristics are poorly understood

7. The primary purpose of the passage is to

(A) illustrate the wide range of Tutuola's body of work
(B) explain the significance of the literary genre of the folktale and to defend it as a valid art form
(C) provide an account of Tutuola's body of work in order to help establish appropriate criteria for its evaluation
(D) distinguish accurately between the genre of the novel and that of the folktale
(E) summarize the disagreement among critics regarding Tutuola's place in world literature

In certain fields of human endeavor, such as music, chess, and some athletic activities, the performance of the best practitioners is so outstanding, so superior even to the performance of other highly experienced individuals in the field, that some people believe some
(5) notion of innate talent must be invoked to account for this highest level of performance. Certain psychologists have supported this view with data concerning the performance of prodigies and the apparent heritability of relevant traits. They have noted, for example, that
(10) most outstanding musicians are discovered by the age of six, and they have found evidence that some of the qualities necessary for exceptional athletic performance, including superior motor coordination, speed of reflexes, and hand-eye coordination, can be
(15) inborn.

Until recently, however, little systematic research was done on the topic of superior performance, and previous estimates of the heritability of traits relevant to performance were based almost exclusively on
(20) random samples of the general population rather than on studies of highly trained superior performers as compared with the general population. Recent research in different domains of excellence suggests that exceptional performance arises predominantly from
(25) acquired complex skills and physiological adaptations, rather than from innate abilities. For example, it has been found that the most accomplished athletes show a systematic advantage in reaction time or perceptual discrimination only in their particular fields of
(30) performance, not in more general laboratory tests for these factors. Similarly, superior chess players have exceptional memory for configurations of chess pieces, but only if those configurations are typical of chess games.

(35) The vast majority of exceptional adult performers were not exceptional as children, but started instruction early and improved their performance through sustained high-level training. Only extremely rarely is outstanding performance achieved without at least
(40) ten years of intensive, deliberate practice. With such intensive training, chess players who may not have superior innate capacities can acquire skills that circumvent basic limits on such factors as memory and the ability to process information. Recent research shows that, with the clear exception of some traits such as height, a surprisingly large number of anatomical
(45) characteristics, including aerobic capacity and the percentage of muscle fibers, show specific changes that develop from extended intense training.

The evidence does not, therefore, support the claim that a notion of innate talent must be invoked
(50) in order to account for the difference between good and outstanding performance, since it suggests instead that extended intense training, together with that level of talent common to all reasonably competent performers, may suffice to account for this difference.
(55) Since sustained intense training usually depends on an appropriate level of interest and desire, and since those who eventually become superior performers more often show early signs of exceptional interest than early evidence of unusual ability, motivational factors
(60) are more likely to be effective predictors of superior performance than is innate talent.

14. Which one of the following most accurately states the main point of the passage?

(A) Researchers have recently found that many inborn traits, including a surprising number of physical characteristics and motivational factors, can be altered through training and practice.
(B) Recent research into the origins of superior performance gives evidence that in sports, music, and some other fields of activity, anyone can achieve exceptional levels of performance with sustained intense practice and training.
(C) Contrary to previously accepted theories of the development of expertise, researchers have now shown that innate characteristics are irrelevant to the differences in performance among individual practitioners in various fields of activity.
(D) Recent research involving superior performers in various fields indicates that outstanding performance may result from adaptations due to training rather than from innate factors.
(E) Psychologists who previously attributed early childhood proficiency in such activities as music and chess to innate talent have revised their theories in light of new evidence of the effectiveness of training and practice.

December 2013, Passage 3

15. Which one of the following most accurately represents the primary function of the final paragraph?

    (A) It makes proposals for educational reform based on the evidence cited by the author.
    (B) It demonstrates that two consequences of the findings regarding superior performance are at odds with one another.
    (C) It recapitulates the evidence against the supposed heritability of outstanding talent and advocates a particular direction to be taken in future research on the topic.
    (D) It raises and answers a possible objection to the author's view of the importance of intense training.
    (E) It draws two inferences regarding the explanatory and predictive roles of possible factors in the development of superior performance.

16. Which one of the following can most reasonably be inferred from the passage?

    (A) In at least some fields of human endeavor, it would be difficult, or perhaps even impossible, to ascertain whether or not a superior performer with extensive training has exceptional innate talent.
    (B) Performance at the very highest level generally requires both the highest level of innate talent and many years of intensive, deliberate practice.
    (C) Exceptional innate talent is a prerequisite to exceptional performance in some fields of human endeavor but not others.
    (D) Exceptional innate talent is probably an obstacle to the development of superior performance, since such talent results in complacency.
    (E) The importance of motivation and interest in the development of superior performance shows that in some fields the production of exceptional skill does not depend in any way on innate talents of individuals.

17. Which one of the following does the passage say is usually necessary in order for one to keep up intense practice?

    (A) desire and interest
    (B) emotional support from other people
    (C) appropriate instruction at the right age
    (D) sufficient leisure time to devote to practice
    (E) self-discipline and control

18. Which one of the following most accurately describes the author's main purpose in the passage?

    (A) to illustrate the ways in which a revised theoretical model can be applied to problematic cases for which previous versions of the theory offered no plausible explanation
    (B) to argue that the evidence that was previously taken to support a particular theory in fact supports an opposing theory
    (C) to show how a body of recent research provides evidence that certain views based on earlier research are not applicable to a particular class of cases
    (D) to defend the author's new interpretation of data against probable objections that might be raised against it
    (E) to explain how a set of newly formulated abstract theoretical postulations relates to a long-standing body of experimental data in a different, but related, field of inquiry

19. The passage says that superior chess players do not have exceptional memory for which one of the following?

    (A) some sequences of moves that are typical of games other than chess
    (B) some types of complex sequences without spatial components
    (C) some chess games that have not been especially challenging
    (D) some kinds of arrangements of chess pieces
    (E) some types of factors requiring logical analysis in the absence of competition

Physicists are often asked why the image of an object, such as a chair, appears reversed left-to-right rather than, say, top-to-bottom when viewed in a mirror. Their answer is simply that an image viewed in a mirror
(5) appears reversed about the axis around which the viewer rotates his or her field of sight in turning from the object to its reflected image. That is, the reversal in question is relative to the position and orientation of the observer when the object is viewed directly. Since we ordinarily
(10) rotate our field of sight about a vertical axis, mirror images usually appear reversed left-to-right. This is the field-of-sight explanation.

However, some physicists offer a completely different explanation of what mirrors "do," suggesting
(15) that mirrors actually reverse things front-to-back. If we place a chair in front of a mirror we can envision how its reflected image will appear by imagining another chair in the space "inside" the mirror. The resulting reflection is identical to, and directly facing, the original chair. The
(20) most notable thing about this explanation is that it is clearly based on a false premise: the chair "inside" the mirror is not real, yet the explanation treats it as though it were as real and three dimensional as the original chair.

(25) This explanation appeals strongly to many people, however, because it is quite successful at explaining what a mirror does—to a point. It seems natural because we are accustomed to dealing with our mental constructs of objects rather than with the primary sense perceptions
(30) on which those constructs are based. In general, we can safely presume a fairly reliable equation between our perceptions and their associated mental constructs, but mirrors are an exception. They present us with sense perceptions that we naturally construe in a way that is
(35) contrary to fact. Indeed, mirrors are "designed" to make a two-dimensional surface appear to have depth. Note, for example, that mirrors are among the few objects on which we almost never focus our eyes; rather, we look into them, with our focal lengths adjusted into the
(40) imagined space.

In addition to its intuitive appeal, the front-to-back explanation is motivated in part by the traditional desire in science to separate the observer from the phenomenon. Scientists like to think that what mirrors
(45) do should be explainable without reference to what the observer does (e.g., rotating a field of sight). However, questions about the appearances of images can be properly answered only if we consider both what mirrors do and what happens when we look into mirrors.
(50) If we remove the observer from consideration, we are no longer addressing images and appearances, because an image entails an observer and a point of view.

20. The main point of the passage is that an adequate explanation of mirror images

(A) must include two particular elements
(B) has yet to be determined
(C) must be determined by physicists
(D) is still subject to debate
(E) is extremely complicated

21. According to the passage, the left-to-right reversal of objects reflected in mirrors is

(A) a result of the front-to-back reversal of objects reflected in mirrors
(B) a result of the fact that we ordinarily rotate our field of sight about a vertical axis
(C) explained by the size and position of the object reflected in the mirror
(D) explained by the difference between two-dimensional and three-dimensional objects
(E) explained by the mental constructs of those who observe objects reflected in mirrors

22. According to the passage, the fact that we are accustomed to dealing with our mental constructs rather than the primary sense perceptions on which those constructs are based facilitates our ability to

(A) accept the top-to-bottom explanation of what mirrors do
(B) understand the front-to-back explanation of what mirrors do
(C) challenge complex explanations of common perceptual observations
(D) reject customarily reliable equations between perceptions and their associated mental constructs
(E) overemphasize the fact that mirrors simulate sense impressions of objects

23. It can be inferred that the author of the passage believes that the front-to-back explanation of what mirrors do is

(A) successful because it is based on incongruous facts that can be reconciled
(B) successful because it rejects any consideration of mental constructs
(C) successful because it involves the rotation of a field of sight about an axis
(D) successful only to a point because it is consistent with the traditional explanations that physicists have offered
(E) successful only to a point because it does not include what happens when we look into a mirror

24. In the passage the author is primarily concerned with doing which one of the following?

(A) evaluating the experimental evidence for and against two diametrically opposed explanations of a given phenomenon
(B) demonstrating that different explanations of the same phenomenon are based on different empirical observations
(C) describing the difficulties that must be overcome if a satisfactory explanation of a phenomenon is to be found
(D) showing why one explanation of a phenomenon falls short in explaining the phenomenon
(E) relating the theoretical support for an explanation of a phenomenon to the acceptance of that explanation

25. With which one of the following statements would the author of the passage be most likely to agree?

(A) The failure of one recent explanation of what mirrors do illustrates the need for better optical equipment in future experiments with mirrors.
(B) Explanations of what mirrors do generally fail because physicists overlook the differences between objects and reflections of objects.
(C) One explanation of what mirrors do reveals the traditional tendency of physicists to separate a phenomenon to be explained from the observer of the phenomenon.
(D) The degree to which human beings tend to deal directly with mental constructs rather than with primary sense perceptions depends on their training in the sciences.
(E) Considering objects reflected in mirrors to be mental constructs interferes with an accurate understanding of how primary perceptions function.

26. The author would be most likely to agree with which one of the following statements about the field-of-sight explanation of what mirrors do?

(A) This explanation is based on the traditional desire of physicists to simplify the explanation of what mirrors do.
(B) This explanation does not depend on the false premise that images in mirrors have three-dimensional properties.
(C) This explanation fails to take into account the point of view and orientation of someone who is observing reflections in the mirror.
(D) This explanation assumes that people who see something in a mirror do not understand the reality of what they see.
(E) This explanation is unsuccessful because it involves claims about how people rotate their field of sight rather than claims about what people can imagine.

27. The author mentions the fact that we rarely focus our eyes on mirrors (lines 37–39) primarily in order to

(A) contrast our capacity to perceive objects with our capacity to imagine objects
(B) emphasize that it is impossible to perceive reflected objects without using mental constructs of the objects
(C) clarify the idea that mirrors simulate three-dimensional reality
(D) illustrate the fact that we typically deal directly with mental constructs rather than with perceptions
(E) emphasize the degree to which the psychological activity of the observer modifies the shape of the object being perceived

27/keepPRACTICING

We hope that over the course of those ten passages you became confident in the Blueprint methods. But if you still feel like you don't have everything down, don't worry! This chapter is devoted to continued study.

There are two important components to doing well on Reading Comprehension:

1) Mastering the correct technique
2) Implementing the correct techniques in a timed environment

We've spent the previous chapters discussing how to master the Blueprint methods for Reading Comprehension, but the second issue deserves some discussion as well. Obviously, these two issues are related. As you improve your skills, you will naturally get faster.

In fact, the primary way to improve the speed at which you accurately complete Reading Comprehension passages is to get better at understanding them.

This fact cannot be overstated, which is why we've given the sentence its own space, put it in bold italics, and placed a unicorn next to it.

We often hear students state that, "just given enough time" they'd get the questions right, they just need some tips for moving faster. This is a confusion that must be squashed as ruthlessly as a cockroach in a gourmet kitchen. *The number one reason that students don't finish all the questions in Reading Comprehension is that they haven't mastered the techniques.*

What sometimes happens is that students try the Blueprint methods but don't practice them until they become second nature. They then stop using the Blueprint method and return to their old, uninformed way of tackling the passages, or do a sort of hybrid between Blueprint techniques and theirs.

This way lies madness, and it can result in less accuracy and longer times than before you started this book. If you find yourself in this position, STOP. Start the Blueprint methods again without timing yourself and learn them over the course of twenty or so passages. Then start worrying about timing.

So how do you make sure you have our methods down? You need more practice. But practice doesn't make perfect. Perfect practice makes perfect. In this book, outside of exercises, we use only real, honest-to-goodness passages and questions from real past tests. You can find replica passages online and elsewhere, but they suck. Make sure to use only genuine LSAT passages when you study.

On your *MyBlueprint* account, you can buy prep tests a la carte that come with detailed explanations of all sections of the test, including Reading Comprehension.

You can also buy full prep tests through LSAC or other bookselling websites like Amazon. All tests are helpful, but focus on the more recent ones since they are likely to look more like what you will see on test day.

When you continue to practice, don't just start taking full practice tests. You should work through the following stages.

Stage 1: Individual Passage Types

In this book, we focus on individual types of passages, divided into primary structure and secondary structure. You should continue to do the same. By repeatedly doing the same type of passage, you will become more comfortable with its important features and how to identify and understand them.

Lucky for you, you don't have to read each passage from previous tests to determine their structures. We've done it for you!

The appendix at the end of this book characterizes passages dating back to Prep Test 1 by primary and secondary structure, as well as passage placement and difficulty.

Bear in mind that you also don't have to spend the same amount of time on all passage types. Synthesis passages, for instance, do not require as much attention as Antithesis, and Classification structures don't require as much attention as Cause and Effect. You have to play the odds. Spend your time mastering the types of passage you are most likely to see. The following is a chart that shows the prevalence of each passage type dating to 1991 (and since 2007 for more recent numbers).

Passage Type	# since 1991	Percentage	# since 2007	Percentage
Thesis	99	33.45%	30	32.61%
Antithesis	149	50.34%	34	36.96%
Synthesis	25	8.45%	5	5.43%
Comparative Reading	23	7.77%*	23	25.7%

Secondary Structure	# since 1991	Percentage	# since 2007	Percentage
Cause and Effect	42	14.19%	14	15.22%
Example	28	9.46%	11	11.96%
Question & Answer	28	9.46%	6	6.52%
Classification	15	5.07%	7	7.61

* Comparative Reading began in 2007, which is why this number is not 25%.

The post-2007 numbers should be read with a large proviso. This is because we didn't track either the passage type or the secondary structures for Comparative Reading passages. Since there are two, they would have skewed the data even more by leaving them in than by taking them out.

Even so, there's enough information here to help you inform your plan of study. It's clear, for instance, that Cause and Effect reigns supreme with regards to secondary structures, so it warrants putting in a lot of time to making sure you've mastered the skill of spotting them and using them to your full advantage.

Stage 2: Full Sections
When you feel comfortable with individual passage types, it's time to attack entire sections. The new challenge will be jumping between passage types. Warning: Do not time yourself yet. Give yourself plenty of time to understand the structure of the passage and anticipate questions.

At this stage, you might find yourself remembering key structures in the passage and not taking the time to write everything down. That's fine, as long as you're remembering everything you're supposed to. If you find that you didn't tag a local Cause and Effect structure and wasted time in the questions hunting around for it, however, return to tagging everything.

Stage 3: Timed Sections
When you feel comfortable working through sections, then it's time to apply the timing pressure. However, don't crank it up to 35 minutes right out of the gate. It can be helpful to give yourself extra time to begin with. Forty five or fifty minutes is a good starting point. You can lower the time incrementally as you get more comfortable.

28/TIMING

Once you have the methods down, then it's time to focus on timing. On test day, you will have 35 minutes to read four passages (five, if you count comparative reading as two passages) and answer between 26 and 28 questions.

> **Cleetus:** Well, shoot! That ain't even enough time to gut and clean a squirrel! Haha, just kiddin'. I could do prolly a dozen squirrels in that time. Still, though, that's pretty quick!

The following tips are the best way to practice on timing *once you have the method down*.

1. Do not time yourself until you can implement all the Blueprint methods without reading a reminder (i.e. going back and referring to the book).

2. Once you have the techniques down (and only then!), time yourself on a Reading Comprehension passage. Remember, your target time per passage is roughly 8 minutes and 45 seconds. However, some passages take longer and some don't take as long so your goal is anything in the 7-10 minute range. However, for this exercise, give yourself as long as you need to complete the passage correctly.

3. Based on your time (say 20 minutes), do more passages, giving yourself 20 minutes (or whatever your time is) to complete them. You should find yourself moving faster in the later passages.

4. If you aren't completing passages correctly (only missing 2 or fewer questions per passage) by your original time or faster after completing 10 passages, figure out what methodology you're not implementing and review. Return to doing untimed passages to practice technique until you have it down. Return to Step 2.

5. If you are moving faster after Step 3, reduce your time. The closer you are to your target time, the less you should reduce it by. For instance, if you're completing passages in 12 minutes, reduce it by a minute. If you're completing passages in 20 minutes, reduce it by two minutes. Tackle 10 more passages.

6. Repeat this process until you are consistently finishing passages in 7-10 minutes, depending on their difficulty. We've rated the difficulty for all passages and placed it in the appendix of this book so you can check your timing against the difficulty level for each passage.

7. At this point, you are ready to drill using entire sections of tests and to take practice tests, provided you've prepped for the other sections of the LSAT* with the same assiduousness.

Ditz: I looked up assiduousness!

Oh, Ditz, we're so proud.

---

* Did we mention we have a great Logic Games book?! You can find it at blueprintlsat.com/lsat/books

29/TIPSforsavingTIME

The previous chapter was devoted to giving yourself enough time to thoroughly master the Blueprint Reading Comprehension methodology, then slowly introduce timing for test day. This chapter is about advanced time-saving devices should you need them on the day of the test. The following is a list of techniques to use when you are near the end of your LSAT study, perhaps two weeks before the exam. They are ways to save time on the test or pick up extra points when you're running out of time, or need to formulate a game plan for the test that doesn't involve doing all four passages in order.

To be clear, we do not advocate these techniques as the best course of action. The best course of action is to understand the passages well enough to answer all the questions in the time allotted. (See previous chapter for how to accomplish this.)

However, some students, for whatever reason, feel they must take the next LSAT even though they haven't truly mastered the Reading Comprehension section. We don't want to leave them in the lurch, even though we'd like them to prep more. This discussion is for them.

1. Anticipate

The best way to improve your speed is to anticipate questions and their answers. Most students rush through the passage, only to get bogged down in the questions. Anticipation allows you to save time overall because you can quickly choose the correct answer choice, rather than going back to the passage and re-reading the information you missed the first time.

There are two places where you should anticipate the answers to questions:

   A. Anticipating the Main Point, Purpose, Author's Attitude, whatever the passage lends itself to, and summarizing the passage in a sentence BEFORE you reach the questions can save you a ton of time in the questions. On average, doing these five steps should yield the answers to four or five questions. If you find that your tagging and anticipation is only yielding the correct answer to one or two questions, *this is not a failure of the method*. Tough news, we know. But it means you haven't yet perfected the Blueprint method and need to practice the full method, without time constraints, on more passages before moving on to timing.

   B. Anticipating the correct answer to the question before moving to the answer choices. By framing the answer choice before you get to the answers, you'll be able to skim the answer choices to find the correct answer quickly, rather than painstakingly reading each answer choice. You'll also be less likely to fall prey to alluring incorrect answer choices, thus minimizing mistakes.

   There are some questions for which anticipating the correct answer choice is more difficult. For instance "Which of the following can be inferred from the passage" is quite open-ended. However, it's still possible to move through these answer choices more quickly than the average test-taker by skimming the answer choices for things you've marked in the passage or tagged in the margin. Often, the correct answer choice will pull from a localized structure, such as a Cause and Effect, or from a strong instance of author's attitude. By looking for such items, you won't need to painstakingly read each answer choice and can find the answer more quickly.

2. Skip difficult questions

If you find that you're running out of time on a passage, the following questions are the first to skip. You can always go back to them if you have time, later.

Ninja: Never skip a question without bubbling in an answer choice, grasshopper. Remember, there's no penalty for guessing on the LSAT.

A. Parallel Questions
These questions are long. They require you to understand the dynamic of the prompt, then check every long answer choice to see if it's replicated. Time suck-arooni. Do them last.

B. Open-ended Inference Questions
These are the types of questions with prompts like "Which of the following can be inferred from the passage?" Like Parallel questions, they require you to read every answer choice and can be a time suck. However, they're better than Parallel questions because it's often the case, as mentioned in the "anticipation" section, that you can skim through the answer choices to find something that accords with your markup. For this reason, skip Parallel questions first and skim the answer choices to these if you have time.

C. EXCEPT Inference Questions
These are questions like "Each of the following is supported by the passage EXCEPT?" Because the answer choices are often small details in the passage rather than big picture ideas, you can end up checking back with the passage for all four incorrect answers. This means you have to go back and re-read parts of passage up to four times for one question. Definitely a time suck, and definitely a question to avoid if you don't have the time.

if your running low on time skip...
① parallel questions
② open-ended inference questions
③ except inference questions

3. Don't go back and read the passage unless it's absolutely necessary

This is what the whole markup thing is all about: minimizing the number of times you need to go back to the passage. The typical student when tackling a Reading Comprehension passage with seven questions does so in the following manner:

A. Reads the passage, fairly quickly and without really understanding it in 3-5 minutes.
B. Moves to the questions.
C. Goes back to the passage for every question to find the answer to the question in the passage. Each question takes approximately 2 minutes.

Total elapsed time for the passage: 17-19 minutes. Otherwise known as wayyyy too long.

Here's how we want you to read the passage:

A. Read the passage thoroughly and efficiently, tagging important information as you go. This should take 4-6 minutes.
B. Anticipate the Main Point, Primary Purpose, Author's Attitude, and anything else specific to the passage. 1 minute.
C. Tackle the questions, using your markup and question anticipation techniques to answer five of seven questions.* 2 minutes.
D. Go back to the passage to check on the two questions not answered by the markup (typically Specific Reference questions) to make sure you've answered them correctly.** 1 minute.

Total elapsed time for the passage: 6.5-10 minutes. Right on target. (Remember, some passages may take 10 minutes but you'll still hit your 8 minute 45 second per passage deadline when an easier passage only takes 6.5 minutes.

BP Minotaur: A good way to practice this skill is to cover up the passage when tackling the questions in order to force yourself not to re-read parts for every question. Some questions require going back to the passage, but practice answer every question you can that doesn't require it. That's typically 5 of 7.

---

* This number varies per passage. On some passages, your markup will answer every question. On others, it may only answer three. On average, however, your markup should answer five of seven questions. This means that for these questions *you should not have to look back at the passage*.

** Again, there may be more or less, depending on the passage. But one or two is the norm.

4. Go in with a game plan

We've put together a scenario for students who plan on finishing four, three, or two passages on LSAT day. Again, we recommend studying until you can do four, but that's not always possible for some students for whatever reason.

First, the amount of time that should be allotted to a particular passage is influenced by two factors:

> 1) the difficulty of the passage, and
> 2) the number of questions it contains.

Some interesting facts:

A. The third passage is historically the most difficult

A clear pattern emerges when you look at the difficulty of passages across the section. The first passage is much easier than the rest, the second passage is a bit more difficult, and the third and fourth passages are essentially tied for difficulty, with the third passage a bit more difficult than the fourth.

Blueprint rated the difficulty of every passage since 1991 (the year of the "modern" LSAT). The scale ranged from 1 (Cleetus handily answers it) to 5 (it makes even the Minotaur sweat into his velvet smoking jacket!).

This graph should teach you an important lesson: the passages in the beginning of the section should take significantly less time than those at the end.

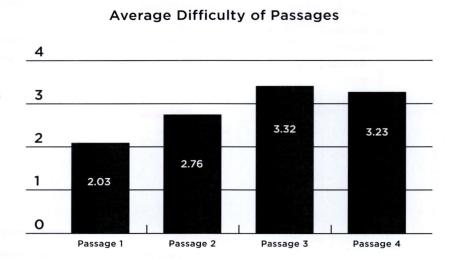

Average Difficulty of Passages
- Passage 1: 2.03
- Passage 2: 2.76
- Passage 3: 3.32
- Passage 4: 3.23

B. Some types of passages are harder than others

While the graph we just looked at may indicate to you that if you can't finish all the passages you should attempt passages 1, 2, and 4 first, that's not correct. There are other factors that will influence which passages to tackle on game day.

Below is a chart that breaks down the relative difficulty for passages by primary structure. This is another factor that affects the amount of time a passage should take.

Passage Type	Average Difficulty	
Thesis	2.66	①
Antithesis	2.93	③
Synthesis	2.56	②
Comparative Reading	3.26	④

It's interesting to see how close many of the difficulty ratings are to each other. Each of the categories is less than a point apart. However, there is a clear outlier: Comparative Reading is the most difficult passage type. This may not accord with everyone's intuition – some of our students luuuuv Comparative Reading. They want to have its babies. But many more find it difficult. If you've got to skip one passage, Comparative Reading may be your guy, even if it's the first passage, which our "Average Difficulty of Passages" graph would indicate you should never skip.

C. Some students find some topics more difficult than others

You may notice as you work through Reading Comprehension passages that certain topics just leave you cold. If you find your eyes glaze over every time you read a legal passage, or the terminology in science passages gives you the chills, then you should know you struggle with these. Practice them so they're not your weak point, but should you get close to the LSAT and you're still struggling, you can use this knowledge to help you formulate your game day strategy.

D. A note on structure

It's not a good idea to use structure to determine whether or not to skip a passage. After all, you probably won't know if a passage is a Thesis, Antithesis, or Synthesis until you're well in it. By then, you've put so much time into the passage that it's too late to back out. To that end, some tips on how to best develop your game plan.

DEVELOP A GAME PLAN

To maximize your performance on Reading Comprehension, you need to have a plan. Most students walk into the test vowing to finish as much of the section as they can and praying to the LSAT gods for easy passages. That's not a plan, that's wishful thinking.

Does the hero in the coming-of-age movie confront the quite attractive but ultimately mean bully without a plan? Heck no! And neither should you. (Confront Reading Comprehension without a plan, that is.)

Before we discuss various plans for the section, we need to get something out in the open. It's a brutal truth that most students don't want to hear. For some students, it's a good idea to plan on skipping at least one passage. Frantically rushing through four passages with low accuracy can be detrimental to your overall score.

BP Minotaur: Completing less passages with better accuracy can improve your overall score. Rushing to do more can be stressful and counterproductive.

You don't need to settle on a strategy right now. It's too early for that. You will continue to improve as you practice more passages. But, as the test approaches, it's vital to develop a game plan you are going to use to attack the section. Here are three strategies that work well for students.

Plan 1: Push for four

If you are capable of completing all four passages with a high degree of accuracy, that's great. But you still must have a plan for managing your time appropriately. If you spend too much time on the early passages, you won't have enough time to complete the later, more difficult passages.

Some students think a Reading Comprehension section on the LSAT looks like this:

Passage 1	Passage 2	Passage 3	Passage 4
8:45	8:45	8:45	8:45

This is actually a terrible plan. Not all passages are created equal, and it's dangerous to think they should take the same amount of time.

Here's a rough idea of how the section should look:

Passage 1	Passage 2	Passage 3	Passage 4
7:00	8:00	10:00	10:00

10.   12   15.   15   =52

430 / Chapter 29

The goal is to complete the first half of the section in roughly 15 minutes, and so you should push yourself to move quickly in order to reduce stress and minimize mistakes on later passages.

Also, you don't have to complete the four passages in order. Odds are that the first two passages will be easier, and you should always complete them no matter what. When pushing for four passages, however, different strategies work for different students.

Some students like to attack the most difficult passage, which is usually the third passage, first because it allows them to read the passage with a fresh mind rather than having already taxed themselves on three passages. Others do the easier passages first in order to make sure they've picked up all the "easy" points before fatigue starts to set in. Still others do the Comparative Reading passage first or last to get the difficult (for them) passage out of the way or to tackle it last. The same tips might help someone with subject matter: keeping the science or legal passage, for example, for first or last.

Plan 2: Aim for three

For many students, the best plan is to attempt to complete three passages. It's important to do this the right way, however.

How to choose your three

Here is the criteria for you to decide which passage to skip.

1. **To compare or not to compare**
   The first thing to decide is whether or not you find Comparative Reading passages difficult. If you find the difficulty level varies depending on the Comparative Reading passage, go to the second step. If you always struggle on them, they're the one to skip no matter what the order.
2. **Topic**
   If there is a particular topic you just can't seem to master, skip it, whatever its placement.
3. **Passage order**
   If you're fine with Comparative Reading passages and don't have particular issues with topic, then the average difficulty of passages becomes a factor. Here is where you would skip the third passages, since it's historically the most difficult.

Ninja: In the weeks before the test, you should try this method several times and average the number you are getting right tackling three passages as opposed to four. If your overall score for the section goes up, this might be the right game plan for you.

WHAT CAN I DO WITH FIVE MINUTES?

Some students find that they reach passage four with only five or so minutes left. This is not enough time to complete a passage, and these students are not managing their time optimally. If you find this happening regularly, it could be a sign that attempting three passages is a better strategy for you. That way you can use those five minutes to ensure that the first three passages were answered correctly, maximizing your points. However, if this happens to you on test day, try the following techniques.

- *If there are Author's Attitude questions, skim the passage looking for the attitude to answer them.*
- *Answer Specific Reference questions that direct you where to look in the passage.*

Plan 3: Ace two

Some students can't get through passages quickly, no matter how much they try. They can read and understand and anticipate, but not while rushing.

If, after heavy practice with the strategies and tips you've learned up until this point, you are still having a tough time completing three passages, you should aim to complete two passages perfectly.

In such a case, use the method outlined for three passages, this time eliminating two. If you find science passages difficult, skip that one as well, regardless of order. If Comparative Reading passages bother you but topic doesn't, skip the Comparative Reading passage and the third (traditionally the most difficult passage),
and so on.

> **Ninja:** If you are attempting three or fewer passages, you can still increase your odds of getting a point or two on the passage(s) you choose not to attempt. Use the same tips for what to do with five minutes left for a passage. Some Specific Reference questions point you to a particular part of the passage with line numbers. Read a few sentences above and a few below for context, and there's a good chance you can get the right answer. Author's Attitude questions are similarly attainable. Eliminate answer choices that describe the author's attitude in extremes.

Pro tip: If, while guessing, you use the same letter, (B) for instance, every time you guess, you should pick up about 20% of the questions that you don't even read. Add that to two or three passages that you complete, and you'll still be on target to get a great score, even without finishing all four passages.

HOLD YOUR HORSES!

Even though this chapter is devoted to timing, we want to again stress that you not incorporate timing into your studies prematurely. We cannot stress enough that, while you are learning the techniques, it is important to work slowly and focus on the details. Only once you have internalized the Blueprint approach can you bring it up to speed.

As you progress, introduce timing pressure into your practice slowly and in stages. As test day approaches, settle on a personal strategy and practice that strategy repeatedly.

Well, that's it from us at Blueprint. After 434 pages, there's literally nothing left to say about Reading Comprehension. Except that we hope you kick some LSAT butt on test day.

We hope you enjoyed the journey. At Blueprint, we strive to provide the absolute best LSAT preparation that has ever been created. Hopefully, you will think we fulfilled that mission.

For more information about the LSAT, and for more wonderful resources, just stop by our website. Best of luck from the Blueprint team. Sayonara.

blueprintlsat.com

30/APPENDIX

In order to help you with your continued studies, we've analyzed the structure of every Reading Comprehension passage since 1991. This is so that if you find you'd like additional practice on Thesis passages or Cause and Effect secondary structures, you'll know which prep tests to purchase in order to find them.

We've also rated their difficulty on a scale of 1 to 5 with 1 being very straightforward and 5 being exceedingly difficult. If you're introducing timing into your studies, the difficulty rating will also help you with that. Easier passages (those ranked 1-2) should take 6 1/2 to 7 minutes, average passages (those ranked 2-3) should take 7 1/2 to 8 1/2 minutes, and difficult passages (those ranked 4-5) should take 9 to 10 minutes.

BP Minotaur: Remember, only introduce timing into your studies after you have the methodology down.

Good luck with your continued studies, Blueprinters! Remember you can always contact us at info@blueprintlsat.com if you have any questions. We'll see you on the other side!

Comp = Comparative Reading
C&E = Cause and Effect secondary structure
Ex = Example secondary structure
Q&A = Question and Answer secondary structure
Class = Classification secondary structure

Blueprint favorites are highlighted. These passages will provide you with particularly good practice on Blueprint fundamentals.

Prep Test	Subject	Primary Structure	Extensive Secondary Structure	Local Secondary Structure(s)	Author present?	Difficulty
1	**Phyllis Wheatley**	**Thesis**			**Yes**	**1**
	Biochemistry	Synthesis	Ex	Class	Yes	4
	Criminal procedure	**Thesis**		**Ex**	**Yes**	**3**
	Medicine	Thesis	Q&A		Yes	4
2	Langston Hughes	Antithesis		Class, Ex	Yes	3
	Public attitudes about railroads	Antithesis	Ex	C&E, Ex	Yes	2
	Adaptive responses	**Thesis**	**Ex**	**Class, Ex**	**No**	**5**
	Legality of troop deployments	Synthesis		C&E, Ex	Yes	2
3	Asteroid satellites	Antithesis	Ex	Q&A	Yes	4
	Robert Boyle	Thesis	Q&A	C&E, Ex	Yes	3
	Monopoly power	Thesis		Ex	Yes	4
	Navajo weaving	**Antithesis**	**C&E**	**Ex**	**Yes**	**2**
4	Sovereign control of territorial waters	Thesis		C&E, Class	Yes	3
	Biodiversity crisis	**Thesis**		**C&E, Class, Ex**	**Yes**	**2**
	History of women and the French Revolution	Antithesis	Class	Class, Ex	Yes	4
	Impressionism	Synthesis	Ex	Class, Ex	Yes	4
5	**Economic development**	**Antithesis**		**C&E, Class, Ex**	**Yes**	**3**
	Emotional art	Antithesis		C&E, Class, Ex	Yes	4
	Bacteria	**Antithesis**	**Q&A**	**C&E**	**Yes**	**4**
	Mandelbaum	Thesis		C&E, Ex	Yes	2
6	Right to work	Antithesis		C&E	Yes	2
	Women physicians	**Thesis**	**C&E**	**C&E**	**Yes**	**2**
	Early Music movement	Antithesis		C&E, Ex	Yes	3
	Steel industry	Thesis	C&E	C&E, Class	Yes	5
7	Effect of parenthood on the labor force	Thesis		Class, Ex	Yes	2
	Webster's plays	Antithesis		Ex	Yes	3
	Genetics bacteria	**Antithesis**		**C&E, Ex**	**Yes**	**4**
	Dawes Act	Antithesis		Class, Q&A	Yes	3
8	RDNA tech	Antithesis		C&E	No	3
	Grey marketing	**Synthesis**	**Class**	**C&E**	**Yes**	**2**
	Autobiographies	Antithesis	Q&A	Ex	Yes	4
	English history	Synthesis		Class	Yes	4

Prep Test	Subject	Primary Structure	Extensive Secondary Structure	Local Secondary Structure(s)	Author present?	Difficulty
9	**Technology and art**	**Antithesis**		**Ex**	**Yes**	**1**
	Readjustment	Antithesis	Ex	C&E	Yes	2
	Greek society	Antithesis		Ex	Yes	4
	Political vocab	Antithesis		Ex	Yes	4
10	Oil platforms	Thesis		C&E, Ex	Yes	3
	Narrative painting	**Antithesis**	**C&E**		**Yes**	**4**
	Legal indeterminacy	**Antithesis**		**C&E, Ex**	**No**	**3**
	Classical theory on the civil rights movement	Antithesis		C&E, Ex	Yes	5
11	**MLK**	**Antithesis**	**Class**	**Ex**	**Yes**	**1**
	Polyarchies	Antithesis		Ex	No	3
	Amazon diversity	Antithesis	C&E	Q&A	Yes	3
	Women in medieval medicine	Thesis		Class, Q&A	Yes	4
12	**Architecture**	**Synthesis**		**Ex**	**Yes**	**1**
	Socioeconomics	**Synthesis**		**C&E**	**Yes**	**3**
	Legal systems	Antithesis		C&E, Ex	No	3
	Carbs	**Thesis**	**C&E, Q&A**	**C&E**	**Yes**	**4**
13	Neurons	Antithesis		Ex	Yes	5
	African American history	Thesis	Ex	Q&A	Yes	3
	Watteau portrayal	**Antithesis**		**Ex**	**Yes**	**4**
	Jury errors	Antithesis		Ex	Yes	3
14	**Geophysics**	**Thesis**	**C&E, Q&A**	**Ex, Q&A**	**Yes**	**4**
	Language	Thesis	Ex		Yes	5
	James Burke	Antithesis		Class	Yes	3
	Slaves and serfs	**Thesis**		**C&E, Ex**	**No**	**3**
15	**Dinosaur extinction**	**Synthesis**	**C&E, Q&A**	**C&E**	**Yes**	**2**
	Folklore	Thesis	C&E	Ex	Yes	3
	Political thought	Thesis		Ex	Yes	4
	Discrimination	Antithesis	C&E	Class	Yes	4
16	**Studies of Byron**	**Synthesis**		**Ex**	**Yes**	**3**
	Native Americans and the Supreme Court	**Thesis**			**Yes**	**4**
	Catastrophes	Antithesis	C&E		Yes	4
	English women	**Antithesis**		**Ex**	**Yes**	**3**
17	Zora Neale Hurston	Antithesis	Q&A	C&E, Ex	Yes	2
	Hard cases	Synthesis		Ex	Yes	4
	Governments and air pollution	Thesis	Q&A	Ex, Q&A	Yes	3
	Saharan drought	**Antithesis**	**C&E**	**C&E**	**Yes**	**4**
18	Law and literature	Antithesis	Ex	C&E	Yes	3
	Accepted views	Synthesis		Ex	Yes	3
	Missionary influence	**Antithesis**		**Ex**	**Yes**	**4**
	Luminist painting	Antithesis		Ex	Yes	4

Prep Test	Subject	Primary Structure	Extensive Secondary Structure	Local Secondary Structure(s)	Author present?	Difficulty
19	**Crime novels**	**Synthesis**			**Yes**	**2**
	Native Americans and artifact ownership	Thesis	Class		Yes	4
	Species distribution	Antithesis	C&E, Class		Yes	5
	Eric Williams	Antithesis		C&E	Yes	4
20	**Miles Davis**	**Antithesis**		**C&E, Class**	**Yes**	**2**
	Canon lawyers	Antithesis		C&E, Ex	Yes	5
	Bird social status	Thesis		C&E	Yes	3
	John Lowe	Thesis		C&E, Ex	Yes	3
21	London piano school	Thesis		Ex	Yes	4
	Study of law	**Antithesis**	**Class**		**Yes**	**1**
	Oil formation	**Antithesis**		**Ex**	**No**	**4**
	Immigrant education	Thesis		C&E	Yes	3
22	**Frida Kahlo**	**Thesis**		**Class, Ex**	**Yes**	**3**
	Narrative and law	Antithesis		C&E	Yes	3
	Corporate responsibility	**Antithesis**		**Ex**	**Yes**	**2**
	Language	Antithesis		Q&A	Yes	4
23	Rembrandt	Antithesis		C&E, Ex	Yes	3
	Medieval law	Synthesis		Class	Yes	2
	George Marsh	Antithesis		C&E, Q&A	Yes	3
	Fugita and O'Brien study	**Thesis**		**C&E, Ex**	**Yes**	**4**
24	Risk Communication	Antithesis		Ex	Yes	1
	Pico Korea Block	Thesis	C&E	C&E, Ex	Yes	1
	Sex discrimination	Antithesis		Ex	Yes	3
	Mark Jones fake	Thesis	Q&A	Ex	Yes	4
25	**Email**	**Thesis**	**Q&A**	**Ex**	**No**	**2**
	Homeric poems	Antithesis		Ex	Yes	4
	Intertribalism	Antithesis		C&E, Ex	Yes	3
	Complex systems	Antithesis			Yes	5
26	National service	Antithesis		Q&A	Yes	1
	James Porter	Thesis		Ex	Yes	2
	Dolphin die-off	**Antithesis**		**C&E**	**Yes**	**3**
	English marriage	Antithesis		Ex	Yes	4
27	**Juror prejudice**	**Antithesis**			**Yes**	**2**
	Personal names	**Synthesis**	**Ex**	**Ex**	**Yes**	**3**
	Homing pigeons	Antithesis	C&E, Class		Yes	3
	Fairy tales	**Antithesis**		**C&E, Q&A**	**Yes**	**4**
28	**Mashpee**	**Thesis**	**Ex**		**Yes**	**1**
	Volcanoes' climate	Antithesis	C&E	Ex	No	5
	Schools of Economics	Antithesis		Ex	No	2
	Movies' influence	Thesis		C&E	Yes	2

Prep Test	Subject	Primary Structure	Extensive Secondary Structure	Local Secondary Structure(s)	Author present?	Difficulty
29	Prophetic artists	Antithesis		Ex	Yes	4
	Tribal Languages	Thesis	Ex		Yes	2
	Platypus	Thesis		C&E	No	3
	Medieval women	**Thesis**	**C&E**	**C&E, Ex**	**Yes**	**2**
30	**Okapis**	**Thesis**	**Q&A**	**C&E, Q&A**	**No**	**1**
	Greek drama	Synthesis		Ex	No	4
	Orthodox theory	Antithesis		Ex	No	4
	New World rice cultivation	Thesis	Q&A		Yes	1
31	Waste production	Thesis		Ex	Yes	3
	Thurgood Marshall and Brown v. Board	Thesis		Ex	Yes	3
	History of science	Antithesis			Yes	4
	Philosophy of mind	Synthesis	Q&A		Yes	3
32	**Defense lawyers**	**Antithesis**	**Q&A**		**Yes**	**1**
	Multicultural education	Antithesis			No	3
	Native Amer autobiography	Antithesis	Class	Ex	Yes	3
	Psychological effects of alcohol	**Antithesis**		**C&E, Ex, Q&A**	**Yes**	**2**
33	Economic health	Antithesis		C&E, Class, Ex	Yes	1
	Harriet Jacobs	Synthesis			Yes	3
	Effects of CO2	**Antithesis**	**C&E**	**Ex, Q&A**	**Yes**	**4**
	Jeremy Bentham	Antithesis		Ex	Yes	4
34	Authoritarian rule	Thesis	C&E	Class, Ex	Yes	2
	Blues	**Thesis**		**C&E, Ex**	**Yes**	**2**
	Adaptation	Antithesis		Ex	Yes	3
	Refugees	Thesis		C&E, Class	Yes	2
35	French memoirs	Antithesis		Ex, Q&A	Yes	3
	Romare Bearden	Thesis		Q&A	Yes	2
	Views of science	**Antithesis**		**Ex**	**No**	**2**
	Ronald Dworkin	Synthesis			Yes	3
36	Computer conferences	Antithesis		Class, Ex, Q&A	Yes	1
	Renaissance history	Thesis		C&E, Ex	Yes	3
	Hormones	Antithesis	Ex	C&E	Yes	5
	South African law	**Antithesis**			**Yes**	**2**
37	Unanimity	Antithesis	C&E	C&E	Yes	1
	Marie Curie	Antithesis			Yes	2
	Invisible Man	Antithesis	Ex		Yes	2
	Decision Making	Antithesis		Ex	Yes	4
38	Burning	Antithesis		C&E, Ex	Yes	3
	Intellectual authority	Synthesis		Ex	Yes	3
	Historical sociology	Synthesis		Ex	No	3
	Medical empathy	**Antithesis**			**Yes**	**3**

Prep Test	Subject	Primary Structure	Extensive Secondary Structure	Local Secondary Structure(s)	Author present?	Difficulty
39	Mexican art	Thesis		C&E, Ex	Yes	2
	Fairy tales	Antithesis		Ex	Yes	3
	Wave theory	Antithesis			Yes	5
	Internet	Antithesis		Ex	Yes	3
40	International systems	Antithesis		Ex	Yes	1
	Spanish poetry	Antithesis		Ex	No	2
	Dark matter	Thesis	Q&A			5
41	**Leading questions**	**Thesis**	**C&E**	**Ex**	**Yes**	**4**
	Copyright law	Antithesis	Q&A	C&E	No	2
	Cullen poetry	Synthesis		Ex	Yes	3
	Electricity demand	Antithesis		Ex	Yes	2
	Victorian philanthropy	Synthesis		Ex	Yes	4
42	**Marshall's legacy**	**Antithesis**		**Ex**	**Yes**	**2**
	Roy Lichtenstein	Synthesis			Yes	3
	New technology	Thesis	C&E	C&E	Yes	2
	Neuron transmission	Antithesis			Yes	4
43	Oil drilling	Thesis	Ex	C&E, Ex	Yes	1
	Linguistic code switching	Thesis	C&E		Yes	3
	Reader response	Antithesis			Yes	3
	Faculty research	**Antithesis**	**Class**		**Yes**	**4**
44	Canadian auto work	Antithesis		Class	Yes	4
	Historiography	Antithesis	Ex	C&E	Yes	4
	Nerve cell growth	**Thesis**	**Ex**	**C&E**	**Yes**	**5**
	Modernist architecture	Antithesis		C&E	Yes	3
45	**Natural disasters**	**Synthesis**		**C&E, Class, Ex**	**Yes**	**1**
	Hippocratic oath	Synthesis		Class, Ex	Yes	3
	Lichen evolutionary origins	Thesis	Q&A		Yes	4
	Native Canadians	Thesis	C&E	Class, Ex	Yes	4
46	**Prosperity**	**Antithesis**		**Ex**	**Yes**	**2**
	Obasan	Thesis		Class, Ex	Yes	3
	Pronghorn	Antithesis	Q&A	Ex	Yes	5
	Criminal penalties	Thesis		Ex	Yes	4
47	Demonstration	Thesis	C&E		Yes	2
	Mao and art	**Thesis**	**C&E**	**Class, Ex**	**Yes**	**2**
	Family law	Antithesis	C&E	C&E	Yes	1
	Pathogens	Antithesis		C&E, Class, Ex	Yes	3
48	**Cave paintings**	**Antithesis**	**Q&A**	**Ex**		**2**
	Louise Gluck	Antithesis			Yes	3
	Native Canadians' property ownership	Thesis		Class	Yes	3
	Polarity	Thesis		C&E, Ex	Yes	5

Prep Test	Subject	Primary Structure	Extensive Secondary Structure	Local Secondary Structure(s)	Author present?	Difficulty
49	**Computer displays in court**	**Synthesis**		**C&E, Class**	**Yes**	**2**
	African art	Antithesis		Ex	Yes	4
	Ancient women doctors	**Thesis**		**Ex**	**Yes**	**4**
	Corn	Thesis	Q&A	C&E	Yes	5
50	Mexican art	Antithesis		Class	Yes	1
	Bankruptcy laws	**Antithesis**			**Yes**	**2**
	Human bias	Thesis		Ex	Yes	4
	Basins of attraction	Antithesis			Yes	5
51	Ezekiel Mphahlele	Synthesis		Ex	Yes	3
	Moon craters	**Thesis**	**Q&A**	**C&E**	**Yes**	**2**
	TV in third world	**Antithesis**		**Q&A**	**Yes**	**5**
	Computers and legal reasoning	Thesis	C&E	Ex	Yes	3
52	Senegalese film	Antithesis		Ex	Yes	2
	Narrative writing	Comp		Ex, Class	Yes	2
	Spiders	Antithesis	Ex	Ex	No	3
	Philosophical anarchism	Antithesis		Class, Ex	Yes	4
53	Asian poetry	Thesis		Ex	Yes	3
	British law	Thesis			Yes	5
	Intellectual property law and scientific discovery	Comp		Ex	Yes	3
	Predatory mites	**Thesis**	**Ex**	**Class**	**Yes**	**5**
54	Internet trademark	Antithesis	C&E	Ex	Yes	2
	Drilling muds	Comp		Ex	Yes	4
	Cakewalk	Thesis	Class	C&E	Yes	3
	Group cohesion	Thesis		C&E, Class	Yes	4
55	Employee injunctions	Thesis		Ex	Yes	3
	Purple loosestrife	**Comp**			**Yes**	**3**
	Maxine Hong Kingston	Antithesis		Class	Yes	4
	Speculative bubble	**Antithesis**		**Ex**	**No**	**3**
56	Amos Tutuola	Antithesis		Ex	Yes	3
	Kin recognition	**Antithesis**	**Q&A**	**Ex**	**Yes**	**4**
	Definition of national minority	Comp		Class	Yes	5
	French women	Thesis			Yes	3
57	FCC	Antithesis	Ex	C&E, Q&A	Yes	2
	Scientific humanism	Synthesis		Ex	Yes	3
	Willa Cather	Comp		Class, Ex	Yes	4
	Fractal geometry	**Antithesis**	**Ex**		**Yes**	**5**
58	Ancient history	Thesis	Class		Yes	3
	Parallel processing	**Thesis**	**C&E**	**Ex**	**Yes**	**3**
	Copyright law	**Antithesis**		**Ex**	**Yes**	**4**
	Music and feelings	Comp		C&E	Yes	3

Prep Test	Subject	Primary Structure	Extensive Secondary Structure	Local Secondary Structure(s)	Author present?	Difficulty
59	Parallel computing	Comp		Ex	Yes	2
	Statutory law	Thesis		Ex	Yes	3
	Isamu Noguchi	**Thesis**	**Ex**		**Yes**	**5**
	Ultimatum game	Antithesis	Q&A		Yes	3
60	Suburban sprawl	Antithesis	C&E	Ex	No	2
	Animal communication	Comp	C&E	Q&A	No	2
	Luis Valdez and Chicano theater	Antithesis			Yes	3
	Contingency fee agreements	**Antithesis**	**Class**		**Yes**	**5**
61	UN Declaration of Human Rights	Thesis		Class	Yes	2
	Art forgery	Thesis	Ex, Q&A	Q&A	Yes	3
	Animal vs. human communication	Comp		Ex	Yes	4
	19th c. African American Historiography	Synthesis		C&E	Yes	4
62	Dating Earthquakes	Antithesis		C&E	Yes	4
	Medical illustrations in court	Antithesis	Class	Ex	Yes	3
	Tooth decay	Comp	C&E		Yes	4
	Sarah Orne Jewett	Thesis	C&E	Class	Yes	4
63	Legal protection for Native American traditions	Thesis	Ex	C&E	Yes	2
	Kate Chopin	**Thesis**			**Yes**	**3**
	Dating the ocean floor	**Thesis**	**C&E**		**Yes**	**4**
	Objectivity in historical writing	Comp			Yes	3
64	Deliberate crime deterrence	Synthesis		C&E, Class	Yes	2
	Mexican American proverb use	Thesis		C&E, Ex	Yes	2
	Evolutionary psychology	Comp		C&E, Q&A	Yes	4
	Dostoyevsky	Antithesis			No	4
65	**Autobiography of Latin women**	**Thesis**	**Ex**		**Yes**	**2**
	Document preservation	Thesis		Class, EX	Yes	3
	Blackmail	**Comp**			**Yes**	**5**
	Soil restoration	Thesis	Class	C&E	No	5
66	Digital publishing	Thesis		C&E, Class	Yes	2
	Fingerprint analysis	Comp			Yes	3
	Toni Morrison's "Jazz"	Thesis			Yes	4
	1930's physicists	Thesis	Ex		Yes	4
67	Lorenzo Tucker	Thesis		Class	Yes	4
	Marjorie Shostak	Thesis	Class	Ex	Yes	4
	Invasive species	Comp		Ex	Yes	3
	Paradox of omnipotence	Antithesis	Ex	C&E	Yes	4
68	Corridos	Thesis		Ex	Yes	2
	Plants and insects	Thesis	C&E	Class	Yes	3
	Economics and increasing returns	Antithesis		Ex, Q&A	No	4
	Discretionary nonenforcement	Comp	Q&A		Yes	5

Prep Test	Subject	Primary Structure	Extensive Secondary Structure	Local Secondary Structure(s)	Author present?	Difficulty
69	Small farms	Thesis	Class	C&E, Ex	No	3
	Old photo techniques	**Thesis**		**Class, C&E, Ex**	**Yes**	**3**
	Software patents	Comp		Ex	Yes	4
	Dodos and tree reproduction	**Antithesis**	**C&E**		**Yes**	**4**
70	Prions	Antithesis		C&E	Yes	3
	Katherine Dunham	**Thesis**	**C&E**		**Yes**	**3**
	Wealth and happiness	Comp	C&E		Yes	3
	Assumption of risk	Antithesis	C&E	Ex	Yes	4
71	Sam Gilliam	Antithesis		Ex	Yes	2
	Taxing online gaming	**Comp**	**Q&A**		**Yes**	**5**
	Nature/nurture in prodigies	Antithesis		Ex	Yes	3
	Ethnography and video	**Antithesis**	**None**	**Ex**	**Yes**	**1**
72	Methods of firefighting	Thesis		Ex, C&E, Class	Yes	2
	Malian terra cotta sculpture	Antithesis		Ex	Yes	3
	Clinical trial ethics	Antithesis			Yes	4
	Flat tax	Comp			Yes	3
73	Natural selection	Antithesis	C&E	C&E, Ex	Yes	1
	Julia Margaret Cameron	Thesis		Ex	Yes	4
	Herbert Marcuse	Antithesis		Ex, C&E	Yes	4
	Law of ownership	Comp		Ex	Yes	4
74	Perfume as art	Thesis	Class	Q&A, Ex	Yes	2
	Stealing thunder	Thesis		Class	Yes	3
	Neuroscience and free will	Comp			Yes	4
	Mario Garcia	Antithesis		Class	Yes	4
75	Video and cultures	Antithesis		C&E, Ex	Yes	1
	Judge's impartiality	Antithesis		C&E, Ex	Yes	4
	Moral philosophy	Comp		Class, Ex	Yes	5
	Glass	Antithesis	Q&A	C&E	Yes	3
76	Schoenberg	Antithesis		Ex	Yes	2
	Biotechnology patents	**Antithesis**		**Ex**	**Yes**	**4**
	Wampum	**Antithesis**		**C&E, Ex**	**Yes**	**3**
	Negative Evidence	**Comp**		**Ex**	**Yes**	**5**
77	Federal Theater Project	Thesis		Q&A, Ex	Yes	2
	Corporate crime	Antithesis	Q&A	Ex	Yes	3
	Women in history	Comp			Yes	3
	Lamarck and DNA	Thesis		Q&A, Ex	No	4
78	Jury nullification	Comp		C&E, Ex	Yes	1
	Arts and the aristocracy	Antithesis		C&E, Ex	Yes	4
	Clay tablets	Thesis		Ex	No	5
	CFCs	Thesis			Yes	3

Prep Test	Subject	Primary Structure	Extensive Secondary Structure	Local Secondary Structure(s)	Author present?	Difficulty
79	Muscle memory	Comp			Yes	1
	Eileen Gray's art	Thesis			Yes	5
	Mesolithic pathways	**Antithesis**			**Yes**	**3**
	Specific performance	Thesis		Ex	Yes	3
80	Rawls' theory of justice	Thesis		Q&A, Ex	Yes	3
	The Great Migration	Thesis		C&E	Yes	2
	Insider trading	**Comp**		**Q&A, C&E, Ex**	**Yes**	**3**
	Brain scans	Thesis		Q&A, Ex	Yes	4